The Architect & Designer Birthday Book

To Carin, for everything

Published by
Princeton Architectural Press
A division of Chronicle Books LLC
70 West 36th Street
New York, NY 10018
papress.com

Editor: Jennifer N. Thompson

Library of Congress Cataloging-in-Publication Data
Names: Biber, James, 1953– author.
Title: The architect and designer birthday book / James Biber.
Description: New York : Princeton Architectural Press, 2024.
        | Includes index. | Summary: "A day-by-day celebration
        and exploration of the greatest architects and designers
        throughout history" – Provided by publisher.
Identifiers: LCCN 2022061776 (print) | LCCN 2022061777 (ebook)
        | ISBN 9781797224541 (hardcover) | ISBN 9781797226897 (ebook)
Subjects: LCSH: Architects – Biography. | Designers – Biography.
        | Birthdays. Classification: LCC NA40 .B53 2023 (print) | LCC NA40
        (ebook) | DDC 720.92/2 – dc23/eng/20230105
LC record available at https://lccn.loc.gov/2022061776
LC ebook record available at https://lccn.loc.gov/2022061777

James Biber

Published by PA Press
New York

The Architect & Designer Birthday Book

Preface

There is history, and then there is one's personal relationship with history.

This book is not an objective historical document; it is, I hope, mostly accurate, like those "based on a true story" TV shows. It's my personal, often meandering, and highly tangential take on the personalities, the projects, and the issues that have shaped architecture and design for centuries, illustrated by the birthdays of those luminaries. It is both random and curated, with the added hook that everyone has a birthday they share with someone more famous than themselves. For me that's artist Beatrice Wood, architect Eva Jiricna, and photographer Arnold Newman. Oh, and Alexander Graham Bell, Carlo Ponzi (Ponzi scheme), Jean Harlow, Lee Radziwill, one of the Chambers Brothers, Tone Lōc, and Camila Cabello. They're all coming over for dinner next week.

Unfortunately, architects (or, rather, their parents) have not been disciplined enough to spread their birthdays evenly across the calendar. They tend to clump together, as when Jean Prouvé and Richard Neutra share a birthday, or Florence Knoll shares a birthday with Alexander Girard and George Nakashima, both artists/designers she worked with.

So, architects and designers get it together, you need to do better! Do it for me. Or do it to be featured in this book, not passed over because you are born on the same day as a design giant. It's like obituaries in the *New York Times* (although this may be changing now, especially with digital readers): you don't want to die on the same day as someone really famous. Your obit will be tiny at best, probably bumped off the page. A bit more discipline and order in birth dates would be nice, thank you. You're welcome.

Also appreciated would be much, much more diversity. This book reflects the unfortunate (and only slowly evolving) lack of diversity in fields as old and patriarchal as architecture. Worse than this is the lack of diversity on any given birthday, where the choices are often extremely limited, almost always to white men of the Western world.

My goal in this venture was to find the most interesting, creative personalities born on any given day, first among architects, then among designers, and finally among artists (who, apologies, are not even acknowledged in the title!). The struggle of women and people of color to compete with the overwhelmingly white male population of these disciplines is reflected not just in their numbers, but also in their stories. Like that of Paul R. Williams, the Black architect who learned to draft and draw upside down to avoid discomforting his clients by sitting next to them. Or of Helen Binkerd Young who, after graduating in architecture from Cornell University in 1900, taught there, for free, while her husband was fully compensated for his identical work. Or Augusta Savage, who was accepted, then rejected from the art school in Fontainebleau, France, after they discovered she was Black.

And these are the successful creatives. Those who couldn't overcome the deeply embedded racism, sexism, ageism, and all the other "isms" were never even up for consideration; they simply never fulfilled their dreams.

Each subsequent edition of this book will, I trust, be more balanced than the last. Until then I share your disappointment in the lack of diversity these fields have always been cursed with.

This is a pandemic project. Starting in 2021, year two of the COVID-19 era, I needed a daily task to reintroduce some structure into days that were melting into each other. I had written an essay or two on birthday buddies like Florence Knoll, who shares a red-letter week of birthdays with (in addition to Girard and Nakashima) Walter Gropius and Marcel Breuer. My Instagram postings were a lark that became an obsession, or at least a daily commitment. After a couple of months, I was tormented by the thought of stopping or missing even one day, but I was equally terrified of the daunting task of a daily bio for the balance of the year.

Preface

I may have been emulating artists I know (or whose work I know) who, for example, built a chair every day for an entire summer or took a self-portrait every day for years or created any other serially obsessive work. The posting, every morning, was a way to reorder my life, to mark each day, to keep time with the music of the pandemic.

This project started without a book in mind; that was the idea of my former Pentagram partner Michael Bierut, who designed this volume and shepherded it through publication. I am still in awe of making books; it seems to take longer to publish a work of design than to build one. That makes no sense, but just try it.

In the months after I finished the 366 postings, I was in equal parts relieved, disoriented, and grieving for the loss, in what must be the Instagram equivalent of withdrawing cold turkey (a phrase that makes absolutely no sense to me). Luckily, I had to review and edit it all again, preparing for this book.

I can only imagine writing something of book length as a collection of hundreds of small bits, effectively turning footnotes into a book. (Note to self: My next project? Check to see if Nicholson Baker has already done it.) The idea of writing a continuous, novel length, cohesive composition is bewildering to me. How does one edit an entire book? How can anyone hold an entire tome in one's RAM while editing? Or read a book the forty or fifty times it takes to see it as a single work of art?

There are sequential, linear arts, and there are nonlinear, or simultaneous, arts. Writing, music, acting, dance, and film are all linear, composed and performed in sequential time. Even when flashbacks are involved, it's just reordering the linear landscape.

Painting, sculpture, architecture, and graphic design tend to be simultaneous experiences (though time exists, it is not the metronome of the experience). I usually live in the world of the simultaneous arts, and the linear ones are a bit inscrutable to me. When I dipped my toe in the linear world, it turned into a chapter book, avoiding the larger narrative arc and slicing the composition into bits or bytes that seem so small as to be almost in the simultaneous category. It's a calendar as novel, or A Year of Living Biographically as a datebook.

This is a collection, more like a reference book than a novel; I don't hold out hope that anyone (other than me and my editor) will read the whole thing. It's structured to bounce around from meaningful date to meaningful date. It's most likely to be read on shuffle.

So, enjoy the book, whatever parts you read, and let me know which important figures I've omitted. It won't change anything, but it will be good to know who I missed.

Oh, and happy birthday!

James Biber

01 January
Alfred Stieglitz

Georgia O'Keeffe–Hands, 1919

Maybe it's just me, but I am forever mixing up Alfred Stieglitz and Edward Steichen. Both were photographers, both moved to New York, both took famous photos of the Flatiron Building, and both knew each other well. One of them (Stieglitz) featured the other (Steichen) in his gallery and magazine. One of them (Stieglitz) was Georgia O'Keeffe's partner, taking hundreds of photos of her along the way. One of them curated photographers and photographs at MoMA (Steichen), helping establish photography as art, while the other (Stieglitz) curated shows at his own gallery (291, for 291 Fifth Avenue) and magazines (*Camera Notes*, then *Camera Work*, with a logo designed by Steichen), helping raise photography to an art.

Stieglitz and his gallery were early promoters of modernism in the US, featuring early exhibitions of Rodin, Matisse, Cézanne, Picasso, and Brancusi, and, of course, Edward Steichen. Together with Steichen he moved from thinking of photography as best when it imitated art (paintings) to the modern view, in which honesty compelled the photographer to stop adorning, coloring, and fussing with the prints to make them more like paintings; they were best when they were simply a new art faithful to the

photographic technology and imitative of nothing. No doubt Steichen felt the same way.

O'Keeffe is Stieglitz's most photographed subject, those pictures comprising a genuine series over time. Her remarkable hands often appear in the portraits; twisted, gnarled, clutching, they are like another subject in the frame. They take over; they transmit all the angst, all the passion, of the images.

They are the closest thing to a mirror of Stieglitz that we have. He is the absent yet ever-present artist in the images. In some ways the images help define photography as well as any compendium might, and in other ways they define Stieglitz himself.

That is more than we should expect from any single image.

02 January
Marcello Nizzoli

The author's Olivetti Lettera 22, his first (and most beautiful) typewriter, circa 1950

How many things you loved as a kid do you still admire?

Nizzoli designed my first and still my favorite typewriter, the gorgeous Olivetti Lettera 22. It was enough to establish his fame, but Nizzoli went on to work at every scale, from buildings to letter openers, from posters to exhibitions.

His stint at Olivetti, starting in the 1930s as a copywriter and eventually becoming a designer and later the head of product design in 1936, was the beginning of the company as a design-driven manufacturer (a new consciousness among corporations). The Lettera 22 was the only typewriter of its kind in the 1950s: a sleek icon rated the number one design of the modern era (1900–1959, as they defined it) in 1959 by the Illinois Institute of Technology. It was extraordinarily compact, came in a range of sophisticated hues that were as cool as 1950s car colors, and revived Italy's postwar industrial design reputation.

Olivetti was the Apple of its day. It hired the best, including Figini and Pollini, Le Corbusier (whose unbuilt 1963 headquarters design defined a moment in architecture), and James Stirling (whose built 1972 training center in the UK defined a moment for him).

Nizzoli did build a headquarters for Olivetti, the Palazzo Uffici Olivetti in Ivrea, a three-winged concrete and glass affair with an incredible hexagonal stair at the center.

Nizzoli, like virtually every designer of the time, worked for Campari and for the Fascists; that's just what Italian designers did. He was responsible for the never-built facade decoration at the Casa del Fascio in Como by Giuseppe Terragni. It is a remarkable building that is far better without the applied decorative images of Mussolini and friends, which Il Duce deemed insufficiently monumental.

Nizzoli's designs for the Necchi sewing machine and the Safnat telephone are still exciting today, though telephones that are not cell phones are looking increasingly absurd, especially those with dials rather than buttons. That might be true of typewriters too, but somehow they persist as stand-alone machines, ready to be called into action whenever we need to pound the keys to dissipate our aggression. Try it, it works.

Marcello Nizzoli, another great, relatively unknown design genius.

03 January
Walter Herdeg

Graphis covers by Thomas Eckersley, 1950, and Jacques Nathan, 1948

Walter Herdeg was one of those Swiss dudes who figured out what modern graphic design should be, and it stuck. After admiring the German magazine *Gebrauchsgraphik*, Herdeg decided to create his own, *Graphis*, which is still in publication and is still the standard by which all graphic design magazines are measured.

Herdeg founded *Graphis* in Switzerland in 1944 before World War II ended, saying, "When Stalingrad fell, I came out with the dummy [of *Graphis*]!" He had already created a virtual corporate identity program in the 1930s for the resort town of St. Moritz, no small feat in a world that hadn't much thought about identity programs, much less for a Swiss town. More than anyone, he celebrated and legitimized graphic design (as opposed to advertising) as the profession it is today.

The level of influence Herdeg achieved could come from a school, like the Kunstgewerbeschule in Zurich that he attended, or magazines like *Gebrauchsgraphik* and *Graphis*, but few other places had the international audience and influence of those venues. Herdeg was smart enough to know that authority could derive from promotion of one's own individual excellence or from the celebration of excellence in others. Herdeg's *Graphis* was more than a glossy mag filled with cool design; its authority extended to annuals (mostly developed after its sale in 1986 to B. Martin Pedersen) and books. Herdeg's legendary *Graphis Diagrams* from 1974 was published nearly twenty years before Edward Tufte published *The Visual Display of Quantitative Information*.

It's an interesting contrast. Tufte (a statistician) seemed amazed that information can be beautiful and communicative; Herdeg seemed equally impressed that beauty can be so informative. I'm pretty sure Peter Saville never cribbed any images from Tufte, but his cover of the Joy Division album *Unknown Pleasures* is a direct lift from Herdeg's book. Just sayin'.

Herdeg was also smart enough to get his son, Marcel, involved in the *Graphis* business. Marcel brought the magazine to profitability and managed the 1986 sale to Pedersen, who continues to publish it today. By 2028, Marty will have matched Walter's tenure at the helm (he has already matched his dedication), a landmark achievement for a landmark publication.

04 January
Helmut Jahn

ThyssenKrupp Elevator Test Tower, Rottweil, Germany, 2017

Helmut Jahn was the eighth member of the Chicago Seven (not *that* Chicago Seven) architects, a group loosely defined as the Midwest's answer to the New York Five. Jahn's earliest and latest work skews to Mies van der Rohe and "less is more," while the postmodern work in between is decidedly "more is more." The latest includes 50 West Street (the most elegant new downtown Manhattan tower) and, in Germany, the world's tallest freestanding elevator test tower (who knew that was even a thing?) for ThyssenKrupp.

Jahn was born in Nuremberg, Germany, when that city was the site of the Albert Speer–designed massive Nazi rallies, which included the remarkable Cathedral of Light. Mostly, though, he witnessed the rebuilding of a city devastated by bombing, when Nuremberg was meticulously reassembled and the evildoers were meticulously vanquished. The postwar years were an era of erasure in the formative period of Jahn's youth.

It may be too easy a formulation, but Jahn's adoption then rejection of Mies and the Germanic rigor of his style (learned at Illinois Institute of Technology, where Jahn studied under Myron Goldfinger and others) may follow this same leitmotif of erasure and sanitized revival. It's why I never took to Jahn's work. It never seems to me to have an ideological center; it is more like an affected rejection disguised as a style.

Somehow he returned to the purer formal language later in life; 50 West Street is one of those towers whose elegance makes it a lot less individual than its competition (and I mean that as a compliment), but whose design will undoubtedly look better longer than its zany competitors. And the ThyssenKrupp elevator test tower is like a building stripped of everything but its core; the windowless form is a unique opportunity to make sculpture rather than occupiable building, and Jahn does that admirably.

Erasure and sanitized revival apply to Jahn's own career as well, moving from one style to another without a glance over his shoulder. Except, that is, when he argued to save one of his own early buildings, the Thompson Center in Chicago; erasure was out of the question in that case!

05 January
JingJing Naihan Li

CCTV Headquarters, inspiration for I Am a Monument–CCTV wardrobe, 2012

Turning buildings into furniture has a long tradition. Paul Frankl did it a hundred years ago, and even Biedermeier furniture seemed to do it two hundred years ago.

Jingjing Naihan Li is doing it today, with a refreshingly specific approach. Her furniture isn't vaguely like some building or other, but based on very specific originals. Li has fashioned the CCTV Headquarters by Rem Koolhaas as a large standing armoire and Steven Holl's Simmons Hall dorms at MIT as an enormous horizontal cabinet. She's turned SOM's Jin Mao Tower and I. M. Pei's Bank of China into candles that can be found at (gasp) Walmart.

Li claims her work is based on the "moody impracticality of globe-trotting," whatever that means. I just see it as appropriation. The Boxes series addresses the shipping of furniture, where the shipping box becomes the furniture itself. It is situated somewhere between Enzo Mari's DIY Sedia 1 chair and the cleverest Louis Vuitton trunks. It is found art as an idea, meticulously thought out as unfolding furniture.

Not every idea needs to be completely new to be successful, just as not every recipe needs to be completely new to be delicious. Li works in well-worn paths, refining ideas, exploring variations, and attempting to straddle the line between furniture and art. It's a world that has spawned a thousand Salone del Mobile Milan outposts; a display of cleverness at the furniture scale is meant to reference talent at every scale.

Li's objects, and those like them, are the "artification" of our furnished lives. Things pretend to be other things: cabinets as buildings, sofas as lips, chairs as sculptures, flooring as landscapes, lighting as events. They may work in the context of Milan's competitive exhibitions, but don't try this at home!

Like nearly everyone, I've toyed with these ideas: buildings shrunk to the scale of furniture and packing crates as part of the finished work, for example. My own attempts tend to be one-liners, cleverness trumping substance.

Does Naihan Li's work transcend the temporal, becoming a meaningful addition to the design landscape? Or will her designs be relegated to one-hit wonders? Ask me in twenty-five years.

06 January
Jean Badovici

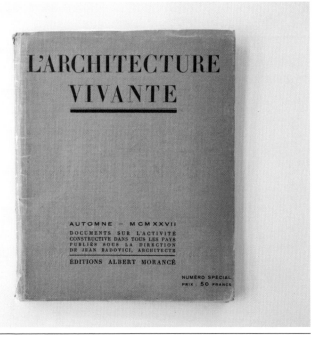

L'Architecture Vivante, Autumn 1927

Eileen Gray's famous E-1027 Villa was named for her initials (E plus 7, for the seventh letter in the alphabet) bookending her paramour Jean Badovici's (J, the tenth letter, and B, the second), but it was Badovici who alone allowed Le Corbusier to slather its walls with his sexualized murals that so offended Eileen Gray that she never returned. So, really, fuck him.

I visited E-1027, following a long tradition of architects trespassing to see, in person, the objects of their affection. It can be thrilling, humiliating, frightening, or humorous, depending on circumstance. My visit to Carl Sagan's house as a stoned-out student left Sagan so annoyed he called the architecture school to put a stop to it (my classmates and I were actually there to mock the house, though he missed that subtlety). As a kid, I used to hop the wall (now raised several feet) with my father on Ponus Ridge Road to wander Philip Johnson's compound. In Rome I passed several *ingresso vietato* signs to find myself in the incredible monks' homes built against the Baths of Diocletian.

At E-1027 I scaled a high wall to wander with my then architectural partner to quietly enjoy the serenity and deft craft of Gray's best project. Now it can be

seen by appointment, but my visit was before the renovation was complete. It is one of those places you really want to inhabit (unlike many of the former examples). It is so perfectly scaled (pun intended) and so complexly assembled as to be a true marvel.

What hand Badovici had in it is disputed. Like nearly all the collaborations of men and women in architecture (Mies-Reich, Venturi-Scott Brown, Corbusier-Perriand, et al.), it's usually assumed that the guy was the prime designer and the gal the supporting one. Doubtful in the case of E-1027.

Corbusier became Badovici's friend (and fellow vandal) because Badovici, starting in 1923, edited *L'Architecture Vivante*, promoting Corbu along with other burgeoning modernists. That's back when Corbusier needed promoting, and he returned the favor by marking, like a cat, anything he deemed competitive. It's a mixed legacy; the murals were famous enough to save the house from destruction, while destroying the house themselves. So, thanks, Badovici? (Or, as above, fuck that guy?)

07 January
Charles Addams

"Normal is an illusion."

Dialogue for Morticia Addams, *Addams Family Musical,* 2009

Chas Addams (as he signed his cartoons) was, of course, the creator of the Addams Family cartoons, which begat the 1960s TV series, the 1992 animated TV series, the 1991, 1993, and 1998 feature films, the 2019 animated feature film, the musical, and probably twenty or thirty other versions in various media right up to the current Netflix series *Wednesday*, released during the "late pandemic period" (an appellation Addams would no doubt have enjoyed). So it still has legs.

When he first assembled the Addams Family in 1937, five years after his cartoons first appeared in the *New Yorker*, he invented what today seems like an easy formulation but was a real transformation of the then-current horror craze. In those days the cartoon macabre (a word that seems to have been invented for Addams) was highly cartoonish, and Addams managed an almost-real family with twisted perspectives that landed as comedy. *King Kong* or *Dracula* or *Bride of Frankenstein* may look like satire today, but they were deadly serious when created. Addams made even the inherently evil look funny, even charming, and relatable.

Of course, we all understand the urge to pour boiling oil on annoying Christmas carolers. And if our children were to be delivered home from summer camp in pet carriers, that makes sense on a certain level. A friend of ours, a jewelry designer, has an absolutely innocent fascination with all things seemingly macabre, frightening, or gory. Her family lives in a church in our small upstate New York town (and maybe that is burying the lede) where once, in their belfry bedroom, a bat landed on her chest while sleeping. Naturally it woke her, and she not only was fascinated but actually stroked the bat gently while it rested there. That is very Chas Addams; the image almost demands a caption! We all found that incredibly funny, like an Addams cartoon, because it didn't happen to us!

In fact, his comics don't celebrate gore, they preempt it. Addams's job after college was at *True Detective* magazine, where he was tasked with retouching crime scene photos to remove the blood and gore. He claimed the photos were often better unretouched, but the job perfectly prepared him for a career making the unspeakable speakable. Addams defanged the horrific, finding the underlying humor in the least funny subjects, giving us all permission to laugh, even at a funeral.

08 January
Poul Kjaerholm

PK25 lounge chair, designed as Poul Kjaerholm's graduation project, 1952

Everything Poul Kjaerholm designed was a weightless refinement of what came before.

His take on the Mies Brno chair removed every unnecessary gram of material. He invented Verner Panton's S chair ten years before Panton did, playing off Harry Bertoia and Charles and Ray Eames on the way.

His works are so meticulously detailed in such an utterly reductivist way that they begin to seem like almost nothing. When a bar of steel is sliced and bent in different directions, as he did for the legs and frame of the PK25 chair, the point of maximum stress (at the end of the slice) ends with a small circle cut out to visually stop the slice, but also to distribute stress-preventing tears. A detail as perfect as that demonstrates Kjaerholm's understanding of both the physics of materials and the visual logic of design.

Another trademark detail employs a rubber ring that not only elegantly secures the seat to the steel frame but also provides a bit of flex to the whole unit. Flex, it turns out, is a design element for Kjaerholm, sometimes to an almost unsettling degree! His chairs can move in reaction to us, the ultimate call and response for furniture.

My fave Kjaerholm piece is a candelabra of thirty-two candles in the form of a hanging helix. Designed in 1956, just three years after the helical structure of DNA was discovered, it's not just a reference to that shape but also a clever way to keep a stack of candles from melting those above them. Just like the sly reference to the Brno chair, all of Kjaerholm's work strips an object down to its absolute essence.

He did that, in part, by using steel when his contemporaries preferred wood (a la Danish modern). As he said, "Steel's constructive potential is not the only thing that interests me; the refraction of light on its surface is an important part of my artistic work. I consider steel a material with the same artistic merit as wood and leather."

Sadly, Kjaerholm died at fifty-one. But he produced several lifetimes of brilliant work, collectively called "profound essays on the relationship between the body, materials, and space."

09 January
Massimiliano Fuksas

Main concourse, Fiera Milano Rho, Milan, Italy, 2005

Massimiliano Fuksas worked for Giorgio de Chirico, Jørn Utzon, and Archigram, which either explains his work or makes it even more confusing.

I get the de Chirico influence; there is an occasionally surreal, charged emptiness to some of Fuksas's work. Utzon seems a bit harder to place in the Fuksas oeuvre; maybe the connection is about parabolic form-making. And Archigram may have given him a taste for the megastructure; his Milan Trade Fair is a nearly mile-/1.5-kilometer-long strip covered in undulating glass, gathering dozens of buildings along the way. If it moved, it would be the best Archigram building ever!

Arriving at the Fiera is a pretty overwhelming experience, but my fave Fuksas designs are the Princi bakeries in Milan (and now elsewhere) fashioned as long stone halls, with the fire at one end and the finished loaves at the other; some occasionally even pop through the facade. But then I may be influenced by their amazing bread, pasticcini, focaccia, and pizza.

Massimiliano heads Studio Fuksas with his wife and partner, architect Doriana Mandrelli Fuksas. She was omitted from a recent lifetime achievement award, once again demonstrating that what bills itself as the most collaborative creative discipline hasn't figured out how to recognize collaboration, especially with women.

It's a bit like that embarrassing 1956 TV interview when Ray Eames was patronizingly called "the woman behind the man" as she stood, literally, behind Charles. And this was an interview conducted by Arlene Francis, who should have known better.

But somehow no man (as far as I know) has rejected these patently sexist awards…while (under different circumstances) even John Lennon returned his MBE. There's still time, Mr. Fuksas!

10 January
Massimo Vignelli

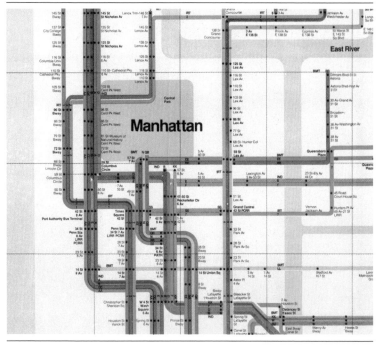

New York City subway map, 1972

Massimo Vignelli was the most delightful, funny, gracious, and charming designer imaginable and at the same time the most dogmatic, definitive, controlling, clear, precise, and unyielding designer ever. These traits only mesh because of his genius. Plus his quotes are perfection:

"If you can design one thing you can design everything."

"If you do it right, it will last forever."

"Design is not art. Design is utilitarian, art is not."

"A grid is like underwear. You wear it but it's not to be exposed."

In the subway, in the air, buying furniture, reading books, making dinner, or sitting down to eat, we are constantly graced with Vignelli's design, and better for it.

Massimo and Lella Vignelli designed just about everything: dinnerware, clothing, jewelry, brand identities, subway signage, maps, books, posters, a church, a restaurant or two, logos and livery for airlines, logos for modern furniture companies, lighting fixtures, chairs, tables, calendars, watches, and dozens more designs I am sure I am forgetting. Massimo even designed his own funeral (and the church in which it was held), down to the music, the speakers, and the black cube urn on the central table draped with crossed linen runners.

They were design polymaths, not in the sense of having multiple unrelated talents (like hockey and applied physics) but in the sense of having a single talent they applied to multiple unrelated things. Truly committed designers, finding there is something missing in their life, don't necessarily look to buy a solution; they simply design it. Massimo and Lella wanted to simplify their clothing choices, so they designed them. Needed a bench for their new home? Designed it. Casual dinnerware? Designed it. It is the trap of being an architect/designer; everything becomes a problem to be solved...by design. And if a great solution doesn't exist, then that is the perfect opening to fill that void.

Massimo Vignelli's genius extended to language; he managed to explain, in as few words as possible, complex ideas with astounding clarity. He was a lifelong professor at large for the design profession. His quotes are nearly all worthy of repeating, but my fave is, "If you can't make it good, make it big!... and if you can't make it big, make it red!" In the right hands this is priceless advice.

11 January
Mary Bright

Mary Bright sporting her hat and dress accessory made from mini-blinds, circa 1982

Mary Bright was everyone's favorite fabric person. She designed curtains that I am reluctant to even call curtains because they were really pieces of textile art. Sadly, she died nearly twenty years ago, and I still miss her.

It wasn't just that Bright could imagine fabric doing things no one else could imagine, it's that she could fabricate these things at a level of perfection that never failed to make picky architects happy, all the while being a charming, funny, impatient, tall, and lovely Scotswoman.

I met her when we worked on the suspended, parachute-shaped fabric light fixtures at Gotham Bar and Grill that she refashioned from the rather flaccid ones I designed originally. The change was the difference between the haircuts I got during the pandemic and a real haircut. Night and day.

Bright started as a hatmaker when she couldn't find a hat she wanted to wear. (This, by the way, is what designers are driven to do: design their lives. That's why my shelves are filled with dinnerware I designed twenty years ago; SQ.WARE wasn't yet made, so I had to design it.) Bright then started amending her wardrobe with unlikely

accents, like metal mini-venetian blinds or other industrial trinkets.

Curtains were next for her, after proclaiming her respect for people who hated curtains. When designs seem stuck in the last century or two, as with most curtains, it's ballsy to think you can affect real change. But she was, and she did. If you're looking to break a mold, it's not a bad strategy to start with something that is: a) badly designed, b) under the radar, and c) ubiquitous. Or, as Bright said, "I decided that if I was going to do something out of the ordinary, that I'd better start with something ordinary." Nice quote, Ms. Bright. Not sure it makes sense to everyone, but it works for me.

Twenty-eight years after Bright did the Gotham parachutes, it was time to change them. Lighting guru David Weeks worked in fabric for the first time, and I think Bright would be pleased. His version is nothing like her parachutes, but brilliant nonetheless.

My only regret about Bright is that she made me realize my own limitations. Now I can never again design things made of fabric, because I know they will never be as good as what she would do. Not even close.

12 January
Raf Simons

Raf Simons at the Calvin Klein runway show, New York, New York, 2018

The problem with writing any bio of a fashion designer is that no matter where you say they are designing, they will not be there by the time you finish typing the sentence. Peripatetic, one might suggest. Fickle, others might offer. Prone to firing is a third possibility. All are true.

Raf Simons has made the rounds, starting as a furniture designer, later heading fashion at Jil Sander, Dior, Calvin Klein, and Prada. He found a middle ground between fashion and furniture and is designing fabrics for Kvadrat (a name that couldn't possibly be spelled this way, but it is). Kvadrat has, at least, a sense of humor about the pronunciation of its name, even going so far as to make a video of famous designers explaining how they (mis)pronounce it. The video includes Simons, Peter Saville, Ronan and Erwan Bouroullec, Patricia Urquiola, and a host of others.

Simons and Saville have collaborated, or at least Raf has appropriated Peter's early record covers, for his collections. They occasionally show up at auction for tens of thousands of dollars, raising the question, "Whose art is this?"

Starting with Saville (with whom I overlapped at Pentagram for a year or two), whose appropriation of imagery is a huge part of his early work on the Factory Records covers he is rightfully famous for: he reproduced (rather a vague term) an 1890 Henri Fantin-Latour painting of a basket of roses (called *A Basket of Roses*) for the 1983 cover of New Order's *Power, Corruption and Lies*. I may be misremembering his description, but I think Saville actually re-created the image as a photograph. It may be much simpler than that; he may have just secured the rights to use the painted image.

Twenty years later, Simons appropriated (with consent) a series of Saville's covers for reproduction on the back of outerwear. Fifteen years after that, in 2018, Simons re-reappropriated Saville (or appropriated himself?). This time he included an image from a Joy Division cover that appropriated an image from *Graphis Diagrams*, the 1974 book by Walter Herdeg. I know; this gets complicated.

Again, whose art is it? And does it even matter? Raf Simons is a collector of images, firms, fabrics, and ideas; that it all finds its way into his work is exactly what you expect and love.

17

13 January
Bernard Hoesli

The Texas Rangers: Hoesli, fourth from right; Colin Rowe, fifth from right, 1950s

Bernard Hoesli worked for two of the most famous Le's: Leger and Le Corbusier (it would have been hard for him to work for Ledoux, as he practiced two hundred years before Hoesli). His tenure included work on Corbusier's Unité d'Habitation in Marseille and the Curutchet House in Argentina.

The Paris gigs make sense for Hoesli. But his next stop at the University of Texas at Austin, as one of the Texas Rangers (not the baseball team) in 1951, was a bit of a wild card for a Swiss architect. The group included Colin Rowe, Robert Slutzky, John Hejduk, Werner Seligmann, John Shaw, Lee Hodgden, and Jerry Wells (five of whom were later my professors, but far from Texas, and a couple of whom later colonized Cooper Union). Together, over the next decade, they developed a pedagogical structure for teaching modern architecture that is still in use.

The idea that modern architecture education (which was systematized at the Bauhaus more than twenty years earlier) needed to be somehow codified in 1951 may seem superfluous. But the Texas pedagogy marked the transition from a fine art/craft-based educational model to a rigorous, analytical, academic, and historically informed process. It was a big deal.

Hoesli led the architecture department at the ETH Zurich for the next twenty-five years. He carried the pedagogical rigor with him, and it continues to define the ETH today. That educational structure endures, as a foundational underlay, even sixty years after it was devised.

Peter Drucker has said, "Teaching is the only major occupation of man for which we have not yet developed tools that make an average person capable of competence and performance. In teaching we rely on the 'naturals,' the ones who somehow know how to teach." There is no good reason that the stars of architecture (or design or art) are inherently good teachers; it happens but it is more coincidence than assured expectation.

Hoesli generated, perhaps unwittingly, several generations of architects who, by virtue of his educational constructs, are connected by a set of common understandings and touchstones; they share a language. That may seem like a small thing, but when a twenty-two-year-old student and an assortment of thirty-, forty-, fifty-, and sixty-year-olds can engage in a vigorous discussion about architecture, it is as much because of Hoesli as anyone.

14 January
Cecil Beaton

Self-portrait reflected in a mirror of the Jain temple, Calcutta, India, 1944

Even his name is perfect: Sir Cecil Walter Hardy Beaton. Raised in wealth but not in the society he felt he belonged, Beaton created not just a persona but an avenue into the class he was certain he was entitled to join. He attended the right schools where, at one, he was bullied by Evelyn Waugh. Ironic, as Beaton essentially documented the world that Waugh wrote about in *Brideshead Revisited* with his Bright Young Things (BYT) images of England between the wars.

Beaton used photography, and his considerable talent, to celebrate a libertine world finally freed of war and Victorianism. These photographs are a catalogue raisonné of the upper classes of BYTs and celebrities, starting with their publication in *Vogue*. His career there ended when he inserted anti-Semitic slogans into an image featured in the February 1, 1938, edition, causing the entire issue to be recalled, pulped, and reprinted. Of course, Beaton was fired. Not unlike Philip Johnson (another wealthy gay man of precisely the same era who similarly flirted with the wrong politics), Beaton did his penance for his transgression; he photographed the wartime blitz damage in London for the British Ministry of Information. In more than ten thousand photos, he redeemed his reputation and learned to photograph things that were neither bright nor young.

He broadened his work to set design and costume design for stage and screen, and he even acted in one of his productions. It was a perfect transition from photographing the stagey and flamboyant BYTs to dressing and designing for the stagey and flamboyant on Broadway and in Hollywood. He won Tonys and Oscars for his efforts, and he lived, during those postwar years, and died in Wiltshire, England, at Reddish House (recently for sale for four million pounds), which isn't Red House (by William Morris) but a little less red and a lot more formal. There he hosted every famous icon from Garbo to Hockney, from Jagger to the Queen Mum.

His 1968 retrospective at the National Portrait Gallery was the first in any British museum of a living photographer, and the museum's recent BYT exhibition has kept alive the enduring (and periodically extremely relevant) allure of that particular age of excess.

15 January
Pablo Ferro

Still of opening sequence to *Dr. Strangelove,* directed by Stanley Kubrick, 1964

Pablo Ferro's observation, to Stanley Kubrick, that all things mechanical seem in some way sexual led to one of the greatest movie opening title designs ever made, for *Dr. Strangelove.* Using stock footage of the midair refueling of a bomber, the metaphor worked, but early designs using large type moved the focus from the airborne sex to the type, so Ferro used his own hand-drawn line and outline text to create a more transparent foreground. It was a bit of innate brilliance that, paired with the velvety soundtrack, announced an entirely new kind of film: allusive, ironic, crafted, and very, very funny.

The title sequence was the opposite of the trailer Ferro made for the same film, which is fast, loud, sharp, and cut together as a collage of its iconic moments. They have two entirely different jobs to do; the trailer is the ad to sell the product, the titles are the foreplay to the action. Kubrick understood that Ferro, whose commercials he had seen, was right for both and later called him a genius.

Kubrick was right, and Ferro went on to do some of the most lasting titles ever (of course, it didn't hurt that the films were classics): *Dr. Strangelove, Psycho, L.A. Confidential, Napoleon Dynamite, Bullitt, The Thomas Crown Affair, Men*

in Black, *Stop Making Sense,* and more. He was the cool kid for cool directors to hire.

Ferro admits learning to draw cartoons (which led to animation and ultimately to film titles and ads) from a 1949 book by a Disney cartoonist, Preston Blair. Ferro produced a comic book that even his coworker Stan Lee had to admit had a too-dark ending. (Spoiler alert: the antagonist's head was used as a bowling ball to knock down an array of his body parts used as pins...as I said, too dark.)

From those amateur beginnings, Pablo Ferro fashioned a career of arresting images and fast-paced sequencing that helped define an entire genre of movies through their titles. He became the resource that a generation of title designers (and filmmakers) have used as their own how-to guide.

16 January
Samuel McIntire

Peirce-Nichols House, Salem, Massachusetts, 1782

There's an entire canon of work based on the instructive manuals of architecture. The first, Vitruvius's *Ten Books on Architecture* (from the first century BC, but not discovered until the fifteenth century AD), or later, Alberti's version from the fifteenth century, or Palladio's from the sixteenth century, all based on the Vitruvian text, have been the pattern books of classical architecture.

For those with access to actual Roman ruins, like Michelangelo and his posse, the education could be firsthand; they crawled all over the remnants of the ancient past for clues on how to build. More than the standing buildings, more than images of those buildings, more than the ruins themselves, these books defined five hundred years of classical building as a codified system. It's not an exaggeration to consider these works the bible of architecture as a system of thought, not just a local tradition or decorated engineering.

These books are how someone like Samuel McIntire, a furniture maker born to a housewright, became a celebrated architect in eighteenth-century Salem, Massachusetts. The translation he made was from the stone and masonry buildings described in all the didactic texts to the wood-frame structures common in the US. This required real invention, not just replacing one material with another; the entire methodology (detailing, mass, technology, and longevity) of the wood frame is worlds away from that of the originals.

While McIntire did design brick buildings, his wood ones are part of a tradition of dematerialization (e.g., wood standing in for stone) that early American architecture embraced. At George Washington's Mount Vernon, wood is cut into chamfered blocks that imitate cut-stone facing. McIntire, a wood carver of both sculpture and furniture, helped translate classicism into wood, establishing a new, uniquely American, neoclassical language.

McIntire built enough to define an entire district, but he is best known for creating the vase-back chair that set a record price of $662,500 at auction. (Mies van der Rohe take note: sometimes it's the furniture that makes you famous!)

17 January
Bob Gill

Bob Gill, Alan Fletcher, and Colin Forbes, photographed by Robert Freeman, 1962

A very smart and talented designer, Bob Gill claimed to be a founder of Pentagram, but he actually joined with Colin Forbes and Alan Fletcher in 1962 and left Fletcher/Forbes/Gill in 1965, seven years before they and others created Pentagram. If he founded something, it would have been called Triangle, not Pentagram, which was founded in 1972 by five designers: Forbes and Fletcher, plus architect Theo Crosby, graphic designer Mervyn Kurlansky, and industrial designer Kenneth Grange.

Nevertheless, Gill adhered to the very Pentagram notion that a good design idea can be described on a phone call. At an early pitch for Citibank's sound mark, he arrived with just a coin, spinning it on edge on a table, and listening to the sound as it, eventually, fell (genius).

His proposal for a peace monument was war machinery (tanks, guns, etc.) piled in a heap forty feet/twelve meters high and painted matte black. Again, brilliant.

His real genius, however, was marrying Sara Fishko, creator of National Public Radio's *Fishko Files*.

I personally found Gill to be enormously annoying, but that might be my wounded ego speaking; after meeting me at least a dozen times, he still introduced himself every time we remet as though we had never met. Or it might be that he really was annoying. Hard to tell. Could be both.

Gill and his colleagues were responsible for pushing graphic design away from a mere decorative or illustrative art to a discipline based on ideas. It is the most significant transformation of that discipline in the twentieth century, perhaps ever, and Gill was a part of both inventing and teaching that change.

A picture of Gill from 1962 that periodically appears is really a crop of a Fletcher/Forbes/Gill portrait by Robert Freeman shot shortly before Freeman photographed the *Meet the Beatles* cover (Google it). The long lens, stacked composition of the three design partners is a model for the much more famous stacked image of the four Beatles.

Bob Gill later wrote and produced the Broadway musical *Beatlemania,* a re-creation of the Fab Four that ran for more than a thousand performances in New York City. So he may be the bookends to the Beatles, in addition to writing the book on design.

18 January
Philippe Starck

Louis Ghost chair, 2002

I first encountered Philippe Starck's work in 1984 (the year after he designed François Mitterrand's private apartments at the Élysée Palace) at the Café Costes in Paris and was gobsmacked (and, really, what a great word). The café looked just barely post-Memphis, both a bit surreal and a bit stagey, but very cool and without the aggressive coloration and highly patterned surfaces of Memphis. Cool luxe. Smart without being elitist (or so I thought).

Since then, Starck has designed products, probably numbering in the thousands, that range from utterly unusable and trivial to truly inventive, genius, and hyperelegant, all from one basically conflicted mind. On the one hand, he is constantly proclaiming the end of design, or the uselessness of material possessions, or how irresponsible it is to add anything to a world crowded with objects. On the other hand, he has been furiously making things for forty years, owns at least nineteen homes, and has had at least four wives. The man is consumed with consumption! It's no wonder he's a bit conflicted.

As much as I find him overly performative (and that may be the point), I may own more of his work than that of any other designer, in part because of the ubiquity, in part because nearly every single design is an actual invention (as opposed to a style makeover), and in part because his work is generally so accessible. Yes, eyeglasses need a flexible hinge. Yes, furniture needs a place to hold your drink. Yes, pools should have music underwater. Yes, yes, yes. And yes, I suppose he does need to personally appear in virtually every promotion, just so we can face our annoyance with him in order to love the things he makes.

Even his mass-market designs manage an occasional elitist pretense. I remember a certain pudgy gallery owner in New York City, who was wearing the same Starck-designed glasses I was (but his in polished chrome), telling me there were only four people with those specially finished frames: Starck, Elton John, Mr. Gallery himself, and probably Richard Branson or Mick Jagger or fill-in-your-own boldface name. It was important to him, anyway, and I'm sure Phillipe didn't mind a bit.

19 January
Sophie Taeuber-Arp

Sophie Taeuber-Arp on the Swiss fifty-franc banknote, 1995

Sophie Taeuber-Arp's work still looks as fresh, as crisp, and as inventive as if it were made today, not, shockingly, a hundred years ago. The work is so perfectly refined and expressed that you can almost see her thinking it through while you look at it.

Much is made of Taeuber-Arp being overlooked as the important artist she was; certainly she was as innovative as her more famous husband, Jean Arp. Originally classified as a "girlfriend member" of the Zurich Dadaist movement (though she was a founding member and signed the manifesto), she produced more interesting work in her brief fifty-three years than most of her colleagues did in twice that time.

Like Anni Albers, she was fluent in (and likely expected to make) textile art, and, like Albers, she made no distinction between traditional fine art and the less-respected applied art. Part of her skill (and charm) is in the overlap of craft and art, of performance and art, or of utilitarianism and art. It makes her unique in the Swiss group that officially marginalized her role but equally admired her work.

Taeuber-Arp graced the Swiss fifty-franc note in the same series that pictured Le Corbusier on the twenty-franc note,

so she wins that one by thirty francs! She is connected to another famous Swiss designer, Max Bill, but for the saddest of reasons: she died while spending the night in his summer cabin. In midwinter 1943, she missed the last tram home and camped temporarily in Bill's snow-covered cabin, where a faulty wood stove leaked carbon monoxide and asphyxiated her. Her bereft husband spent a good part of the rest of his career promoting her work, cataloging it, and keeping her name alive, though without much demonstrable success.

Sophie Taeuber-Arp was rediscovered with massive shows at the Tate and MoMA, but there are still attribution issues that blur credit between Jean and Sophie. That is unfortunate, but understandable, as Dada was not known for precise recordkeeping. It may be that her lack of celebrity has preserved her work; what else could explain hundred-year-old textile art that looks perfectly new?

20 January
Julia Morgan

Roman pool at Hearst Castle, San Simeon, California, 1934

Julia Morgan, an extraordinary architect and engineer, has a long list of firsts: first woman to graduate from University of California, Berkeley, with an engineering degree with honors; first woman admitted to the École des Beaux-Arts; first woman licensed as an architect in California; first woman awarded the American Institute of Architects Gold Medal (a mere fifty-six years after her death).

Each first was a much more complex accomplishment than it might seem. She applied three times to the École des Beaux-Arts, failed once on her own, failed once due to an "adjustment" in her exam by the school, and finally was admitted so late that she exceeded the acceptable age requirement, resulting in her having to finish the entire program in three years instead of five.

That was typical Morgan: so smart, talented, and driven and (of necessity) so unperturbed by the obstacles scattered in her path. Because Berkeley had no architecture school, she became a skilled engineer. After the 1906 San Francisco earthquake, her unique talent in engineering concrete structures was highly valued, and she finally succeeded financially as she had already artistically. Until then she had often been hired initially because she charged less than her male competition. After that, it was pure talent.

She designed more buildings as a single architect than any other American, seven hundred in all. Most were for clients for whom she built over and over and over (dozens for William Randolph Hearst alone). It's an astonishing record, still intact, and it would be impressive even if the buildings were not as extraordinary as most of them are.

She didn't publicize her work or her life; media often pursued the "woman architect blah blah blah" angle, which didn't interest her. As she said, "My buildings will be my legacy...they will speak for me long after I'm gone." And, of course, they have.

Our lives overlapped only four years, but I would have loved to have known Julia Morgan; seems like she would have been a force of nature.

21 January
William Adams Delano

Epinal American Memorial at the American Cemetery, Epinal, France, 1956

Before opening my own firm, I worked for architects whose offices were in the Dakota (home to John and Yoko, Lauren Bacall, Leonard Bernstein, etc.). The firm was headed by a well-connected architect whose family, and whose life at the Dakota, led to a wealth of clients and projects. It's how it used to work for nearly every successful architect: family name and network were everything. (Maybe it still does, despite the success of some on their merits, not their names.)

William Adams Delano was born into those connections and led the comfortable professional life of an architect whose livelihood wasn't entirely dependent on his business. His educational CV has all the markings of Gilded Age class and power: an elite prep school, then Yale, Columbia, and the École des Beaux-Arts (which in those days was the ultimate education in, well, Beaux-Arts architecture).

Then there's the name, Delano, which he shared with his distant cousin Franklin Delano Roosevelt. Together with his partner, Chester Holmes Aldrich (who shared his last name with Senator Nelson Aldrich and that other Nelson Aldrich...Rockefeller), Delano became the in-house neoclassical designer to the American

moneyed class. They designed Kykuit for the Rockefellers (of course) and Oheka, the insanely large Gold Coast home for banker Otto Kahn (the second-largest American home at more than 100,000 square feet/9,290 square meters).

They also designed what might be the worst national pavilion at the Venice Biennale Gardens, the USA Pavilion. Sadly, their design is from a moment when the US lacked the international mojo to do anything radical, modern, or distinctly American. The pavilion is a sad mimic of classical heroics at a scale so small it fails to be either intimate or monumental. The 2021 Venice Architecture Biennale did it the favor of completely concealing it behind a wooden facade.

Delano's 1932 sketch for a "Govt Building for a Metropolis" seems most out of step with his conservative character. It's a corner building with rippling US flag facades and (this is where real commitment to an idea shines through) a plan that is also a US flag! Bravo, Billy! Turns out you had both a clever streak and a great sense of humor!

"Good taste is as tiring as good company."

Francis Picabia, quoted in *Yes No: Poems and Sayings*

As a young painter, Francis Picabia painted his own copies of valuable paintings his father owned, swapped them for the originals (without permission), and sold the originals (in order to finance his own stamp collection)! This may be his earliest Dada act, questioning what constitutes value in art. Or it may be just Picabia's earliest felony.

Picabia was trying to work out cubism from 1909 onward; he was there along with all those other artists in Paris (you know, Picasso, Braque, etc.) trying to figure out a new way of seeing. Picabia even traveled to New York City several times to promote the movement, and was the only cubist painter to attend the 1913 Armory Show. Alfred Stieglitz gave him a solo show at his Gallery 291 (at 291 Fifth Avenue) and devoted a double issue of its magazine, *291*, to him. Picabia's New York work shifted to a mechanical phase (the *portraits mécaniques*), on the way to Dada. He named the Dada magazine he created *391* (in a very *Spinal Tap* "this goes to eleven" kind of competitiveness).

My favorite client bought several original issues of *391* and named his postproduction studio after it. For the color scheme of the studio's editing suite doors, we took the numbers three, nine, and one and used every Benjamin Moore color with a combination of those digits. Color 391 (now called Sweet Vibrations – and I don't envy the people who have to make up these insane, and totally unhelpful, names) is still among my faves!

Somehow Picabia, whose work is simply fantastic, never had the profile of his contemporaries, even though he worked hard to promote himself and the various movements he joined. Maybe he enjoyed the *succès de scandale* a bit too much, as when his new cubist work was called "ugly" and "incomprehensible." He said, "The world is divided into two categories; failures and unknowns," which may confirm his enjoyment of criticism and his tendency to incomprehensibility.

His cantankerous personality may be why he was thought to be a Fascist and was arrested after World War II as a collaborator with the Vichy government. He was released (possibly using the "he's not a Fascist, he's just an asshole" defense), and the charges never went further, but it was far from his final act as a provocateur.

23 January
Jože Plečnik

Clock interior and building, Most Sacred Heart of Our Lord, Prague, 1932

If Plečnik had designed only the Church of the Most Sacred Heart of Our Lord in Prague, that would be enough; the building's 25-foot/7.5-meter glazed clock set in a flat tower, with one of the most modern ramped spaces inside (rarely seen, just for clock maintenance and architectural tourists), is a marvel. Looking suspiciously like a Michael Graves concoction but built before Michael Graves was born, it is a sourcebook for postmodern architecture.

The ever-grim-looking Plečnik (though he did love dogs) must have had a perverse sense of humor: his droopy lights on an Ionic column, his witch's hat on the (unbuilt) National Parliament, and, of course, the church that is really a clock. His work is actually sublime, once you get past the quirkiness. And when you learn that he was a student of Otto Wagner, it all begins to make sense, especially knowing that Plečnik had a portrait and inscribed motto of Wagner on the wall of his home.

Plečnik's work, like Wagner's, makes a point of departing from classical/ traditional norms just enough to get your attention, but not enough to flatten you with its radicalism. And the work never fails to reference (quite abstractly) the time he spent in Italy after winning

the Prix de Rome in 1898. His triple bridge over the Ljubljana River slyly nods to Michelangelo's Campidoglio as well as Mike's Laurentian Library stairs.

If you think that reference is a stretch, too much of an inside game, too obsessive, consider that when a woman wrote to ask him to marry her, he wrote back, "I am already married to my architecture." (He was twenty-eight.) That could be his devoutly Catholic "married to god" thing; there is a touch of the fanatic in him, as there was with Luis Barragán. Both ascetics, both without families, both Catholics, both producing unique work that came to define a time and place. Plečnik is the face of Ljubljana the way Antoni Gaudí is of Barcelona (just to jump geographically for a moment).

Slovenes (like Melania Trump) love his work so much they put his never-built National Parliament building on a coin, which must be a first. His portrait was on the five hundred Slovenian tolars banknote (worth a couple of dollars) because Plečnik is so money.

24 January
Phyllis Lambert

Seagram Building, New York, New York, 1958

Phyllis Lambert CC GOQ FRAIC FRSC RCA (she has more letters after her name than in her name) is the legendary daughter of Samuel Bronfman who steered her father to enlist Mies van der Rohe to design his New York City headquarters, the Seagram Building. It was the first of a lifetime of contributions to the art of architecture.

Much is made of Lambert's influence at age twenty-seven; she effectively managed to get Mies the job and then ran it as the client, while working on it as a mentee. What is remarkable (and quite fortunate) is that she, as a recently divorced artist living in Paris, had no architectural training at that point. Had she just finished architecture school (she entered Yale, then Illinois Institute of Technology after the Seagram Building was nearly complete), she would have likely tried to get the commission for herself. Or at least that's what nearly everyone I know, including me, would have done!

To be both as insistent as she was (there's a famous eight-page letter she wrote to her father to convince him to abandon the quite creditable firm he had already retained, to let her research and recommend an architect) and as respectful to Mies as she was required a balancing act of extraordinary

confidence and understandable deference.

A lesser person might have robbed us of the chance to have the premier example of Mies's modern urban tower. She pursued the role of patron saint (both demanding and supportive), essentially the same role that has moved architecture forward in any age.

Like lots of urban modernism, Seagram works best in the context of what Park Avenue was, not what it became as a result of Seagram. The spread of lesser Seagrams has not been to the advantage of Park Avenue, nor the city at large. But as with postmodernism, can you really blame the originators for what the imitators have wrought?

Phyllis Lambert, likely to her eternal dismay, is also the aunt of Clare Bronfman, sentenced to eighty-one months in prison for her role in promulgating the NXIVM cult affair. Imagine if it had been Lambert instead of Bronfman; NXIVM cofounder Keith Raniere wouldn't have stood a chance!

25 January
Aino Aalto

Side Table 606, originally designed as a shoe-changing stool, 1920s

Looking down a list of famous Finnish women architects in the twentieth century (not the shortest list ever, but pretty short), the first two are the only recognizable names (to me). Both are Aaltos: Aino (Alvar's first wife) and Elissa (his second wife after Aino's death in 1949 at fifty-four). The list is alphabetical (and nothing can beat Aalto for the top position), but they are first in importance as well, though we will never know precisely how important.

Aino Aalto was an architect and designer in her own right. She often submitted her own entries for competitions, even though Alvar seemed to win them all. She was a critical part of the Aalto architecture office, eclipsed in fame by her husband in part because she died so young and in part because men ran that world. Though, if you look at a project known to be hers, the couple's own Villa Flora, it's clear she was not the architectural genius Alvar turned out to be. Her early death means we have no proof of her contributions to the architecture she and her husband created together (though some projects like Villa Mairea clearly show her hand).

But it's also clear that many (most, really) of the pieces we simply call Aalto furniture (including, reputedly, the Aalto stool and Aalto table) are really

Aino Aalto furniture. The iconic glassware for Iittala is hers as well. She was a cofounder of Artek, its first design director, and its managing director. Most people who couldn't name a single Aalto building would know the Aalto stool and the Aalto vase. Burnishing the Aalto brand, these are the artifacts we can own and live with (so few of us have Aalto buildings to live in!).

It may be apocryphal, but when the now-famous Model 60 Aalto stool first appeared in the US, it was sensibly priced at $5 and didn't sell; when the price was raised to $25 (equal to about $250 today), it sold out. Lesson: the perceived value of design can be manipulated by prices, inverting the normal laws of supply and demand.

It's time that Artek and Iittala gave Aino Aalto her due with at least co-credit on the hundreds of items she shepherded through these still-successful design businesses. Aino does come before Alvar in the alphabet, so maybe top billing is in order!

26 January
Jules Feiffer

Jules Feiffer at work, 1958

Jules Feiffer's big bald dome seems to barely contain his big ambidextrous brain. Still working in his nineties, Feiffer is one of those polymaths who can both write and draw a cartoon, and write plays and screenplays, employing both his left brain and right brain in an impressive range of projects. Naturally, like nearly every other successful New York City artist, he attended the Art Students League, but that hardly explains how literate he has become.

The whole left brain/right brain thing must be working for him, given his Oscar, Obie, Pulitzer, and membership in the American Academy of Arts and Letters. In fact, Arts and Letters may be the best description of his talents.

In addition to creating more than forty years of cartoons in the *Village Voice* (where I first encountered him), he has written for some of the rare geniuses of film: Stanley Kubrick, Robert Altman, and Mike Nichols. Kubrick had "unqualified admiration" for his comics and asked him to write a screenplay; Nichols directed the film of his play *Carnal Knowledge*; for Altman he wrote *Popeye*.

If he had done only his *A Dance to...* comics in the *Village Voice*, it would be enough to eternally endear him to me. That and his wonderfully merciless

Richard Nixon comics. The *Dance* comics may be so authentic because he lived through the Beat era, designing the poster for *The Nervous Set*, a Beat musical from 1959. His sense of humor must have gelled during this era, but was born more of anxious satire than obeisance to the spirit of the times. (Feiffer's autobiography was reviewed as "invading Jack Kerouac territory," so maybe not all satire.)

His anxiety and his politics never seem to grow old. He said, "Nixon seems to be us" in the 1970s, and "Let's stop fucking around, this is who we always were" about the Trump years. Cynical, yes. Cyclical, of course. We need more cultural intellectuals like Jules Feiffer, and we definitely need more consistent criticism of the hypocrisy that seems to invade virtually all politics. I would say "these days," but Feiffer has proved that hypocrisy is eternal.

Living from FDR to JRB (Joe Biden and I have the same initials) has its advantages; Feiffer gets to recycle his observations and be right about 100 percent of the time.

27 January
Luigi Figini

Villa Figini, Milan, Italy, demonstrating Le Corbusier's five points of architecture, 1935

Born just eight days after his future partner Gino Pollini, Luigi Figini may be the most famous Italian modern architect you've never heard of.

He designed a house in Milan, a small house tucked away in a quiet neighborhood, that is as good an example of Le Corbusier's "five points" (his abbreviated manifesto of the elements of style – his style, of course) as exists anywhere. If Corbusier's Villa Savoye is a horizontal slab levitated, Figini's Milan house is turned on its side, a slim urban house rather than the suburban Villa Savoye. Most remarkable is the 14-foot-/4.3-meter-high space under the occupiable portion of the house; it is completely empty but for the columns and a floating staircase to the box above. It is so pure it looks like the house could walk away.

Figini checks off all the five points (piloti, roof garden, free plan, horizontal windows, independent facade), but manages it 1) in the middle of the city; 2) with an entirely open ground floor; and 3) for the working class (well, it was for Figini, an architect, famously not rich). Corbusier's villas (and virtually all similar examples) are for captains of industry, forever associating the best of modern architecture with the moneyed classes, not exactly how it was sold to the public at events like the 1929 experimental Weissenhofsiedlung! Figini's project at the 1933 Triennale in Milan was a demonstration of how the masses could live in rationalist homes (just as Marcel Breuer proposed at MoMA fifteen years later).

Figini and Pollini (the firm he founded with his mate Gino) followed Gruppo 7, which they founded with Giuseppe Terragni, Adalberto Libera, and others. Figini and Pollini were the ultimate *razionalistas* in 1920s–30s Milan, as demonstrated at EUR (Esposizione Universale Roma, Mussolini's urban escapade that captures the only thing that is good about Fascism: its architecture and design), Olivetti (perhaps the first design-driven manufacturer), and Cimitero Monumentale (a who's who of the architecture of death).

Figini and Pollini built the remarkable Chiesa della Madonna dei Poveri (at the same time Corbusier built Ronchamp). It is a church rendered as a factory, in a country where churches are the most exalted buildings imaginable. "A church is a machine for praying," to paraphrase Le Corbusier? Figini, an iconoclast until the end.

28 January
Wallace Neff

Experimental Bubble Houses in Los Angeles, circa 1940–1949

Wallace Neff is responsible for what we (and *Architectural Digest* and every other house-as-competitive-sport publication attests) think of as the Hollywood celebrity home. They tend to be vaguely Spanish (but really Italian inspired), beautifully detailed, very grand, and perfectly sited. They are easy to love as dramatic pastiches of everything from Tuscan farmhouses to more formal monuments like Rome's Villa Giulia, whose hemicycle Neff borrowed for his Misty Mountain House. Of course, what at Villa Giulia is a garden loggia becomes a circular driveway in Neff's hands, but that's how Hollywood works: by appropriating and collaging.

Neff's grandfather was the McNally of Rand McNally, and he started his career with work for his family in Altadena, California, just north of the restricted city of Pasadena (restricted as in WASPs only). This forced celebs like the Marx Brothers to seek land elsewhere, hence Altadena. Neff's mash-up style worked well in a climate even warmer and steadier than Italy's. The loggias, outdoor rooms, porches, and other transition spaces encouraged the indoor-outdoor life that is so perfectly tuned to the climate and lifestyle of LA.

Wherever Neff built, it was nearly always for the likes of Groucho and Charlie (Chaplin) and Cary (Grant) and Daryl (Zanuck), now coveted by Jen and Brad and Reese and Diane and Madonna and everyone else including Rupert (Murdoch), who owned Misty Mountain, later selling it to his own son. Never mere houses, they were always called mansions.

Interestingly, Neff was proud of quite the opposite: the Bubble Houses he invented as a low-cost solution to housing after World War II. A house-sized inflated balloon was sprayed with gunite (concrete) to produce an igloo-like house before the balloon was deflated, pulled out through the door, and inflated for the next bubble. Brilliant and visionary, odd and ultimately undesirable all at the same time, Bubble Houses have never been called mansions!

Wallace Neff's mass-market forays might be limited, but they demonstrate what his mansions never had: a social conscience and a fascination with new technology.

29 January
Barnett Newman

Barnett Newman as the Monopoly Man, 1969

If there was ever an artist who looked like the Monopoly Man, it was Barnett Newman. In the age when artists aspired to dress like successful captains of industry, Newman said, "My struggle against bourgeois society has involved the total rejection of it." Maybe, but he and other artists kept the business attire. Think early Beatles in their matching suits or late David Bowie as an elegant rake. The uniform proclaimed art as a profession.

Newman failed exam after exam to teach in the New York City public schools, wrote art criticism, and published magazines while painting in a vaguely impressionist style. Until, that is, the beginning of World War II, when Newman wrote, "Painting is over, we must all abandon it." He lived up to his creed by refusing Works Progress Administration funding, thinking it foreshadowed politically approved art (which it did).

Newman then abandoned his impressionist style, starting anew with extreme abstraction: intensely colored canvases divided and joined by vertical lines he called zips. Watershed moments can do that, force artists to reconsider their art. That reinvention for Newman meant leaping over abstract expressionism, going directly to an elemental, almost mathematical system of painting. His most reductive moment is *The Wild*, a painting of just the zip, 8 feet/2.4 meters high and just 1.5 inches/4.1 centimeters wide. The contact sheet of pictures by Hans Namuth of Newman and Betty Parsons standing on either side of *The Wild* is revealing, as Barney barely moves while Betty adjusts her pose for each shot.

Watershed number two happened after a heart attack in 1957, with a series of paintings called *Stations of the Cross*, perhaps signaling a conversion from his Jewish upbringing to the true universal man. Or maybe he was relating to the suffering of a fellow Jew, with one painting's subtitle (in Greek), "Why have you forsaken me?"

As he said, his work should, he hoped, "signify the end of capitalism and of the totalitarianism of the State. My work, in terms of social impact, suggests the possibility of an open society, of an open world and not of a closed institutional one." Seems like quite a lift for an art he declared to be over just a few years earlier.

Barnett Newman branched out into sculpture with *Broken Obelisk*, which sat for years in the atrium at MoMA; I still miss it.

30 January
Finn Juhl

Judas table with silver inlays indicating seating positions, 1948

I grew up dining at a Finn Juhl (pronounced *yule*) table (the oval one with round silver inlays) at my mother's home and playing records in a rosewood Finn Juhl wall unit when visiting my father at his Upper East Side bachelor pad, all without having any idea who Finn Juhl was.

I know now, and he was a genius. Like Hans Wegner, he helped define Danish modern, which helped define the house I grew up in. My brother has the Finn Juhl table, I have the Hans Wegner daybed, he has the generic Danish dining chairs, I have the Womb chair, he has the anonymous china cabinets, I have the custom coffee table (that my parents preposterously told me was the pair to the one the Queen of Denmark had!).

I grew up hating these designs but love them now. It's irritating when your parents turn out to be right or have good taste, but teenage rejection can only go so far. At some point I even stopped hating the orange, mustard yellow, brown, and olive green palette I could barely bear growing up. So annoying.

When the midcentury design craze started (decades ago, with no end in sight), I was ready to concede. There is something beyond nostalgia that drove my conversion; these pieces represent change: technological, cultural, and lifestyle. They are artifacts of the postwar world order, of modernity, of accessibility, and of the diffusion of design beyond the doctrinaire early modernism.

Juhl is emblematic of that transformation, especially in the US, where he produced his designs in the 1950s. His US presence led to designing interiors at the United Nations Headquarters, articles in US magazines, and teaching at the Art Institute of Chicago. Still, he is hardly a household name, and it is hardly ever pronounced correctly, but his pieces have risen steeply in value. The oval table is listed for $72,000 on one auction site.

That table was inlaid with different size silver disks (and called the Judas table for thirty pieces of silver) in a pattern completely inscrutable to me. I now know the disks mark the seating positions for various numbers of diners at the table. Oh, how very droll, Mr. Juhl!

31 January
E. Fay Jones

Thorncrown Chapel, Eureka Springs, Arkansas, 1980

E. Fay Jones apprenticed with Frank Lloyd Wright after meeting him in 1949 as Wright got the American Institute of Architects Gold Medal. Jones was awarded the Gold Medal forty years later, the only of Wright's disciples to receive it. It's not surprising that Wright's acolytes were light on the awards; Wright, it turned out, was the only one who could do Wright. In anyone else's hands they never look (W)right. One could say that even with Wright they rarely looked (W)right, but that might be churlish. Or it might be true.

Jones, after serving in World War II, returned to the University of Arkansas and graduated with the school's first class in architecture. He returned to teach and lead the school for thirty-five years; it is now named the Fay Jones School of Architecture and Design or just Fay (as in "Why Fay?"). Amazingly, Fay (the school, not the man), while house-proud, fails to mention the architect of its latest award-winning building anywhere on its website (though the building's funders and its AIA Honor Award are referenced everywhere). It was Marlon Blackwell, who teaches at the University of Arkansas. Amazing omission...at an architecture school. No wonder the rest of the world undervalues the work of architects when even the institutions

that promote architecture don't seem to promote its practitioners.

Bill Clinton, when teaching law at UA, lived in a Fay Jones house he rented for $150 a month. It was destroyed by fire in early 2017, which seems like a perfect architectural reaction to Donald Trump ascending to power.

Jones is famous for one of America's most beloved buildings, apparently one of the four most beloved (yes, there is actually a numbered list of these), namely the Thorncrown Chapel. It is a breathtaking world unto itself and the only Jones building I really like. There are certainly moments in other projects that I truly admire, but overall they still look like second-rate Wright or, worse, ordinary suburban homes.

Designing one remarkable building is enough for me; adding extraordinary value to the built environment isn't easy, and every instance should be acknowledged. Fay Jones got the acknowledgment throughout his career, even if it was only for the fourth most beloved.

01 February
Vivian Maier

Rolleiflex 3.5F, twin lens reflex, similar to one of the cameras used by Vivian Maier

It's hard to understand how an enormously talented photographer, one whom people have compared to Robert Frank and Garry Winogrand and Diane Arbus, would work for more than forty years at her art and never show a photograph she took...to anyone! Not just refuse gallery and museum shows, not just avoid publicity, but never share an image with a soul and leave thousands of rolls of film undeveloped.

We are not talking about a tiny body of obscure work from unknown places; Vivian Maier spent two years traveling around the world, lived in New York and Chicago, and took hundreds of thousands of pictures. That translates to almost a roll of film every day for forty years. With astonishing endurance, persistence, and fearlessness, she spent time in some of the least savory areas of cities to document a time and place that was often hidden from public view. The photographs are nothing less than remarkable; this is not the accidental greatness we all (as a matter of odds, and a point of pride) occasionally achieve. This is a body of mature work so accomplished it would look at home in any museum. The proof, of course, is the more than fifty international exhibitions of her work, all after her death in 2009.

Though she may have had reasons for her shyness about the work, she was not shy about creating self-portraits. We are lucky to see her in full-on portraits in mirrors or reflections, but also lingering in the margins, or as shadows, or captured in a moment (such as in a mirror being carried by men at a rakish angle) that existed for only a fraction of a second.

Maier was employed as a nanny for most of her life, and she often took her charges with her, even to the seediest neighborhoods, while she did her photographic work. They recall her as a Mary Poppins figure with boundless energy and patience, never without a camera around her neck, ready for any adventure. She used a Rolleiflex for most of her photography; not placing a camera in front of her face at eye level, she could assume a posture of discretion that didn't immediately announce her intentions.

Luckily for us, Vivian Maier's medium-format camera (and her extraordinary skill) give us a precise and fine-grained view of a world long gone and barely noticed.

02 February
Theodate Pope Riddle

Bridgeport Evening Farmer

CUNARDER LUSITANIA SUNK BY TORPEDO OFF COAST OF IRELAND; PASSENGERS SAFE

Bridgeport Evening Farmer on the day of the *Lusitania* sinking, Friday, May 7, 1915

Theodate Pope Riddle was born Effie Brooks Pope, changing her name at nineteen to Theodate in honor of her grandmother Theodate Stackpole (who was also Philip Johnson's great-grandmother). She graduated from Miss Porter's School in Farmington, Connecticut (still in operation today!), where she got her first education in architecture by hiring faculty to privately tutor her. She became the first woman licensed as an architect in both New York and Connecticut. Of course, there's more.

She was on the *Lusitania* when it was torpedoed on May 7, 1915, jumping from the deck with her maid, saying, "Come, Robinson," rather than join the incompetent crew in a lifeboat. Another passenger jumped and landed on her, nearly drowning her and knocking her unconscious. She was pulled from the sea as dead, until someone noticed signs of life, and after two hours of resuscitation, she was alive again.

Pope Riddle's work in architecture began (as it has for many architects) with a home for her parents, Hill-Stead, in Farmington. At McKim, Mead & White, she managed an early internship while designing her first project. The house mimics, in part, Mount Vernon, George Washington's home, and

signaled her interest in referential architecture.

She went on to found and build a number of schools and even rebuilt the long-demolished home of Theodore Roosevelt on East Twentieth Street as a memorial/museum upon his death. This is the house in which the seven-year-old Teddy, as one of the million people viewing the parade, was photographed (and, really, how is this even possible?) hanging out the window to watch the catafalque bearing Abraham Lincoln's body rolling up Fifth Avenue.

When Theodate Pope Riddle's younger cousin Philip Johnson put together the first modern architecture show in the US, her reaction was dismissive. Her review was, "It was purely intellectual without regard to the emotions....Men who worked with machinery during the day might rather not sleep in a machine at night," comparing her preferences to Le Corbusier's "a house is a machine for living." Take that, Mr. Johnson.

03 February
Alvar Aalto

Door pull at the Säynätsalo Town Hall, Säynätsalo, Finland, 1951

Alvar Aalto is one of those architects every student of architecture is taught to love, holding down one corner of the Corb/Mies/Wright/Aalto pantheon. His furniture, especially, is easy to grasp, but his buildings are meant to be seen not in photos or drawings but IRL. Way too late (or just in time), I had that experience, and it was seismic.

Aalto seems to be everywhere in Finland, not just in Helsinki, where it's hard to walk for fifteen minutes without seeing at least a few of his buildings. His furniture is ubiquitous, not just in every project he designed, but as a national standard. Aalto defines design in Finland, and Finland is the beneficiary.

As a true devotee, I even stayed overnight in Säynätsalo Town Hall in one of the bedrooms the Aaltos created for themselves (imagine roaming a town hall, completely alone, at night, without any supervision. Ahh, Finland.). Every detail, every light fixture, every door handle, every column, every truss, every handrail, every skylight is worth a lifetime studying, so start early.

His residential masterpiece is the Villa Mairea, built for the family that would eventually join Alvar and Aino Aalto in creating Artek. It is the equal of the Villa Savoy, the Farnsworth House, Maison de Verre, Fallingwater, and the Kaufmann Desert House (and I could go on, but these are the canon in my book). His less-well-known Maison Louis Carré outside Paris is similarly remarkable.

Alvar Aalto died the day I graduated from architecture school. (I don't mean to imply anything by it; architecture did not die the day I graduated! I was also born the day Stalin died and don't draw any inference from that either.) Aalto was the last of the great first generation of heroic modernists, all born before 1900, to die. Like everyone who outlives their peers, it must have been lonely at the top. But lucky for us, as we got to see Aalto evolve for yet another decade.

04 February
Lorenzo Apicella

Adshel (now Clear Channel) Research and Design Centre, London, England, 1998

Born in Ravello, Italy, educated in London, sporting an English accent, and practicing as Apicella Studio in Rhode Island, Lorenzo Apicella was one of my architectural partners at Pentagram. Renzo (as no one calls him) was asked to join Pentagram by Kenneth Grange, who said upon suggesting him, "I'm just flattered he was interested in talking to me," which belies Grange's healthy sense of self and Apicella's charming affability. They met as Apicella was designing the Adshel Research and Design Centre (still my favorite of his buildings) in London (Grange was designing bus shelters for London).

The Adshel, now Clear Channel, building is one of those rare designs for which the unprogrammed part becomes the main story; it's the enormous, diaphanous canopy that provides a dry (did I mention it's in London?), softly lighted, outdoor space to display their bus shelter, newsstand, and kiosk designs in plein air. The gently inflated ETFE canopy in its exposed truss not only covers the plaza but also diffuses light and manages to look a little bit like geometric clouds. The first time I saw the material (which is now ubiquitous) was in this building.

Renzo's work often privileges the extra-programmatic to make a point,

architecturally. It's part of the architect's (any architect's, really) instinct to rewrite the program to shift the center of the idea, to own the brief rather than be subservient to it. Redefining the problem turns out to be the best way to solve the problem! Adding insight, experience, and (gasp!) wisdom to a project is the true role of the architect, something internally inscrutable that transforms a mere list into a scaffold for actual ideas.

Apicella's work manages to be much like him, including not being in the least bit self-centered, but instead elegant, clever, direct, inventive, and occasionally quite humorous. Intentionally.

When I joined Pentagram, I was suggested to the group by Paula Scher with words that now seem to be more about my profession than me: "I know an architect who is not an asshole." We all moved down a notch when Lorenzo arrived.

05 February
Ken Adam

War room set for *Dr. Strangelove*, directed by Stanley Kubrick, 1964

Steven Spielberg called the war room set that Ken Adam designed for Stanley Kubrick's *Dr. Strangelove* "the best set that's ever been designed" (after first telling Adam it was the best set Adam had ever designed). Adam worked both sides of the high/low street, doing production design for Kubrick films and James Bond films. In both he was remarkable; think *Clockwork Orange* and *Goldfinger*, *Dr. Strangelove* and *The Spy Who Loved Me*, *Barry Lyndon* and *Diamonds Are Forever*. He skipped working on *2001: A Space Odyssey* when he found out that Kubrick had been talking to NASA for a year before asking him to get involved, but it freed him to work on a few more Bond films. He managed that high/low dichotomy perfectly, both in his ninety-five years of life and in his work designing more than forty movies.

Born Klaus Hugo George Fritz Adam in Berlin, he was sent to boarding school in Edinburgh as Nazis took power. Klaus became Ken, one of only three German-born Royal Air Force pilots serving in World War II (one other being his brother Denis, born Dieter). He started in the RAF designing bomb shelters, a safe assignment; while he was a pilot he risked execution as a traitor if he was captured in Germany. (Immigrants really do get the job done.)

Adam studied architecture under fellow expat Erich Mendelsohn, who taught him the rendering style that he used his entire career. His sets really were architectural marvels. The gold vaults in *Goldfinger* were an insanely vertical jail-like affair (gold is very, very heavy, so not really practical, but still). In *The Man with the Golden Gun*, the partially sunken RMS *Queen Elizabeth* ship that, at a rakish angle, becomes MI6 Hong Kong HQ is pure genius, with the two geometries (the angle of the ship and the level spaces installed within them) colliding in every space. The set for the Korova Milk Bar in *Clockwork Orange* is an utterly fantastic 1971 vision of trippy London, while the newly built brutalist housing estate in Thamesmead needed no modifications to play its role as a dystopian background in the same film. Adam, as much as any designer, promoted brutalism as the preferred style of the evil criminal mastermind. We now see it everywhere, but Adam saw it first.

06 February
Robert Maillart

Salginatobel Bridge, Schiers, Switzerland, 1930

Robert Maillart is the best engineer you have never heard of, one who built, in Switzerland, the most beautiful concrete bridges that have ever existed. He did it starting in 1900, and for the next forty years, until his death, he produced increasingly refined and elegant examples of concrete's latent potential. The designs look nearly new today, and they should; the physics of his bridges are still the physics of bridges, and the engineers' creed of "economy of means" drove the designs toward the slimmest, most elegant profiles. His gracefully curved arch shapes are still beautiful; it's the pure engineering you see even today, absent the thirty to forty (or three to four hundred!) style changes that have come and gone over the past hundred years.

Maillart won state contracts based on cost; he winnowed down the price to a minimum, including the hidden cost of monolithic concrete construction, the formwork. For every concrete structure, forms (usually wood planks in those days) are built to contain the reinforcing, shape the pour, and support the concrete before it reaches full strength. The entire structure must be built first in negative, then filled for the positive. Maillart never managed (as Brunelleschi did at the Duomo in Florence) to eliminate the support altogether, but he came close.

Without complex mathematical analysis (he wasn't about the numbers), Maillart intuited what would work, and proving his confidence, he tested the bridges by crossing them first himself! He invented the mushroom column you've seen in factories and warehouses: columns that flare out at the top to distribute load with less concentration. But in all other things architectural, his work is much less compelling; he was a bridge builder, where his art was at its best. His Salginatobel Bridge was voted the most beautiful bridge of the twentieth century (so stand aside, Mr. Calatrava!).

MoMA exhibited his work in 1947, a few years after his death (of course) and as part of the 1964 *Twentieth Century Engineering* exhibit, whose catalog (bought by my parents at the show) was my first exposure to Maillart and to his world of elegant genius.

07 February
Bernard Maybeck

Hearst Hall, UC Berkeley, Berkeley, California, 1899

Bernard Maybeck was one of those difficult-to-pigeonhole architects, called by one a-bit-too-clever writer "not Wright but not wrong." I'm not sure how to reconcile that with the building he designed called the Mistake House. It does highlight the essential unknowability of Maybeck, at the very least.

His most famous work is the Palace of Fine Arts built for the 1915 Panama-Pacific International Exposition in San Francisco. An intentionally temporary building, it was constructed (as nearly all Expo buildings were then) out of plaster reinforced by burlap over a wood frame. It was so beloved that it was rebuilt in 1964–74 in concrete. Lucasfilm studios are nearby, which might explain why the city of Theed on Naboo in *Star Wars* has a very similar building.

Maybeck's most ironically named house is the Kennedy-Nixon House in Berkeley, named for the family that built it (Nixon) and the piano teacher for whom it was built (Alma Kennedy). Nixon (Richard M.) famously, but uncharacteristically, played the piano, so its name is even more confusing than it seems. It's now a music venue called the Maybeck Studio for the Performing Arts, sensibly.

Appropriating virtually any style in service of his projects, Maybeck was an alchemist, turning other's visual languages into his own. His buildings are occasionally craftsman style, sometimes classical, a few are rustic or half-timbered or Mission or even Gothic, and others are a mash-up of all the above. That eclecticism feels right at home in Berkeley and the whole Bay Area. His attempts to create a simulacrum of an English town seem more Disney than dialectic, and that is my problem with Maybeck. As serious as he might have been as an architect, picturesque is not as cogent as style, and style is not as substantial as an actual idea. But that's just me.

He mentored Julia Morgan and others while teaching at University of California, Berkeley, and he even worked with her on a project for William Randolph Hearst's mother, while Morgan spent the rest of her career working for the son.

The American Institute of Architects awarded Maybeck the Gold Medal in 1951 (six years before his death). Julia Morgan finally got hers more than half a century after her death.

08 February
Alvin Lustig

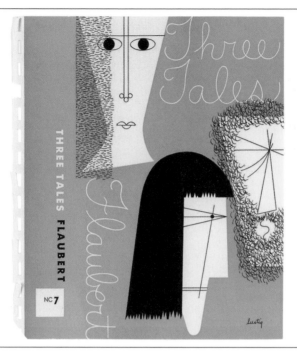

Cover of Gustave Flaubert's *Three Tales*, 1945

Alvin Lustig died at forty, and were it not for his wife, the accomplished designer Elaine Lustig Cohen, he might have faded from view. She kept his legacy intact and growing. Elaine continued to promote Alvin fifty years after his death, when she was nice enough to allow me to create rugs from his fabric design Incantation (a pattern of glyphs) for our renovation of Richard Neutra's 1934 Sten-Frenke House.

It was not a random choice; Lustig befriended Neutra in 1934 and gained access to the older architect's library as well as his sage advice. When Lustig went to Taliesin (briefly), he followed a path that Neutra had taken.

It's a habit of mine to always ask, when we are having something cool made for a client, "And if you were to make another one at the same time, what would that cost?" That's why I have (and love) my Incantation rug!

Lustig's book covers for New Directions are legendary; for ten years, he changed the way book covers were designed, creating a catalog of inventiveness that looks cool even today, seventy-five years later.

He designed the opening credits for the cartoon series *Mister Magoo* (maybe the first place I encountered his work) and interiors for his art department at *Look* magazine. There are those for whom lack of training is the best ingredient of great work. That was Lustig.

Like Mr. Magoo, he was nearly blind (from the diabetes that eventually took his life) when Philip Johnson asked him to design the signage at the Seagram Building. Elaine finished the job after Alvin's death, and a new graphic design career was born.

For me, Lustig's most surprising work is the Beverly-Carlton Apartment Hotel, now the Avalon Hotel. While working in LA on projects (like the Sten-Frenke House), the Avalon was my second home. Touted as home to Marilyn Monroe, Lucille Ball and Desi Arnaz, Mae West, and others, it was always the coolest, friendliest, most convenient hotel in LA (plus it was just steps from my sister's apartment on Olympic Boulevard). When last there I spotted Omarosa confabbing with a bevy of Hollywood types, just before she was "escorted" from the Trump White House. Maybe the Avalon is where all the wicked in Hollywood still like to congregate!

09 February
Gerhard Richter

Gerhard Richter in Düsseldorf, circa 1970

Everyone knows who Gerhard Richter is, nearly everyone loves his paintings, and many consider him to be among the twentieth and twenty-first centuries' most important living artists (if not *the* most important artist). The 2018 film *Never Look Away* by Florian Henckel von Donnersmarck (who also directed *The Lives of Others*, another amazing film about life in East Germany) is, even if only "inspired" by Richter, a remarkable narrative of a famously private obscurant.

Richter lived in, and left, East Germany for the West shortly before the Berlin Wall was built. He burned nearly all the work he had made to that point, an act of separation that allowed him to become the Gerhard Richter we know. While we may mourn the loss of his personal history, he has said, "Who knows what would have become of me had I succeeded with those paintings?" Not so of his subsequent work, which has made him spectacularly rich and respected.

If his early painting explored social realism, his later painting evolved to nearly always be about painting. He applies his prodigious skill to a kind of abstraction that always seems to be, ironically, content heavy. His paintings of newspaper articles, his blurry

paintings, the stripes, the almost-tacky abstracts, the color charts, the landscapes, the shadow paintings (I could go on) are each phases Richter has evolved through. His well-known ability to paint at an extraordinarily photo-realistic level seems to inform our understanding of his work after his East German phase.

I was in Rome celebrating my sixtieth birthday (I believe in being in very old places when one is feeling a bit old) and had dinner with friends at Piperno in the Jewish Ghetto. During dinner, the lights went out (I assumed it was a blackout) as a cake with candles was brought in. The entire room sang "Happy Birthday" (in English, which seemed odd) to my everlasting embarrassment, and when the lights came back on one of my dinner companions leaned over and whispered, "You are sitting next to Gerhard Richter." He was at the next table, literally next to me!

Gerhard Richter singing "Happy Birthday" to me is the best birthday gift I have ever had.

10 February
John Alcorn

Augustus Saint-Gaudens medal awarded by the Cooper Union in 1970

John Alcorn was called "the fifth Beatle of graphic design" by Steve Heller, which doesn't quite make sense; wasn't Brian Epstein the fifth Beatle? Was Alcorn the manager of Push Pin Studios? And what about Billy Preston? So many questions...Alcorn joined Milton Glaser, Seymour Chwast, and Reynold Ruffins at Push Pin after Edward Sorel departed. So maybe the Ronnie Wood of graphic design?

It was a perfect design fit; Alcorn's work is so easy to date because it so defines its time. That time may not have come back into fashion yet (or it did, and I missed it) so I'm not (yet? again?) a fan of his work, but wait a while, and I likely will be.

Alcorn moved to Great Neck, New York, as a child, graduated from Cooper Union, worked with Lou Dorfsman (Lou!) at CBS, designed books and book covers, moved to Italy, received the Augustus Saint-Gaudens Award from Cooper, and eventually settled north of New York City. He foreshadowed, by thirty years, my wife Carin Goldberg's career point by point in an eerily precise way, except that she left Long Island as a child. The rest matches up. Weird.

Alcorn got his Saint-Gaudens Award two years before Seymour Chwast did,

which I am sure the older Chwast was less than sanguine about. Glaser got his four years before Alcorn, and Sorel the year after Chwast. Twenty-three years after Alcorn, Ruffins was finally honored with the same award, so a four-peat! It's a five-peat if you are into the fifth Beatle thing.

Along the way, Alcorn designed movie opening sequences and posters for the Fellini movies *Amarcord, Ginger and Fred,* and *And the Ship Sails On*. But it is his 1960s illustrations that define him; vaguely Peter Max, soft psychedelic, *Yellow Submarine*-ish (he, in fact, illustrated a book of Beatles lyrics, so kind of related), they were more a mirror of the times than its avant-garde. His style evolved, with each decade reflecting (or possibly creating) a new cultural zeitgeist.

Alcorn died at fifty-six, while the rest of the Push Pin partners have lived into their nineties. It may be that the Saint-Gaudens Award doesn't guarantee a long life, or it may just be that the fifth Beatle always dies young.

11 February
Arne Jacobsen

Series 7 chair, 1955

The eight-hundred-pound gorilla of Danish design, Arne Jacobsen created some of the most iconic furniture, lighting, timepieces, buildings, and other accoutrements of life "from spoon to city," as Ernesto N. Rogers of BBPR (Milan architect and relative of Richard Rogers) said. Somehow tiny Denmark has produced a string of famous modern designers like Jacobsen: Finn Juhl, Hans Wegner, Poul Kjaerholm, Verner Panton, Poul Henningsen, Jens Risom, Georg Jensen, Jørn Utzon, all from a population about half of New York City's today.

Jacobsen's Series 7 chair remains the most beautiful, lightweight, comfortable, and iconic chair of the twentieth century (though some may nominate other designs). His other instantly recognizable and instantly iconic chairs include the Swan chair, Egg chair, Drop chair, Grand Prix chair, and Ant chair, a remarkable series of era-defining work.

And that's just chairs; he was an extraordinary architect and industrial designer, creating nearly all the Stelton products as well as Vola faucets (ask an architect friend), flatware, clocks, and watches, and a spectacular gas station prototype.

The Series 7 chair is emblematic of the inflated cost of "authentic" designs and raises questions when the licensed manufacturer, for example, invents new colors. In the case of the Drop chair, the licensee, Fritz Hansen, decided to reimagine the luxurious leather-upholstered chair...in plastic. Manufacturers vigorously object to knock-offs, of course, to protect their market (though they will couch the protection in the language of quality, royalties, reputation) and to protect their right to profit perpetually on their license. The intent of the designer to produce affordable furniture for the masses can be warped by the manufacturer's intent of the largest possible profit. In at least one case, perfectly crafted knockoffs prompted Herman Miller to reissue Charles and Ray Eames furniture they had long dropped from their line. The story is that they had to go out and buy pieces at auction because they didn't even have an archive of them. Amazingly.

Arne Jacobsen, who hated the label *designer* and considered himself only an architect, was a genius designer, and the products he made to ship around the globe will improve more lives than a town hall or hotel in Denmark ever could, but they will continue to only if the masses can actually afford them!

12 February
Auguste Perret

Palais d'Iéna, Paris, France, 1937

If your father is a stone mason (as Auguste Perret's was), perhaps the best filial rejection possible is to become a master of concrete (as Perret did) and celebrate the material's exposed finish (gasp!), saying, "My concrete is more beautiful than stone" (OMG). The first office Corb worked in was Perret's, where he learned to love concrete, later becoming the public face of *béton brut* (whence brutalism is derived) for the twentieth century.

Perret stands at the crossing of the old and new; trained at École des Beaux-Arts, he had one foot (on which he wore spats!) in symmetry and classical space and one in the brave new world of modernism. But unlike his contemporaries, like Adolf Loos, his name is nearly forgotten. On the other hand, if Loos himself is ever forgotten, at least his pithy proclamation "ornament is a crime" is well-known (if incorrectly quoted and misunderstood). Perret's work always seems, for its time, way too modern or not modern enough, though it is always remarkable and never without genuine and deep inquiry.

Perret is to Corbusier as, say, Muddy Waters is to the Rolling Stones: earlier, rougher, less accomplished at marketing, but more authentically pure than their progeny. Perret left his concrete exposed, while Corbusier and others plastered their early concrete buildings to create more abstraction and less materiality, eschewing cornices, while Perret understood their function of protecting facades and included them, albeit in modern form. Corbusier championed horizontal strip windows; Perret loved large vertical ones. Perret accused Corbusier and others of demagoguery in support of their beloved abstract volumes that rivaled the classical demagoguery they detested. He wasn't wrong.

Just as Perret developed (and used for his entire career) concrete in defiance of his father's beloved trade, Corbusier rejected Perret's brutal structural honesty in favor of dematerialization and abstraction. The conflict is the oldest story there is, well developed in both Greek tragedy and the Bible; happily, it produced at least two (and possibly hundreds of) remarkable bodies of architectural work for eternity.

13 February
Verner Panton

VP Globe light fixture, 1969

Why has Denmark, a country with a lot fewer (nearly half) the population of New York City, produced so many towering furniture designers? I don't know why, but Verner Panton is yet another (much younger) one, working in injection-molded plastic rather than the wood favored by (much older) Wegner, Juhl, and Jacobsen (for whom Panton worked in the 1950s).

Panton marked Denmark's transition from midcentury modern to 1960s pop. His first and most famous chair, the one-piece swoopy Panton S chair, was so complex to produce that it took ten years after the design for manufacturing to catch up; it was the first all-plastic chair. (Fellow Dane Poul Kjaerholm produced a model/prototype in wire and papier-mâché of a nearly identical design in 1953, at least ten years prior to Panton, before Kjaerholm moved on to his better-known steel-framed pieces; it was an idea that may have been in the air those days.)

In color, form, pattern, and exuberance, Panton's work explicitly occupies the more aggressive end of a design spectrum, an exception to the Danish notion of modesty and social conformity, as in the Law of Jante (a literary notion, now cultural). His

work also breaks from hygge, the Danish idea of coziness and comfort.

It's hard for us to see just how much an iconoclast Panton was in his native land. He was like Andy Warhol coming after abstract expressionism or Memphis following Italian modernism. His Cone chair is a visual joy; the upholstered cone replaces the stem of an ordinary chair to beautifully comic effect. It's a formal rather than material invention, but as clever (and easily produced) as anything he designed. The all-wire version is even better – a wonderfully transparent chair in which users seem to float on an impossibly frail construction.

He produced a modular tiny-home kit (Quonset hut style), inflatable furniture, buildings and interiors, and public art, all overshadowed by his very first chair.

Panton, Kjaerholm, Jacobsen, and Juhl all have birthdays within days of each other, which can only mean that Danes get very frisky in the spring. Or at least Danish designers' parents do. The month of May in architecture school (in the Northeast) is when everyone sheds several layers of clothes when spring (and end of term) finally arrives.

Good to know.

14 February
Katherine Stinson

KATHERINE STINSON   3457-15

Katherine Stinson and her airplane, circa 1910–1915

Architecture is not always a first career. The Wright Brothers first flew in 1903 (and it wasn't their first career, either). In 1911 (at nineteen) Katherine Stinson was the fourth woman to get an international pilot's certificate. She set flying records, was the first woman US Postal pilot, was among the first pilots to fly at night, was the first to skywrite in a plane (writing CAL after attaching flares to her plane), was the first to fly over London, was the first woman to fly in Canada and in Japan, and more.

Stinson started flying and learned to fly a Wright Brothers Model B after just four hours of instruction. Those early planes were a bit like extremely large box kites and still had the "tail" in front. Stinson was a flying savant and an accomplished daredevil of the sky.

She raced her plane against cars at Indy, performed endless stunts (including five hundred loops without an accident), and opened a flight school before contracting tuberculosis and marrying another aviator, both promising never to pilot a plane again! But that was after traveling the globe and being (condescendingly) nicknamed "America's Sweetheart of the Air," "The Flying Schoolgirl," and, in Japan, "Air Queen."

She wasn't accepted as a pilot for the US during World War I (even though she was one of the most accomplished pilots then alive), but she did raise two million dollars on a fundraising flight for the war effort. She was admitted into the National Aviation Hall of Fame...in 2019, a mere fifty years after her death.

Stinson went on to design award-winning homes in her adopted Santa Fe (where she recuperated from tuberculosis). One was for Dorothy McKibbin, who was the gatekeeper at the Manhattan (atomic bomb) Project in nearby Los Alamos.

My friend likes to hire, for his design firm, people on their third or fourth careers; he says they are smarter and better at design after doing other things (though I could argue that someone on their fourth or fifth career is either really old or has trouble focusing). Stinson would have fit right in. After being a pilot, a teacher, and an ambulance driver (during World War I when she wasn't permitted to fly), she finally became an architect. Given her past heroics, I am guessing she was pretty great at that too.

15 February
Shepard Fairey

Obey logo, transformed from the original *Andre the Giant Has a Posse* of 1989

It's hard to be a young rebel over fifty, but Shepard Fairey has consistently hooked his politics to the left and worked to create a visual language for activism. His quasi-Soviet-style propaganda is to the 2000s what psychedelic artwork was to the 1960s, long after his OBEY/ Andre (the Giant) street art spotted the urban landscape and became memes.

Fairey's high and low moments are linked to his Obama *Hope* poster; it made him famous (being the first modern campaign poster?) and infamous (as he appropriated an Associated Press photo for it and then lied about the source of the photo). Chastened, he made *Obey Giant* and *Facing the Giant*, a pair of documentaries attempting to explain, and humanize, his error while promoting a body of work that is more interesting than the single-most-humiliating event of his life.

If fifty is the new thirty, Fairey seems to have transcended his seventeen-times-arrested-bad-boy rep to become a committed post-felony activist. It works for some, irritates others, but the only question for me is whether Fairey cares what we think. I'm pretty sure his grandparents didn't when they named his father Strait Fairey, which is one of the coolest names imaginable.

Fairey does seem to care what everyone thinks, but hopefully he will outlive that unfortunate drag on any artist's progress. He developed an entirely post hoc justifying philosophy about his earliest work (the Andre faces he plastered everywhere); he now couches it as an experiment in phenomenology! Let's keep Martin Heidegger out of it; Fairey did what he did as a teen not for the sake of some Nazi enthusiast's philosophy (Heidegger joined the party in 1933) but because it was his art.

Art isn't made better by fitting it to a philosophical framework to give it heft. Others may ascribe some external intellectual associations to one's work, but better to leave that to the professionals. Artists make art, the art stands mute to the viewer, and the viewer gets to decide what they think. You can quote me on that (but I wish you didn't need to!).

Shepard may be missing one of the great things about getting older: not giving a fuck what others think.

16 February
Lawrence Murray Dixon

Postcard showing the McAlpin Hotel, Miami Beach, Florida, designed 1940

Lawrence Murray Dixon worked for Schultze and Weaver in New York City, whose commissions included the Breakers in Palm Beach and the Waldorf-Astoria Hotel in New York, as well as the Sherry-Netherland and the Pierre, which stand next to each other on Fifth Avenue at the corner of Central Park. It's reassuring that the same firm designed both, just as it's reassuring that they aren't a matched pair. Seems like anyone doing the same thing today would be sure everyone knew the same architects designed both (as I did not until writing this bio).

Dixon moved to Miami to design a spate of art deco hotels in the 1930s and '40s that continue to prove that a consistent style can indeed cohere a city (despite the previous paragraph). In less than ten years, Dixon designed the Tides, the Victor, the Marlin, the Tudor, the Senator, the Raleigh, and the Betsy Ross, among others, all in a relatively unadorned version of art deco. He designed hundreds of buildings in Miami Beach, especially in South Beach, effectively remaking the city as we see it today. That one man, one firm, could have that impact on a city is extraordinary. We're lucky it was someone as talented and as restrained as Dixon (and not, say, a Donald Trump).

The idea that buildings can be background buildings (like background actors in movies) and still have an enormous impact on the sense of place, especially in urban contexts, is kind of lost on us today. Imagine a movie with only the featured talent, and you get the idea. There is no movie without backgrounders, and there is no city fabric without background buildings: a movie without background talent is a stage play, and a city without background buildings is a world's fair.

Now everyone wants to be a star, which means no one is a star. Buildings that try too hard, that assert dominance in order to be valued, that prefer to break urban norms rather than reinforce them, are emblematic of our culture. Everyone now has their own truth, their own unimpeachable (well, for some) view of the world, and norms be damned. And how has that been going for us? Lawrence Murray Dixon would be horrified.

17 February
Thomas Heatherwick

Spun chair, 2007

Thomas Heatherwick started with some extremely clever and admirable work and has evolved, in my view, past his comfort level of expertise and scale. I loved his Rolling Bridge in East London, a very clever little walkway over a trough of water, that furls and unfurls in the cutest possible way.

Heatherwick's UK Pavilion, the Seed Pavilion, at the Expo 2010 Shanghai was a work of genius (and the star of the Expo) as an unexpected, enigmatic, fuzzy box with an image hiding in plain sight; a Union Jack can be seen as a shadowy subtext in the porcupine exterior. Hard to explain, but once you see it, it's indelible.

His Spun seating must be experienced to understand just how fucking cool it is. It evokes both incredible insecurity (as in, "I will be flung out of this thing") as well as great comfort, knowing you are not going anywhere, except around and around.

But it all starts to fall apart a bit after that. His new London buses are less than great looking, the now-closed Vessel in New York City's Hudson Yards is nearly as disliked as Hudson Yards itself, and Little Island, the little floating park in the Hudson, is, well, meh.

I date Heatherwick's devolution to the quite beautiful (and intimate) retrospective show at the V&A in 2012, where the then-forty-two-year-old was seen as the fashionable choice for larger projects. Great for him, possibly less great for us.

Not everything can be scaled up and still maintain the embedded genius of a simple, great idea. The Rolling Bridge could likely not span the Thames and still be as purely effective; the Vessel is kind of monstrously large; the Seed Expo Pavilion is so successful in part because the leap of scale from seed to building is measured and manageable (it might not be successful at four times the scale, for example).

Computers are partly responsible; once, when changing scales of design drawings, you had to redraw the set. Now there is no redrafting needed, unfortunately; you can just print at a larger scale and forgo the rethinking that redrafting requires.

Nevertheless, Heatherwick's best work is enough to establish his reputation, and he is young enough to steer it in even more successful (hopefully smaller) directions.

18 February
Paul R. Williams

Theme Building, Los Angeles International Airport, Los Angeles, California, 1961

Paul R. Williams, born in pre-twentieth-century Los Angeles, was raised in a foster home after both his parents died of tuberculosis. He was the only Black student at his elementary school and became, in 1921, the first Black architect certified not just in LA, but west of the Mississippi! He was also the first Black member of the American Institute of Architects.

Williams described his realization that it was his color, not his talent, that condemned him: "I passed through successive stages of bewilderment, inarticulate protest, resentment, and, finally, reconciliation to the status of my race....I wanted to prove that I, *as an individual*, deserved a place in the world."

And he did, unquestionably. Williams designed more than two thousand private homes (!), many for the most famous celebrities of the time, including Frank Sinatra, Lucille Ball, Lon Chaney, Barbara Stanwyck, Bert Lahr, Zasu Pitts, and Bill (Bojangles) Robinson. Many were designed on land with segregation covenants, meaning that he could design the houses, but not live there himself.

Williams, it is said, learned to draw renderings and even draft upside down because he realized that many clients would not feel comfortable in a meeting

sitting next to a Black architect. This is a desirable skill for entirely different reasons; being able to talk and present work while looking directly at a client's reaction is invaluable. Plus it's easier on the neck.

Williams was interested in low-cost housing and joined Wallace Neff in the Airform (also called Bubble) houses effort, definitely more Williams's modern style than Neff's traditional one, though they were both the same age. Together they designed a huge portion of the houses for the rich and famous in Hollywood, but in radically divergent styles.

If you have ever been to LAX, you've seen Williams's work at the Theme Building: the spacey, UFO-looking, revolving restaurant pavilion in the center of the airport.

In 1957 Williams was the first Black architect to be inducted into the AIA's Fellowship (FAIA) and a mere sixty years later was awarded the AIA's Gold Medal. Thirty-seven years after his death. In 2017 (sigh).

It took years for institutions to acknowledge what clients had already, immediately, recognized: Paul R. Williams indeed had a "place in the world."

19 February
Edward Austin Kent

Universalist Unitarian Church of Buffalo, Buffalo, New York, 1906

Edward Austin Kent, a Buffalo, New York, architect, designed a number of charming, even beautiful, buildings there, as well as the mosaic floor, composed of twenty-three million pieces of Italian tile, in Daniel Burnham's (of Flatiron Building and World's Columbian Exposition fame) Ellicott Square Building. His (now destroyed) Temple Beth Zion and Unitarian Universalist Church were both more exuberant than refined and much less doctrinaire (and spectacular) than, say, the Larkin Building by Frank Lloyd Wright, built the same year a few miles away.

Kent's educational pedigree (Yale and École des Beaux-Arts) and professional standing were impeccable. He formed the Buffalo Society of Architects, which later joined the American Institute of Architects as the first local chapter, and Kent himself was elected as president.

He traveled to Europe and elsewhere frequently, including a two-month 1912 trip to Egypt and France. He delayed his return just long enough, until mid-April, to travel first class on the world's newest and fastest ship's maiden voyage (pretty sure you know where this story is going).

En route he befriended writer/feminist/ interior decorator/geographer Helen Churchill Candee, whom he helped into the first lifeboat as their ocean liner hit an iceberg. By all accounts he spent the rest of his time onboard the *Titanic* helping passengers into lifeboats and going below deck and up again to assist. Candee gave him an ivory-framed portrait for safekeeping, and it was still in his pocket when his body was recovered.

We mostly hear about people who were late to work just that once at the World Trade Center on 9/11, or just missed TWA Flight 800. Edward Austin Kent may have chosen badly, or at least unluckily, but as the Royal Institute of British Architects said upon his death, he was "the very best type of American gentleman." While this seems just a tad snarky (especially about the rest of American gentlemen, those below "very best type" status), it perfectly describes Kent's architecture as well.

It's a question of manners that even a sinking ocean liner in the cold, dark North Atlantic was not enough to shake him from his habitual politeness. *Manners* is a word that barely describes what it takes to ignore one's own safety to help others, but surely that behavior achieves "very best type" status.

20 February
Harold Van Buskirk

Dazzle camouflage, USS *West Mahomet* in port, circa November 1918

Technically, Harold Van Buskirk was an architect, but really the most interesting things about him are that he was on the US Olympic fencing team three times (épée, for crossword enthusiasts) and a national fencing champion and that during World War I, he ran the US government's Camouflage Section, which produced "dazzle camouflage." This was the most counterintuitive method to defend oceangoing ships from submarines; instead of being painted with patterns that blended in with their surroundings, ships were painted with loud abstract patterns designed to perplex the enemy.

Today, you might consider painting the sea, or something digital and relatively subtle, or even transformable graphics, on enormous floating objects to conceal them. But no single disguise works in all conditions; the sea can be gray, black, or blue, and the sky is equally fickle. Dazzle's idea was not to hide the ships, but to make them visually confusing enough to render them hard to attack. It's the difference between James Comey pretending he could blend into the blue curtains to avoid Donald Trump, and, say, Bjork.

U-boats were slaughtering ships (like the *Lusitania*, plus about 5,700 others) before radar, sonar, and guided torpedoes. It was basically point and shoot. If you could confuse the U-boat just a hair, you had a chance, but it's unclear how often the trick worked.

The dazzle designs seem to us today so bizarre and bold that they look like an attempt to execute cubism on an industrial scale (in fact, cubist painters claimed authorship of the designs). It was more than just camouflage; it became fashion, as bathing suits were patterned on razzle dazzle.

One puzzling aspect is dazzle's black-and-white color palette. Was it because black-and-white photography, the closest way to simulate the view of the targets, eliminated colors from consideration? Or was it a style choice, just as the current vogue with newborns' toys is black-and-white patterning?

Today the closest analog is when car manufacturers wrap newly shaped prototypes for real-world test driving in patterned vinyl (and if you've ever encountered them on the road, they are more than a bit mysterious and hard to decipher). Auto makers try to prevent car-paparazzi (carparazzi?) from selling images of not-yet-released autos, albeit with lower stakes. Though a real dazzled car would be a sight!

21 February
Hendrik Petrus Berlage

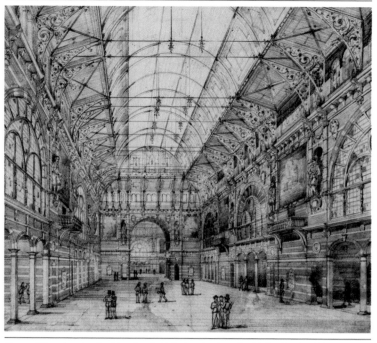

Competition drawing for Merchant's Fair, Amsterdam, the Netherlands, 1885

"Modern" is not the first thing that comes to mind seeing most of H. P. Berlage's built work. It appears to be tightly constrained by tradition, by conservatism, and by charting a fairly narrow path through the design world.

But that would be a misunderstanding of the role of architects like Louis Sullivan or Otto Wagner or Josef Hoffmann or, for that matter, Gustave Eiffel. Later work was better packaged and marketed as modernism, as in the 1932 *Modern Architecture: International Exhibition* and the companion book at MoMA, which established a clear brand, something the earliest modernists, like Berlage, never had. He has it now, of course, that he is called "the father of modern architecture" (and the many who are called this should be a list in its own right) and his Exchange Building in Amsterdam is now named the Berlage Bourse.

Berlage traveled widely in Europe after graduating from architecture school and later visited the US, where he saw work by Frank Lloyd Wright and Louis Sullivan. He promoted Wright in Holland after he saw the then five-year-old (now demolished) Larkin Building in Buffalo, New York. It was a remarkable building (whose 1950s demolition permit was signed by a witless former professor of mine. He should be in architectural jail.)

Peter Behrens (who I always seem to confuse with Berlage) was of the same generation, also designing brick-and-iron buildings in northern European countries and could certainly be considered a FoMA. Behrens employed Le Corbusier, Mies van der Rohe, and Walter Gropius, so maybe the moniker fits him a bit better.

There is modern (which to me has always been Modern), there is modernist (and modernism), and there is modernistic – words that have no carefully defined meaning (but should). I'm not sure where Berlage fits on that spectrum, so maybe we need to add proto-modern or premodern or some other appellation. Is he like Henri Matisse? Or Paul Cézanne? Certainly not Pablo Picasso or Georges Braque or Fernand Léger.

I'll go with John Singer Sargent, born just weeks before Berlage and similarly considered both a master and iconoclast, even though to some he is more connected to the past than to modernism. Berlage, meet Sargent. I think you'll find you have a lot in common.

22 February
Justus Oehler

Justus Oehler's home, Berlin, Germany, designed by Arthur Korn, 1928

Justus Oehler, for reasons I forget, was born in Tokyo, schooled in Marseille and Athens, attended college in London and Munich, and speaks way too many languages to count. He joined Pentagram as a partner in London and eventually moved to Berlin to open an office there. Somehow that was home, after a peripatetic youth.

For quality of life, his Berlin office can hardly be beat; it's in an enviable Altbau (old style building) apartment with an enfilade of generously proportioned rooms. The New York equivalent is the prewar apartment, but which war? The question makes the Berlin version easier just to call old. "Old" isn't a pejorative in Berlin, but maybe "prewar" is.

All the Pentagram partners once met in Austin, another outpost of the firm. The Austin office was founded as they all were: disgruntled partners branched out and founded new offices in somewhat random cities, in what can only be called a growth-though-divorce expansion plan. It seems to work.

In Austin, Oehler and I stopped by the Charles W. Moore Library, a University of Texas building that was formerly Moore's house. It is also where Colin Rowe's archive is kept as a tribute to the Texas Rangers days in the 1950s, when Rowe

and others created a new pedagogy about teaching architecture. In the library sat a beautiful wood model of Le Corbusier's Unité d'Habitation in Marseille (these wooden models were/ are the gold standard of scale models), and when Oehler saw it, he pointed to the rooftop extravaganza and said, "Oh, that's where I went to nursery school." (Mind blown!)

This early architectural inculcation (or brainwashing, depending on your point of view) obviously had an effect. Oehler now lives in a truly lovely early modern home in Berlin by Arthur Korn, which inspired a very moving Pentagram Paper no. 37 called *Forgotten Architects*, featuring Jewish architects whose careers in Berlin were ended by the Nazi regime.

My only question, I guess, is why Oehler didn't decide to live in Corbusierhaus, the Unité d'Habitation in Berlin. Maybe a bit too close to home.

23 February
Woody Pirtle

The Letter Y, Ambassador Arts alphabet poster series, 1994

Woody Pirtle makes graphic design look easy. He actually thinks it *is* easy; he once told me, after a career designing every imaginable type of project more than a few times, "It's not that hard; anyone can do this." No, not really!

I may be the most graphic-design-educated and graphic-design-loving architect alive (I would challenge anyone to a competition), but even I wouldn't dare show my attempts at graphic design to a real graphic designer. When surrounded by brilliance, it's best to stay in your lane, a lesson I wish some archi-aspirants would learn.

Plus, Woody can actually draw, once a requirement but now just a lost art. Combine all that with a sense of humor (plus a degree of impatience with typologies he has already done, and done) and you get to enjoy work that ranges from brilliant reductivist logos to lushly layered artwork to charming drawings to clever visual insights (and I could go on).

Pirtle was once, long ago, in the hospital after some issue, and I visited him in recovery or his room or somewhere post-op. It was like an episode of *General Hospital*; he looked better after surgery than I looked at my wedding.

That's about the most annoying thing I can say about Woody; he's just too well put together!

A small bunch of Pentagram partners used to ride motorcycles, and after we designed the Harley-Davidson Museum we thought an exclusive motorcycle club would be cool. We called ourselves the 99s because the most reprobate Harley riders call themselves the one percenters (ironically, the inverse of whom Bernie Sanders calls the 1 percent), even sporting "1%" patches on their leather jackets. We needed a logo and T-shirt, of course (really, that was the whole point), and Woody came back in like eight seconds with an upside-down Route 66 shield. Fucking genius. Plus, true to the Pentagram credo, he could describe it on a phone call. A short phone call.

So, yes, when Woody Pirtle designs it, he makes it look easy. And, no, it isn't easy. And, yes, it's his birthday. And, no, he doesn't look a day over fifty. And, yes, that is really annoying. And, no, you can't blame him! Though I never looked for the aging painting in his attic.

24 February
Steve Jobs

Steve Jobs introducing the iPhone 4, San Francisco, California, 2010

Who has done more to reshape the last four decades (crazy, I know) of design than Steve Jobs? Jobs, perhaps more than any actual designer, has completely altered the design landscape, and the effect may continue for the next forty years as well.

It was his obsessive sense of perfection, his need to organize the entire universe, that gave us the phone that (most) designers use, the computers that (most) designers use, and the watch that (some) designers wear. He proved we could be moved by design to the point of obsession, remaking us in his own image. He embedded design so deeply in his products that it seemed to be part of their soul, not just a superficial skin, as it seems to be with most car design.

If he had only mentored the design of a stream of Apple products it would be a remarkable, if somewhat limited, legacy. But he forced everyone, especially in technology, to define themselves based in large part on design. No one has elevated global design culture more than Jobs.

One could argue that his products were an assemblage of existing technologies cleverly repackaged as unique tools, but it is his design ethic that transformed mere technology into objects of desire, of love, and of faith.

Jobs grew up in an Eichler home in northern California, living in a design created for an accessible mass market. He idolized Edwin H. Land, another design genius who never studied design. Painting a fence with his father, including painting the back of the fence because Jobs would know if it wasn't painted and wouldn't be able to bear it, supposedly led him to design the unseen insides of his products as thoroughly as the seen exterior. The Jobs origin story is too neat to be true, but still you can love it anyway.

He believed that design improved everything, so of course the discipline of designing a total work of art was as much about morality as the guilt of expedience.

His record was hardly perfect; the half melon iMac was ridiculous, and the desktop icons are stuck in a bizarre realm. But as I write this on my MacBook Pro, occasionally checking my iPhone, I can look around the room to see how Jobs shaped my entire world. For the better.

25 February
John Wood the Younger

The Royal Crescent, Bath, England, 1774

Back when "the Elder" or "the Younger" was a way to publicly establish your place in the artistic firmament, John Wood the Younger was assumed by some to be just that: the lesser architect, essentially executing the Elder's work. But look again.

The Younger designed the finest building in a city of extremely fine buildings, the Royal Crescent in Bath, England. The Elder had brought Palladian-style buildings to Georgian Bath and had merged the roles of architect and urban designer (though it was never called that) by designing streets, squares, and circuses (round squares) as well as the principal and secondary buildings that defined them.

But the Younger extrapolated that introverted, intensely urban work into extroverted buildings like the Crescent that mediated between the city and the landscape. There is an openness to the Crescent due in part to the site and in part to the geometry. It faces a park (protected by a ha-ha to keep animals at a picturesque distance) and the view beyond, creating a gorgeously designed connection of city to landscape. But the geometry is equally suggestive: a semi-ellipse, as described by some, that has none of the rigid interiority of a circle or orthogonal squares.

The 500-foot-/152.4-meter-long Crescent with its giant order of Ionic columns is utterly palatial yet utterly democratic (and, yes, I use that term advisedly when describing a collection of very grand houses) in its almost insane lack of hierarchy. Virtually all the homes are the same, except at the very center, where the columns are doubled just to let you know there *is* a center!

The Crescent center has, for a long while, been a hotel and spa that must have a guest book entry for every architect in the last two hundred and fifty years, including me. It must have the same effect now as then; walking out of the hotel you feel, in architectural terms, as royal as the name implies.

Theo Crosby (Pentagram partner/founder/architect) said, when I asked how it was that an eighteenth-century city still works as well as it ever did, "Because people are essentially the same." It's a radical provocation, yet I'm pretty sure John Wood the Younger and I could have a perfectly modern conversation, maybe over tea at the Royal Crescent.

26 February
Peter Guzy

House in Stowe, Vermont, 2021

If you eat out in New York City, even a bit, you have almost certainly been in at least one of the more than fifty restaurants Peter Guzy designed: any Blue Ribbon restaurant (of the more than twenty of them, including Sushi, Bakery, Brooklyn, Market, Downing Street, Chicken, Brasserie, and Federal Grill), Blue Hill New York and Blue Hill at Stone Barns, Misi, Redd, Shukette, Alison on Dominick Street, WD-50, Back Forty, Los Feliz, Sullivan Street Bakery, Vic's, Meadowsweet, and I could go on.

His work includes hotels like AKA, retail like Moss Gallery (for Murray Moss, the design maven of New York City), offices like Kirshenbaum and Bond and (gasp!) Trump's modeling agency, T Management (and, yes, he was paid!).

Guzy's later work culminated in a truly gorgeous Aalto-reminiscent house in Stowe, Vermont, that is a hidden gem of high design. Not a single project, from this latest house to his earliest work, is the slightest bit dated or out of tune with the times. They all look as refreshingly modern, airy, and well-conceived as the day they were completed. They are stylish without being overly stylized, high design without being fashion fads. I wish I could say the same about my own projects!

Guzy and I realized that before we met, we had both competed for the same residential project, a loft on East Twelfth Street that eventually became the first of twelve homes for the same couple (technically for two couples, after a divorce and remarrying, but, really, the same money). Though I won that first commission, and benefited greatly from it and the next eleven, Peter never flinched.

After college (we both attended Cornell), Peter worked for our professor Werner Seligmann, then moved to Switzerland to teach at the ETH Zurich, to practice, and to live in a house overlooking the Heidi Weber Pavilion, the last of Le Corbusier's work, on Lake Zurich.

I'm not sure why a certain class of architect has very low, bass register voices, but Peter was one of those. Gravitas ensued. Éminence grise. His work has all the wisdom of an elder statesman without any of the crustiness or aging of projects that one would expect.

Peter died in 2022. He lived up to his oft-quoted Mies van der Rohe claim, "I don't want to be clever, I want to be good."

Guzy managed to be both.

27 February
Paul Schuitema

Chair no. 55, tubular aluminum, created for a competition, 1932–1933

The Guggenheim exhibition *The Great Utopia: The Russian and Soviet Avant-Garde, 1915–1932* viewed Russian constructivism not through the lens of a few iconic practitioners but as a mass movement in which *everyone* was a constructivist. It included a lot of really lovely paintings, but none of the artists were brand names you would recognize. It made a point (to me, at least) that beyond the iconic figures in any movement there are hordes of working artists (or graphic designers or architects or musicians or sculptors…) making quite creditable and often excellent work supporting any cultural design movement.

Paul Schuitema is one of those talented, not terribly well-known worker bees who made some great, but not revolutionary, work. Without Schuitema (and people like him), there would be only the stars and their scant effect on the design landscape.

Schuitema's work is remarkable, if sometimes a bit parodic; his furniture almost competes with the landmark pieces (but not quite), and his graphic design and photography look familiar (because they are!). He was part of de Stijl and constructivism as an adherent, not a pioneer. But that is still noble work; reinforcing and disseminating ideas rather than originating them is a necessary part of any artistic movement. Otherwise, they aren't movements; everything is just sui generis work.

Part of what always makes Schuitema's ads and posters and ephemera feel so abstract is that you rarely know what the hell they are for. Or if you do, they are long-gone brands or companies or look so ancient. (What is that thing they are calling a camera? Or a car? Or a telephone?) Except, that is, for his work for Berkel, which made, and still makes, the most beautiful hand-cranked prosciutto slicing machines ever devised, in the most gorgeous deep red color, which has essentially remained unchanged for a hundred years. When we see Schuitema design for a familiar brand, his work, all of a sudden, looks as revolutionary as it must have then.

I am not damning with faint praise; I am praising with a coda!

Paul Schuitema's work plays a critical role in the early modern Dutch and Russian movement, even if his is a role as follower rather than leader! s.

28 February
Frank Gehry

Walt Disney Concert Hall, Los Angeles, California, 2003

Frank Gehry's career echoes Louis Kahn's career in some of its milestones; both changed their too-Jewish names (Frank Owen Goldberg and Itze-Leib Schmuilowsky) early in life; both had a midcareer revelation that propelled them into extraordinary fame; both were called "the most important architect of our age." (But only one died in the men's room of Penn Station, or let's hope.)

Gehry was basically a shopping center designer, living in his wacky Santa Monica home, when he invited his mall-developer client to dinner. "Do you like this kind of thing?" his client asked, gesturing to the house. When Gehry said yes, the client asked, "Then why are you working for me?" That was all it took.

Gehry essentially closed his office and restarted life as the Gehry we now know (the movie version would have him change his name at just this moment).

Where Kahn adored weight and mass, Gehry adores their dissolution and distortion. Kahn condensed, Gehry evaporates. And if you like that kind of thing (and I often do), Gehry's is a remarkable portfolio of complicated work made to look, well, difficult. He didn't necessarily start there, but he was (luckily) pushed to embrace what he *really* liked.

Underlying the sometimes frilly exteriors Gehry slathers and layers on his work is a carefully arrayed programmatic composition, sometimes hard to see but almost always solidly executed, if one takes the time to uncover it. The shapes have made him famous, but the underlying sanity of the work, the well-functioning spatial compositions under the shapes, have kept him in business. The buildings really work (mostly), though they don't look as ordered as they actually are. That's the opposite of many buildings, whose careful exterior can wrap a less-ordered interior.

Those famous exteriors are complex and difficult to design and build, but Gehry (like Frank Lloyd Wright, famously, at the Johnson Wax Headquarters in Racine, Wisconsin) took full responsibility to get his work built. That is a remarkable position to take, especially in the US (though Gehry is Canadian), where distributing liability sometimes seems central to an architect's process.

So, bravo, FOG, for taking risks to be the architect you wanted to be and building the work you wanted to build.

29 February
Augusta Savage

Augusta Savage with sculpture *Realization,* commissioned by WPA, 1938

Augusta Savage (and what a great name) was, like her mentee Selma Burke (31 December), a sculptor and part of the Harlem Renaissance. Sadly, she didn't achieve the deserved acclaim, the longevity, and the success of her progeny. While Burke met (and sculpted) a president, Savage retreated to Saugerties, New York, as the victim of a legendary insane writer Joe Gould, who was obsessed with her and supposedly writing the world's longest book. Clinically psychotic, Gould stalked Savage and drove her from her carefully organized life in New York.

Savage was truly brilliant; she was accepted to Cooper Union in 1921, receiving a special additional scholarship to cover expenses she couldn't afford. She won the Otto Kahn Award, but travel costs prevented her from accepting a fellowship at the American Academy in Rome. Applying to the French Fontainebleau School of Fine Arts, she was accepted, then rejected in 1923 when they discovered she was Black.

Her early life was brutal: beatings from her minister father, who prohibited her from creating "graven images" (that is, art); three marriages to men who died or whom she divorced; with a daughter she introduced as her sister to "adjust" her age. Yet in Harlem she opened two galleries and more than one school of art that together attracted some fifteen hundred of the brightest in her orbit. She lived to create a legacy by inspiring a generation of students.

For the 1939 New York World's Fair, she was one of only four women (and the only Black woman) to be commissioned to create sculptures, and hers was among the most photographed in the fair. Yet she couldn't afford to cast the plaster in bronze or store it after the fair, and it was bulldozed with all the temporary items there.

Augusta Savage's life was thwarted at so many points, it is remarkable just how extraordinary, in the end, it was.

01 March
Jan Duiker

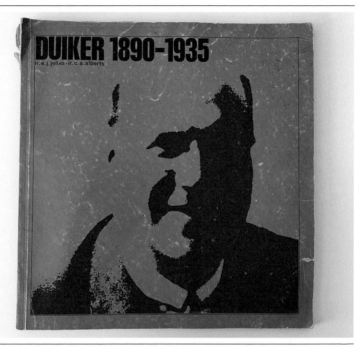

Cover of *Duiker* 1890–1935 by E. J. Jelles and C. A. Albert, 1972

If you're like me, you think Dutch modernism simply kills.

The Dutch may be the world's most design-obsessed modern culture for the longest period of time, producing the biggest raft of name-brand architects: Berlage, Bijvoet, Van Doesburg, Dudok, de Klerk, Oud, Rietveld, Van der Vlugt, Wils, Arets, Van Berkel, Blom, Bos, Brinkman, Coenen, Van Eyck, Hertzberger, Maas, Soeters, and, of course, Koolhaas, to name a few (and, really, it's just a fraction) of the remarkable modern Dutch architects. Plus, the Netherlands has artists Piet Mondrian, De Kooning, Van Gogh, Rembrandt, Vermeer, and Escher, much more than any comparable country, especially one that is only twice the size and population of New Jersey. It doesn't have a Bruce Springsteen, but other than that, well done, Holland.

I know that Denmark also has an outsized club of (mostly) furniture designers from a country with fewer people than New York City, not to mention Danish modern as a brand/type, but Holland is different; it has not just one midcentury period, but a 150-year record of the culture of design.

Duiker was partners with Bernard Bijvoet until Bernie went off to work with Pierre

Chareau on some little house in a Paris courtyard (wink, wink, the Maison de Verre). Duiker went on to design some iconic and some unknown works that the Dutch still take considerable pride in: Zonnestraal Sanatorium, a sprawling, land-based cruise ship of a rehab spot (but not that kind of rehab); Open Air School, a carved-away cube set at forty-five degrees in an Amsterdam courtyard, the school we all wished we went to; Nirwana Apartments, which looks like it could have been built in Miami, recently (and check out those balconies!); Cineac Theater, a movie theater surgically inserted into an impossibly irregular space with an insanely large sign that is the best of all those de Stijl drawings that never got built, except this one was built and still exists; and Grand Hotel Gooiland, the very definition of seaside 1930s resorts, unfortunately not at the seaside.

Bernie Bijvoet came back to finish the Gooiland after Duiker died at forty-four, as a bookend to their early-career partnership. So, those two were not only talented and design obsessed, but also loyal, generous, and sharing friends. Dutch treat isn't just for dining.

02 March
Howard Garns

Sudoku, invented by Howard Garns, first published 1979

There are those people who, despite spending a life doing one thing, become immortal (well, famous) for something else entirely. Imagine that Einstein remained a Swiss patent examiner or David Sedaris still cleaned houses (though he does still pick up roadside trash, so I guess that counts) while managing to do those other things that made them famous. Garns's architecture is completely unknown, but he did invent sudoku (though didn't live to see it explode internationally).

Another architect, Alfred M. Butts (which sounds like a *Mad* magazine mascot) lived in my little upstate town and invented Scrabble. John Lloyd Wright (son of Frank) designed some buildings of minor note, but invented Lincoln Logs. It's almost as though being an architect was not enough (gasp!).

In the office where Garns worked, there were, apparently, some extra drawing boards (Google it), and he was often seen drawing some kind of grid with numbers. As soon as anyone approached, he would just cover it up and say it was a game he was fooling with.

That game was first published as "Number Place" in May 1979 but without an on-page credit. It was Will Shortz

who connected Garns's name to the puzzle and Japan that renamed it sudoku ("single digit" in Japanese). Crossword puzzles in Japan are difficult (Japanese words aren't constructed of letters), making number puzzles popular there. In 2004 the *Times of London* published a sudoku puzzle, and the rest is obsessive-puzzle history.

The nine-square grid (composed of smaller nine-square grids in classic sudoku) is an architectural obsession: John Hejduk used it as a teaching device and the point of departure for seven houses he designed in 1954–1963. It has roots in Schinkel's Neuer Pavilion and Palladio's villas. It has a magical resonance with architects, becoming its own platonic geometry in two-dimensional and three-dimensional (cubic) forms and a potential fractal at the same time.

Sudoku and crossword puzzles are touted as brain stimulants in later life, but for those of us who live in gridded cities, the street grid structures our physical universe as surely as sudoku, and crosswords structure our intellectual one.

Thanks, Howard Garns, for adding one more (occasionally frustrating) grid to our mental sphere!

03 March
James Biber

Entrance to USA Pavilion, American Food 2.0, Expo Milan, 2015

The Bauhaus and my father were both born the same year, but I grew up in Rob and Laura Petrie's town, New Rochelle, at precisely the time *The Dick Van Dyke Show* was on the air, in a suburban home completely furnished in Danish modern. I knew we had a Womb chair before I knew what a womb was.

Our family homes were ordinary on the outside but their interiors were filled with names like Wegner and Juhl, woods like teak and walnut, and "interesting" ceramics. Even our dinnerware (by Heath, of course) and tablecloths (Marimekko, of course) couldn't escape my family's need to make every decision a conscious jab in the eye of normalcy.

My mother was a graphic designer, working at one point for Lubalin, Burns & Co. at the traffic desk. She attended Pratt University and took courses at the Art Students League of New York and the New School. My father won drawing contests as a kid and could paint signs (when that was a thing) after teaching himself to paint straight lines by practicing on columns in newspapers. Naturally, he opened an office-supply store, which must be like an aspiring sculptor owning a lumberyard.

After Philip Johnson's Glass House was published in *Life* magazine, my parents

called to make an appointment to go see it. When my mother asked how Johnson could move the enormously heavy rug he used as a bed spread, he answered, "Well, I have a house boy to do that... doesn't everyone?" He was a snide dick even then.

My parents' art-adjacent life meant dragging the kids to MoMA and to SoHo in the 1960s and '70s. In 1969, when MIT Press published Hans M. Wingler's landmark book *Bauhaus* (a book about as large, solid, and heavy as a building), my father bought a copy for his cool bachelor pad. As a miserable college biology student, I borrowed the book and pored over it, page by page, for the entire extremely cold and snowy housebound winter semester. That was all I needed to change lanes and avoid an oncoming collision with organic chemistry, which I knew would not end well (for me).

My father could be a bit of an asshole, so he insisted I return the book that had completely changed my life. Years later, I bought my own first edition.

(Slip)case closed.

04 March
Edgar Tafel

Church House of the First Presbyterian Church, New York, New York, 1960

Edgar Tafel was the last-surviving original disciple of Frank Lloyd Wright (FLLW) and proved that being a disciple is no guarantee of talent. His work was recognizably suburban and mostly undistinguished, but his advanced age eventually meant he was the only tangible remnant of the great man. He was therefore accorded the accolades intended for Wright. In one oft used portrait, he looks more like a magician than an architect (the Great Tafellini!).

A Scarsdale house Tafel designed was scheduled to be demolished until the town architectural board deemed it worthy of rescue because he was a master (!). Maybe they thought he was actually FLLW or one of the genuine luminaries that descended from the master (like John Lautner, Bruce Goff, or E. Fay Jones), but Tafel was more sycophant than independent talent.

So, no genius, no master, certainly not an original, but he kept the flame alive for the fifty years between Wright's death and his own. He wrote books about his apprenticeship and about Wright, quite skillfully working his nine years at Taliesin into a lifetime of work, writing, and praise. Obviously he was a very smart, or at least a very clever, guy.

The weirdest artifact he left is a handwritten list of architects, matched with their particularly gruesome deaths and perhaps a building or two they designed. It is pricelessly eccentric:

> [Antoni] Gaudí: hit by streetcar
> (Cathedral, Barcelona)
> O'Gorman. Juan: [suicide by]
> poison, hanging, and pistol...
> 3 at once! Synchronized
> Carlo Scarpa: model on platform,
> stepped back, viewing, fell
> backwards [down staircase]
> [J. André] Fouilhoux: Radio City -
> fell off steel framing

But the punch line is Stanford White, who, we know, was shot by Harry K. Thaw on the roof of his own Madison Square Garden in a dispute over Evelyn Nesbit (White's one-time mistress and later Thaw's wife). Tafel quotes FLLW as saying, "H.K. Thaw killed S.W. for the wrong reason"!

That pretty much sums up the Wright camp's attitude toward everyone who wasn't in the Wright camp (which, of course, they saw as the Right camp). You were either in it, or you deserved to be added to the list of gruesome deaths.

Edgar Tafel's book *Apprentice to Genius* kept him squarely in the (W)right camp.

05 March
Louis I. Kahn

Louis Kahn onstage, auditorium of Kimbell Art Museum, Fort Worth, Texas, 1972

Louis I. Kahn was born on March 5, 1901, on our current Gregorian calendar or February 20, 1901, on the Julian calendar (in use in Estonia, where he was born), foreshadowing a life of multiple realities. At age fourteen, after ten years in the US, his name was changed from his birth name, Itze-Leib Schmuilowsky, to Louis I. Kahn; it seems cruel to allow a child to get nearly all the way to high school before removing what must have been a debilitating social handicap. On the other hand, the change allowed a reinvention that might not have happened at, say, age three (at which age he burned his face, literally scarring him for life).

Decades later, his time at the American Academy in Rome prompted another reinvention, at nearly fifty years old, transforming him into who some called the most important living American architect of his time. In Rome and Egypt and Siena and Greece, Kahn discovered light and mass and the power of the geometry of the circle, square, and triangle in revelations that would carry him through the next twenty-five years.

His maxims about talking bricks and arches were Kahn working out how to create the weighty geometry of mass and light in compositions that were more like de Chirico than the weightless abstractions obsessed over by most early modern architects.

The best thing built in New York City in this century (so far) is almost certainly Four Freedoms State Park, which finally explains why Roosevelt Island has FDR's name. Unlike buildings with interiors and exteriors, the park's architecture is entirely unconcealed and open to the public, even from across the East River in Manhattan. Stupidly, the culmination of the trip to the apex of the design, an open room facing the city, the river, and the UN, is roped off because of accessibility issues. Consider, for a moment, that a monument to FDR has, specifically, wheelchair accessibility issues! And consider that despite nearly fifty million dollars and hundreds of architects, engineers, consultants, and builders, no one seems to have noticed that irony.

Kahn may be most famous for his living arrangements with three entirely separate families, in what might be the most lasting geometry of his career: the triangle.

06 March
Colin Forbes

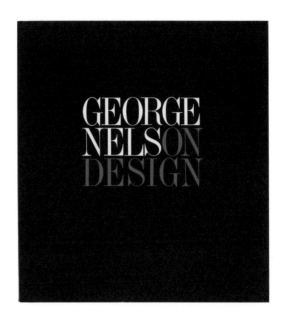

Cover of George Nelson on Design, Whitney Library of Design, 1979

In a life filled with remarkable accomplishments, perhaps the most amazing thing about Colin Forbes was how he maintained his ability to change his mind. At an age when most (we know who we are) become more and more ossified, Forbes was still evolving and still rethinking everything in his sphere.

Colin, who as a young man had a definite Daniel Craig vibe going on, started with his best friend, Alan Fletcher, a series of London design partnerships (Fletcher/Forbes/Gill, Crosby/Fletcher/Forbes) culminating in Pentagram in 1972. Forbes moved to New York City in 1978 (there was one partner in London he simply couldn't abide) and shared an office with George Nelson. He eventually corralled a small set of local partners, including Woody Pirtle and Peter Harrison, to form an independent and growing US presence.

Colin was, in those days, just taciturn enough to be intimidating, especially as he focused on you through those thick eyeglasses (I sat next to him for years, so believe me, I know). But really he was as gentle, generous, and warm as anyone could be. And just as he recognized the extraordinary talent of Alan Fletcher, he was able to spot young talent at precisely the moment they were

ready, with his assistance, to flourish. He loved complexity and designed a system of finances for Pentagram that was nearly beyond the comprehension of most members but perseveres. His system, it turns out, was as adaptable as he was and remains a glue that holds the group together.

Colin Forbes lived his final years in North Carolina on a horse farm he and his wife, Wendy, and son, Aaron, turned into a sanctuary for older horses (and maybe someday older designers?). When I visited him there, he pointed out Mitt Romney's lame horse living out his own late years. I suppose the horse didn't fit on the roof of Romney's station wagon, but I have to admit it was a fine-looking horse. Every bit as good looking, and lame, as Romney himself.

When I visited Colin last, he bounded around with more energy than I had, despite having twenty-five years on me.

07 March
Baldassare Peruzzi

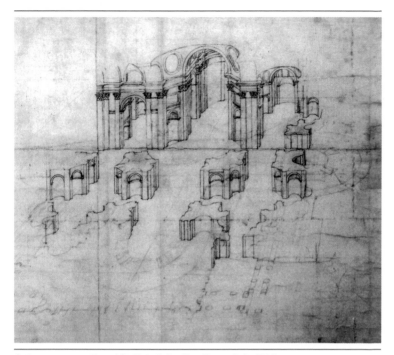

Cutaway perspective of St. Peter's Basilica, Rome, Italy, 1505

If Baldassare Peruzzi had designed only three things during his career in Rome, he would be a major star. But somehow his name isn't as boldface as his friends (Bramante, Raphael, Sangallo, Sebastiano Serlio, and Giulio Romano). It should be; he is the Joey Bishop of his Rat Pack. Or maybe the Peter Lawford.

The Villa Farnesina (considered a suburban home when Peruzzi built it, though in the middle of urban Rome now) is a jewel of space, painting, and sequence; the loggia alone (originally the open-air entrance) is an encyclopedia of food, illusion, and mythology.

For the Palazzo Massimo alle Colonne, Peruzzi needed just a *little bit* more frontage to make the elegantly curved facade as perfect as it is. He persuaded the client's brother who owned the adjacent site to swap a bit of land, and voilà. That tiny adjustment centered the facade and portico on the approach from Via del Paradiso, creating one of the truly magical moments of emerging from the darkness onto the Corso. Palazzo Massimo is one of the great examples of recentering and rationalizing an awkward site as well as reworking the idea of palazzi, which were previously based on fortified dwellings where an open public portico at ground level just wouldn't do.

Finally, Peruzzi worked on St. Peter's Basilica and drew what is one of the greatest renderings of plan, section, and three-dimensionally realized space, in effect, a building constructing itself in a drawing. That it is so clearly a drawing made to figure out a building (as in math tests, "show your work") is all the more remarkable.

Peruzzi became instantly more famous in death than in life, being interred in the Pantheon (literally, he is buried in *the* Pantheon, near Raphael) and with an epitaph that spelled out his fifty-five years, eleven months, and twenty days of life with florid praise. But it didn't stop there, calling him equal to "the ancients." Then, like now, marketing mattered, and Peruzzi was too modest and unambitious to compete successfully with Michelangelo or Raphael for fame and legacy. But being buried next to Raphael is really all one needs to establish artistic cred.

Almost better than a flash of fame while alive. Almost.

PACK MY BOX WITH DZEN & FV LQR JUGS

1234567890

Lining Gothic typeface, from Frederic Goudy's *Elements of Lettering,* 1921

Walk down Rue Jacob in Paris, look up, and you can still see the sign at #56: Typographie de Firmin Didot. I imagined Frederic W. Goudy as Firmin Didot, a French eighteenth- to nineteenth-century craftsman typographer. Or maybe like Giambattista Bodoni, even older than Didot (of course) and living in Italy.

Nope. Goudy was all-American and self-taught, born in Bloomington, Illinois, a hundred years later. He even taught at New York University and the Art Students League of New York. His most famous, and most misquoted, utterance, "Anyone who would letterspace lowercase would steal sheep," seemed utterly inane until I learned that he said it as he was accepting a hand-lettered award, glanced at it, and seemingly commented that anyone who would letterspace the Gothic typeface Blackletter (think *New York Times* logo) would fuck ("shag" was the original utterance) sheep. That I understand.

Fred Goudy, all-American, designed more than a hundred usable typefaces, more than all the Gutenbergs and Garamonds and Bodonis and Didots put together. I suspect that it might be a typical case of American quantity over quality. Like food. Or house size.

Or Donald Trump's gigantic suits and ties.

His work might also be a typical case of Americans creating a false sense of history to compensate for having so little. The biggest complaint about Goudy was his tendency to be persistently old-fashioned, rarely designing a sans serif typeface (Copperplate Gothic being almost sans serif, more like micro-serif) and favoring lower case e's with a tilted cross bar.

And one more complaint: it's not a font if you are talking about the design of letters and numbers; it is a typeface. A font (when type was made of metal) was a complete set of letters and numbers. Like car and fleet. Or puppy and litter. Or ape and shrewdness.

And while I am at it, it's not a beam if it stands upright; that is a column (even if it is made of exactly the same shape of steel). Beams are horizontal (nominally, anyway).

Also, it's Daylight Saving, not Savings, Time (really, catch up on *Veep* if you weren't aware of that).

Glad we got through all that

09 March
Edward Durrell Stone

Huntington Hartford Gallery of Modern Art, New York, New York, 1964

Edward Durrell Stone is a hard one. He produced some of the most admirable and some of the least admirable buildings on both sides of World War II, including two museums a short stroll from each other in New York City: MoMA and Huntington Hartford's Gallery of Modern Art (now Museum of Arts and Design).

Nearly all his 1920s, '30s, and '40s work (large houses for wealthy patrons, smaller ones for the masses, his work at Radio City Music Hall, and, of course, MoMA) is pure corporate International Style and usually quite good. His later work includes the Kennedy Center, the US Embassy in New Delhi, and a raft of suburban houses virtually indistinguishable from the most banal of that genre. Plus there's the Huntington Hartford, one of the strangest and least-loved buildings in New York City but one that perfectly represented its very odd benefactor.

That Frank Lloyd Wright called the US Embassy in New Delhi "one of the finest buildings in the last hundred years" is more a testament to Wright's advanced age and failing eyesight (I have no evidence of this, but it's the only explanation for his praise) than to the building itself.

It seems that Stone's difficulty was moving on from the International Style. That evolution affected other devotees, like Philip Johnson, who was nimbler, but Stone (just slightly older) seems to have lost his bearings.

It is also possible that Stone, who then ran one of the nation's largest architectural offices, just had too much work to invent something for each project and so fell into tropes at just the wrong moment. Whatever the cause, the results are the same. You all know architects (and filmmakers and writers and painters) whose accumulated wisdom continues to improve their work as they age, and you also know those artists whose early work is exuberant and whose aging produces a kind of calcification, set in stone.

Edward Durrell Stone is the latter. But luckily much of his early work remains, so you get to choose the buildings you want to remember him by, whatever your taste and interests. His prolific career, like that of Frank Lloyd Wright, produced enough work for several ordinary lives, so you can just circle those you like and put on sunglasses for the others.

It's amazing what you can live with if you just stop looking.

10 March
Hector Guimard

Entrance to Paris Metro, detail of signage, Paris, France, 1900–1913

Hector Guimard might be forgotten (like, for example, his Paris contemporary Henri Sauvage) if not for MoMA's acquisition of one of his Paris Metro entrances. I remember seeing it in the Sculpture Garden as a kid and for the longest time it defined for me, having barely left New York, Paris. Not a bad way (nor an accurate way) to imagine Paris as a place infinitely more elegant than New York City, one with public art that was fucking cool.

The Metro entrances are among the purest expressions of Guimard's style because they weren't buildings but more like scaled-up jewelry, furniture, or railings. His buildings are clever in that with only a few appliqués they completely transform an orthogonal construction into a flowing art nouveau one. The plans for these buildings are almost prototypical, but the layer of swirl, curve, and flourish creates the dreamlike interiors and gestural exteriors.

Like Frank Gehry's work, Guimard's appliqués define the image (where a rigorous programmatic assemblage often undergirds the frills of the exterior). Guimard forged iron railings, castings in metal, plasterwork, and woodwork as well as stained glass that were easy to reshape, mimicking the

posters, typography, and decorative work becoming the style du jour.

Some of the first expressions of art nouveau, not unlike those of other modern movements such as the Bauhaus or de Stijl, were graphic. Printed ephemera and decorative artwork were a low-investment laboratory for design movements. Buildings take time, capital, and technology to change, while shaping a poster, cabinet, or painting is just a matter of drawing or carving or brushwork.

Guimard, Gaudí, Goff, Gehry: these G architects all worked to free architecture from the tyranny of the right angle, but in the end their designs became personal style rather than cultural dogma.

Guimard's (and the other Gs') work is almost too easy to like. The compositions appear to be less empirically determined and more personal and arbitrary (though they are not), disarming the viewer into a kind of well-lubricated acceptance of the visual language. It's ice cream, not the main course. It's more rather than less. And it's smooth rather than sharp. Soft rather than hard. It's why, as a nine-year-old, I understood the Metro entrance at MoMA, and why I still love it today.

11 March
Thomas Hastings

New York Public Library, Fifth Avenue, New York, New York, 1911

Everyone knows the name of architects McKim, Mead & White and ascribes nearly every Beaux-Arts building of note to them. But some of the most famous classical structures were designed by other architects, who must have been constantly annoyed at their own lack of equal prominence. But if you have to be murdered on the roof of your own building to maintain your firm's fame, it might be better to be anonymous.

Thomas Hastings, of Carrère and Hastings, was one of those misattributed architects who nonetheless designed some of the most glorious buildings in New York and beyond: the New York Public Library at Fifth and Forty-Second Street, for example, or the Frick Museum, built as a private house for Henry Clay Frick, or Woolsey Hall at Yale (completely mangled by the Beinecke Library).

To be fair, both Hastings and John Merven Carrère worked for and met each other at McKim, Mead & White, leaving to start their partnership.

Even the temporary World War I Victory Arch at the head of Fifth Avenue at Twenty-Fifth Street is misattributed. I always thought it was Stanford White's, and I always thought there was only one Victory Arch. There were five, in fact,

and the one White designed is the only one remaining (rebuilt in stone after the plaster original) at Washington Square Park. The four capturing the stretch of Fifth Avenue at Madison Square Park were all by others, and the last and most spectacular was by Thomas Hastings.

It was both spectacular and spectacularly criticized. Fiorello La Guardia, in his quest to become head of the New York City Board of Alderman, was particularly pointed in his critique of the wasteful and corrupt process of building the arches. Hastings avoided being accused by La Guardia in his *New York Times* article because another designer (incorrectly called the architect of the boondoggle) was in charge of contracting the arches and skimmed a fat 10 percent of all monies spent.

Hastings's own funeral monument is remarkably modest, especially in light of the more elaborate one he designed for his partner (whose funeral was on my own birthday, in 1911). As someone quipped, "If John M. Carrère had been shot rather than dying in a car accident, Carrère and Hastings might be better known!"

12 March
Anish Kapoor

Black circle, as seen in some works by Anish Kapoor

Anish Kapoor pursues a variety of sculptural modalities, but almost always at XL to XXXL size. They never fail to attract the informed and the uninformed, which might make him seem highly commercial (and that is certainly true) but also occasionally quite esoteric.

At the Royal Academy in London, his red wax works included a train-size block moving (very slowly) on rails through doorways and creating an enormous, messy extrusion of the doorframe, moldings, etc., while a cannon in an adjacent room periodically fired a huge slug of red wax from one room to splat on a wall in the next. It was spectacular.

His Vantablack (the least light-reflective, blackest pigment at one time) work creates a false sense of the infinite. While most viewers hover around the edges of the illusory Vantablack hole Kapoor created to the next dimension, one visitor thought it was a black circle of paint on the floor (which is quite a stretch if you've ever seen it) and decided to walk across it (mistake #2. I mean, who does that at an art gallery?). Fortunately, the hole was just a few feet deep, but part of me wishes the trespasser had, in fact, dropped into the sunken place.

Vantablack is another kind of trap as well; only Kapoor can use it, according to the deal he made with the producer. On the one hand, artists through time have had secret formulas for their pigments; on the other hand, what a dick. Stuart Semple, pissed-off artist, was so irritated that he produced an eponymous Pink that anyone in the world, except Anish Kapoor, could buy. Kapoor fired back with a pink middle finger. Literally.

I believe the phrase "none more black" (uttered by Nigel Tufnel of Spinal Tap upon seeing the cover of *Smell the Glove*, the black album) captured the concept long before Kapoor's dickish monopoly. I think the pigment's name should be None More Black.

Myriad cartoons have created a portable hole that characters conveniently slip in front of their pursuer, and I assume the Acme Company would like to challenge Anish Kapoor's exclusive deal. The company is already involved, as I am sure you know, in the *Coyote v. Acme* lawsuit (Wile E. Coyote is suing Acme for faulty merchandise), so with lawyers already on retainer, it may be time to take the fight to Kapoor.

13 March
Karl Friedrich Schinkel

Altes Museum, Berlin, Germany, 1830, photograph 1890–1905

Without Karl Friedrich Schinkel, it is hard to imagine there would have been a Mies van der Rohe, and not just because Mies worked for Peter Behrens and Behrens obviously adored Schinkel (and by the transitive property...). Behrens never actually met Schinkel (who died twenty-five years before Behrens was born), but Schinkel, if you lived in Berlin, was alive everywhere, and his work was (and is) simply stunning.

Schinkel's buildings seem to fall into two categories; the romantic compositions are related to his first career, painting, and his third career, stage set design. They are atmospheric and picturesque (yet still crisply drawn) in a Wes Anderson kind of way, precisely the opposite of his classical, Teutonic, almost late-Enlightenment work like the Altes Museum.

The military posture of those classical buildings might seem overbearing, as they later would with the work of Schinkel's biggest fan, Albert Speer, and his architecture-school-reject friend Adolf. But Schinkel understood scale and grandeur, foreground and background, detail and precision and proportions, which make all the difference in his work. It may be the regal insouciance of those classical buildings, if that doesn't seem oxymoronic.

The Altes Museum (Old Museum) was, of course, once the Neue Museum (New Museum) but aged out of that moniker. Opposite the museum, and in conversation with the museum, is (or rather was) the East German Communist-era Palace of the Republic, a gold-glass-clad, marble-lined fun palace for the volk. Stripped to its rusted steel frame, it was the most inventive and remarkable (ad hoc) museum in Europe, with exhibits in which entire areas were flooded for ships. It was the perfect counterpoint to the Altes Museum, but some didn't see it that way.

Sadly, the fun palace was removed to build a reconstruction of the site's previous palace, the Berliner Schloss. What a missed opportunity; Berlin chose to exhume the past and re-create a monumentally anodyne pile rather than acknowledge the history of the place and formalize an informal adaptation of Berlin's (and Germany's) division.

Schinkel's museum overlooks it all and stands respectfully mute as the machinations proceed.

14 March
James Bogardus

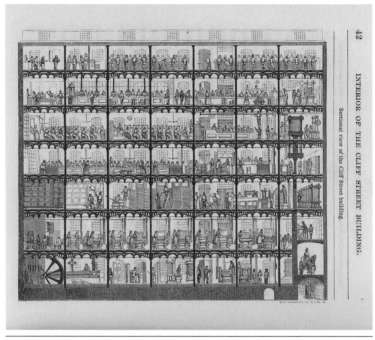

Sectional drawing of Harper's Building, Cliff Street, New York, New York, 1858

James Bogardus, who trained as a watchmaker, had a pile of disparate patents before patenting ways of making cast iron buildings. In a kind of meta-move, he manufactured the first cast-iron building in New York City, which itself became a factory for manufacturing cast iron buildings.

Cast-iron building in 1850 was revolutionary. Its prefabrication and bolt-together assembly took much of the craft out of decorative facades and buildings, saving money and huge amounts of time. While masonry couldn't proceed in freezing weather, cast iron was unaffected by weather (though I suppose it could rust in the rain).

Interestingly, the world's largest (and best) cast-iron and glass building, the Crystal Palace in London, opened just twelve months after Bogardus patented his process. This was an idea in play in the mid-nineteenth century.

Cast iron was a necessary step to the steel frame, which was a necessary step to tall buildings, and therefore a necessary step to the modern city. Cast-iron buildings were as advanced in their day as supertall billionaires-row buildings are today. Technological marvels, all of them.

Cast iron's slender frames allowed enormous windows that admitted copious amounts of natural light when the only alternative was gas lamps or candles. Cast iron, Bogardus believed, was less prone to collapsing in a fire, which gave people a chance to leave safely and fight the fire more easily. The eerie image Bogardus created of a skeletal building (actually, his own building) on fire pictured an imagined survival of a facade as the building dissolved in flames.

Bolted-together, kit-of-parts buildings were fast to assemble, but also to disassemble. When the Bogardus Building at Washington and Murray Streets (a corner that no longer exists) was to be demolished, the entire cast-iron facade (as per the New York City Landmarks Preservation Commission) was disassembled and stored to be reincorporated in an urban renewal project. It would have been, but it was stolen! And recovered. And stolen again. For scrap.

I feel for James Bogardus. My USA Pavilion for Expo 2015 in Milan was stolen (well, moved) and reopened as a tech hub in Hamburg!

15 March
Philip Powell

Skylon, erected for the Festival of Britain, London, England

Philip Powell CH OBE RA FRIBA was a British architect educated at the Architectural Association and responsible for some rather unimaginative modern postwar housing, beginning with a commission he won when he was twenty-three.

But he famously designed a popular feature of the Festival of Britain, the Skylon. The Skylon was a tall, suspended, vertical, entry feature at an event that was meant to create a sense of optimism in a depression-ravaged nation, still in ruins from World War II.

The 1951 festival marked the hundredth anniversary of the very first World's Fair, London's Crystal Palace Exhibition. Unlike that exhibition, the festival featured only Britain, but like it, it focused on the technological, industrial, scientific, cultural, and artistic (but not political) issues of the day. The Crystal Palace was a single-building exposition, while the Festival of Britain was a distributed one, with exhibitions all over the UK.

The Skylon sat on the South Bank of the River Thames (near where the London Eye is today) next to the Dome of Discovery, at a time when names like Dome of Discovery were not ironic

or laughable. Shaped like a pointy cigar and cleverly suspended on cables (it's called a tensegrity structure), the 300-foot-/91.4-meter-tall tower appeared to float with no visible signs of support, as some joked that England's Labour Party was at the time! Others thought it was too obviously supported and should have floated on magnetic power. (Everyone's a fucking critic.)

Winston Churchill, back in power after a six-year absence, couldn't wait to dismantle the Skylon (to him a symbol of Labour Party power). Powell said it would be like scrapping a watch for the tin; there just wasn't enough metal to warrant the cost of dismantling. Most wanted it to stay, but it was demolished and, some said, thrown into the River Lea (cue Adele).

Even worse, it turns out it was sold for scrap to a firm that made it into commemorative ashtrays and letter openers (a fate almost as bad as the stone eagles from Penn Station that were dumped in the New Jersey swamps like some mafia hit).

There was recently a movement to rebuild it, but unlike the bombastic Berliner Schloss or the sublimely beautiful Barcelona Pavilion, it never was resurrected.

16 March
Aldo van Eyck

Amsterdam State Orphanage, Amsterdam, the Netherlands, 1960

Aldo van Eyck is most famous for the 1960 Amsterdam Orphanage, a building made from the aggregation of mostly identical units. It's very seductive in plan; from a single module, a building can grow, more or less infinitely, into any building shape necessary (as long as it's one story high, has space around it, and remains navigable and humane). It's bit less seductive in reality, but it's still the opposite of our stereotypical (for example, *The Queen's Gambit*) orphanage. And it was a fringe idea in a world of more unitary buildings (packaging everything into a more elementary form), which was the norm those days.

Van Eyck started his career as the Amsterdam architect in charge of playgrounds and built more than two hundred of them after World War II. His work was based on the denunciation of austere modernism with a humanist approach to building that was particularly attuned to children. His perspective was valuable yet marginalized in the design community, and his actual buildings (not playgrounds) were so few that their impact was limited. That's why his one iconic project has been featured so often; it's an idea that barely works in other contexts.

It turns out the idea didn't even work for his signature building; the orphanage was closed, and to save the building the Berlage Institute took over the space. In fact, the Berlage Institute was *created* to fill the building; it didn't exist before the building needed a tenant!

Van Eyck said, "A house must be like a small city if it's to be a real house, a city like a large house if it's to be a real city," which is one of those slightly ridiculous reciprocal propositions that look so good and mean so little. (And BTW, "look so good and mean so little" may be another of those ridiculous reciprocal propositions, so I know of what I write.)

In the end, the question is whether his designs, after all the philosophical positing, are as good as his quips. Mostly they are, especially his open-air pavilions (you know, like playgrounds). But Aldo van Eyck proved that it takes designing only a single cool building to become important to the history of architecture, with influence far beyond the scale of the built work.

17 March
Herb Lubalin

Avant Garde typeface, special characters and ligatures, 1970

When I was a teenager, my mother worked for Lubalin, Burns & Co. and Typographic Communications (TGC), and maybe Herb Lubalin's other companies like Visual Graphic Communications (VGC) and Typographics Inc. (TGI); it's all so confusing. It was a male-dominated world (except for the secretaries) and it's possible she started smoking her small mustard-yellow suede-covered pipe to be "one of the boys" (and somehow to stop smoking cigarettes). Not sure it worked in either pursuit.

I grew up with Lubalin's poster of the entire book of Genesis and his "word pictures" of pithy type interpretations, and magazines like *U&lc* and *Fact*, and probably a lot more artifacts I don't remember. They were the height of cool back then, and I kind of hate them now (though they seem to be making a comeback). They may have sensitized me to a certain stripe of typographic expression, but impressing a thirteen-year-old suburbanite was not, I would guess, his aim.

I know Lubalin was an important designer, part of the "Sitz Pack" (a group of mostly Jewish graphic designers who always seemed to be photographed in a Russian bath or steam room) and much adored.

The typeface Avant Garde says it all: super cool when it was designed for *Avant Garde* magazine but entirely of its time. The sexually liberated magazines in the late 1960s (like *Eros* and *Avant Garde* in New York and *Nova* in the UK) seemed sophisticated then, but they look a bit like vintage porn now. But with a modern sense of style.

I am completely unqualified to judge Lubalin, but Massimo Vignelli wasn't, and here is what he said:

> I remember when I came to the States, I thought that Herb Lubalin was the best thing that this country ever had in terms of graphic design, but was also the worst danger. His graphics were absolutely personal, and therefore only he could do it. Meanwhile, I was advocating a kind of typography which was nonpersonal and therefore could be used by many people, regardless of their degree of talent. Of course, it could be bastardized by someone who had no talent. That happens everywhere. But Lubalin's direction was very, very slippery ground. It was like drugs: fascinating but lethal.

Perfect. Thanks, Massimo.

18 March
Mollie Parnis

Lady Bird Johnson wearing Mollie Parnis dress, with President Johnson, 1968

Mollie Parnis was a major force in the democratization of women's wear. In 1933, she established her line under her own name (rather than allowing department stores to brand her clothes as their own), for everywoman. She dressed first ladies, including Mamie Eisenhower and Lady Bird Johnson (one of those rare designers dressing both sides of the aisle!), and sold the same dresses as ready-to-wear.

Parnis sold to everyone. Mamie Eisenhower experienced that democracy while wearing a blue-green shirtwaist dress on a receiving line, only to greet a woman wearing the same dress! A national crisis ensued (not really), but, as Parnis said, that's what was great about a democracy. I've never quite gotten the social faux pas of two people wearing the same outfit, and I suppose neither did Parnis.

Her dresses seem like the kind of thing Lucy Ricardo, but probably not Laura Petrie, would wear. She had, apparently, an unfailing sense of what would sell and was interested in clothing the entire public (or, rather, half of the public).

Parnis unwittingly designed her first dress when, after a high school football rally, she was invited to a party. She had no other dress to wear except the one she had on, so she raced home and reworked it with a few clever flourishes and, voilà, a (seemingly) new dress! She later started to study law at Hunter College but soon found her way into fashion.

Sundays she would hold a salon at her home in New York City or Katonah, New York, gathering all the interesting people she knew and ending with a viewing of her Matisse or Cézanne or Utrillo (and which one doesn't belong in that sentence?).

Still, she was very Seventh Avenue, something that today doesn't seem like a compliment but should be. Making design accessible is the noblest of all pursuits. The Jil Sander line at Uniqlo or the Rachel Comey line at Target sell out instantly, for example. Design democracy is possible; it just takes designers and retailers who believe in it.

If only people liked good design, in general, as much as they liked a Mollie Parnis dress.

19 March
Josef Albers

Drawing class, Black Mountain College, circa 1939–1940

Josef Albers, along with his wife Anni Albers, taught at the Bauhaus before fleeing Germany in 1933. At the Bauhaus, Anni was pushed into the textile arts by Walter Gropius and Josef was told to first take an introductory course, but they persevered and became a famous pair. Philip Johnson got them to Black Mountain College, where Josef's "wonderful inability with English" forced him to take a more theatrical approach to art; "art is performance" was his credo. Anni pursued textiles more as an architect than an artist, using them as a palette for material studies and experimentation; no less an icon than R. Buckminster Fuller said she had a complete "realization of the complex structure of fabrics."

Josef and Anni transformed Black Mountain College (with students including Robert Rauschenberg, Cy Twombly, Ray Johnson, and others) before moving to Yale, where Josef headed the design department and began his *Homage to the Square* series of color studies and wrote *Interaction of Color*.

Albers became so famous for his *Homage* series that much of his other work, including his prolific album cover designs for Command Records, has been neglected. *Homage* is easy to understand, an effective teaching tool, and repetitive enough to have drilled into the public conscience. Its infinite variations also push the definition of what is art, what is design, and what is quasi-scientific experimentation.

His work is, of course, all of those.

But his greatest achievement was probably the faculty and students of the Yale design program. He invited Alvin Lustig and Herbert Matter to Yale and taught students including Richard Serra, Richard Anuszkiewicz, Eva Hesse, Jay Maisel, Victor Moscoso, Harry Seidler, Robert Slutzky, and (I assume) Alan Fletcher, who was there during Albers's reign.

When the couple arrived in the US, it was Anni who was the main attraction, and in time she has finally gained back some of the recognition she deserves. At the Bauhaus, as a woman, she was barred from the heavy arts by Gropius and was fated to work with "these limp threads," as she called them. But as the exceptional artist she was, she transformed that art into a highly technical, highly experimental, and now highly regarded discipline.

Thanks, Anni.

20 March
Mike Mills

Album cover of *Butter 08* by Butter, 1996

Mike Mills is annoyingly talented in an annoyingly broad set of artistic endeavors. We are all lucky that talent is not a zero-sum game, or we might have to do something drastic just to leave a bit of talent for the rest of us. Fortunately, there is no limit on the total amount of talent at any one time, but, still, Mills has too much.

Films, skateboards, album covers, documentaries, clothing, book jackets, posters, music videos, and probably twenty or thirty other things I don't even know about. Even more annoying, I really like almost all of it. If only he were also a billionaire, a model, lived in the Maison de Verre, drove an Aston Martin DB5, cured multiple sclerosis, and had been married to Miranda July would he be even more unbearable. As far as I know, only one of these is true.

I will not use the phrase Renaissance man (damn, just did) because that implies a kind of genius that doesn't seem quite right in Mills's case. Polymath might be right. But really it looks like a case of someone with a way of seeing the world that can be applied in lots of venues and lots of modalities. His expertises with language and image combine to make not only engaging film but also some very funny graphic design.

Being good, very very good, at all these endeavors is one thing, but being successful is another, and successful he is. Success brings the ability to choose what one's next project will be, what you don't want to do, and to wait for opportunities (or make them) rather than waste time and creativity on projects that have less potential. And if you are making things in six or seven fields at the same time, waiting can be just switching, for a time, to another art. It's like a painter who works on a variety of canvases so the paint has a chance to dry.

I seem to like every graphic designer who ever worked for Tibor Kalman at M&Co, so Mike checks that box. It's satisfying to discover someone whose work you like, whose humor you get, and whose next project will likely be a pleasant surprise. Having seen his latest project, the movie *C'mon C'mon*, I am even more annoyed. It is amazing.

Carry on, Mike Mills.

21 March
Claude-Nicolas Ledoux

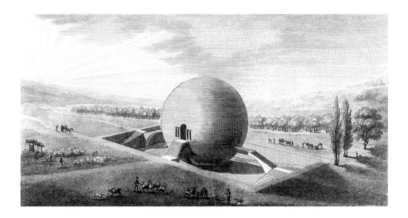

Maison des Gardes Agricole, ideal house design, 1770

Claude-Nicolas Ledoux was, and is, one of my favorite architects, even after someone described him as the "Albert Speer of revolutionary France" (Speer's birthday was two days ago). Like Speer, Ledoux escaped death, was imprisoned, and produced a stripped-down neoclassicism. In Ledoux's case, it was a welcome relief from the baroque work in fashion at the time.

After his year in prison, he began documenting his designs and modifying them to suit his later proclivities. It's the kind of personal revisionist history we would all like the chance to indulge in!

Ledoux was despised by the French (people) because of his complicity in the taxation and control of salt. Salt was like oil is today. It was crucial for the preservation of food, was an antiseptic, was used for manufacturing silver, and was a marker of social class. "Not worth his salt" references soldiers' pay in salt. "Above the salt" refers to the position at a dining table nearer the salt cellar and host, as opposed to below, where you just didn't matter much.

Ledoux's best built works were 1) the Royal Saltworks in Chaux, the processing plant where mined salt brine was pumped from a great

distance, and 2) the sixty or so Barrières de Paris, the customs houses/gates and wall surrounding Paris that collected salt taxes. It is remarkable he was not guillotined.

Chaux is genius. Based on an ideal city, it is filled with highly charged symbolism: water (brine), fire (to evaporate the brine to salt), earth (forests for the wood fires), and air, all the primal elements. Plus it encompasses all the human typologies (directors, farmers, workers, coopers, blacksmiths, keepers of the woods, etc.) plus some functional types (like hospitals and gates), all of whom were distinguished by individuated architecture together composing an entire town.

The Barrières de Paris, too, are each distinct, usually built in pairs, and were differentiated to respond to place; those still standing are worth a visit.

With no work after his prison stint, and lots to draw, Ledoux speculated on the future and sometimes made (architectural) jokes of his ideas. All his works are divine, but the House of Pleasure is simply outstanding. Or upstanding, depending on your point of view (hint: it's a phallic-shaped brothel). NSFW in my view.

22 March
Pierre Jeanneret

Pierre Jeanneret House, Chandigarh, India, 1954

Poor Pierre Jeanneret. Not only did he have to put up with his cousin's preposterous name change from Charles-Édouard Jeanneret to Le Corbusier (which would be like Frank Gehry – who changed his name from Frank Owen Goldberg – declaring he was henceforth the Golden God), but Corbusier, having left his family's name behind, similarly left his cousin off the credits after World War II. He also managed to forget Charlotte Perriand's contribution as well. Corbusier must have been very forgetful.

It's no wonder the cousins parted; Jeanneret left their office to work in the French Resistance, while LC collaborated with the Vichy government. That pretty much sums it up. It's amazing they ever worked together again, but when LC designed Chandigarh, Pierre, encouraged by Charlotte Perriand, who knew a thing or two about cousin Corb, became his on-site representative.

It is impossible to see where Corbusier's design ended and Jeanneret's began. PJ and LC worked together on all the iconic prewar projects: Villa Savoye, Villa Garches, Ozenfant Studio, Pavillon de l'Esprit Nouveau, etc., etc. (and of course, with Perriand, on all their famous furniture as well). Jeanneret was said to be the "hand" while LC was the "intellect," but architecture succeeds or fails based on its execution, not just its conceptualization. Without the "hand," all their work would be just ideas, sketches, proposals, or unrequited work. Maybe Pierre preferred to stay out of the spotlight, in which case he succeeded admirably.

No one ever claimed to love Corbusier (his work, yes; him, not so much), but apparently Pierre was much adored in India. He spent more than fifteen years there, working on the city designs and buildings (especially the housing) and furniture (which has lately become highly valued once again).

His later furniture, the ones he can call his own, are wood and cane/rattan, the opposite of the studio's machine-driven tubular steel pieces of the 1920s and '30s. They are elegant nonetheless, exhibiting a bit of the 1950s penchant for tapered legs but none of the tendency to make furniture thinner or lighter than air, more in line with Perriand's late work.

Pierre Jeanneret and Charlotte Perriand were the hidden powers behind the early volumes of the *Oeuvre complète*, more respected for their modesty than Le Corbusier was for his narcissism.

23 March
Ruth Biber

Ruth Biber posed on flexible modular daybed of her design, 1950s

Ruth Frances Biber (or Mom, as I knew her) was raised in Mount Vernon, New York, until the Depression, when her family lost its house and moved to a New York City apartment at 235 West Seventy-Sixth Street that few would consider a step down; it was palatial by today's standards.

She took trolleys to the Art Students League of New York and the New School and the subway to Pratt Institute to study art, eventually landing on design and forming a small studio with Millard Francis Biber (Dad), where they designed a very 1950s daybed system with lots of configurations. Confusingly, both their middle names were Frances/Francis, and, weirdly, they both had nose jobs before they met. Their grandparents were all Orthodox Jews, their parents Conservative, they were Reformed, and we children, of course, are atheists (with surprisingly okay noses, probably disproving Darwin, or Mendel).

After their divorce, Ruth started working full time (though she always worked) for Lubalin, Burns & Co., for advertising agencies, and finally for the March of Dimes. We lived in a house filled with Danish modern furniture by Finn Juhl and Hans Wegner, a Womb chair, Herb Lubalin posters, a letterpress and

darkroom in the basement, and a collection of owls (drawn, sculpted, whatever) that drove me nuts.

Ruth had a penchant for going to other people's houses and rearranging the furniture (still the best metaphor for her that I know). Once I was watching her and a friend demolish a huge wall of those awful antiqued mirrors with sledgehammers, when the slightly drunk husband arrived (it was the suburbs, and the ladies may have had a few martinis as well). He didn't find it amusing and chased us as we ran to the car. That was fun.

All that furniture (and the rearranging) and posters and museum visits and weird colors must have had some subconscious impact on me. After studying biology (and finding I was more of a PBS *Nature* scientist than the real kind) I pursued architecture, something I had never seriously considered (consciously).

That seems to have worked out, and so I have Ruth Frances Biber to thank. (Thanks, Ruth!)

While I and her myriad friends miss her terribly, I still have all her cool furniture and a life that would never have been as good but for her.

24 March
Robert Mallet-Stevens

Spiral stair in Robert Mallet-Stevens house, Paris, France, 1927

If Robert Mallet-Stevens hadn't insisted that all his archives be destroyed upon his early death in 1945, we would all know a lot more about him, and he might not have disappeared for decades from design annals.

Mallet-Stevens grew up in Château de Maison-Laffitte, a fucking seventeenth-century villa designed by François Mansart (whose name was later defiled as the creator of the mansard roof), so he knew a bit about architecture. And because he was born to wealth, he not only could afford to be an architect (the first requirement) but had strong connections to the world of wealthy patrons (the second). He hung out with all the right Dadaists, Cubists, Surrealists, and others for his avant-garde cred; he even designed movie and stage sets for their productions.

Then there's the Rue Mallet-Stevens, a private street filled with houses of his design, a kind of wealthy artistic ghetto in the middle of Paris. It includes houses for Mallet-Stevens, a Dreyfus (distant relative of Julia Louis-Dreyfus), two sculptors, and a few others. It was a street museum of modern houses when there was no such thing. Rue Mallet-Stevens was built in 1927, the same year that the Weissenhof housing estate was built for the Deutscher

Werkbund exhibition in Stuttgart and a few years after Le Corbusier and Pierre Jeanneret tried a similar thing, with two connected houses, a few blocks away on Square du Docteur-Blanche (a name almost as good as Rue Mallet-Stevens!).

Mallet-Stevens's work was more luxurious (and probably easier to love) than that of his dogmatic competitors. For one of his projects (Villa Noailles), the clients also interviewed Corbusier and Mies van der Rohe. It's not hard to see why the viscount and viscountess settled on one of their own, though one critic complained that the titled couple deprived Corbusier of another potential masterpiece. Yes, architecture is viciously competitive, apparently even decades after the protagonists' deaths!

Mallet-Stevens's main talent was assembling teams of the best designers in France: Pierre Chareau, Eileen Gray, Man Ray, René Lalique, Fernand Léger, Gabriel Guévrékian, Jean Prouvé, Theo van Doesburg, Sonia Delaunay, Marcel Breuer, Constantin Brancusi, Alberto Giacometti, Piet Mondrian, Georges Braque, etc.

It pays for an architect to be collaborative, elegant, and soigné. Oh, and rich. That helps too.

25 March
Aline Saarinen

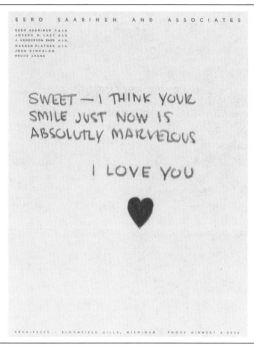

Note from Eero Saarinen to Aline Saarinen, circa 1950s

It would be a mistake, a big mistake, to assume Aline Saarinen (née Bernstein) was made famous by her last name; it is more likely that she made Eero Saarinen, her husband, as famous as he is today. She was an art critic at the *New York Times*, was managing editor of *Art News*, appeared on NBC's *Sunday* and *Today* (prior to and with Barbara Walters) shows, and was a Guggenheim Fellow, but she turned down an offer by President Lyndon B. Johnson to be the ambassador to Finland (just a few years after Eero died).

She met Eero when she was on assignment for an article called "Now Saarinen the Son" for the *Times* magazine. Eero, a cool Finn, must have simply exploded when he met the super-smart, attractive, independent, Jewish, Vassar-via-Fieldston, New York writer. They fell in love and were married the next year. She stopped writing architectural criticism (an obvious conflict of interest, with the last name Saarinen) but managed the press for the Saarinen office.

They met shortly after Eero won the competition for the St. Louis Gateway Arch. (When the telegram to E. Saarinen arrived at Cranbrook Academy of Art, it prompted a celebratory party…for the father, Eliel, who assumed the E was his! A few days later, there was another party for the actual winner.) Aline's article properly acknowledged what was already evident to anyone who was paying attention.

She was there for all of Eero's mature works: TWA Flight Center, Dulles International Airport, Bell Labs, John Deere Headquarters, CBS Building, Yale Hockey Rink, even the Vassar College dorms. When Eero died, with many unfinished (and amazing) buildings in the works, Aline calmed CBS's Frank Stanton and William S. Paley and approved the stone color for the Building. She did the same with all the other projects, vouching for a small office no one was sure could complete the work. She wrote the definitive catalogue raisonné of Saarinen's work and tied a bow on his professional fame.

The story of Aline and Eero has a pair of bittersweet endings. Eero died in 1961 at fifty-one (just seven years after they married) and Aline a decade later at fifty-eight, both of brain cancer. I'm not sure I have ever seen a picture of Eero smiling, but I know I have never seen a picture of Aline where she wasn't smiling. That seems to have worked for them!

26 March
Philip Freelon

National Museum of African American History and Culture, Washington DC, 2016

There's a great Roz Chast cartoon of someone perusing the obituary pages on which each obit is labeled "ten years older than you" or "five years younger than you" and one labeled "exactly your age." Philip Freelon, who died at sixty-six, was exactly my age, and, believe me, I noticed that fact. Painfully.

Freelon died of ALS after an amazing career designing exactly the kind of important architecture we all wish we could make: the National Museum of African American History and Culture on the Mall in DC, the Museum of the African Diaspora in San Francisco, the National Center for Civil and Human Rights in Atlanta, and many more.

He was appointed to the US Commission of Fine Arts by President Obama. He was a Loeb Fellow and professor at MIT. He received the Thomas Jefferson Award for Public Architecture, and he founded, with his wife, Nnenna Freelon (renowned jazz singer, composer, producer, and arranger), the NorthStar Church of the Arts in Durham, North Carolina. NorthStar is housed in a building that was once a church serving the Deaf community.

I didn't know Freelon personally (and didn't realize he was African American until writing this piece), but what

emerges from the laudatory obits is a picture of a profoundly good man doing profoundly good architecture for the good of communities (often underserved communities), with a sense of purpose, a sense of humor, and a warm countenance. While so many architects are overly ambitious, or obnoxious, or just plain assholes, Freelon was the other kind of architect: talented, dedicated, decent, and sadly in the minority (in a few senses of the word).

Nnenna, with a dozen albums and a half dozen Grammy nominations, was married to Phil for forty years. Marrying a creative partner is a great idea. Marrying someone who pursues the exact same creative path can be a mistake. Obviously, Phil and Nnenna got it right.

The only things about Philip Freelon (and I'm sure others could add more) that I find hard to relate to are his viewing of *The Matrix* more than fifty times and his commitment as a Trekkie. I will, therefore, avoid any "beam me up" references regarding his early death. But clearly he was the One.

27 March
Mies van der Rohe

Dr. Edith Farnsworth House, Plano, Illinois, 1951

Mies van der Rohe changed his name from Maria Ludwig Michael Mies (Ludwig Mies is roughly translated as "lousy warrior") and cleverly included the Dutch "van der" at a time when "von der" was legally reserved for nobility. Adopting his mother's maiden name, Rohe, which is an adaptation of the regal *roi*, he injected just enough class pretension to give himself a name befitting his ambition. And ambitious he was, pleading repeatedly with the Third Reich to christen modern architecture as the official style of the realm. It didn't work, and he just barely escaped Germany, eventually landing in the US.

It took me decades to fully appreciate the genius of Mies; his work can look so mechanical, so cold, so Teutonic, until you see just how refined and elegant it really is (and just look at the poseurs' imitations to see the difference – and, yes, I mean Philip Johnson). The Farnsworth House is an entire world in a single house. The Seagram Building is the finest tower of its type in New York City, maybe anywhere. Villa Tugendhat is remarkable, and the rebuilt Barcelona Pavilion is a secular temple. The simplicity can seem simplistic, but less is not only more, it's the hardest thing to realize. Mies's projects reference a world, a utopia, that we are all thankful

he imagined, but also happy to see in small bites.

In the 1990s, Pentagram held a meeting in Miami, and we invited Morris Lapidus to dinner. He was in his midnineties and came with his granddaughter, who ordered him a large vodka on the rocks as soon as he arrived. About halfway through the drink he became fully animated. I asked him about Mies (I don't remember why), and he replied, "Oy, Mies, what a pill!" which is the funniest thing I have ever heard about a famously unfunny man. I later learned that Lapidus had designed the earlier Seagram offices and was undoubtedly miffed at losing the big Park Avenue commission.

I wrote a piece, "When Mies Designed a Drive-In," looking at the least likely project he might have built (but didn't) and the gas station he did build. They confirm what he said: "I don't want to be interesting. I want to be good." But I think there may be one too many o's in that last word.

28 March
Viktor Vesnin

Likhachev Palace of Culture (aka ZIL Cultural Center), Moscow, USSR, 1930

Viktor Aleksandrovich Vesnin was a third of the famous Vesnin brothers (the others being Aleksandr Aleksandrovich and Leonid Aleksandrovich), a Russian firm spearheading the constructivist architecture movement in the Soviet Union. Building constructivist architecture was hard, but it was the images that had the greatest impact, and the Vesnin brothers produced one of the most enduring and oft-quoted building designs of the age: the Moscow headquarters for the *Leningrad Pravda* newspaper.

Designed for a tiny plot (twenty by twenty feet/six by six meters, smaller than that of a brownstone), the tower was more a piece of identity and advertising than a serious attempt to house and print a newspaper. It still captures our imagination nearly a hundred years later, because it manages to predict so many modern tropes; the large Times Square–scale signage (theirs on a revolving wheel, to change headlines), the exterior elevators, the exposed steel frame and large glass areas, even the searchlight (or is it a Morse code device?!) on the roof and the extreme verticality seem familiar. And this was designed when cars looked like antiques (to us), penicillin was still a few years off, the wireless (radio) was exploding, some homes were being

wired for electricity, Aeroflot was nearly ten years away, and the Russian Revolution had occurred only seven years before. These were very primitive times, by our standards, and yet the architecture was quite sophisticated and modern.

Viktor Aleksandrovich Vesnin built much more as the Soviet Union's head of infrastructure (People's Commissariat of Heavy Industry) where all the projects had the Soviet imprimatur of both name and form: Palace of Culture, Communal Housing, Lenin Library, Palace of Labor, Palace of the Soviets, even the club for the Society of Tsarist Political Prisoners.

But none really live up to the promise of constructivist architecture, a new world defined by architecture (not unlike the promise of the Russian Revolution itself). Still, you can't build utopia without first imagining it through images, so we owe the Vesnin brothers thanks for providing us with a view of the future to aspire to, even if it is a hundred years old.

29 March
Raymond Hood

30 Rockefeller Center tower seen through "Channel Gardens," 1939

When visitors to New York City ask me what buildings to see, I usually demur, saying that New York is a city of streets, not of buildings. But when pressed, I point people to Rockefeller Center. It's effectively a rearranged city in miniature, with the Fifth Avenue buildings cutting the city grid in half, and the RCA (30 Rock) Building viewed on edge to accentuate its height-to-width aspect ratio. It is a fucking marvel, and Raymond M. Hood designed it.

He also designed the American Radiator Building across from the New York Public Library (the black one) and the McGraw-Hill Building (the green one) on West Forty-Second Street. Its lobby was recently threatened by demolition, which would be an unnecessary, but seemingly inevitable, loss.

Hood designed the Tribune Tower in Chicago, winning a competition that attracted virtually every important architect of the day. His win was remarkably like that of the easily influenced Peter Keating (playing the amoral foil to Howard Roark, modeled on Frank Lloyd Wright) in The Fountainhead. But Ayn Rand, in the end, loved the McGraw-Hill Building and even conceded that Rock Center was not so bad.

Hood also designed the Daily News Building in New York City, which is fairly dumb in overall form (basically a built zoning diagram) but pretty spectacular in its entry sequence. The facade, the entry rotunda, and the huge globe are so theatrical that it seems like a set for the Daily Planet more than a real newspaper (it was, in fact, used in the first Superman movie).

The lobby at 30 Rock is equally remarkable, slathered in black marble and bronze detailing and leading to the underground version of the Rock Center scheme: a small city within a building. Rem Koolhaas described Hood in typically obscure praise, saying, "The secret of [his] success is a radical command of the language of fantasy-pragmatism that lends Manhattanism's ambition – the creation of congestion on all possible levels – the appearance of objectivity." Whatever the fuck that means.

But really, Hood managed to stay just slightly ahead of the times, not so much as to be truly radical, and not so far behind as to feel derivative.

30 March
Werner Seligmann

Entrance to Willard State Hospital Administration Building, Willard, New York, 1971

It is axiomatic that a student truly graduates after returning to their school as a teacher. Werner Seligmann was the enabler of my return. He led the first-year studio in alternately excoriating and paternal ways (while barely forty), and his impact is one of those things that echoes throughout my career. How many times does a tossed-off phrase redound decades later and guide your action? (More often than makes sense.)

After he departed Cornell, Seligmann invited me to teach at Syracuse University, where he was the dean. He showed up years later at a building dedication in Rochester, joined my own thesis review, was on a jury awarding some project I did, and was generally paternal and only occasionally excoriating to me. I took it as high praise.

Seligmann somehow implied he was Swiss, though he was German (he was born and lived there, in part in camps, through World War II and after); he was Jewish (see camps above), though nonsecular; his face was always in a permanent scowl/grin, though he was jocular in countenance. He was a walking contradiction, producing scholarship on Frank Lloyd Wright and Le Corbusier (and who else has done that?), seeming both energetic and depressed, extroverted and yet somehow sad and withdrawn, an enigma wrapped in a riddle inside a mystery, or however that phrase goes.

His work was often overdetermined. He was so intent on jamming as much didactic content as possible or so focused on issues of form (rather than material reality) that his work was ultimately compromised, but at least two were absolutely outstanding.

His teaching, on the other hand, was clear-eyed, direct, consistent, and dogmatic in all the (W)right ways. He was maniacal about the rigor of some fundamental skills, forcing a class (well, mine) to repeat exercises again and again and again until he deemed the work of sufficient quality to move on. It was painful (even had me searching for other schools to attend) but ultimately critical to being an effective architect.

Werner Seligmann lives on through his progeny: a generation of architects imitating his dedication and drive, with a voice in our heads that has that same bass register and vaguely German accent.

31 March
William Golden

CBS eye logo, 1951

William Golden designed what is commonly thought to be among the most perfect logos ever: the seventy-year-old CBS eye. And like any icon of modernity, it has a variety of possibly apocryphal backstories (all surrounded by legends). The most likely one is a Shaker drawing with a similar eye, published in the first issue of *Portfolio*, the legendary Alexey Brodovitch design magazine.

Golden married legendary graphic designer Cipe Pineles, who worked at legendary (I'll stop now) Condé Nast. Golden moved to CBS in its radio days and returned after World War II to its nascent TV era. Promoted to art director under Frank Stanton and owner William S. Paley (when something like CBS could be owned and run by, essentially, two people), he developed the eye and the Didot typeface that defined CBS.

Golden produced thousands of other graphic bits, but none have had the staying power or cultural assimilation of the eye. Since then the typeface has changed and the eye has been drawn in neon, in colors (with images inside), but it has never changed its essential form. Remarkably. The latest variation deconstructs the eye's geometry, in motion, and adds a sans serif face and a four-tone sound mark. It still works,

and works well, after seventy years, which might be unprecedented for a modern logo (although I'm happy to hear of other examples).

Golden was clear-eyed about the role of the designer versus that of the artist and was good enough with language to concoct some very quotable quotes:

> If he is honest enough, [the designer] becomes a professional who can do something special. I think the trouble comes when he tries to make it a work of art, too.... A lot of designers who are talented and intelligent don't find this very satisfying. But they're not going to find it more satisfying by pretending it's something it isn't.

And his variation on less is more:

> It is sometimes frustrating to find that hardly anyone knows that it is a very complicated job to produce something that is very simple.

Just like the eye, these quotes remain true and current. For a guy who died at forty-eight, William Golden did a lot of timeless work.

01 April
Dan Flavin

Lithonia Lighting, fluorescent strip light, low profile, 120V, UL listed, T8, 32 watts

Dan Flavin (whose last name became the first name Donald Judd cadged for his son) spent five years at seminary studying to be a priest (!) only to leave to join his twin brother in the US Air Force as a meteorological technician. That alone is an entire movie...but wait, there's more.

He returned to New York City to attend the Hans Hofmann School of Fine Arts, the New School, and Columbia University before getting a job as a mailroom clerk at the Guggenheim Museum. He moved on to MoMA as an elevator operator and guard (where his wife was an office manager), and finally worked as a guard at the American Museum of Natural History. That sounds like another movie (Days at the Museums?) or maybe just a live-action short.

Flavin's early works were abstract expressionist paintings and mixed-media collages, often with crushed cans he found on the street. At thirty he began the work we know him for: standard fluorescent tubes on white industrial steel boxes in every imaginable form, exploring the combinations and effects of light.

The fixtures were just vehicles (as neutral, repetitive, and ignorable as possible) to make the lines of white and colored light the actual sculpture. The limitations of available tubes (two-, four-, six-, and eight-foot-long and, later, rings) as well as identical white back boxes are just the kind of rigid vocabulary he and his friends (Judd, Sol LeWitt, Robert Ryman) reveled in. Reduced material palettes also, cleverly, gave each artist a visual brand that they could own.

It is hard to imagine how Flavin, having once been a mailroom clerk at the Guggenheim, must have felt in 1992 when he returned there to install his work throughout the entire rotunda. Like so much of his work, the installation explained the architecture and made it legible in a new way.

When I first saw Flavin's work, probably in the late 1960s, I thought it was clever. I admired the elevation of standard, off-the-shelf hardware to art, and I appreciated the elementary way he employed the fixtures as basic building blocks as an almost atomic approach to art. It is, of course, way beyond merely clever and much more than the objects themselves.

The way the light changes the world is more to the point. And light is how we know the world.

02 April
Jan Tschichold

Sketches for Sabon typeface, 1963

The son of a sign maker, twenty-one-year-old Jan Tschichold visited the Weimar Bauhaus and was instantly converted from traditional to modern type design. He published, a couple of years later, *Elemental Typography*, which codified modern typography and produced dozens of posters, books, and other Bauhaus-influenced work.

Ten years after his Bauhaus visit, he was arrested in Germany and jailed; he escaped to Switzerland in 1933, just as Hitler consolidated power. Thus began his conversion *back* to more traditional design, culminating in his denouncing his prior conversion and even calling modernism Fascist and authoritarian.

Maybe he was bipolar, maybe he regretted his youthful modern indiscretion (!), or maybe he just liked change. Not sure, but in whatever style he practiced, he always found admirers. He claimed to be one of the most profound influences on twentieth-century typography, though which period he was referring to I don't know. We might be tempted to add narcissistic personality disorder to the diagnosis if his work, in any style, wasn't so good.

Tschichold went on to design the cover format for Penguin Books in the UK, just ten years after the publishing house was founded. It set the bar for uniform brand design in books. The covers used a standard design with colors indicating book types: green covers were generally for crime novels, pink for travel and adventure, dark blue for biographies, red for drama, purple for essays, and yellow for miscellaneous titles that did not fit into any of the previous categories. And the most common and most famous color was orange for fiction. And gray was used for "important books."

The book design has that familiar, easy, and comfortable look and could be spotted from yards away, due to the uniform design and color coding. Founder Allen Lane said he wanted Penguin Books to be "bought as easily and casually as a packet of cigarettes." The books were sold for six pence, the price of a pack of cigs, and Lane even imagined they would be sold in vending machines. Penguin sold three million books the first year and transformed paperbacks from pulp fiction to serious literature. In short order, it had published a thousand titles.

So maybe Jan was right.

03 April
Theo Crosby

Theo Crosby with model of Shakespeare's Globe Theatre, London, England, 1986

Theo Crosby was a founder of Pentagram and was still at the firm when I joined in 1991, though he died just a few years later (the first founder to retire!). He once referred to his "late wife" (who was still alive), clarifying, "She just hasn't been my wife lately" (they were divorced). But in his case, being hit by a bus after suffering heart issues earlier that year, he is "my late partner Theo Crosby." Full stop.

Crosby was a bundle of contradictions. A committed modernist who devised *This is Tomorrow*, a landmark exhibition in 1956 at the Whitechapel Gallery, but later re-created Shakespeare's Globe theater. He joined Monica Pidgeon to transform *AD* magazine into the powerhouse it became, but he also published (among his many, many books) *Let's Build a Monument*, heralding his Battle of Britain entry, a decidedly unmodern design. He was interested in prefabricated housing, yet he joined the Prince Charles's (now King Charles III's) anti-modern Foundation for the Built Environment.

I loved arguing with Theo, who never raised his voice and always had a clever, well-thought-out answer, delivered with the most charming (perhaps self-satisfied?) smile and devastating logic. And he was rife with quotable

quotes, my fave being, "Don't look for clients; look for friends."

He was great with words (though his students might disagree), but his work never achieved the level of importance or public acclaim he might have hoped. Possibly because while he was facile with ideas, his design work was always intensely quirky and personal.

What he was very good at was promoting other talents, a valuable talent in itself. Alison and Peter Smithson, James Stirling, Norman Foster, Richard Rogers, and especially Archigram, along with scores of others, benefited from his promotion of their work, including at *This Is Tomorrow* and in *AD*, but also in books like *An Anthology of Houses* and the first exhibition on Le Corbusier in the UK.

And he promoted me as well, of course, in 1991 when I, as a young architect, visited Pentagram's London office to consider becoming only the second architect at the firm. I stayed for nineteen years. It was an act of generosity repeated many times in his life, so there are many of us out there who owe Theo Crosby quite a bit.

04 April
Mary Elizabeth Jane Colter

Desert View Watchtower, Grand Canyon National Park, Arizona, 1932

At a time when there were only, perhaps, thirty women who were architects in the US, Mary Elizabeth Jane Colter produced some of the most influential works of any architect: the original buildings that defined National Park Service Rustic, a style intended to harmonize with America's national parks.

At the 1935 Bright Angel Lodge on the south rim of the Grand Canyon, Colter created the geologic fireplace out of stone mimicking the stratigraphy of the canyon itself. Stacking local materials (in the correct geologic order), she created a teaching moment and an iconic element within the lodge; it is genius. Even more presciently, she pioneered experiential architecture (and created narratives for a mythical backstory for her buildings) in service of a commercial enterprise.

The Fred Harvey Company, where Colter was chief architect for nearly forty years, developed hospitality (Harvey House hotels, stores, restaurants, and even souvenirs) along the path of the Santa Fe Railroad. Colter developed and broadened styles respecting local contexts through the twenty-one landmark hotels and other buildings she designed for it. Her group of buildings in the Grand Canyon is now called the Mary Jane Colter Buildings

and are National Historic Landmarks. Her buildings that were demolished during her lifetime prompted her to say, "It is possible to live too long."

Fortunately, she didn't live long enough to read the recent book *False Architect: The Mary Colter Hoax* in which Fred Shaw claims all of Colter's claims of authorship are fabricated, possibly due to her narcissistic personality disorder. Nearly one hundred years after the work was built and more than fifty years after her death, it is hard to understand how, suddenly, all the prior history can be a hoax. Shaw's self-published story (on Kindle only; is it still a book if there is only an electronic edition?) offers a whopping ten thousand dollars to anyone who can prove him wrong. For a year after the publication date of his book. To his satisfaction.

Why, one might reasonably ask, is one of the few, lauded, inventive architects of the Southwest in the early twentieth century being dogged by claims of hoax?

Oh, right...woman.
Oh Mary.

Architype Bayer typeface, based on Bayer's 1927 Universal typeface

It's amazing what Herbert Bayer did while just in his (and the twentieth century's) twenties: attended the Bauhaus (in Weimar), taught there (in Dessau), and designed about half of the graphics we think of as Bauhaus. At twenty-five, he designed the typeface Universum, which was startlingly modern (lowercase only, eliminating most atypical letters) but also was intended to change the way German was displayed typographically at a time when Blackletter, Fractur, etc. (think *New York Times* logo) were used for everything! The idea that an alphabet could change the world was part of the optimism promulgated by the Bauhaus and probably what seduced Bayer into working for the Nazis after the closing of the Bauhaus. (He later professed profound regret, but believing that with good design the Third Reich could be tamed does seem a common trap for German modernists.) After his artwork was included in Berlin's *Degenerate Art* show, he wisely fled to the US to design a Bauhaus show at MoMA.

And it was not just graphics; he was a pioneering photographer, collage artist, painter, architect, and sculptor. He seemed to change things within whichever art he focused his talent on (he said that printers were already being asked to make their work "more like the Bauhaus" just a few years after he revolutionized that work). He defined modern Aspen, redefined the Container Corporation of America, and curated an art collection at the Atlantic Richfield Company that approached thirty thousand pieces. He created earthworks that rival those of Robert Smithson, modern monumental sculpture. His enthusiasm and optimism were infectious.

He even created an atlas that, in 1953, paved the way for infographics and corporate identity beyond the typical logos and letterheads. The *World Geo-Graphic Atlas* was nothing less than an entirely new, postwar way to see the world. Graphically rich and gorgeous, dense and brimming with serious data, the atlas was unequaled, perhaps ever. We are now accustomed to data displays in the *New York Times* and online, and they all owe a debt (long before Edward Tufte) to Herbert Bayer.

06 April
Raphael

Marriage of the Virgin (Lo Sposalizio), Citta del Castello, Italy, 1504

One could make the case that Raphael, in addition to being the GOAT finalist painter we know, was an accomplished architect based solely on the buildings in his paintings. But he did more than paint in the thirty-seven years he spent on earth.

After the death of Donato Bramante, Pope Julius II turned over the design of St. Peter's Basilica to Raphael, despite his youth and inexperience. He produced a transitional design, altering Bramante's Greek cross into the Latin cross we see today. Raphael died midproject, and the work was handed to Michelangelo; we're lucky Raf was involved but equally lucky the older Mike Angel got the gig.

Raphael adorned the loggia of the Villa Farnesina with 360-degree frescoes that define the space as fully as Peruzzi's architecture. The formal scheme of his Villa Madama precedes Vignola's similar Villa Giulia by more than twenty-five years. Raphael's Palazzo Jacopo da Brescia, which was demolished and sort of re-erected in the 1930s, was a sophisticated commentary on Bramante's Palazzo Caprini that Raf bought and lived (and died) in.

Raphael's painting *The Marriage of the Virgin* devotes as much canvas to the idealized (and exquisitely rendered) temple as to the marriage in the title. Painted just two years after Bramante's (built) Tempietto, it posits an entirely different approach to idealized architecture. The collection of luminaries in Raphael's *The School of Athens* is nearly dwarfed by the architecture, suffused in gorgeous light and extending the architectural context of the Stanza della Segnatura (not unlike Leonardo da Vinci, who is rendered as Plato in Raphael's painting, did in *The Last Supper*).

The focus on who's who in these crowded compositions is like the IMDb for Renaissance painting; it's understandable, as these paintings were the literature, cinema, and history channels of their time. The game of *Where's Waldo* (finding Raphael's self-portrait in the crowds, as we do with Alfred Hitchcock) or guessing which famous contemporary icon is playing which famous historical icon (the *Lincoln* or *Midnight in Paris* game) turns Raphael's epic paintings into giant romans à clef.

Maybe Raphael was Andy Warhol (or Werner Heisenberg), chronicling (and therefore changing) the society in which he lived because he was chronicling that society. Meta-Raf!

07 April
Leon Krier

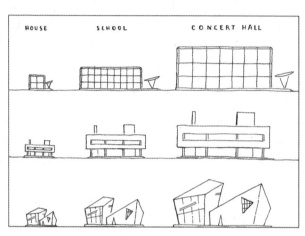

Leon Krier's polemic diagram about scale in architecture and the city

If you believe in birthday buddies, it's interesting that Léon Krier and Theo Crosby have birthdays just days apart. And Krier and Heinrich Tessenow share a birthday (not too far from that of Albert Speer, for that matter). Crosby criticized modernism after a genuine engagement with the origins of postwar modernism, as separate from political commentary. Krier, only twenty years younger than Crosby, has the moral detachment to praise Speer, and his teacher Tessenow, with an intellectual appraisal (apologia?) of Fascism and Fascist architecture.

Krier and Crosby are connected by their involvement in the Prince of Wales's (now King Charles III's) retrograde embrace of the past via his Foundation for the Built Environment. The prince/king, in all his wisdom, even forgives the Nazis for only destroying the buildings of London, not replacing them with dreaded "modern carbuncles." Theo would never embrace that kind of blind spot, but Krier seems happy to reconsider Speer as an apolitical animal. Yikes.

Krier appears to base most of his legitimate criticism of early modernism on the old and long-discarded tenets of its sterile and destructive urban ideas, ones that no one has seriously

supported for more than fifty years. Fighting against long-dead ideas may seem noble, but really it's a head fake for his rather limited view of alternate solutions.

I remember Krier, teaching at Cornell University, from nearly fifty years ago, when it was quaint, if only slightly more timely, to rail against "towers in a park" and other discredited notions. Now it seems like he's fighting the wrong war

Krier seems to have trouble dealing with the modern world as a whole: cars, computers, messiness, media, and, of course, design as it is currently practiced. He actually uses 9/11 as a case study to say that the loss of tall buildings (the World Trade Center) is inherently more destructive than horizontal ones (the Pentagon) and so therefore tall buildings, and all modern architecture, are totalitarian and absurd.

Krier has produced a few actual buildings, and some are quite lovely, if a bit on the Disney side of life. They may work as fantasy, but they don't get us far if we include reality. We all love old buildings and old cities, but living in the past is another thing entirely.

Petrol Station for Mobiloil Socony-Vacuum, installed at Vitra Campus, 1953

Jean Prouvé is a miracle. Any single thing he designed would be enough to make any single designer famous. But he designed hundreds of things: chairs, houses, buildings, doors, tables, beds, lighting, desks, stools, benches, prefab houses, demountable houses, gas stations, schools, prefabricated facade systems, and lots of things I am forgetting. And he didn't just design them; he built them in his factory/shop, saying, "Never design anything that cannot be made."

As Renzo Piano said, anyone can build using a maximum of materials, but Prouvé's ethic included economy of means; everything he made used materials (and labor) to their maximum efficiency. In other hands this idea might produce ugly efficiency, but in his the results are artful in a way that makes you forget the efficiency altogether and marvel at the pure invention, the pure elegance of highly refined form.

If I had to pick a single project to highlight (and luckily I don't), it would be his 1956 prefab Maison des Jours Meilleurs (House for Better Days) that he designed and fabricated in a matter of weeks and erected in seven hours by the Seine in Paris. Someone not known to throw around praise lightly

(Le Corbusier) said of it, "On Quai Alexandre III Jean Prouvé has built the handsomest house I know of: the most perfect object for living in, the most sparkling thing ever constructed. It's all the real, built outcome of a lifetime of research."

Prouvé created his solution to France's serious postwar housing crisis after a woman died of exposure one winter. It was a suburban solution to an urban problem but appropriate as an emergency solution Prouvé could realize immediately. Of course, it wasn't accepted.

His longest lasting impact may be leading the jury for the Centre Pompidou and selecting Piano and Rogers, forever changing the landscape of Paris and of architecture.

Jean Prouvé said, "There is no difference between the construction of an item of furniture and that of a house," and apparently of a museum as well; a Prouvé house now sits atop Pompidou.

09 April
Giambattista Nolli

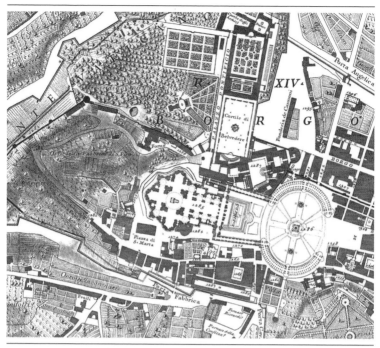

Nolli Map of Rome (Pianta Grande di Roma), detail showing Vatican area, 1748

There was a time (and it may still be true today) that every architecture student had a famous twelve-part map of Rome as the only large-scale (nearly 6 by 7 feet/1.8 by 2.1 meters) art we could afford. Sometimes framed, but usually unframed, these pages were pinned to students' and graduates' apartment walls.

Giovanni Battista Nolli created that insanely beautiful plan of Rome in 1748 after starting his survey twelve years earlier. He built upon the Bufalini Map of nearly two hundred years earlier, adding greater accuracy and more aggressive detailing of the interiors of public buildings. The Nolli Map posits an important idea about the city: the outdoor public spaces and the indoor ones (churches, ancient relics, covered passages, etc.) are parts of a single, continuous network of urban spaces. Roofed and unroofed public spaces are still public spaces: a revolutionary idea, and one exquisitely rendered by the Nolli Map.

Nolli accomplished this before any aerial options (even hot air balloons were decades in the future) and with, essentially, compass, chain, and theodolite. The task seems monumental: surveying, with extreme accuracy, the entire city plus the interiors of

hundreds of civic buildings. It must have taken an army of surveyors; it's hard to imagine the complexity of the task, even for the much smaller city Rome was 275 years ago. And it's so accurate that the Rome city planning department used the map until 1970!

Nolli oriented the map with magnetic north up (previously east was the cardinal orientation point, hence the word orientation), eschewing the religious and promoting the Age of Enlightenment's secular view. The densest part of the map fills only a third of the pages' area; the borders, engraved views, dedication to Pope Benedict XIV, and ancient and modern monuments fill the rest. Putti are even shown surveying (with appropriate tools).

A contemporaneous map of Paris commissioned by Michel-Étienne Turgot is equally remarkable; it is a building-by-building three-dimensional rendering of every single structure in Paris. As spectacular as it is, it didn't change the way people see cities; it documented the way people already saw cities.

By treating all public space as connected, Nolli redefined the role of space in the city, a revolution that is still being fought today.

10 April
Judith Turner

Peter Eisenman, House VI, Frank Residence, Cornwall, Connecticut, 1975

The only reason you may know about the New York Five is because of Judith Turner. That's not her brag (though why not?), but what they (they being architects Peter Eisenman, Michael Graves, Charles Gwathmey, John Hejduk, and Richard Meier) said to her about the publication of her 1980 book, *Judith Turner Photographs Five Architects*. The name Five Architects was coined earlier, around 1972, when their eponymous book was published. They had little built work to show at the time, but the book included some of their best projects, as first projects often are (ironically). Did Gwathmey ever do better than his parents' house and studio?

By the time Turner started photographing them, they were certainly well-known among the architectural community (mine especially, as two of them were alums of my school, and another two were colleagues of my first employer). But Turner put them in a (gasp!) coffee table book that was about her abstract view of their buildings, not the architects' own intellectualization of those buildings. That may seem like a distinction without a difference, but it was actually the first time their work, as a group, was in a book interesting to more than just architects.

In some cases, her pictures are better than the buildings; they rework the architecture into images that emphasize the abstract qualities of the projects. As she has said, she is not an architectural photographer, but a photographer who uses architecture as her subject. Forty years later, she has applied her vision to a staggering range of buildings, and always with the same ability to undo the general in favor of the specific.

I met Turner more than forty years ago, introduced by a mutual Dutch architect friend, and she is essentially the same person today as when we first met. She is living in the same Upper West Side apartment, wearing her hair in the same parted style (though possibly grayer), still using a 645 medium-format camera, shooting with film rather than digitally. I find that reassuring. The same could be said of Julius Shulman when I worked with him at age ninety-four. He was still using the same view camera (though with more assistants), living in the same house, using the same tricks to craft his images.

Turner isn't stuck, she just hasn't finished yet!

11 April
Dody Weston Thompson

Ghost Town Kitchen, Rhyolite, Nevada, 1940s

Dody Weston Thompson was one of those figures in art who worked in the seams between her own work and that of her mentors, getting a bit lost in the process. She apprenticed to Edward Weston, who trusted her to write about him and even to print the last set of images he showed publicly, and seemed happy for her to marry his son Brett, though that only lasted four years.

Weston Thompson, who sometimes signed her work simply "Dody" to avoid leaning on her ex-father-in-law's fame, was Weston's assistant, Ansel Adams's assistant, and a member of f/64, the San Francisco photographers' group founded by Adams and others. She was awarded only the second Albert Bender Award (after Adams) and cofounded *Aperture* magazine, yet somehow she never found the fame she deserved.

She was stunning in her youth, destined to be a famous actor, when she transferred to Black Mountain College and met the world she would embrace. It didn't hurt that her father was a filmmaker, but she was truly converted at a Weston retrospective. She sought him out and telephoned when she was near his home, getting an invitation to meet and see Weston's platinum prints.

That one could just look up a telephone number and call one of the most famous photographers (and be invited over for a viewing!) seems utterly inconceivable today. But the telephone book was once the great leveler in society. In the 1980s, I was trying to find Benny Goodman's address (to send him something or other, I forget) and there he was in the phone book. Not as Benjamin Goodman or B. Goodman (which might have made me wonder if I had the listing for Bergdorf Goodman), but as Benny Goodman, just to make it absolutely clear who he was.

Dody wrote extensively about photography, documenting both the history and the methodology she had absorbed (after a year assisting Adams and learning his zone method, for example). She had worked as a riveter during World War II and was unwittingly photographed by Adams leaving a plant in California long before they met in person.

Dody Weston Thompson made the transition to color, and to small handheld cameras, after a life lugging those enormous view cameras for herself and for her mentors.

12 April
Antonio da Sangallo the Younger

View down Pozzo di San Patrizio (St. Patrick's Well), Orvieto, Italy, 1537

Who can understand names from the Renaissance? Antonio da Sangallo was born Antonio Cordiani to Bartolomeo Piccioni (and his grandfather was Francesco Giamberti). He adopted his uncle's name, making the original "the Elder" (which I suppose was an honor, unlike today). He apprenticed to a carpenter, rather than a painter/sculptor as was the traditional path to architecture, but eventually apprenticed to Bramante. Good move, Tony da Younger (his rap name).

Bramante was tasked with St. Peter's Basilica, which young da Sangallo eventually took over after he died. He had lots to do at the Vatican, including the Scala Regia and Sala Regia, while working on St. Peter's. He didn't live to see his work at St. Peter's completed, and Michelangelo, who succeeded him there, dismantled it (and the world is better for it).

Michelangelo also bested da Sangallo at the Palazzo Farnese, the enormous block in Rome, when Alessandro Farnese was dissatisfied with the cornice da Sangallo had designed. He held a competition (and, really, who does that? a competition for a cornice? with heavyweights like Mike Angel submitting? what a world...) that da Sangallo lost to Michelangelo,

much to his eternal shame. It is said, by the way, that the shame of losing was what killed him, but that sounds a lot like the stereotypical Jewish grandmother clutching her heart because her grandson wasn't going to be a doctor. But maybe cornices were really important to da Sangallo!

He worked with Raphael on Villa Madama and had lots of other remarkable constructions, but the one I didn't know was Pozzo di San Patrizio (St. Patrick's Well) in Orvieto. This is no ordinary well; it's 175 feet/53.3 meters deep and more than 40 feet/12.2 meters wide with a central open cylinder surrounded by double helix ramps. The ramps allow mules to travel down to the water and back up without passing each other. And the open central cylinder has windows all the way down to light the ramps.

Francis Crick (of Watson and Crick fame) visited Orvieto in the 1940s, so it is possible that after five hundred years Antonio da Sangallo the Younger played a role in the discovery of the structure of DNA (which, of course, is a double helix just like his well)!

13 April
Leendert Cornelis van der Vlugt

Connecting bridges at Van Nelle factory, Rotterdam, Netherlands, 1931

On a day that is also Thomas Jefferson's birthday, I decided to focus on non-slaveholders, hence Leendert Cornelis van der Vlugt. He deserves it, and not just for his moral superiority of not enslaving humans; he did the opposite, reserving the best rooftop spot at the Van Nelle Factory for a workers' tearoom!

Van Nelle is the Ur-modern glass and steel factory replete with glass transport bridges connecting the factory to the warehouse. It was, said Le Corbusier, "A poem in steel and glass" and "the most beautiful spectacle in the modern age."

I visited in the late 1970s, while it was still occupied by Van Nelle (but with empty factory floors). As the elevator opened to each level, an overwhelming aroma of that floor wafted in: coffee, tea, or tobacco, permanently embedded from decades of processing. Plus, the incredible concrete structure and the light from a full-glass facade delineated an overwhelming architectural experience I will never forget.

Van der Vlugt went on to design houses for each of Van Nelle's executives (they were aficionados; Richard Neutra's VDL House in LA was built with a loan from one of the execs at Van Nelle!), including the remarkable Sonneveld House, which

I visited in 2007, completely restored. The exterior may be white, but the interior is an explosion of color: gold leaf walls, powder blue kid's room, red kitchen, orange chairs, all planned in gorgeous gauche drawings.

You can overlook color in early modern architecture, as almost all were photographed in black and white. But few were limited to that in reality. Convenient color film wasn't available until the late 1930s, and even after that, black and white dominated architectural photography. The advanced development of black-and-white film meant faster, finer grain, less-expensive images that were easily developed and printed in a small darkroom. But it is the film's ability to isolate form and light in images, absent the distraction of color (which tended to look even more artificial then) that architects and photographers found so seductive. Paintings (*Guernica*, for example) even mimicked this colorless view of the world.

In ten short years (until his early death at forty-two) from the Van Nelle factory (which looks black-and-white even in person) to the Technicolor Sonneveld House, van der Vlugt crystallized the poles of modernism.

14 April
Anthony McCall

Solid-Light Works, Pioneer Works, Brooklyn, New York, 2018

When I met Anthony (who spells it with an *h* but doesn't pronounce it), he was in his middle period, designing books, mostly for artists. Had he not returned to his real calling, I might never have realized what an incredible and incredibly important artist he was, and is.

We met as parents of two boys going to the Village Community School do; we looked around at all the class parents and said, "Those guys." Plus our sons Julian and Hardy were friends. But, really, Anthony and his wife, Annabel McCall, looked like the only interesting *and* sane people there. They are lovely: funny, smart, interesting, charming, and almost entirely sane.

McCall decided, after facing down a health issue, that life was too short and picked up his art where he left off; he used film in the original iterations of his solid-light works, but he had digital tools the second time around. During the twenty-year gap in his art, smoking inside buildings more or less disappeared, as it did from all those atmospheric jazz club black-and-white photographs. Light was no longer reliably *visible* in the way it once was.

Big difference. But the atmosphere was easy to create with some kind of mist- or fog-generating devices, giving the air an even more manageable materiality. And the freedom of digitally generated images allowed McCall to proliferate what was once an arduous task of stop-action photography.

The result is a marvel to see; His light sculptures allow (encourage, really) the viewer to physically engage with the seemingly solid, evanescent light forms, changing slowly in time, and wrapping the visitor in a highly personal world in a remarkably intimate way. It is as though you can feel the light, and the galleries seem to hush in response to the power of the pieces.

McCall also revived his 1970s films of fire pieces. In one he walks (in white bell bottoms, to establish the period!) a large field at night carrying a lit torch and setting a grid of firepots alight, to stunning effect.

There is a kind of asceticism in Anthony McCall's work; it is all made of light, time, and motion. These are, as he says, the elements of any motion picture. But no film I have ever seen has done what McCall has: he includes the viewer in the art.

15 April
Leonardo da Vinci

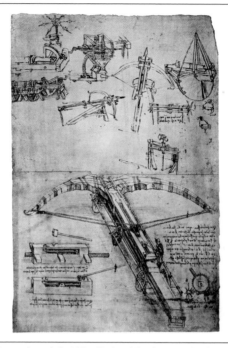

Sketch for giant crossbow, folio 149a, *Codex Atlanticus* notebook, circa 1480s–1490s

The first time I visited Florence, I met, and spent a few months with, some Americans looking for *The Battle of Anghiari*, the long-lost da Vinci painting for the Salone dei Cinquecento (Hall of the Five Hundred) in the Palazzo Vecchio. It was copied by many, including Peter Paul Rubens, and was lauded as a marvel of equine power.

Da Vinci worked slowly, so fresco, where paint is applied to wet plaster and bonds chemically to the ground, was not his favorite medium. *The Last Supper* attests to this conundrum; frescoes from two thousand years ago have survived intact, but Leo's oil-based concoction began to self-destruct almost immediately.

It seemed to my new friends inconceivable that when Giorgio Vasari (who wrote *Life of Leonardo da Vinci* and designed the Uffizi) overhauled the Salone, he would simply demolish the Leonardo. They surmised that Vasari built a new wall (on which he then painted his own frescoes) over *The Battle of Anghiari*. They even, secretly and illegally, pulled a core sample that proved (to them) that the painting was still there. It felt like I was as close to da Vinci as possible, but the full story of the painting is even more remarkable.

Jonathan Jones in *The Lost Battles* describes the vicious rivalry between Leonardo and Michelangelo and their competition for the painting commissions (for two different battle scenes) and for personal reputation. Both set new benchmarks for the art of battle paintings: Michelangelo's in sketch form only, and Leonardo's, now lost but known through the Rubens.

Jones tells a story of the two artists meeting in front of the Palazzo Spini Feroni, across from the Santa Trinita church. These are two incredibly famous gay men in sixteenth-century Florence. Leonardo, older and gayer, typically wore robes of pink or purple velvet or satin, a genius dandy. Michelangelo was younger, rougher, messier (sculpture is a messy business), brasher, and angrier. Some men asked Leo to help explain some Dante passages, when Mike walked by and Leo demurred, "He will explain it." Somehow (anger management issues?) this enraged Michelangelo, who insulted the older artist about his unrealized monumental bronze horse and stormed off, leaving Leonardo as red as his cape.

This is how I will always think of Leonardo (and Michelangelo): framed by the poles of their personalities as much by the battle for GOAT status.

16 April
John Chamberlain

Source material for John Chamberlain sculptures (!)

John Chamberlain's best-known works (painted car parts torn, flattened, bent, and welded into fantastic constructions), simply beg to be criticized (as a car wreck or junk pile, for example). This was demonstrated when two of his pieces were mistakenly hauled away as scrap while sitting in front of a Chicago warehouse. But it's the same brand of criticism leveled at Jackson Pollock, Franz Kline, Andy Warhol, and Jeff Koons (and I could go on): how is this art?! Marcel Duchamp answered that long ago ("because it is made by an artist"), and eventually the world agreed.

The path Chamberlain took to the work we know was circuitous. After enlisting (at age sixteen!) in the US Navy, he studied hairdressing (to meet women), attended the Art Institute of Chicago (which he left), and landed at Black Mountain College (where he hung out with poets). Visiting Larry Rivers in 1957, he discovered car parts and began making art from them. Early in Chamberlain's career, Donald Judd opined that he would be recognized as the best American sculptor under forty, if that designation meant anything.

It must have been hard for Chamberlain to respond to the same fucking criticism over and over (to paraphrase these insightful observations, "It's like a car wreck"). His work is more like three-dimensional abstract expressionist painting than more consciously assembled pieces like David Smith's or Mark di Suvero's. Just to prove it was not really about auto parts, Chamberlain changed media and did foam rubber and aluminum foil sculpture before returning to the prepainted metal scraps.

Chamberlain wasn't the only artist working in car parts. When in college, I drove a 1960 Mercedes 190D (it cost six hundred dollars), a Berlin taxi–style car with two-by-ten wood planks for front and rear bumpers (the originals had long ago rusted away). I would sneak it behind the sculpture foundry to park. Jason Seley taught and worked in the foundry, and he made his sculpture from shapely chromed car bumpers, artfully assembled and welded to re-create classical Roman sculpture (from the life-size plaster casts that dotted the college) like *Herakles in Ithaka*, a bit of an Ithaca/Ithaka joke. He stopped me one day to say I had to stop parking behind the foundry because everyone assumed he stole my bumpers!

I'm just glad John Chamberlain wasn't teaching there too...

17 April
Andrew Geller

Cover of *Beach Houses: Andrew Geller* by Alastair Gordon, 2003

Working at a firm like Raymond Loewy's was a way to do virtually every kind of design imaginable: cars, houses, exhibitions, products, TV show sets, packaging, graphic design, trains, and even planes (like Air Force One, until the idiot-in-chief decided to redesign it in 2019).

Andrew Geller was one of Loewy's designers, part of a quaint time when an argument between nations could be about washing machines and "beach house" meant a shack by the water. He designed the display at the 1959 American National Exhibition in Moscow, where Richard Nixon and Nikita Khrushchev argued about whether it was truly a typical, affordable American house (it was, and it was split in half to allow more room for crowds and so christened "Splitnik").

Geller went on to redefine the modern beach house with a series of very small, very simply assembled, and very dramatically shaped homes that are still beloved. They are more like tents than what you would call houses today: often uninsulated, inexpensive, stick-built, geometric constructions that were unmistakable in any landscape at a time when most houses were low-slung suburban affairs.

These were weekend party, not work-week, abodes, and their design said just that.

I remember seeing some of Geller's beach houses on Fire Island when I was a kid. They were famous even then, not for their architect (whom we didn't know) but for their shapes – the box kite house or the double diamond house or the A-frame house. But by that time, "beach house" was beginning to mean something very different: they were becoming elaborate competitions in size, proximity to the ocean, architectural provenance, and high (not low) cost. It's a shame that they have become like every other house type rather than remaining simple and clever, but I am as guilty as anyone in helping to promote that version of home.

Geller's most reductio ad absurdum proposal was the *Esquire* Weekend House, an ultra tiny (about 50 square feet/4.6 square meters), slightly raised cabin that cost three thousand dollars and could be towed behind a bachelor's three-thousand-dollar Chevy Impala. Architects ("real" ones) were incensed that Geller (being "not in the canon") got the attention and glossy mag press he did for this beach house, but then architects really haven't changed!

18 April
Giuseppe Terragni

Casa del Fascio, Como, Italy, 1936

I'm beginning to think that architects who designed for Fascists may get a pass when they are really good architects, and Giuseppe Terragni was one of the best. Or maybe I can tolerate their misdeeds if they die young (Terragni didn't even make it to forty) but not if they enjoy a long life. However it works, Terragni benefits from these bespoke new rules.

I still call his most famous building the Casa del Fascio, without irony or hesitation, maybe because it doesn't have any explicit Fascist mottos (like "Roma o morte!") and has been stripped of contemporary decorative flourishes (like swastika banners or huge portraits of Benito Mussolini). What remains is an amazingly deft manipulation of a cubic volume with an interior glass block–lit atrium that feels like being at the bottom of a swimming pool. The light from the glass block ripples on the polished floor like water, and the space is two or three stories high, surrounded by interior spaces; it's like being bathed in modern light.

The facade alone is incredibly evocative, especially for architects who are enthralled with blank facades and asymmetry (as in the Ca' d'Oro in Venice or Villa Schwob in La Chaux-de-Fonds). It was a canvas for propaganda but functions now as a stunning architectural element. The front piazza allows you to back up and appreciate the building as an abstract object and really see the decisive way it meets the ground.

Terragni's most important unbuilt work is the Danteum, commissioned by Mussolini and arranged to reflect the divisions in the text of *The Divine Comedy*. It is, as much as any building (built or unbuilt), the progenitor of building as narrative, something very much in vogue for at least the last several decades. The idea that a thirty-five-year-old could produce a work of such conceptual clarity and constructional precision is remarkable.

From a career that lasted only thirteen years and produced only a handful of buildings, Terragni has had an outsized impact on architecture. During World War II, the Italian army sent him to the eastern front, Stalingrad, where he was surrounded by, and drew, the depths of human misery. He returned to Como, where he died before the war ended.

19 April
Helen Binkerd Young

Home Economics Department, Cornell, 1918–19. Young is third from right, middle row

It's hard not to invoke *Promising Young Woman* (the title, not the plot) in the case of Helen Binkerd Young. She graduated in 1900 from Cornell University's College of Architecture with a BArch as the only woman in her class and the winner of design medals and other approbation. She was only the eleventh woman to get that degree at Cornell and one of only thirty-nine women in the US who had graduated from any architecture school.

It's hard to know whether to praise or shame Cornell, but when she returned ten years later with her husband (George Young Jr., a graduate of the same class), he was hired to teach at the College of Architecture and she was relegated to the School of Home Economics, where she taught for free. (There are similar echoes today, with some teaching at the now-renamed School of Human Ecology as a farm team for the College of Architecture, Art, and Planning. Though hopefully not for free.)

At a time when the Cornell dean, the Architecture Department chair, and (not quite) half the department's professors are women, it is easy to forget what the prior 120 years was like. Helen Binkerd Young was an outstanding architect and educator, a writer of important texts (some still referenced in scholarly work), and a published architect, yet even she

convinced herself that she needn't fight to be paid to teach (she said her husband might not appreciate hearing she was uncompensated!).

This was ten years before she could even vote in US elections, but still it's outrageous. In 1920 she could both vote and call herself a full professor, and she left Cornell to pursue her architectural career while her husband continued to teach there until 1946. It's no wonder she looks rather cross in most photos.

Helen Binkerd Young's design work was, of course, buried within her husband's, so we don't really know how much she was responsible for. But together they designed numerous homes in Cayuga Heights (the nearby tony neighborhood for professors and other school leaders) that give it the World War I–adjacent character it now has.

About 50 percent of all current architecture students in the US, though only 17 percent of registered architects in the US, are women. Since the 1970s, Cornell has boosted enrollment by women to approximate parity to that of men, but it will take decades or more to shift a profession that has been ingrained as male, essentially, forever.

20 April
Rachel Whiteread

Nameless Library, Judenplatz Holocaust Memorial, Vienna, Austria, 2000

I think the reason so many architects (and not just architects) are in love with Dame Rachel Whiteread's work is that it reverses the figure-ground of object (primary) and space (secondary). Architects spend their careers juggling these two physical imperatives, solid and void, by conceptually privileging space over solids, but the rest of the world, in a kind of space blindness, sees only solids. I used to say that space is the one thing we are left with after everything else has been value engineered, so it had better be damned good!

Whiteread wasn't the first to cast the voids of objects (Bruce Nauman cast the space under his chair in concrete just around the time Whiteread was born), but she took this idea to worlds no one had attempted. It's not just the meaning loaded into her work (her inverted library at Judenplatz in Vienna is fairly rich with embedded inferences) but also the sheer scale of the endeavor.

Casting an entire house or an NYC water tower or a staircase (making the voids solid) is making the imperceptible perceptible at a scale beyond ourselves. Whiteread's work makes space both material and inaccessible at the same time. As one writer said, "Rachel Whiteread reveals...what the eye cannot see but the mind knows."

Equally seductive are her materials: first concrete and later resin, a kind of gelatinous rendering both material and ethereal. A Jell-O mold of life! But no matter its material, her art reminds us that the universe is almost entirely space; atoms may maintain an illusory rigidity from our perspective, but Big Bang tells us the entire universe, everything that exists or has ever existed everywhere, was (before the BB) somewhere between the size of a soccer ball and a soccer stadium! The rest is emptiness, void, space.

It may be aggrandizing to ascribe that level of insight, or import, to Whiteread's work (or to the architect's view of space), but that is what art is. Art describes while it explains, provokes and questions while it suggests connections, and fucks with the most elemental aspects of the imaginable universe. Pretty heady stuff for a concrete ghost house.

21 April
Eve Arnold

Malcolm X during visit to Muslim-owned enterprises, Harlem, New York, 1962

Eve Arnold studied photography at the New School with Alexi Brodovitch and in 1951 became the first woman to join Magnum Photos.

In the 1990s, I designed the Magnum offices; I forget the details, but I will never forget my visit to their old offices. It was pretty basic: some desks and lots and lots of metal shelving and filing cabinets filled with boxes, binders, and books. It could have been a movie set for a disheveled genius's filing system (much less organized than the archives of, say, Stanley Kubrick or Andy Warhol, who mastered the box method).

There was an end cap (retail speak for the shelves at the end of aisles) with old, black-textured binders, each labeled, with one of those slip-in labels in a small metal frame, the typed name "Cartier-Bresson." It was kind of mind-blowing to think that this 4-by-8-foot/1.2-by-2.4-meter shelving contained all or part of the Henri Cartier-Bresson opus (I assumed there was more). I pulled one at random and flipped through the contact sheets. The best frames were marked by Cartier-Bresson himself, but even more interesting were the outtakes, the shots he never wanted anyone to see (or wanted everyone to see, but not while he was alive, which he was when I perused the binder).

Eve Arnold was there somewhere, but I didn't know enough about her to seek her out. It's a shame, because her images have a kind of rare intimacy, and contact prints are about as intimate a view of a photographer's eye and brain as any catalogue raisonné. If the one contact sheet I've seen is representative, she took very few images (often three) of any composition before moving on. She knew when the moment had passed, which is why she most often shot in natural light with a handheld camera.

Some images are posed, but one of Malcolm X in 1962 Chicago is so dense with information as to make posed portraits seem irrelevant. The crescent and star ring, the watch, the hat rakishly tipped forward, his iconic glasses, all giving a sense of the man that few posed shots could.

That was Eve Arnold's genius: finding the moment that defined the subject in a single image. "It is the photographer, not the camera, that is the instrument," she explained, as though that was enough to make any of us her equal.

22 April
Craig Ellwood

Bridge Building, ArtCenter College of Design, Pasadena, California, 1976

If Craig Ellwood's work weren't so good, our fascination with him might begin and end with his almost cinematic identity issues. There's more than a bit of Don Draper in Ellwood. Architects change their names (Le Corbusier, Mies van der Rohe, Frank Gehry, Louis I. Kahn) almost as a rite of passage, but I'm pretty sure none other than Ellwood took the name of a liquor store across the street from their office!

He and partners created a business with the name Craig Ellwood (after the Llord's & Elwood liquor store), and Jon Nelson Burke eventually adopted the name to give a face to the studio (and, of course, to reinvent himself). His marketing savvy remained a part of his career until the end; every single photograph published (and there were lots) was controlled by Ellwood.

He wasn't trained as an architect but learned the trade working as a construction estimator on postwar housing; eventually he designed homes for clients rather than build the predrawn plans. He had a brief style flirtation with Frank Lloyd Wright and Richard Neutra before he discovered Mies van der Rohe and adapted his work to the West Coast.

Ellwood was who Mies might have been if he had landed in Los Angeles rather than Chicago and smoked weed rather than cigars (and wasn't German, or imperious or, well, Mies). Ellwood's louche life of Ferraris and tennis at 3:00 (after a long client lunch) drove his office mad.

Despite his shape-shifting, Ellwood became quite dogmatic about his work. The Mies part of his psyche was completely and unmovably committed to structure as the generator of all architectural form. "Structure is the only clear principle," Ellwood declared in 1966. That faith, and the Los Angeles light and culture that Mies lacked, drove his work at the domestic scale.

His first Case Study House in 1953 featured translucent glass fences to curtain (wall) the house from the road. The fences permitted slim details freed of the requirements for actual building envelopes. The period from that house until his final great work, the 1976 ArtCenter bridge building in Pasadena, was his second of three acts, filled with an endless series of great work.

After being tossed from his office, Ellwood spent his last act in Italy, painting and restoring a villa, dying there in 1992.

23 April
Lee Miller

Self-Portrait, 1932

It's no wonder that the movie *Lee* is being made about Lee Miller; she lived a life that was so extraordinary, so layered, and so broad that it could fill several movies.

After being booted from every school in the Poughkeepsie area, she moved to Paris to learn stage lighting. She returned to attend the Art Students League of New York (like everyone else). Nearly stepping in front of a streetcar, she was saved by Condé Nast (not by a magazine, but by Mr. Condé Nast himself!), who naturally turned her into a model for *Vogue.* She was absolutely beautiful, photographed by all the best, and her interest in photography started to grow.

She left New York and returned to Paris to be Man Ray's assistant; she became his mistress and, later, his friend. She discovered the solarization technique Ray used when she accidentally turned the lights on while in the darkroom. She started her own studio and, with Ray's help, photographed everyone, met everyone, and befriended everyone. Pablo Picasso was deeply affected by her; he painted six portraits of her, while she took more than a thousand photos of him.

Returning to New York, she began her US career working for *Vogue* and became their credentialed war correspondent, probably the only woman photographer in the field. From (and for) the world of fashion, she became the most remarkable war photographer, documenting Buchenwald and Dachau, bathing in Adolf Hitler's tub (long story, but, obviously, as Germany was being defeated), shooting Henry Moore in the London Underground as he sketched those gathered there, and recording the death and destruction that surrounded her and everyone else. The war traumatized her, and she suffered from PTSD before there was a name for it.

At this point we are about 20 percent through her story.

Skipping ahead to her marriage to a surrealist painter, collector, and author of books on Picasso, Miró, etc., she continued to photograph everything and everyone but locked her wartime work away (along with the PTSD) in the attic at her farm. About sixty thousand photos of the war were found there by her flabbergasted son, who has managed to revive her story and reputation.

Just wait for the Kate Winslet version. It'll be mind-blowing.

24 April
Bridget Riley

Study for *Blaze*, 1962

When I was twelve, there was a show at MoMA, *The Responsive Eye*, with a catalog I pored through constantly, not realizing that Bridget Riley was the cover artist (her art was under a title, used as a background, but still...). She was just thirty-four and photogenic; her paintings were perfect backgrounds for a series of (black-and-white) portraits in front of or surrounded by her art. The whole point of her art was to be engaged, surrounded, or absorbed, or simply to stand in the illusory space created by it.

When MoMA tagged her work, along with that of dozens of others, as op art, the name too neatly packaged a set of seemingly similar but quite different art. The MoMA catalog used only last names when identifying the artists, maybe responding to Riley's idea that art was genderless or at least unaffected by gender. Or maybe it was an attempt to hide, during the beginning of the women's movement, the lack of women artists in the show (pretty sure you could count them on one hand in a show with ninety-nine artists). Op art was treated like a gimmick or a cross of science and art, but this trivializes the art and Bridget Riley, who attempts to create an almost vertiginous spatial relationship between art and viewer.

She studied Georges Seurat and even repainted *The Bridge at Courbevoie* in 1959 to try to understand how it worked. The exercise was transformational for her. In his twenties, Hunter S. Thompson typed, word for word, *The Great Gatsby* and *A Farewell to Arms* just to see how it felt to write a masterpiece. Copying paintings is a familiar homage (or heuristic device) for visual artists, but retyping a novel seems daft; I am not sure why.

Riley was the first woman and first Brit to win the international prize for painting at the 1968 Venice Biennale with *Cataract 3*, where she employed color in work similar to that which had previously been colorless. It was, she said, the instability of color that was her insight into exploring it in the context of her monochromatic work.

She moved to painting multicolor stripes in the 1980s (from no color to all colors in about twenty years) and used color rather than shape to create space. Still painting, still inventing, even into her nineties.

25 April
Herbert Matter

America Calling, civil defense poster, 1941

Herbert Matter is a magician. To satisfy the needs of industry, that's what you have to be. Industry is a tough taskmaster. Art is tougher. Industry plus Art, almost impossible....His work of '32 could have been done in '72, or even in '82. It has that timeless, unerring quality one recognizes instinctively. – Paul Rand

Who am I to argue with Paul Rand?

The whole idea of timelessness is fraught. I doubt that Matter's goal was to create timeless images (and how would he do that if he wanted to?) but rather to create new, modern, beautiful images to satisfy himself. When they last, it's as much luck as intention.

Cultural tastes change, our own tastes change, and when the two overlap it's more kismet than endurance. I've often wondered what it is that makes things last: simplicity versus complexity, fame versus invisibility, golden section versus square, fashion versus design? It's always seemed impossible to me to plan for timelessness.

That Matter seems to be perpetually current is in part about us; we see his art, and it changes us. It changes the way we see going forward, and that includes seeing his art as seminal, classic, and timeless.

He, as much as anyone, is responsible for the merger of photography and graphic design. It seems obvious now, but there was once plenty of illustration and typography, but rarely modern graphic design and photography together. Matter was messing with a new kind of visual space, and it stuck, or proliferated as art moved forward.

This was probably in large part due to whom he worked with and for: Amédée Ozenfant, Le Corbusier, Cassandre, Alexey Brodovitch, and Charles and Ray Eames, as well as his friends: Alexander Calder, Jackson Pollock, Willem de Kooning, Robert Frank, Alberto Giacometti, Paul Rand, and John Cage.

But his success wasn't about self-promotion or aggressive marketing skills. As Rand said, "The absence of pomposity was characteristic of this guy."

And how many timeless geniuses can you say that about?

26 April
Peter Zumthor

Saint Benedict Chapel, Sumvitg, Switzerland, 1988

Peter Zumthor doesn't have a website, but somehow that has worked for, rather than against, him. He prefers in-person to telephone interviews, but, again, that works for him; better to summon journalists to his world rather than try to conjure it with only audio.

Twenty years ago, I had an idea to ask Vincent Scully (the architecture historian, not the baseball sportscaster) to join a post-9/11 project, and I called him, leaving a message on his answering machine. I know it was an answering machine because when I had to write or call again to reach him, he apologized; without a touch tone phone he couldn't navigate my voice mail menu. Scully had only a rotary landline. And as my friend Aki said when she heard that, "I don't want to have any phone that can't receive a call from Vincent Scully."

That's pretty much how Zumthor works, and his occasionally monastic buildings support that image. The Therme Vals, public pool/baths in the Swiss Alps, are really a *Divine Comedy* of water. The inferno is the sauna, a path to hotter and hotter (and redder and redder) chambers, separated by heavy black leather curtains. A therapeutic shower area has industrial-strength streams of water in differing temps, pressures, and forms. The pools (Paradiso?) are separated by temperature and eventually lead to an outside pool (entered from inside) where one can swim in a snowstorm. It's all built of stacked local quartzite and dotted with skylights, an orderly cave of almost Roman proportions.

Zumthor's work forces you to re-see what you thought you knew in entirely unknown ways, making the experience as much transformational as admiring. What I always admire, and am a bit jealous of, is his way of managing his life/work: a small office and home in a gorgeous landscape, with a smallish staff and only a few (carefully selected) projects at any time. It's ideal, seductive, and elusive.

And not terribly easy to get to from anywhere. Like Vincent Scully, it takes a bit of effort to reach him, and like Scully, he is worth every moment.

27 April
Norman Bel Geddes

Norman Bel Geddes, 1925

Norman Bel Geddes (who combined his name, Geddes, with his wife's middle name, Belle) designed, in the streamline style of his day, lots of things: cocktail shakers, cars, airports, airplanes, cities, stage sets, movie sets, radios, and ocean liners. These all used one of his talents at a time, but his greatest multitalent achievement was at the 1939 New York World's Fair (The World of Tomorrow), where the most-loved pavilion was his General Motors Futurama.

This was GM, after all, on its way to being the largest corporation in the world, and its vision of the future was heavily auto-centric. Bel Geddes subscribed to GM's vision and used his theatrical background to create a powerful narrative to methodically unveil the future. Robert Moses organized the fair, and it undoubtedly fed his own automania (though Moses never learned to drive).

The future, according to Bel Geddes, was streamlined, curvy, and undecorated. Futurama was built around the big reveal climax: a full-size urban intersection replete with cars, car showrooms, stores, people (the visitors), and the futuristic fair beyond, seen at the end of a ride that was like flying above the world of the future (defined as 1960!).

The ride started, after a long wait on the sizzling asphalt, with a curving ramp to the interior, where visitors got into moving pods (a first) and clacked along a track to a position high above a one-acre (!) animated model of the future landscape of America. Planes flew above five hundred thousand individual building models (and one million model trees), where ten thousand cars (out of fifty thousand in the model) moved as the pods surveyed the remarkable model, with narration piped in.

The future included huge multilane highways (nonexistent at that point) with cloverleaf exchanges, self-driving cars, circular airports (Bel Geddes designed a floating one for New York City), and other unimaginable trappings.

As the pod clacked past the countryside toward the city, the scale incrementally grew until visitors exited into the full-scale, open-air intersection on elevated sidewalks a level above the roadway below, filled with the newest GM cars.

What is so refreshing (if we ignore the damage the auto has done) is Bel Geddes's optimism; Futurama is no Fritz Lang dark dystopia, but a bright and shining future in service of humankind. If only...

28 April
Bertram Goodhue

Nebraska State Capitol, Lincoln, Nebraska, 1922–1932

These dates must be wrong, but here they are: Bertram Grosvenor Goodhue was fifteen years old when he moved to Manhattan from Connecticut to apprentice at James Renwick Jr.'s (of St. Patrick's Cathedral fame) architectural firm. Wasn't that illegal? And he was all of twenty-two when he won a competition to design a church in Dallas.

That's when he formed the firm Cram, Wentworth and Goodhue, later Cram, Goodhue and Ferguson (at a mature twenty-nine years old!) with Ralph Adams Cram (great name, great architect; I think he starred in *The Honeymooners*...not 100 percent sure).

At twenty-seven, Goodhue created the typeface Cheltenham, later used as the headline typeface for the *New York Times*. I could go on, but, really, must I?

He died at fifty-four (I mean, he had done it all by then) with more than fifty important projects completed. No kitchen renovations, houses for his parents, or lost competition entries (though he didn't win the Chicago Tribune Tower Competition; his former employee Raymond M. Hood did). Just tons of churches and other serious stuff.

The old saw is that architects don't really start their careers until they turn fifty, but that is frankly bullshit, likely promoted by those slackers who didn't achieve what Goodhue did!

By fifty he was basically done.

I remember Michael Bierut working on Celebration, Florida, and convincing Robert A. M. Stern that Cheltenham was the right typeface for the town. "It was designed by Bertram Goodhue," was all he had to say. That proved a bit easier than approval for the silhouette of the golfer midswing on the course signage... too bad Goodhue wasn't a golfer.

Goodhue designed projects that were really good, some even exceptional. For example, St. Thomas Church on Fifth Avenue is a clever sleight of hand. It's a party-wall church, not wide enough for full aisles and chapels on both sides of the nave, but some shifting symmetries manage a very wide nave and one set of side chapels, while the lack of the opposing chapel is barely noticed. And it's all built in stone, as Gothic cathedrals were supposed to be built.

Bertram Grosvenor Goodhue was a prodigy who died suddenly, leaving us a huge pile of good work to think about. Perfect.

29 April
Jacob Jensen

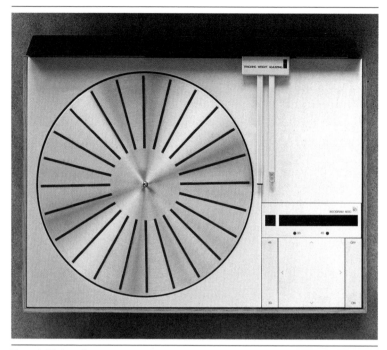

Bang & Olufsen Beogram 4000 turntable, 1973

MoMA has held only a few exhibits for a corporation's design: Olivetti in 1952, Thonet in 1953, Braun/Chemex in 1964, and Bang & Olufsen/Jacob Jensen in 1978. That should establish Jensen's bona fides, but being Danish (modest, a bit out of the mainstream), he is the least known of giants like Dieter Rams who hail from larger economies.

Jensen designed nearly all of B&O's products from 1964 to 1989, when it was established as a high design company. Like Rams for Braun, or Ken Grange for Kenwood, or Jony Ive for Apple, Jensen for B&O was a huge plus. The constancy of a single (good) designer gives an innovative firm a visual identity and language to match its brand identity. Jensen said:

> Constructing a fountain pen, writing a poem, producing a play or designing a locomotive, all demand the same components, the same ingredients: perspective, creativity, new ideas, understanding and first and foremost, the ability to rework, almost infinitely, over and over. That "over and over" is for me the cruelest torture.

And while I am not sure I agree with the idea of iterative design as torture, I do agree that all "making" is related and relatable. Making is the center of my life, and I am not sure what I would do without it.

Jensen did more than design for B&O; he designed the original melamine bowls for Rösti (those multicolored nesting bowls with handle and lip and rubber bottom ring) that I use every day. And the watches he designed compete in the class of designer watches architects wear, starting with the Mondaine (Swiss Railway clock watch), some M&Co editions, the Max Bill Junghans watches, the Braun watches, and the Jacob Jensen watches. (And yes, I have at least one of each. Hello, my name is Jim, and I am a watchaholic.) The Jensen is the one I still wear these days.

The Danish TV series *Borgen* is about a female prime minister who still rides her bike to Parliament, lives (mostly) at home, and cooks meals for her kids while being an exceedingly clever and effective politician. On set, Artichoke lights, Arne Jacobsen clocks, Stelton servers, and other mod items abound. But it is the sensibility of Denmark that seems most in line with Jacob Jensen's design work. Clear, simple, honest, and beautiful.

30 April
Antonio Sant'Elia

"La Citta Nuova," from *L'architettura futuristica*, 1914

Antonio Sant'Elia sets the died-too-young bar at a ridiculously low level: twenty-eight years. There's a photo of him posing with fellow futurists Filippo Tommaso Marinetti and Umberto Boccioni, who were soldiers together in World War I, fighting to "cleanse the world through warfare." This is how Futurists would describe the undoing of the world order. "A racing car is more beautiful than the *Winged Victory of Samothrace*" was another tossed-off idea that seems commercial today but in 1914 seemed simply insane, or at the very least irritating.

Sadly, World War I cleansed the world of Sant'Elia, and we are left with only the drawings of his version of the future. Modern renderings, computer models, and three-dimensional models attempt to "help" us understand his vision, but these "more accurate" third-party renderings just suck the life out of his remarkable hand-drafted drawings. All the comparisons to Ridley Scott's *Blade Runner* or Fritz Lang's *Metropolis* are an attempt to enlist Sant'Elia's ideas in the cause of dystopia, when they are actually quite optimistic, if a bit overstated! Hugh Ferriss might be more responsible than Sant'Elia for Anton Furst's dark version of Batman's Gotham.

Sant'Elia celebrated technology, which in 1912–1914 was the elevator, the car, the plane, and the bridge, a pretty primitive and paltry palette for a machine-age obsessive. Still, his fascination with machines is beautifully played out in heroic idealism. His work is part of a very young modernism; early works like Walter Gropius's Fagus Factory and Peter Behrens's AEG Turbine Factory and Otto Wagner's Post Office Savings Bank had just been built. Sant'Elia's ideas are even more monumental and heroic than those early industrial attempts. Henri Sauvage was building apartments in Paris with similar forms, but otherwise Sant'Elia was on his own.

The power of Antonio Sant'Elia's imagery is the power of his drawing. He built almost nothing (and certainly nothing with the power of his futurist ruminations), but he left a permanent impression. The drawings, not the buildings, are the artwork. Degraded into CAD models or photo-quality renderings, they just look like bad ideas. It's his hand, like Ferriss's, that makes the images sing.

Libertad de Palabra, 1942

There's that great line in some Steve Martin movie where he, playing a downtrodden advertising executive or something, competing for partnership, is told by his boss: "Dazzle me." Alexey Brodovitch was famous for saying to his students, "Astonish me," but they didn't seem as undone by that as Steve Martin was; they just rose to his challenge.

Brodovitch's students at the Pennsylvania Museum and School of Industrial Art (as the University of the Arts was then called, and I wish they had kept the name) and the colleagues he attracted to *Harper's Bazaar* included so many important photographers (Diane Arbus, Eve Arnold, Richard Avedon, Lillian Bassman, Robert Frank, Hiro, Lisette Model, Joel Meyerowitz, Hans Namuth, Garry Winogrand, Irving Penn) and artists (Jean Cocteau, Raoul Dufy, Art Kane, Marc Chagall, Man Ray, and Cassandre) that he must have done something right.

Brodovitch is credited with inventing modern magazine design. White space, text and image, cropped photos, editorial flow, plus the technique of laying out magazines with all the pages on the floor to allow the right pacing and sequencing was all Brodovitch. It changed the entire idea of a magazine.

He started figuring out what he wanted to do with his life while in Paris, where he won a competition for a poster for an artist's soiree, Le Bal Banal (Picasso took second prize). The famous photo of all the posters on the wall high above a single seated figure is like a poster in itself (and the seated figure really does look like Woody Allen doing Zelig), making a sweet little meta moment in 1924.

Brodovitch had a big moment at the 1925 International Exhibition of Modern Decorative and Industrial Arts (whence art deco was named) with five medals for various work (jewelry, kiosk, fabrics). This was the moment modernity became manifest, quite literally, as the brief for the fair was modernity; no historical styles would be permitted. Nearly all countries exhibited, but the US declined to participate; Secretary of Commerce Herbert Hoover explained that there was no modern art in the United States, so why participate?

Alexey Brodovitch would help fix that with nearly twenty-five years at *Harper's Bazaar* and hundreds of acolytes, all attempting to dazzle him.

02 May
Edmund Bacon

Edmund Bacon with model of Society Hill Towers, Philadelphia, Pennsylvania, 1960s

When I was in college, Edmund N. Bacon's *Design of Cities* was the best, maybe only, reference book on urban design (not really the same as urban planning). Bacon couldn't escape the 1967 era of its publication; his view of the future was bound by that moment of megastructures and insensitivity to context. But his analysis of the historical precedents is simply thrilling and far ahead of what was seen then as the roots of urban design.

This book was released a few years after Jane Jacobs published *The Death and Life of Great American Cities* and almost a decade after her epic battle with Robert Moses; the drift away from grand projects that destroyed cities was underway. The last hurrah of urban renewal, as it was called, was ending, but there was nothing to replace it, and Bacon attempted to inject some sophisticated spatial notions into the discussion.

The book is (unfortunately) addicted to big ideas and big redevelopment projects, but at least it connects those interventions with a historical background, which was anything but obvious at the time. Stylistically, the book is also very much of its time, filled with Paul Klee drawings as analogs to the points Bacon is making. And

because he headed the Philadelphia City Planning Commission then, Louis Kahn (and why not?) pervades as well. But when it came to drawing historical cities, explaining how urban space worked, analyzing the success of particular urban icons, and looking at cities as chess games (with each move leading to or blocking avenues of development), Bacon was unequaled.

He received an architecture degree from Cornell University in 1932 and returned to lecture more than forty years later, while I was studying there. He seemed ancient even then, but he kept at it for another thirty years.

What I never realized until just this year is that Edmund N. Bacon is Kevin Bacon's father! Six degrees of separation Kevin Bacon. Kev was opining in some doc about an urban something or other, and I couldn't figure out what the fuck he was doing there until I looked it up. I'm counting that as one degree of separation, though some may disagree.

03 May
Aldo Rossi

Ossuary at San Cataldo Cemetery, Modena, Italy, 1971

It seems unfair, and somewhat trivializing, to categorize Aldo Rossi as postmodern when he was really more like a straight up de Chirico. He might have been the second wave of Italian Rationalism, the School of Kahn, or lots of other things, but postmodern? That seems a bit lazy.

Rossi started as a writer in the 1950s, as an editor and journalist for *Casabella* and other architectural magazines. That he graduated from writing to building is the inverse of others (like me) who started making and came late to writing as a way of addressing issues that built work often cannot. Rossi came to built work as an expression of the ideas he developed in words.

I first saw his work at the Gallaratese Housing campus in Milan soon after it was built, and it can hardly be classified as anything but brilliant modernism in search of an ordering system. The ossuary at San Cataldo Cemetery is the most relentlessly modern building ever; a perfect cube of perfectly square punctures that conceal stairs wrapping a grid of recesses (for urns). The Teatro del Mundo is a stage set containing a stage set, explicitly temporary and styled to look back to the nineteenth-century floating theaters in Venice; it is not a piece of retrograde architecture, or pastiche, but a theater as theater.

Ada Louise Huxtable called Rossi "a poet who happens to be an architect," which, for some lesser architect, might be a pan. For Rossi it gets to the essence of how he made buildings: as built ideas, not stylistic machinations. What other (supposed) postmodernists lay claim to "defender of the city"? (Answer: none.)

In Celebration, Florida, we built a stage set called the Temporary Preview Center out of trailers and flat, rendered facades. It was (and still is, in some form) a pointed commentary on Disney's reluctance to let visitors see behind the curtain. It sat opposite Aldo Rossi's administrative building, a flimsy foil to his stolid block. The town was filled with (and an homage to) postmodern follies by every serious claimant that Robert A. M. Stern could enlist. Rossi's building was too serious to be included downtown, but it was a perfect counterpoint to our own wry joke.

04 May
Bruno Taut

Hufeisensiedlung (Horseshoe Housing), 1933

Bruno Taut is most famous for one tiny glass pavilion designed to promote glass as a building material for the 1914 Deutscher Werkbund Exhibition, but he really built quite a bit more. The glass pavilion was brightly colored, but, of course, only black-and-white photos of it remain. His idea was to make the pavilion entirely of glass, something Steve Jobs accomplished on Fifth Avenue in New York a hundred years later. In 1913 Taut designed another pavilion called the Monument to Iron, which pretty much cemented his cred in the steel and glass modern architecture polemic.

His other work is much less ponderous or metaphysical; housing that looked a bit more like *Accidentally Wes Anderson* than the white versions his contemporaries were designing at the time. At the Weissenhofsiedlung, the 1927 housing exposition in Stuttgart (mostly still standing but without Taut's house), he insisted on painting his in primary colors (red, blue, and yellow) possibly just to piss off the younger architects. Le Corbusier, the doyen of white (though there were lots of colors added to his white houses…inside), said, "My god, Taut is colorblind!" Kind of rich coming from an architect who was legally blind in one eye. ("My god, Corb has no depth perception!") Taut may have been the slightly older,

slightly more contrarian, slightly off-brand, and maybe slightly embarrassing participant in this group exhibition, like someone wearing festive garb at a funeral.

Bruno's other housing projects weren't shy about color either, especially on the doors, where I guess ornament wasn't a crime. One project was even called the Paintbox Houses. Theo Crosby may have picked up the Taut mantle when he started veering from modern to, well, colorful not-so-modern work.

Taut was slightly more Jewish than many of his German colleagues, so he fled to Japan and then Turkey in the early 1930s; he died in Turkey in 1938 and was interred in the Edirnekapı Martyr's Cemetery in Istanbul, the first and only non-Muslim buried there. So, I suppose he was slightly off-brand there too.

05 May
Leo Lionni

Model of Unfinished Business Pavilion, Expo Brussels, 1958

Leo Lionni had me at his tiny Unfinished Business Pavilion, a remarkably prescient little sideshow to the main USA Pavilion at the 1958 Brussels Expo. The main American pavilion was an Edward Durrell Stone pile: a massive cylinder with the filigree he was becoming (in)famous for. Despite its enormous size, it just didn't seem to have space for a self-critical look at race relations in the US in the 1950s.

Lionni, working for *Fortune* magazine, which sponsored a side garden, designed a pavilion-ette that addressed race in a photographic essay within a trio of tiny enclosures, all on stilts. The content was forward thinking, and the pavilion looks modern even today.

The forms evolve from crumpled or wrinkled or folded to smooth and unwrinkled (flat) in three steps (illustrating the problem, the efforts toward solutions, and a hopeful future), gesturing to the unfinished but aspirational aspect of race relations in America. This modest little metaphor was exceedingly more eloquent and more humane than Stone's behemoth US flying saucer.

But then it was noticed by US politicians and undone. Georgia Senator Herman Talmadge demanded it be closed for its judgmental view of the South's racist policies, which he claimed were a "matter of choice"! Sound familiar?

It was, as it is today, impossible for some to accept the deep-seated problem we now call structural racism, preferring to whitewash the issue (literally in this case) and present a whiter perspective. Lionni had made the mistake of actually fulfilling the brief: an introspective look at race in America.

Lionni started as a Futurist painter in Italy; went on to be the design director for Olivetti; designed the catalog for the MoMA exhibition *The Family of Man*; created more than forty utterly charming children's books; designed *Fortune* magazine for more than a decade; taught at Black Mountain College, Cooper Union, and Parsons School of Design; and still had time to sculpt, paint, draw, and photograph the world.

Unfinished business then is still unfinished business now, and the ability of strong democracies to be self-critical is still in debate. Lionni dared to make that debate public.

06 May
Carlo Mollino

Self-portrait of Carlo Mollino, pictured over New York, circa early 1930s

Carlo Mollino was able to execute two drawings simultaneously, with two hands, a lovely metaphor for his internal and external identities, or the hidden and the public aspects of his life.

He designed the curviest everything: cars, chairs, tables, lamps, buildings, and every other domestic appurtenance. But he died leaving a trove of erotic Polaroids of sex workers, dressed by Mollino and staged in a hidden apartment he used as a studio for this private work. The pure sexiness of his public designs is often linked to and explained by this private kink. That explanation seems a bit too easy.

These photos have overshadowed his immensely valuable work, becoming the public face of a private obsession. They are, by today's standards, quite tame, even tender, but not so tame that Instagram wouldn't likely censor them.

It's the hidden part of the equation that interests me. He apparently worked by night and slept by day, so the dark was his light. And even though he grew up using a darkroom and was an accomplished photographer, these photos are all instant ones, another contradiction of a man who could draw with both hands.

But put those photos aside, as they were for the time he was alive, and his work is remarkable on its own. He treats structure like anatomy and surface like water, or skin, or plump softness. It's his language of form that has made him famous, with one table selling at auction for more than six million dollars. That table has bent and fabulously shaped plywood legs and a set of wooden ribs that support the glass top (because who would hide the real soul of this table below an opaque top?).

Mollino was a speed junkie, racing cars, flying aircraft, skiing, and generally living an outré life. At the same time, he lived and died in his engineer father's house (never even changing the nameplate to his own name), a retreat into the past (almost into the womb) as a counterpoint to his careless behavior.

It's drawing with both hands at the same time.

As he said, "Everything is permissible as long as it is fantastic."

132

07 May
Edwin Land

Polaroid SX-70 camera, released 1972

Edwin H. Land didn't make art, but he did make a new kind of art possible. And he altered the concepts of time, immediacy, and instant gratification and became indispensable to photography and photographic art. Land invented the Polaroid instant camera in 1947, creating an entirely new idea of what a photograph was.

Perhaps apocryphally, he invented the instant photo when his daughter asked why she couldn't see a photo he took of her right away. He was the kind of genius who worked things out in his head quickly, often forgoing writing solutions down (much to the chagrin of his colleagues and family), though he apparently left enough notes and personal documents that it took his family three years to shred them all (though why they did that, even at his request, and why they declined to specify his cause of death remain mysteries).

Land named his company Polaroid because it started with his invention that made polarizing lenses and films inexpensive. He created a great company that failed, like Kodak (who invented the first digital camera in the 1970s), to see the next future. These giants of industry are now marginal players in a world swamped in images

and powered in part by social media, also dominated by images.

Land created the famous giant-scale Polaroid camera with 20-by-24-inch/51-by-61-centimeter images and made it available to artists for free (copies of the images being the only payment required). Polaroid had, as a result, some twenty-five thousand artist images by photographers like Ansel Adams, Robert Frank, Andy Warhol, Chuck Close, and David Hockney. Sadly, the collection was broken up and sold when Polaroid filed for bankruptcy.

The 1972 Polaroid SX-70 is still the most beautiful camera ever designed, an SLR that folds flat, ejects photos to develop in daylight, and can rapidly shoot in sequence. It's deservedly a cult object. Its images could be manipulated by pressing on their transparent top layer, becoming a medium for even more art.

Edwin Land was an American original, inventing complex solutions that were simple to use, answering the call for things no one knew they needed until he invented them. Maybe that's why Steve Jobs made the pilgrimage to visit Land, twice.

08 May
Saul Bass

Saul Bass signature and logo

There was a time when record albums were packaged in banal book-like binders (hence album), and a time when movie titles, literally the titles, were projected on the curtains in movie theaters before they parted to reveal the screen for the actual movie, and a time when book covers (before there were dust jackets) were just there to spell out the name of the book and author. There was even an expression, "You can't tell a book by its cover," which might have once been true!

Now book covers are a celebrated art form, the elevator pitch for the book, and the first thing you might know about what's inside. And record album covers, even though music is nonmaterial these days, became the artwork we stared at while playing the entire album (over and over and over), making them, perhaps, the artwork with the greatest accumulated eyeball time. And after Saul Bass, movie titles became the mood-setting infotainment we now are coaxed into enjoying (or trained to keep watching, past the action, to wait for a surprise reveal).

In a time when everything is animated, every logo has a motion version, every website has too many bouncy screen transitions, and you can't read the paper (online) without distracting GIFs trying to lure you off topic, the idea that moving, meaningful, artful mini-movies before or after a film was once a new idea seems hard to believe. But, yes, that whole industry was invented, and one of the best early practitioners was Saul Bass.

If he had only done the after-credits for *West Side Story*, that would have been enough for me. But he worked for Alfred Hitchcock (*Psycho*, *Vertigo*, *North by Northwest*), Stanley Kubrick (*Spartacus*, *The Shining*), Otto Preminger (*Anatomy of a Murder*, *Man with the Golden Arm*), Martin Scorsese (*Cape Fear*, *Casino*, *Goodfellas*, *The Age of Innocence*), and *Big* and *Broadcast News* and *Oceans 11* and *The Seven Year Itch*, and I could go on, but you get the idea.

I'm not sure if today's insistence on the overdesign of every event, object, room, building, media, and logo (Saul used a bass, the fish, in his signature) is a good thing, but I am sure that having Saul Bass design film credits has made watching movies just a little bit more fun.

09 May
Gordon Bunshaft

Lever House, Park Avenue, New York, New York, 1952

Gordon Bunshaft joined SOM (Skidmore, Owings & Merrill) even before Merrill did, so technically he joined SO (it might have been called SOB, so I guess we're lucky). From the time he was a partner, he designed perhaps every building of note that SOM did, and he never let them forget it. He also designed a few of the less-than-wonderful buildings they built, but who doesn't have a bad moment now and then?

Bunshaft was notoriously difficult to work with; nevertheless, he managed to produce some truly stunning work. These things don't seem to easily go together, but when they do, the myth of the auteur architect (Howard Roark manqué) is unfortunately reinforced. I was walking by the Manufacturers Hanover Trust Building at Forty-Third and Fifth late one night and saw mini bulldozers demolishing the interior. I took a pic that (in others' hands) eventually enraged enough people to stop the demo and demand the reinstallation of the bronze Harry Bertoia screen upstairs. Sadly, the space was still transformed into a North Face or Joe Fresh or some other retail irrelevance instead of the very image of modern, transparent banking.

Bunshaft's own house in the Hamptons met an even worse fate; he willed it to

MoMA, who sold it to Martha Stewart, who sold it to Donald Maharam, who declared it decrepit and demolished it. But much, or most, of what he designed still stands and marks a time in architectural history of incredibly optimistic, modern-forward, clear ideas.

Lever House (which Bunshaft admitted was turned perpendicular to Park Avenue by Nat Owings) has been in conversation with Mies van der Rohe's Seagram Building (which followed it by six years, and that must have made Mies seriously cranky) for more than sixty years. It is much less the classical temple that Seagram is, but much more the American fun house.

Beinecke Library at Yale is a bit of real genius, using thin slabs of marble to admit low levels of book-preserving beautiful light into the rare-book fortress. The Hirshhorn Museum, built ten years after the Guggenheim, is Bunshaft's attempt to rationalize the circular museum. The Albright-Knox Art Gallery does that design trope of "old and new as equals" that architects love, sometimes out of insecurity.

With a back catalog like that, being difficult might just be acceptable.

10 May
Henri Sauvage

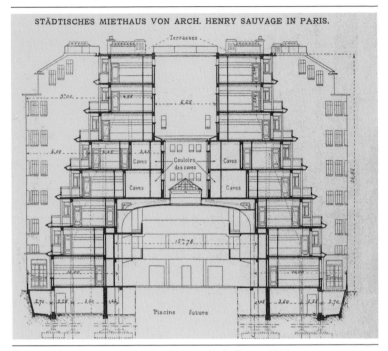

STÄDTISCHES MIETHAUS VON ARCH. HENRY SAUVAGE IN PARIS.

Cross section, Apartments Rue des Amiraux, Paris, France, 1925

In the 1920s in Paris, Henri Sauvage created a series of white subway-tiled apartment buildings with long, stepped terraces that remain unique in that city and anywhere. They were vaguely art deco, and Sauvage aimed at low-cost, hygienic housing that looked, and still looks, like the cleanest, airiest, and sunniest apartments possible. In figuring out what to do with the space captured below the terraced units, he inserted a swimming pool, in keeping with the theme of healthy housing.

Getting there, he designed art nouveau wallpaper, cafés, jewelry, furniture, and houses in full-on Hector Guimard style. He hung with Hector; Henri's father's wallpaper company made wallpaper (that Sauvage designed) for Guimard. After becoming facile in art nouveau, he realized it was coming to an end and adopted art deco early on and became interested in low-cost housing.

In 1911 he built apartments, called Cité de l'Argentine, above a new *passage*, the glazed commercial arcades that fill Paris. These were the object of Walter Benjamin's *Arcades Project*, a massive, unfinished study of the arcade as an active sponsor of Paris's public culture. In the nineteenth century, there were 150 of these arcades, a kind of street-simulacrum that both presages the mall

and explains the mall's eventual demise. Now there are around thirty.

I spent one trip to Paris visiting as many as I could find, and they are a remarkable portrait of an urban form well worth reviving. They range from high elegance to the dusty and unused. Sauvage built a new arcade in the twentieth century, a preview of the skylit caverns he created in his later work. After the passage apartments, but before his research into low-cost housing (Habitations à Bon Marché), was the Spanish flu pandemic, which helps to explain the hygienic slant to his housing proposals. It's amazing how we now understand 1918 as a health (and design) watershed, something I never really considered before our own pandemic.

The tiled buildings are the apex of Henri Sauvage's short career (these guys always seem to die young), but he also built La Samaritaine, the Paris department store, just before he died and was eulogized by his hero, Guimard.

11 May
Henri Labrouste

Bibliothèque Sainte-Geneviève (Sainte-Geneviève Library), Paris, France, 1851

When MoMA has a show about, say, Beaux-Arts architectural drawings or the work of Henri Labrouste, some of the architectural firmament loses its shit and declares the end of modernism or the end of MoMA or the end of architecture. Seems like such a doctrinaire view of "modern."

Some significant fraction of the painting at MoMA is a century or more old, yet no one suggests MoMA divest itself of Picasso's self-portrait at age twenty as no longer modern. The whole point of MoMA (and museums in general) is to accumulate the growing historical context for any set of ideas or objects or people or movements. While a single (dead) artist may have enough art to fill a single museum (as with the Zentrum Paul Klee), the norm is otherwise. Large museums are department stores, not brand boutiques.

Labrouste is a victim of the same hair-on-fire proclamations of the end of modernity, but really his work is so revolutionary, so modern, and so beautifully documented that to ignore him would be shocking. His two libraries in Paris, in addition to being the first to have genuinely public reading rooms, are stunning spaces that explicitly use iron structure to point the way to the future of steel and glass in modernism.

The dates of the libraries bracket (and the buildings are strongly related to) the 1851 Crystal Palace in London, which, as a temporary (and prefabricated and demountable) exhibition building, was then the apotheosis of modern architecture.

Without Labrouste, the very idea that created the New York Public Library (magnificent public spaces for books, reading, and research, not associated with universities or churches or private individuals) might not exist. Yet his buildings are infinitely more modern, constructed fifty years earlier than the NYPL Main Branch on Fifth Avenue; they not only create magnificent spaces but also experiment and invent a language appropriately daring to compete with the texts they contain.

Plus, he could really draw! Like all Beaux-Arts architects, he was schooled in the art of remarkable renderings that put our current photo-realistic ones to shame. Yet another lost art.

MoMA's Labrouste show was a marvel, but I'm still waiting for the exhibit on the Crystal Palace.

12 May
Daniel Libeskind

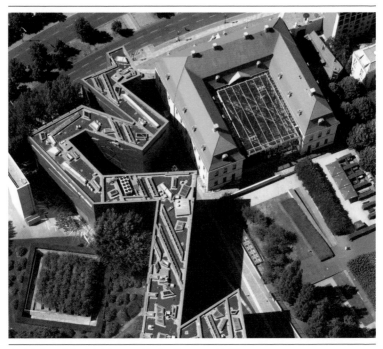

Aerial view of Jewish Museum, Berlin, Germany, 2001

I have a hard time writing about Daniel Libeskind. It's not that he hasn't produced some very interesting buildings, but that the ones I know about are so compromised and emasculated (by others) that it's mostly pity I feel when I think of them. I think this is due in no small part to Libeskind's extraordinarily internal process that seems to filter out much of the reality obvious to us all.

His best (and among his earliest) work is the Jewish Museum Berlin. It is a jagged lightning bolt of a building (not unlike the SS bolts on Nazi collars) with a set of almost sacred and profane spaces evoking real emotional responses, but only when it was empty, as it was for years. Fill it with exhibitions, and the whole thing becomes a laughable study in how to defile a building that is about the defiling of a people. The exhibits (when I saw them) so trivialized the building as to seem to mock the people and culture it purports to honor.

It is a misunderstanding of just what the building was destined to be; Libeskind created a form that only communicated when it lacked content. It's like a restaurant that only works when empty of diners, or an office building that only functions properly without tenants.

When I joined Pentagram, our offices were at 212 Fifth Avenue, a building that eventually emptied of all tenants but us. Still, the building super complained that the building would run well if only the tenants weren't there to interfere.

Libeskind's World Trade Center–winning competition was an even more humiliating exercise. He won because New York Governor George Pataki overruled the jury that elected a much more interesting scheme, which he decried as empty "ghost towers." Libeskind's scheme had a tower 1,776 feet /541 meters high, a clever but meaninglessly pandering gesture, and revealed the original foundations of the WTC (a meaningful but misused attempt to create a new wailing wall).

It was all undone by the corporate powerhouse Skidmore, Owings & Merrill, which steamrolled Libeskind while he cooperated with the castration and continued to claim authorship. The result is beyond awful, a terrible chunk of a tower and a funereal landscape of water-filled holes.

Sad but predictable.

13 May
Paola Antonelli

The at sign (@), "acquired" by Paola Antonelli for MoMA in 2010

Who doesn't love Paola Antonelli? It's not just that she managed to bring the most interesting subjects to light at MoMA, curating exhibitions that would never have existed under anyone else's rule, but that she brings considerable public intelligence to every endeavor. Plus, of course, her charming and eloquent discourse on virtually every topic around modernism and design, always without being arcane or obtuse or attempting to overintellectualize her subject. We barely notice all this because she seems to be perfect in her roles, and it's increasingly hard to remember any of the personalities that preceded her (actually, we do, but we prefer her!).

It's the Museum of Modern Art, but design has always been an integral part of the museum, from the *Machine Art* show in 1934 to Antonelli's acquisition of the @ symbol into the collection. Both of these bookends wink at a Duchampian view of the world; declaring something is art (or design) makes it so. Springs and boat propellers and bolts are unwitting art, just as is Antonelli's selection of the Google Maps pin. All are unselfconsciously made but recognized, as Duchamp did with the urinal, as inherently beautiful and art of their age.

Her view depends on a simple recognition: that everything not part of nature is designed by humans. Everything is designed, and therefore everything can impact our lives and the life of the planet. As Antonelli describes it, in selecting iconic objects (or nonobjects), the question is "whether it would be a pity if this item did not exist," a perfectly subjective assay of, well, everything. Leading the museum away from exclusively self-conscious art to design that matters has been her task for her more than twenty years at MoMA.

The bias of the historical MoMA toward more formal, more monumental, more male work is hard to miss. Paola didn't feminize as much as she broadened the museum's gaze to include the simple but noble elements of modern life (the white T-shirt, video games, a typeface, mutant materials) and to promote people out of the mainstream of male-dominated design.

The Architecture and Design Departments at MoMA have a history of esteemed directors, curators, and chairs, from founder Philip Johnson to Arthur Drexler to Emilio Ambasz to Terrence Riley to Barry Bergdoll. Paola Antonelli is the fitting successor to this long line of luminaries.

14 May
Minerva Parker Nichols

Delaware Children's Theater (or New Century Club), Wilmington, Delaware, 1892

Minerva Parker Nichols has the distinction of being the first woman to start an architectural firm in the US without partnering with a male colleague or husband or mentor. She, after an intern-based education, started her own office focused on domestic architecture, a predetermined track that the profession was willing to tolerate then.

It's amazing how, in the 1890s, the published support for Nichols sounds as sensible and open-minded as it might today: of course women are capable of being just as effective as architects as men are; of course everyone should be judged on their abilities not their gender (or substitute any other cause for discrimination); of course, of course, of course...

But more than a hundred years later, the change to her profession is still shamefully incremental. While 50 percent of students in architecture programs are women, only 17 percent of registered architects in the US are women.

Nichols was born in the middle of the Civil War. Her father went off to fight and died, leaving her and her mother to fend for themselves. Women did exactly that during the Civil War, and, like during WWII, this created a generation of women for whom providing for (and raising) a family was utterly natural. It was also utterly natural for Nichols to be advocating for women's suffrage and civil rights.

Her grandfather, standing in for her father, was an architect and trained her in architectural drawing, and she then apprenticed for Edwin Thorne, a Philadelphia architect. When Thorne decided to move his office, she decided to open her own office in his former space.

Her work was primarily houses and a few clubs, and she won the competition for a building at the World's Columbian Exposition. Nevertheless, she closed her office after fewer than ten years to move to Brooklyn. She died in 1949 in Westport, Connecticut, her life bridging the Civil War, World War I, and World War II. Minerva Parker Nichols had enough distinction to warrant a *New York Times* obituary on Sunday, November 20, 1949, appearing next to Belgian painter James Ensor's obit, not the first time she achieved equity with the male world.

15 May
Gianfranco Frattini

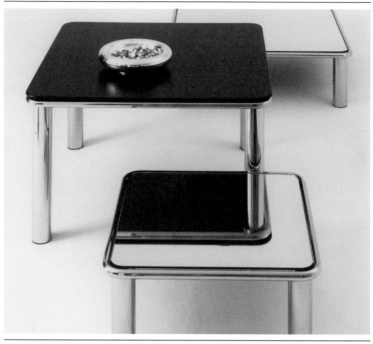

Sesann tables, manufactured by Cassina, 1968

Gianfranco Frattini was one of those admirably hip Italian designers of the 1950s, who created that fantastic Boalum lamp, a squiggly, plastic, vacuum-hose-type thing that would be *so* easy to produce now and so difficult then. It was included in the landmark *Italy: The New Domestic Landscape* exhibition at MoMA, securing his place in the design firmament while suggesting to us all just how cool the future would be, if only Italians designed it.

Frattini apprenticed for Gio Ponti after graduating from the Polytechnic University of Milan (where virtually every important Italian designer was schooled, including his daughter, Emanuela Frattini Magnusson) and worked for almost every Italian design company (Cassina, Artemide, FontanaArte, Poliform, Poltrona Frau, Bernini, ArteLuce) as well as Knoll and others.

Frattini, like his peers, reinvented the idea of modern designed objects in postwar Italy, and companies like Artemide and Cassina manufactured the designs almost as a point of national pride. He founded the Associazione per il Disegno Industriale, which still pursues its original mission of promoting Italian product design, including issuing the prestigious Compasso d'Oro award,

more than sixty-five years later. Design was, of course, part of the postwar revival of the Italian economy (as something more than Parmesan and politics), called Italy's economic miracle. As architect Luigi Caccia Dominioni said, "Quite simply, we are the best!" and he meant all Italian designers.

One item that nearly every Italian designer created that seems so very odd today is the ashtray. Frattini created dozens, and I have to admit that just looking at them makes me want to start smoking again. My fave picture of Frattini is him smoking a cigarette while standing next to a painting of him smoking a cigarette! It's smoking squared. Or metasmoking.

I could live easily in a house designed by Frattini, with his furniture, lighting, and ashtrays, eating off plates and dinnerware designed by him, with doorknobs, textiles, and storage designed by him, and be very happy. Italians don't just know how to design; they know how to live. And filling my life with the joy they create would be a pleasure and an honor.

16 May
Konrad Wachsmann

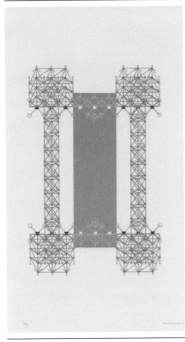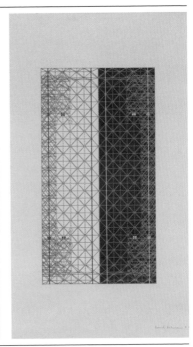

Study for an airplane hangar, 1953

You know how sometimes you borrow a friend's book, then forget to return it? Then discover it a year later and feel so embarrassed that you almost can't return it? Then ten years later, you see it on your bookshelf and almost stop feeling guilty, but still there's a pang of something? Well, about forty-odd years ago, I borrowed a book by Konrad Wachsmann and never returned it. Coming across it reminds me that I may not be quite as upstanding as I imagine. There was a recent story about a woman who took out a VHS tape (*Sabrina the Teenage Witch*) from a local rental place and didn't return it, resulting in a felony embezzlement warrant forty years later. A cautionary tale.

Wachsmann was one of those brainy architects from Germany who found their way to the US via Paris just before World War II. He designed a house for his good friend Albert Einstein, proposed a gargantuan airplane hangar for the Air Force reminiscent of the Galerie des Machines in its heroic scale, and ultimately became obsessed with prefabrication and turning building from an art to a science.

In the US, except for some very tall buildings or some deliberately experimental ones, the idea of subjecting buildings to the process and fabrication rigors of, say, automotive manufacturing has been about as effective (at about 3 percent of US building) as electric cars (3 percent of all cars sold). It is a great idea that somehow is resistant to deep market penetration (so far). That will change with cars, as fossil fuels get legislated out of existence, but buildings are still handmade and more craft (in construction) than efficiently engineered processes.

There's a tale about a very carefully worked-out system of prefabricated houses, designed in the US by a team of German architects, that was exceedingly clever except for one tiny misstep: it included standard wood sizes, like two-by-fours, without realizing that they are not 2 by 4 inches/5.1 by 10.2 centimeters. They are (currently) 1.5 by 3.5 inches/3.8 by 8.9 centimeters, so the entire system fell apart.

Craft (and the peculiarities of the American system of deceptive nomenclature) reasserts itself, derailing the mechanization of construction. This ill-fated prefab system may have been the one Konrad Wachsmann and Walter Gropius developed that could erect a house in nine hours, but that would just make the tale even better.

17 May
Vertner Woodson Tandy

Villa Lewaro (Madam C. J. Walker estate), Irvington, New York, 1918

Vertner Woodson Tandy was the first Black architect registered in New York State, but really that was just one of his life's accomplishments.

Tandy's father, Henry, was born into slavery, but by 1893 he had built a building contracting business in Lexington, Kentucky, which propelled Vertner in the direction of architecture. On the way, Tandy was the first Black soldier to pass the military commissioning exam, leading to his appointment as a first lieutenant in the New York National Guard. He transferred from Tuskegee Institute to Cornell University's architecture school in 1906 and graduated in 1907, but not before he and six others (collectively the Seven Jewels) founded Alpha Phi Alpha, the first Black fraternity.

In Lexington, my firm converted a downtown department store into a large contractor's office. We toured the empty building, including the basement, where staff locker rooms were marked with a painted sign stenciled directly on the wall that said, "Colored Locker Rooms." I was stunned (having never seen anything like that in person). It was a time capsule, a diorama of a world a half century earlier. Astonishing but, like Confederate statues, remnants of Jim Crow live on.

Tandy went on to design some pretty fabulous buildings for some pretty fabulous people, especially his Villa Lewaro, built in Irvington, New York, for Madam C. J. Walker, who developed beauty products for Black consumers, becoming the first female millionaire in the US. The house (named, at the suggestion of Enrico Caruso, for the first two letters of Walker's daughter's names) became the center of Black thought and activism (and apparently Italian opera), with regular visitors like W. E. B. Du Bois, Langston Hughes, and Zora Neale Hurston. Madam Walker died just after its completion and willed it to her daughter, who willed it to the NAACP, who sold it, etc. Just a few years ago, it was purchased by Richelieu Dennis, owner of *Essence* magazine (and founder of Sundial Brands, his own hair and skincare products), for use as a foundation.

Dennis is an immigrant from Liberia. The Liberian Pavilion in the 1939 New York World's Fair was designed by Vertner Woodson Tandy, so coincidences abound.

18 May
Walter Gropius

Fagus Factory, Alfeld on the Leine, Germany, 1913

In the modern canon of Frank Lloyd Wright, Le Corbusier, Mies van der Rohe, and Alvar Aalto, Walter Gropius has always seemed to be at the wrong table; in *Hamilton* he would be "and Peggy" of the Schuyler sisters.

Gropius collected boldface names. He married Alma Mahler, the widow of Gustav Mahler; after divorcing Alma, he married Ise Frank and adopted her niece, Ati, who married one of Gropius's students at Harvard, John M. Johansen. John and Ati lived in my little town in a very crazy little house, and when a friend had dinner there and used the word *modernist*, Ati exploded and said, "There is no modern-ist, only modern!" Fun dinner, no doubt.

Gropius, along with other young Turks Mies van der Rohe and Le Corbusier, went to work for Peter Behrens, leaving to design the 1910 Fagus Factory facades, an example of modernism in its infancy. He was drafted into World War I, injured at the Western Front (all was not quiet there, apparently), and awarded two Iron Crosses.

He returned to life in Berlin and became master of the school that would become the Bauhaus, where he hired virtually every important European artist, architect, and designer, including Paul

Klee, Josef and Anni Albers, Marcel Breuer, Herbert Bayer, László Moholy-Nagy, Mart Stam, and Wassily Kandinsky. He eventually designed all the Bauhaus buildings in Dessau.

He pitched modern architecture as the right style for the rising National Socialist Party (you know, Nazis) and even produced a Reichsbank design before fleeing, with his Jewish wife, to England and ultimately to the US, where he landed at Harvard with Marcel Breuer. Gropius ran the Harvard Graduate School of Design for fifteen years and educated the next generation of modernists like Johansen, I. M. Pei, Ulrich Franzen, Edward Larrabee Barnes, Paul Rudolph, and Philip Johnson.

Klaus Herdeg, in his book *The Decorated Box*, blames Walter Gropius's tenure at Harvard for the vacuous and brutal architecture that seemed to fill the decades in the US following his rule there, and Herdeg may be right (or Wright). For a reputed master, Gropius produced only a handful of buildings, for which we should probably be grateful! And, just to be fair and balanced, we should be genuinely grateful for his tenure at the Bauhaus; he is the undisputed master of that remarkable realm.

19 May
Giovanni della Robbia

Coat of arms of the Franciscan Order, circa 1525

Giovanni della Robbia inherited the workshop for ceramic art of his famous father, Andrea della Robbia, and continued the work of his father, making his own reputation. But Giovanni was also likely the artist for work attributed to Andrea and other della Robbias (it was the family business). Andrea created the famous tondi of swaddled babes set into round recesses in the Brunelleschi arcade surrounding the perfect little Renaissance Piazza della Santissima Annunziata in Florence.

Those renowned roundels are simple blue and white, which comport with our idea of elegant artwork, but Giovanni and other della Robbias were famous for multicolored ceramic sculpture. Those can lapse into what we might see as kitsch, but that is a modern conceit (at least partially influenced by twentieth-century modernism, which we like to think of as the milestone in visual art).

It's not unlike the Parthenon, which may be majestically monochromatic now but was painted in a riot of colors when it was built. We can't really cope with that view of antiquity, and I suspect Giovanni suffers from the same color blindness; just as plumpness once indicated wealth (but now self-indulgence), bright, permanent color was a remarkable

innovation. We accept it in painting, but we see sculpture at its apex when perfectly white (or bronze, or any other solid, material-based color).

The incredible Greek *Boxer at Rest* bronze sculpture in the Palazzo Massimo alle Terme in Rome is colored with inlays of copper to simulate blood or lips, but even that is so subtle as to be essentially monochrome. Greek amphorae were similarly limited in palette (black and red, terra-cotta, and some off-white), like black-and-white photography today. Much else looks, to our eyes, like Neverland Ranch or anime or a visual joke. But it's not (except, of course, Neverland and some pieces by Jeff Koons).

Like color photos or color movies, polychromed sculpture is an art that embraces an entirely different visual language that Giovanni della Robbia mastered. If you've watched any episodes of *The Great British Throw Down* (and I've just discovered it), the art of ceramics can lean toward craft. At least on that show...

Della Robbia kept it squarely in the art column.

20 May
Dieter Rams

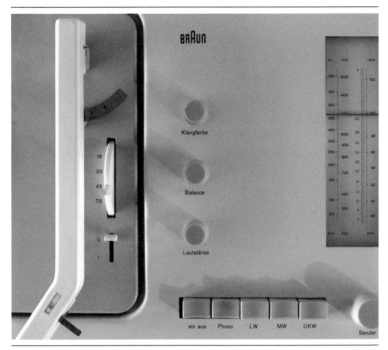

Detail of "Snow White's Coffin" Braun SK61 record player/radio, 1966

Dieter Rams is to modern postwar (often electronics) design what the Bauhaus was to mostly prewar nonelectronic design. He defined, and refined, the art of removing as much as possible to reveal the essence of things, managing it down to a ten-point checklist.

Good design, according to Rams, 1) is innovative, 2) makes a product useful, 3) is aesthetic, 4) makes a product understandable, 5) is unobtrusive, 6) is honest, 7) is long-lasting, 8) is thorough down to the last detail, 9) is environmentally friendly, and 10) involves as little design as possible.

That last item seems the most interesting, along with 4. With books by him titled *Less But Better* and *Less and More* in addition to the ten principles above, I think you get the idea.

It turns out that stripping away all style becomes a style in itself. Pictures of the Rams T3 transistor radio from 1958 next to Jony Ive's first version of the iPod from 2001 abound. The point is clear: they are at least first cousins, if not twins.

It's revealing that Rams was born in 1932 in Germany and lived through the height and downfall of the Third Reich and ultimately the physical (and moral)

destruction of Germany. He grew into an adult rejecting the bombastic pomp of the Nazis; he found a quiet, modest, and utterly simple response to the visual excess of his formative years. It defines a moral dimension beyond the taste for less.

Reductivism is a kind of religion, and Rams (through Braun) created what we think of as moral products: well thought out, definitionally modern, cool, and eventually prestigious as a brand; Braun products were a statement of socioeconomic and cultural acumen.

That was then. When controlling interest in Braun was purchased by Gillette in 1967 (eventually owning it in whole in 1984), it continued Rams's design directorship. In 2005 Gillette was purchased by Procter & Gamble, and the products were distributed across four companies (Braun has control of just one). Some products continue to lean heavily on Rams's design; others have strayed considerably.

Dieter Rams continues to design all the products for Vitsoe, the makers of a shelving system he designed in 1960, and the company remains true to his ethos. But the aura of cool around Braun has evaporated.

21 May
Marcel Breuer

Marcel Breuer in B3 Wassily chair at the Bauhaus, Dessau, Germany, 1925

Marcel Breuer is a birthday buddy with his sometimes friend Walter Gropius (May 18), with whom he landed at Harvard and with whom he built a house in Lincoln, Massachusetts. The relationship wasn't always rainbows and butterflies; when Breuer was at the Bauhaus (that Gropius essentially founded and ran), his famous furniture was a popular product that Gropius thought belonged to the Bauhaus, but Breuer decided it was his own and pursued licensing deals outside the institution. Good for Breuer, bad for Bauhaus.

They both had to leave Germany, eventually; Breuer (though converted) was born Jewish and Gropius was married to a Jew. So they met up again in London at the Isokon Building and eventually reunited at Harvard, where both taught and built their houses on the estate of a patron who was happy for some famous architecture.

Breuer eventually created small, very efficient homes, like the one he designed for MoMA and built in its Sculpture Garden and the one in Croton-on-Hudson, New York, that my brother lives in. Another house he designed is a few minutes from me in Clinton Corners, New York, and was once owned by artist David Diao. It had

this one amazing detail (in addition to the Airstream-trailer kitchen plugged into it): to connect perpendicular cables on its deck (several horizontal railings and one vertical cable to support the railing), Breuer literally wove the two together to create a fixed connection with no external material, fasteners, or welds. It's a lot harder than it seems, and when Diao restored the house, he discovered that he had to unwind the cables and weave them back together. But, still, it's a perfect detail that I have never seen since!

Breuer designed some truly terrific, and some much-less-than-terrific, buildings, but all of them are looking better today than they did when they were built. It's partly our renewed taste for brutalism and for structural heroics and partly just the cycle of taste. When the perfectly lovely Cesca chair he designed became knocked off, ubiquitous, and devalued, we hated it; it's not the design itself, but how that design has penetrated culture.

Breuer was particularly attuned to popular tastes and was always just a step ahead, or ready for the next cycle in case he missed it the first time around.

22 May
Neave Brown

Alexandra Road Estate, London, England, designed 1968, completed 1978

There were once buildings that could only have been built in a particular country at a particular time, before architecture (and maybe everything else) became so internationalized that any building could be virtually anywhere.

A particular kind of housing, one that could only have been built in the UK, is typified by Neave Brown's work. These projects (there are only four of them) are now all "listed" buildings, considered to be part of the national cultural heritage. But when they were built, the reaction was less admiring.

As a young architect, I visited friends in London, and one of them worked for Neave Brown (a name that is so utterly British that I was shocked to learn he was born in the very American town of Utica, New York) on his reputed masterpiece, the Alexandra Road Housing Estate. The 984-foot-/300-meter-long curved street (it followed the arc of the adjacent railroad tracks) was shockingly brutal, yet it is now much beloved.

Staying with these friends introduced me to some British oddities, apart from brutalist housing estates that embraced the ethics of Jane Jacobs. We all bathed in the same bath water (sequentially), hopefully while (Brits would say "whilst")

it remained warm. It was filled from a coin-operated, gas-fueled water heater (no, this was not 1920s London), which seems more like a Harry Potter dream than 1980s reality.

Neave was marginalized in the UK when the Alexandra Road project was investigated by the local council for being over budget and over schedule. They sought to blame the architect, but in the end the blame was their own. Yet just the accusation was enough to nearly ruin Brown. That was in part why he, at seventy-two, returned to art school to study painting.

To a large extent, housing (versus houses) is about one's facility in arranging very minimal space allocations (because they tend to be government sponsored) into apparently spacious homes. Brown was a genius at that. He was also (maybe because of his American roots) prone to rearranging homes and was credited with the first upside-down homes in the UK (ones with the bedrooms below living spaces).

Neave Brown lived for most of his life in the housing estates he designed, living with, rather than scorning, the people for whom he built.

23 May
Max Abramovitz

The Egg, Empire State Plaza, Albany, New York, 1978

Max Abramovitz falls on the fault line between formerly reviled and currently admired. His work was always a bit (or more) bombastic, heroic, and monumental, but veered stylistically, as at Avery Fisher Hall, toward either interpreted classicism or brutal functionalism, two poles that don't easily mesh.

He worked with Wallace K. Harrison for decades, being the lesser-known partner to Harrison's regal (read "not Jewish") presence, even though it was his hand that designed some of their most famous projects.

Abramovitz (before becoming a partner) worked on the Rockefeller Apartments, across Fifty-Fourth Street from the MoMA Sculpture Garden. Now filled with architects and the architect-adjacent, these apartments are among the most luxuriously detailed early modern homes in New York.

Max also worked on the Trylon and Perisphere, the famously abstract centerpiece at the 1939 New York World's Fair. He was integral to the United Nations Secretariat Building and to Lincoln Center. But somehow he was always overshadowed by Harrison, whose name came first, despite the alphabet.

It's not clear whether it is fair to judge architects by their last, or worst, work. In Abramovitz's case, those are the same thing: the Empire State Plaza, Nelson Rockefeller's folly (well, enormous folly) in Albany. It's a shonda (look it up).

To complete it, Abramovitz more or less moved upstate and left his partner, effectively ending the partnership, while he created a massive work that has never become cool. Rockefeller also dreamed up the World Trade Center, which, in time, became beloved, or at least not hated (by New Yorkers, in any case).

Empire State Plaza, I predict, will never soften the hearts of architects nor governmental functionaries. It is a view of the brave new world that proves the timid old world was best. An attempt to out-Brazil Brasilia, it has neither the skill nor the level of abstraction to transcend its worst qualities.

The best and worst thing about architecture is that it exists long enough to get the benefit of time to consider. But when it is bad, it is equally there for all to see for many, many years.

Max Abramovitz knew both extremes.

24 May
Florence Knoll

Florence Knoll and Pedestal Collection prototype with Eero Saarinen, circa 1958

Sometimes birthdays make interesting neighbors and suggest interesting polemics. Take the week of May 18–24, when Walter Gropius, Marcel Breuer, Max Abramovitz, and Florence Knoll all celebrate their birthdays. The linkages are copious: Knoll worked with Gropius and Breuer in their architecture office, she produced Breuer's furniture, and she worked at Harrison and Abramovitz (and studied under Mies van der Rohe at Illinois Institute of Technology, before it was called that).

Knoll (known as Shu, her maiden name being Schust) was orphaned early and ultimately attended Cranbrook Academy of Art, where she was essentially adopted by the Saarinens and spent summers vacationing with them. She met Alvar Aalto, who recommended her to the Architectural Association in London, which she promptly attended. She worked with Charles and Ray Eames and knew, it appears, everyone of any import in the design and architecture world.

As much as any architect, Knoll (both the firm and Florence) promulgated the modern interior by both planning and furnishing it. In the end, no single piece of architecture, nor any architect, made the case for modern interiors at work and home more than Knoll and her firm.

Knoll created a language of furniture that both domesticated the office and professionalized the home. Her pieces (as much as those of the Eameses, Paul McCobb, or George Nelson) define the midcentury renaissance in furniture and interior design, helping to usher in the era of Mad Men modernity. She was virtually alone as a woman designer at Knoll (perhaps Anni Albers kept her company after being invited by Florence to create products for the company), and she remained the sole female voice there for years. She was the face of Knoll not just because her husband (Hans Knoll) died in a 1955 automobile crash but because she was actively engaged in designing and design, not just manufacturing and sales.

Florence gave Knoll, like Ginger Rogers gave Fred Astaire, emotional appeal, no small accomplishment given the cadre of German designers she shepherded. Without creating splashy designs, she crafted a suite of furniture that eventually totaled half the pieces Knoll manufactured.

In her quiet way, Florence Knoll completely transformed the role of modernity in America.

25 May
Aaron Burns

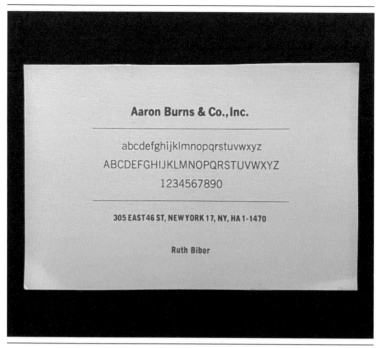

Aaron Burns & Co., Inc.

abcdefghijklmnopqrstuvwxyz
ABCDEFGHIJKLMNOPQRSTUVWXYZ
1234567890

305 EAST 46 ST, NEW YORK 17, NY, HA 1-1470

Ruth Biber

Business card from Aaron Burns & Co. for Ruth Biber, the author's mother, 1960s

Recently, my brother sent me a business card from Aaron Burns & Co.; it was my mother's business card when she worked for Burns at his East Forty-Sixth Street office in New York. It must have been 1965 or so, given the lack of zip code (New York 17 became 10017) and the letter telephone exchange (HA 1, whatever HA stood for; the neighborhood was Turtle Bay). Burns printed the full alphabet on the business card, as he did with a lot of his pieces. It was, after all, his passion.

I remember Aaron from visiting my mother at work; he was a heavy-lidded, soft-spoken guy who was more than happy to show me how cool his new photo Typositor machine was. His enthusiastic explanation was that with metal type a font had a limited number of any particular letter and the physical restraint of the block itself; you couldn't letterspace them closer than the slug allowed and you definitely couldn't overlap them. He then proceeded to produce a strip of capital Rs (in some sans serif face), slightly overlapping and clearly as many as he wanted to produce. Super fucking cool (I thought). Looks like the future to me.

That was, apparently, how he thought of it too. Someone called him the Bucky Fuller of type, which might overstate it a

bit, but the point is made. He understood, even in 1964, that phototype was the transitional phase from metal to digital type. He had a dizzying array of company acronyms for the dizzying array of companies and organizations he founded or led; VGC, ITC, Rapid, ICTA, TDC, ADC, etc.

At the time, my mother worked the traffic desk, or something like that, with big(ish) hair and a stylish wardrobe. About ten years later, there was a gas leak in the building, and it kind of exploded. No one (amazingly) was killed, but seventy people were hurt. A "printing executive" was quoted in the *New York Times* as having lost everything, including five hundred thousand dollars in machinery. Who knows if it was Burns, but by then my mother had moved on. Given the exploding townhouses (Weathermen making bombs), everyone seemed relieved it was just a gas leak!

Aaron Burns died in 1991 of an AIDS-related illness he got from a blood transfusion during open heart surgery a decade earlier. He was the necessary (and mostly forgotten) bridge between the analog past and the digital future.

26 May
Joseph Urban

Main auditorium of New School for Social Research, New York, New York, 1931

Today it seems inconceivable that an architect's work might be independent from their politics. How could an architect designing a New York City office building for William Randolph Hearst also design the landmark building for the most progressive school in the city? No stranger than designing a fabulous Florida mansion for a leftist Democratic philanthropist that became the home to the most virulent right-wing Republican imaginable (hint: the adopted home of 45).

Joseph Urban did all of that and more. He started as a theater set and scenic designer, coming to the US from Vienna to design at the Boston Opera Company, but eventually designed for the Vienna Opera, Champs-Élysée Opera, Covent Garden, and the Metropolitan Opera. It is from that perspective that all of Urban's work makes sense.

The new(ish) Hearst Tower sits atop Urban's amusingly bizarre fantasy, the International Magazine Building, built for Hearst in 1929. Seen as a set design it makes more sense, adopting the same theatricality that Urban's Ziegfeld Theatre had. If you see the city as opera (and why not?), then the streetscape is the set design, the evocative background before which the performance of urban life takes place. It explains so much about the hyperbolic tone of the street, the choreography of transit: dodging tourists, bikes, crossing the street in sync with oncoming traffic, hailing cabs.

Mar-a-Lago was designed for Marjorie Merriweather Post but is now the Xanadu of "he who must not be named." He reportedly roams the halls, occasionally interrupting a wedding or reception to take the mic for a screed of grievances. Post donated the mansion for use as the winter White House in 1972, but the government returned it a decade later.

Joseph Urban's last and best work, among my favorite New York City buildings, is the New School, a striped affair of black-and-white brick, and a fairly straitlaced adherent to modern orthodoxy (occasionally called the first International Style building in New York City). The sequence from the street to the oval auditorium is elegant though efficient; the whole composition must have appealed to a school looking to break the elitist mold of education in New York City. The theater has a strong Radio City vibe, without the pomp. The New School's modernity still looks fully and convincingly modern, even as it approaches its first hundred years.

27 May
Marie Neurath

The Wonder World of the Seashore, 1958

I remember reading somewhere that Massimo Vignelli declared that he would be proud to be called an information architect. Maybe it was in his piece extolling the US Nutrition Facts label, or maybe just Vignelli being Vignelli, but Marie Neurath was precisely that, an information architect, several decades earlier.

Neurath, then Marie Reidemeister, studied math and physics from the end of World War I and took art school courses. She eventually moved to Vienna to join the Gesellschafts- und Wirtschaftsmuseum (and where else would there be a museum of social and economic issues?). She developed, as part of a team including her husband, Otto Neurath, a system of visualizing science and statistical information. This was the birth of data visualization. Maybe I've been out of the loop, but I've never heard Neurath credited for her seminal role in it. Shocking to hear that a woman was not fully credited (she will get my Rosalind Franklin Award for Invisibility).

The Gesellschafts- und Wirtschaftsmuseum was, before it was burned by Austrian Fascists, a kind of marvel of communication; with a significant portion of the population illiterate, the museum was the cultural tool for social and economic information. The displays sat in rows like pews in a churchlike space that helped its credibility. Words (or rather pictures) from God was the effective, if unspoken, implication.

In fact, one reason Marie and Otto Neurath did not simply publish their techniques for wide application was their fear of misinformation being given visual credibility. Marie, as a "transformer," performed the critical analysis and numeration of data to evoke the truth; she understood how the same data could result in different (false) representation.

Echoes of that Fascist past abound today, with information being weaponized against the truth once again: Where is our Marie Neurath of today? (The other side may ask, "Where is my Roy Cohn?")

Former Google CEO Eric Schmidt once said that Google's goal was to make the entire universe of information fully accessible, at which point he predicted that it would be impossible to lie. When Facebook and others permit false news to exist within a context designed to validate all information as equally based in reality, they are proving Schmidt wrong, and playing out the Neuraths' greatest fear.

28 May
Piet Zwart

Bruynzeel modular kitchen, 1931

Piet Zwart was a visual polymath who practiced everything from architecture to typography to graphic design to photography to furniture and industrial design; he referred to himself by the portmanteau *typotect*. He was named the Designer of the Century in 2000 by the Association of Dutch Designers, yet he remains relatively unknown.

It is not surprising that design was once inextricably linked to social and cultural issues, not simply aesthetics. Zwart said, "To make beautiful creations for the sake of their aesthetic value will have no social significance tomorrow, will be nonsensical self-gratification." At the time, most designers would have agreed. Today, given the conflation of art and design, few might agree with that proposition.

Zwart worked for architects H. P. Berlage and Jans Wils, which led somehow to graphics and typography. His naivete in graphics made it easier to design outside the mainstream, and his association with the progenitors of de Stijl gave him the hook he needed.

Some of his most powerful work is for the cable company NKF (and not what we now think of as cable; this was a company that literally produced electrical and telephone wires) and

for a producer of cutting tools (saws, drills, and files), which are just the kind of faceless fabricators for whom so much famous design has been done (think Container Corporation of America or General Dynamics).

Just ten years after Margarete Schütte-Lihotzky conceived the Frankfurt Kitchen (in 1926), Zwart designed a modular kitchen for Bruynzeel. It was a perfectly Dutch response to the original German modern kitchen. The Frankfurt was a Taylorized (time/motion-engineered) construction to make women's kitchen work more rational. The Bruynzeel was about choice and adaptation; the system could be customized according to the consumer. And it solved some issues of the Frankfurt model, like the drawers of staples that were at child height in the Frankfurt, which were moved to a row below the wall cabinets in the Bruynzeel.

The Sonneveld House had a Bruynzeel kitchen, replacing the American-made steel cabinets originally installed. It's a perfect kitchen, one I would be happy to have today, thanks to polymath Piet Zwart.

154

29 May
George Nelson

Vintage Ball clock, Howard Miller Company, 1949

Although George Nelson's name is on a lot of furniture (especially Herman Miller furniture) of a particular period and style, much of it was designed by his staff. Still, Nelson actually did more to support other designers and architects than we generally realize. And he did much more to shape the postwar American domestic landscape than we know.

He discovered architecture at Yale after popping into a building to avoid the rain and finding an exhibition of design work (for a cemetery gate!). He taught a bit upon graduating but quickly won a Rome Prize and spent two years at the American Academy in Rome, traveling Europe and meeting every architect and designer he admired.

Nelson became a design writer and editor and published the work that earned him fame in a variety of design and architecture magazines, ultimately creating books that take a serious look at every aspect of domestic living.

One book, *Tomorrow's House* (which, for some reason, I own two copies of), introduced concepts like "storage wall" (making it to the cover of *Life* magazine!) and "family room." It was an influential *New York Times* bestseller, remarkable for a book about how to conceive, build,

furnish, and live in a house. But reading it is a joy; it's filled with anecdotal narratives, like a chapter called "Home Is a Place to Hang Your Architect," as well as deeply analytical deconstructions of the art of the house as it was in 1945.

The book was very timely and led to the next phase of Nelson's career; the chair of Herman Miller read the book and hired Nelson as a design director, a position he held from 1947 to 1972 while he operated his own firm from 1955 on. Herman Miller allowed Nelson to hire the band of designers he admired and to effectively change the face of furnishings for the next fifty years.

In 1979 a young designer named Colin Forbes arrived in New York City to open a new branch of his newish design firm, Pentagram, and shared George Nelson's office until Forbes attracted other partners. Nelson may even have considered himself a partner of Pentagram. He died five years before I joined the firm, but his influence on American life has never died.

30 May
Alexander Archipenko

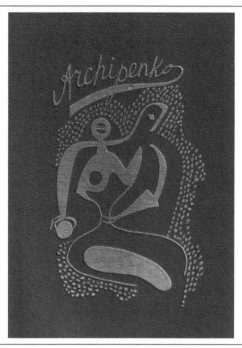

Cover of *Archipenko: Fifty Creative Years 1908–1958,* 1960

Alexander Archipenko is occasionally credited with making the first cubist sculpture (1913), but of course that was Picasso. How much being first matters is the difference between Picasso and someone you barely know about, like Archipenko.

Archipenko was a guy who started an art school in Paris at age twenty-five; was in the 1913 New York Armory Show (the big one) at age twenty-six; moved to the US and exhibited at the 1933 Chicago World's Fair, filling a room at the Ukrainian Pavilion; got a patent for a "changeable picture device"; bought land near Woodstock and established an art school; taught at the Dalton School; moved to Los Angeles; moved to Chicago; moved to Paris; moved to New York; and married a student fifty years his junior, who lived with him for the last eight years of his life and who wrote *My Life with Alexander Archipenko.*

Archipenko made hundreds of works of art, and nearly all are a standing female figure, or his abstraction of that subject. That alone is incredible, but not at all unusual. I recently saw a Richard Meier house from 1967, which is not all that different from a Richard Meier house fifty years later. Some artists (and architects) spend their careers perfecting an idea or playing out the variations of an idea.

Spending a life developing the same pursuit, constantly working to refine something done perhaps hundreds of times, is both utterly reasonable and absolutely insane.

Archipenko was one of those relentless artists. He exhibited in all the right places, alongside the boldface names we know, but remained a secondary figure, respected and talented, but not a superstar. There may be lots of reasons for that; maybe he was not good at promotion (though I doubt that); maybe he was good with things but less good with people (though again I doubt that).

I went to school with friends who had a lot more raw talent than I had, but who haven't managed to convert that talent to success in the world at large. Archipenko had all the talent to be renowned, plus a young enough and devoted enough partner to maintain his legacy (she manages the Archipenko Foundation), but it takes more than talent to succeed at the level of the stars in any discipline.

31 May
Lebbeus Woods

Cover of *War and Architecture,* Pamphlet Architecture 15, 1993

When I was in school, it wasn't uncommon for teachers to be architects who didn't build; actually building (or deigning to supplicate to clients in order to build) was seen as a corruption of their ideas. Really, it was a cover for a kind of professional bitterness. "It's not cool to build" was an unspoken attitude.

That changed when those academic architects began to win competitions, get things built, and enter the much more complicated world of capital and commerce. (Sayre's law is credited with formulating "academic politics are so bitter because the stakes are so low.") Building became cool (again), and now even the assumption that architects' careers begin at fifty is nonsense.

But then there are architects (and one could even dispute whether that is the right term) who intentionally don't build. Lebbeus Woods was one of them, and he deliberately worked in a speculative world where he was free to explore ideas that were about architecture and architectural space, but not bound by pesky issues of physics, economics, materials, or regulations. I don't pretend to understand his work, but I do respect and admire him. In his own words:

Architecture and war are not incompatible. Architecture is war. War is architecture. I am at war with my time, with history, with all authority that resides in fixed and frightened forms. I am one of millions who do not fit in, who have no home, no family, no doctrine, no firm place to call my own, no known beginning or end, no "sacred and primordial site." I declare war on all icons and finalities, on all histories that would chain me with my own falseness, my own pitiful fears. I know only moments, and lifetimes that are as moments, and forms that appear with infinite strength, then "melt into air." I am an architect, a constructor of worlds, a sensualist who worships the flesh, the melody, a silhouette against the darkening sky. I cannot know your name. Nor you can know mine. Tomorrow, we begin together the construction of a city.

Sounds like a futurist manifesto to me. And the work has that feeling too. But then I don't pretend to understand Lebbeus Woods's work.

01 June
Norman Foster

Great Court of the British Museum, London, England, renovation 2000

The account of Baron Foster of Thames Bank, of Reddish in the County of Greater Manchester, is truly rags to riches. On the way to being the iconic architect he now is, he was a clerk at Manchester Town Hall (at age sixteen), contract manager at a local architect's office, ice cream salesman, crumpet maker on the night shift, bouncer, and probably a hundred other jobs.

But really, it was a fellowship to Yale, then led by Paul Rudolph, and a year traveling America with his fellow Eli Richard Rogers that transformed him in his early, pre-fame, life. And it was probably his lifelong addiction to sports and athleticism that saved his life at the other end of his career, when cancer, a heart attack, and other potentially fatal health issues were vanquished by his dogged cycling, skiing, and every other form of competitive racing. He essentially competed his way out of a death sentence.

His friendship with Buckminster Fuller undoubtedly and famously influenced his work and environmental ethics. Foster addresses, as Bucky did, technology in the most heroic and monumental way imaginable. He doesn't shrink his way into conservation of matter and energy; his declarations are bold, occasionally bombastic, never small scaled or modest. This makes sense in the totality of his life; he's highly competitive, highly disciplined, aggressive, and a bit of a tough guy.

He may have just missed meeting Alan Fletcher at Yale (they were a couple of years apart), but they met later, when Fletcher designed signage for Stansted Airport and other Foster projects. To me, they are essentially the same person (aside from their different experiences with cancer and a certain sartorial flair only one of them possesses). They are tough guys with sensitive sides, wickedly smart dudes with working-class backgrounds, designers whose turning point was a Yale fellowship.

Foster worked with Steve Jobs (another colleague with a different cancer outcome) on Jobs's last gesture: the Apple Park headquarters in the form of a giant ring. As someone pointed out, the Spaceship Apple defines an elemental aspect of the brand; you are either in the circle or you are not. Norman Foster's version of that paradigm is simple, and simply gargantuan.

02 June
Carlo Scarpa

Olivetti showroom, Piazza San Marco, Venice, Italy, 1957–1958

There are some architects whose work can only be fully understood (at least by me) when seen in person. All architecture is a surprise; it's either larger or smaller, more finely detailed or less finely detailed, or somehow better or worse than you imagined. But visiting is impractical in most cases, and we tend to see, learn, judge, and internalize most buildings from images. Some buildings are clearly built for photographs, but Carlo Scarpa's work isn't. It may look good in photos, but it is immeasurably better in person.

Scarpa is a son of Venice, born, educated, and working close to the Invisible City most of his life. Never taking the official exam for architecture (which gives you some idea of his contrarian personality), he was known as "Professor." He spent fifteen years as head of design at Venini glass and produced a simply astonishing range of the most beautiful glasswork I have ever seen (hundreds of pieces filled a show at the Met). That was before he began to really build.

His buildings have enchanted architects for decades, and every important architect has something to say about Scarpa. Rafael Moneo said, "I look at any work by Scarpa as if it were a work of a painter." Arata Isozaki asked, "Did

he see a wilderness or ruins behind the gold?" Louis Kahn wrote a poem to him, ending with, "The detail is the adoration of Nature." Egle Trincanato (whose birthday is the day after Scarpa's) said, "Above all, he was exceptionally skillful in knowing how to combine a base material with a precious one," which seems inscrutably specific. Kurt Forster called him "the Architect of the Incalculable." I would add that his 1958 Olivetti Showroom on Piazza San Marco in Venice is certainly the most enchanting typewriter showroom ever! And Scarpa said, "If the architecture is any good, a person who looks and listens will feel its good effects without noticing."

Carlo Scarpa designed an uncommon number of tombs and other works around death. He died in Japan (his other love), falling down a set of concrete stairs, and was buried standing up, wrapped in linen, in a cemetery of his own design, like a medieval knight. Incalculable, and perhaps inscrutable.

03 June
Egle Renata Trincanato

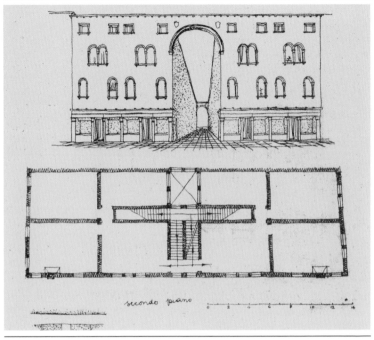

Residential building in Campo San Marina, Venice, Italy from *Venezia Minore,* 1948

While it is hard not to love all of Venice, I most love the Venice of Egle Renata Trincanato.

Her exquisite drawings plumb the relationship between the grand and the modest, between houses and housing in Venice, while exploring the extraordinary rationality behind the seemingly picturesque city. The hidden dimension revealed in her 1948 book, *Venezia minore* (a study of the unstudied buildings of Venice), is as ruthlessly modern and efficient as that of any developer today but with a Palladian sense of proportion, scale, and elegance.

Celebrating the commonplace can be a tiresome, or quaint, exercise, but Trincanato reveals the underlying structural relationships between the palazzo, the casa, and the *casetta*, effectively making every Venetian building a study in grandeur. This may be at odds with our love of the worn, layered, sagging relic that Venice is today. Her book confronts the precision and intentionality, the complexity and the logic of Venetian living.

The revelation changes how you look at Venice. Like an actor playing a drunk but playing it so well you both admire the artifice of the performance and their

intelligence at the same time, Venice is a genius in mismatched socks.

This seems to me to be the essential contradiction of Venice: a place of romance that is as cool and calculating as surgery, picturesque facades masking an unmatched sophistication of plan and circulation, and a city that appears to be a relaxed tourist-driven playground that is in fact a well-tuned machine struggling against incredible contextual odds to function with a sense of normalcy. The illusion of ease and simplicity in the face of difficulty and complexity is an Italian trait, but in Venice it is high art.

Trincanato (and I wish I had met her) was the first female student at the Istituto Universitario di Architettura di Venezia (now the IUAV University of Venice). After graduation, she rose to supervise historical architecture in Venice. She wrote both guides and serious tracts about monuments of Venice as well as *Venezia minore,* her most famous work.

I love Egle Trincanato's Venice because I see it as a Venice stripped of superficial beauty but revealing its deeper beauty. Trincanato describes the hidden intelligence of Venice exercised over centuries.

04 June
Diana Balmori

Diana Balmori in her studio, 2014

Diana Balmori worked within the firm of her husband, Cesar Pelli, until 1990, when she formed her own firm to practice landscape architecture and urban design in an eponymous vehicle. I knew her very slightly, from post-9/11 civic groups, and I didn't know why she separated her professional life from her personal life, but I can guess; it's not easy to attract the work you want when standing in a crowd of other disciplines, especially when those other disciplines are world famous. And I know this truth from personal experience.

It's not unlike her decision to pursue architecture and design, a way of not competing directly with her accomplished parents. Her father was a renowned linguist, and her mother was a musician, composer, and musicologist. Unlike her own son, who is the second Pelli in Pelli Clark Pelli, Balmori drove through the gap in her parents' creativity. They worked in sound, language, and music; she chose the visual arts, architecture, urbanism, and landscape, along with writing books. It was a perfect noncompete clause of a career.

I understand that instinct. My son, looking left and right at his graphic design mother and architect father,

studied classics and later abandoned that pursuit to design clothing. It was an intuitively brilliant move, staking out a territory that is distinct and one's own yet in the same general world (the fashion, not the classics!). Balmori did this while forming her own firm to distinguish herself from her successful husband. It worked better than anyone could have imagined. From the time I met her until the time of her death, I was unaware whose wife and mother she was; she was entirely her own person, celebrated in her own profession for her own talent.

Her work I most like (and really, there is a lot to admire, but much of it is beyond my own taste) may be her least-typical project: the grid of palm trees in the World Financial Center's Winter Garden. It is precisely that kind of decorative use of landscape that she bridled at; her vision was landscape as part of the continuum of designed spaces, buildings, and cities.

It is for that vision that Diana Balmori is remembered, which is precisely what she sought in her move toward a fully independent intellectual life.

05 June
Max Huber

m.a.x. museo, Chiasso, Switzerland, 2005

I first noticed Max Huber when, as part of an unfortunate watch obsession, I bought an Alessi Record watch designed by Achille Castiglioni with graphics by Huber (who knew it took two really good designers to design a watch?). But, really, he was much more than twelve numbers arrayed in a circle.

He bounced back and forth between Switzerland and Milan, working in both places and avoiding the draft and World War II. He seemed to have touched nearly every designer worth meeting in both places, including Castiglioni, Max Bill, Josef Müller-Brockmann, and Ettore Sottsass Jr. His work in the 1950s looks like it was made last week, but that may be our current eye for more naive modernism, when life was a bit less complicated.

The watch Castiglioni designed was done well after Huber's death but was based on a design Huber did with Castiglioni for a clock back in the 1960s. So maybe our taste for Huber's work has just recently matured, so much so that a relatively recent museum in Chiasso, Switzerland, dedicated to graphic design is called the m.a.x. museo as an homage to Huber.

The museum is a very cute little building with a number of au courant tropes.

Channel glass, an extended cantilever, and a glowing floating box are allegedly the architects' interpretation of Huber's design style. The glowing box is purportedly for displaying current exhibitions at night for all to see. Of course, this is all bullshit. The building is very nicely done, very Swiss, and very crisp, but has nothing to do with the design of Huber. And the idea that exhibitions would be displayed in full glaring light, even at night, is absurd. The museum has never been pictured as anything but an empty glowing box, so it appears that it figured out rather late that artwork (especially ephemera) needs to be shielded from extremes of illumination.

That is no knock on Max Huber, who is described in most places as an influential graphic designer but was probably more of a minion than a master. His work is very accomplished but "one of the most influential graphic designers of the twentieth century" may be a bit hyperbolic. But the museum devoted to him, as an idea, is fantastic.

06 June
Ivan Chermayeff

Monumental address icon for 9 West 57 Street, New York, New York, 1972

For years I would buy gas only at Mobil stations, and Ivan Chermayeff is probably the reason. The all-white stations are now being invaded by blue (it is really ExxonMobil, one of the worst polluters in the worst industry on Earth), yet I still am attracted to that damned logo. It proves that 1) logos do matter and 2) if you design one really great thing in your life, you are deemed a great (even legendary) designer. I should be happy about part b, because being defined by your worst or last work would be disastrous for people like, well, me.

Ivan's father, Serge, was a Russian-born English architect, and Ivan is a British-born American designer; each left one home for another at a young age. Ivan said he attended twenty-four different schools; my own youth was graced with twenty-four different cars my father regularly bought and sold (not sure if this explains my Mobil-blindness). Serge was a terrific architect, led a bunch of important design schools, and even joined Erich Mendelsohn in some projects. Ivan attended all the right schools and joined Tom Geismar (and, originally, the unfortunately heroin-addicted but brilliant designer Robert Brownjohn) in his own partnership.

Ivan Chermayeff is like the American Alan Fletcher in that his later style was highly personal, hand-drawn, and collage-based graphics, while his earlier work included some amazingly trim and eternal logos. I really love some of his (and Fletcher's) early work and find his (and Fletcher's) later stuff less interesting. Compare Chermayeff's MoMA logo to his New York Public Library logo and you get the idea. Or Fletcher's V&A logo to his later watercolor flowers and you get the idea. It's an interesting dilemma: how to transform a life of solving other people's problems to making up your own to solve; graphic design ≠ art.

I have to admit my feelings about Ivan are colored by the way he and Tom dissolved their firm, took its name, and left its creative engine, Steff Geissbuhler, to carry on the responsibilities without the firm's assets. As I said, legendary for your best work, not your worst.

07 June
Charles Rennie Mackintosh

Drawing of House for an Art Lover, Glasgow, Scotland, designed 1901, built 1996

Considering architects who channeled a burgeoning modern movement around 1900, you might expect someone like Josef Hoffmann in Vienna (home of Secessionism) to produce a lush, gridded, and slightly floral version of functionalism, and a northerner like the Scotsman Charles Rennie Mackintosh to be much more austere and, well, Scottish. But Hoffmann's work was even more restrained than Mackintosh's, even though sometimes they are easy to conflate and confuse and confound us.

Mackintosh, with his wife, Margaret Macdonald, together (for a brief ten-year window) produced some of the most eccentric and charming architecture, furniture, and decorative arts of the time. Whatever the Scottish word for Gesamtkunstwerk is (not sure. Haggis? Laddie?), Mackintosh and Macdonald created exactly that: a total piece of art from the architecture to the furniture, lighting, decorative flourishes, and, if given the chance, probably the clothes and the conversation!

Maybe that is why so few such thoroughly designed projects exist in America; it is against the grain for clients, who commission and pay for work and rightly consider themselves to be central to the enterprise, to be so completely wrapped in another's design. Frank Lloyd Wright tried, often, to subsume his clients within his work. Mies van der Rohe wanted to, but Dr. Farnsworth declined. Richard Meier may have had that effect on early clients (where, in one case I witnessed, a client wouldn't dare move a stupid Frank Stella print because "Mr. Meier put it there").

Mackintosh's architectural career was so short, really just from 1895 to 1906, that the sheer amount he produced was remarkable. He left the field during a time of economic pressure and eventually moved to the south of France to paint. But that wasn't the end of his building career.

When Mackintosh's reputation and interest revived in the 1980s, some of his unbuilt work attracted interested enthusiasts. They built, in the 1990s, a few of his designs, including the House for an Art Lover in Glasgow and the Artist's Cottage and Gate Lodge in Farr by Inverness.

I love these vague and evocative names as much as I love Charles Rennie Mackintosh's work.

08 June
Bruce Goff

Bavinger House, Norman, Oklahoma, 1950

Today is a dual birthday; Bruce Goff, the disciple, and Frank Lloyd Wright share a birthday. Goff was thirty-seven years Wright's junior but one of the only architects Wright deigned to endorse. Goff's successor is Bart Prince, still at it and celebrating his birthday in a couple of weeks. All of these June babies produced some exceedingly weird (and some extraordinarily great) work, and, yes, that includes Wright.

The whole idea of organic architecture (or organic furniture) is, to me, an oxymoron. Unless we are talking about birds' nests or spiderwebs or beaver dams, no architecture is organic, except insofar as it contains some organic materials (wood, cotton, wool, cork, people) or materials from the earth (concrete, stone, metal ores, glass, porcelain, clay). But all that is not what organic means in this context.

Organic is a formal concept, implying that some shapes, like curves or nonorthogonal geometries, are more natural than others. But all the curves in Le Corbusier's work (and there are lots) don't make it, in the eyes of some, organic. The shapely Philips Pavilion and Ronchamp are still highly rationalized shapes, not bona fide organic, but somehow the white geometry of the Guggenheim Museum is organic?

And the Guggenheim in Bilbao, is that organic? It's certainly curvy enough and made from mined materials (well, titanium), but I doubt it qualifies.

The definition is a bit tribal, like politics today. Organic is a way of creating clubs or cliques. Goff, who used Quonset hut ribs to make one project, somehow could claim to be an "organic architect" while Pierre Chareau, who built a studio for Robert Motherwell out of a whole Quonset hut, is most definitely not. It's a distinction without a difference, or at least without an interesting difference.

What did make a difference to Goff's career (when he chaired the University of Oklahoma School of Architecture) was being gay. He was forced to resign for "endangering the morals" (sigh). This seems unsurprising in 1955, but the university has gone to rather extraordinary lengths to establish that Goff left on his own volition after being encouraged to stay. That might be true (perhaps he was asked to stay but was so uncomfortable with the accusations that he left), but he does seem to be owed a posthumous apology.

09 June
Les Paul

Les Paul, circa 1947

There's that amazing opening scene in *It Might Get Loud* where Jack White, on some Tennessee country porch, takes a plank of wood, a hammer and nails, a Coke bottle, some wire, and some electrical stuff and makes an electric guitar, in real time, then plays it. What I didn't realize was that it was an homage to Les Paul, who made the first (many believe) solid-body electric guitar with a hefty block of wood he later called "the log." The log changed music forever, for good.

Lester William Polsfuss performed as Rhubarb Red and Red Hot Red when playing country music and as Les Paul when playing jazz. He was nearly electrocuted, almost lost his right arm (which, though broken, was set at a permanent angle just under ninety degrees to allow him to continue to play), broke his eardrum, and had a quintuple bypass but still managed to squeak out ninety-four years of playing and inventing.

Before the log, Les made "the rail," which was literally a section of steel railroad track with strings on top. He was trying to do two things: eliminate the feedback caused by hollow-body guitar resonance and prove that sustaining a note was not dependent on the sound box of the conventional guitar. The heavy steel rail eliminated feedback and could sustain a note seemingly forever. Paul said, "You could go out and eat and come back and the note would still be sounding."

Paul's music teacher said that "Lester will never learn music" just before Lester started playing piano, guitar, and harmonica, inventing along the way. He devised a hands-free harmonica holder that allowed him to flip it over to play in a different key. His solid-body electric guitar inventions are legendary. He invented and refined two-track (first on aluminum disks, then on tape), four-track, and eventually eight-track recording (made to his specs by Ampex). He invented echo, slap-back, reverb, and other guitar effects. The custom-built recording studio he made (at the suggestion of Bing Crosby) was lined with custom-made sound deflectors (which he individually shaped) to give the space a neutral ambiance.

Plus, Les Paul was a wizard at playing guitar. Not bad for a kid who would never learn music!

10 June
Jack Masey

Khrushchev and Nixon (Jack Masey at rear), kitchen debates in Moscow, USSR, 1959

Jack Masey was responsible for the US presence in international expos (world's fairs, in our native parlance) and other cross-national pavilions and exhibitions, hiring the best designers of the day in the high renaissance of US soft diplomacy.

Jack was the young man who escorted Nikita Khrushchev around the US exhibition in Moscow, best known for the kitchen debates. The debates were really a discussion between the world's most stilted man, Richard Nixon, and the world's least, Nikita Khrushchev. Khrushchev refuted the idea that everything shown in the typical US kitchen was truly available and affordable, probably claiming that the Soviets had rocket-powered dishwashers or something like that. It was 1959, and the Cold War was very chilly indeed.

I met Jack in July 2014 when the Storefront for Art and Architecture screened *Air Up!*, a film from the 1970 Expo in Osaka about the inflatable USA Pavilion he oversaw. It was an amazing film, and after the screening, I introduced myself as the guy who was designing the 2015 USA Pavilion at Expo 2015 in Milan. He simply couldn't say enough nice things about our project, then about to start construction

(so naturally I immediately liked and respected him). That was, of course, after the thoroughly underwhelming Expo 2010 Shanghai USA Pavilion (anything was better than that), so it was a very low bar.

Masey hired Buckminster Fuller with Chermayeff & Geismar to make the big geodesic dome at Expo 67 in Montreal, and later he hired George Nelson, Charles and Ray Eames, Davis, Brody & Associates, and myriad other designers (all without competitive bidding) for other expos and pavilions to build an image of America in foreign lands. Heady work, this soft diplomacy.

But my favorite part of the Jack Masey story is his part in the Ghost Army, a deception used in World War II to simulate masses of armed forces where there were none. Along with other artists like Bill Blass, Ellsworth Kelly, and Art Kane, Masey created inflatable tanks, canvas aircraft, the sounds of armies on the move, rubber Jeeps, fake airfields, barracks, and traces of nonexistent battalions. The Ghost Army seems insane today, when it would never work in such a crude analog way, but it did work, and it set Masey on a career of creating images for things that, on occasion, were not really there!

11 June
Julia Margaret Cameron

The Mountain Nymph, Sweet Liberty, photo of Miss Keene, 1866

To take a photo in 1863, the year Julia Margaret Cameron was gifted her first camera, was about as complicated as making a meal from scratch today, if we made our meals in complete darkness. She had to mix dangerous chemicals into emulsions, coat them on a glass plate (in the dark), move the plate to the camera (in a light-tight sleeve), set up to take the photo, expose the plate for anywhere from a few seconds to a few minutes (Cameron's subjects have written how impossible that was!), then go back to the dark to develop the plate, wash and dry it and coat it with varnish, and at that point she had one negative. Making a print was another process altogether!

Cameron's male contemporaries mocked her out-of-focus, smudged, and scratched images; they were the technocrats of the day and thought technical quality was paramount. But Cameron wanted, as she put it, "to ennoble Photography and to secure for it the character and uses of High Art...sacrificing nothing of the Truth by all possible devotion to poetry and beauty." Hardly a technical treatise, but among the first to treat photography with the same seriousness and artistic purpose as painting.

Cameron took exclusively portraits of both important neighbors on the Isle of Wight (like Charles Darwin) and others (like her housemaids) in allegorical poses. In a short career of about twelve years, she made nearly one thousand images and changed the face of photography.

Looking through a family album like my own, I recognize that the images from one hundred years ago are more vivid, more revealing, and better preserved than nearly anything we have today in our own photo streams. Artfully posed portraits are now a conceit rather than the way every family (of even modest means) documented their lives. We have massively outphotographed our ancestors, producing in a month an output exceeding Cameron's life's work.

But the images she made, like many of the time, have the ability to connect across the centuries to reveal something deeply real and modern about her subjects (her "victims," as her friend Alfred, Lord Tennyson called them). They feel startlingly alive, which was precisely what Julia Margaret Cameron wanted and subsequently achieved.

12 June
Carin Goldberg

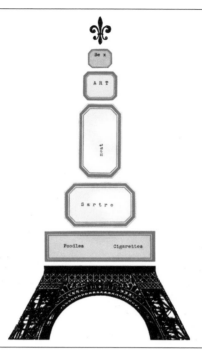

Paris Poster, for Alliance Graphique Internationale Congress, 2017

When I met my wife, Carin Goldberg, in 1980, she was working at CBS Records designing those 12-by-12-inch/30.5-by-30.5-centimeter posters we call album covers. It was the high renaissance of the record jacket, with huge budgets and famous photographers and artists creating the packaging for disks of vinyl. She let me help her spend her thirty-album-per-month allowance and had lots of celebrity stories ("David Bowie stopped by today" or "I'm doing a cover for a new singer named, get this, Madonna!") that made the job glamorous beyond measure. I got to watch Richard Avedon shoot Dexter Gordon and chatted with Avedon while we waited for hours, then watched Gordon play while being photographed. That was some thrilling shit.

But it's only a fraction of what Carin did; she moved on to book covers, magazines, drawing, collage, video, embroidery, photography, advertising, identity, posters, and virtually every aspect of graphic design. I should add her four-decade-long career in teaching, helping lead graphic design organizations (like AIGA and AGI), and her books (plus her role as mother, wife, and co-creator of multiple homes). After a Rome Prize gave her the time and space (and amazing context) to create her own work again, she jettisoned commercial work for the artwork she began at Cooper Union.

Then there's the work itself, which is simply amazing in its thoughtfulness, its depth and range. Carin worked during the transition from almost purely analog to almost purely digital processes. She worked in a darkroom, painted type with gouache, drew and cut out images at one end of her career, and did it all digitally at the other. Through all of this, Carin has had a keen eye for image, for type, for language, for history, and for charting a personal path through it all.

But the thing that distinguishes Carin is just how much better she made life for nearly everyone she touched; students adore her (they kept in touch with her for decades, while becoming among the most famous young designers of the day); clients feel lucky to have worked with her (Kurt Vonnegut once spent an evening thanking her for making him a lot of money!); and her friends and family are the luckiest of all.

The work speaks for itself, but it's the person who has found a place in all our hearts.

13 June
Emilio Ambasz

Acros Building, Fukuoka, Japan, 1990

Emilio Ambasz is such an enigma that I have to admit I wasn't sure he was still alive. He is, though he refuses to say where he lives, except "in his shoes." The one time I saw him speak he had suffered a stroke that partially paralyzed one side of his face, and he spoke as two characters: Emilio would say one thing and Ambasz would posit a response. It was an act of courage and chutzpah (somewhat inseparable in him).

This split psyche fairly describes his career, as it diverges between marketing himself and promoting others. In the same breath that he proclaims finishing Princeton (undergraduate and graduate school) in two years, he then lets us know that at age twenty-five he became MoMA's curator for architecture and design, where he produced a handful of seminal shows on such things as the work of Luis Barragán, Italian design, and the taxi.

If he had only produced *Italy: The New Domestic Landscape* (in 1972), I would be forever indebted. It was the most exciting and influential show I saw at the precise moment I was giving up studying biology and starting a run at architecture. It is still a touch point for what we think of as postwar Italian design; every important designer was

introduced to the US audience at that show, and, if someone missed the exhibit, the excellent book that followed (with an "idea" cover, containing loose cutouts of some of the iconic pieces in the show) perseveres.

Ambasz's claim to be the father of green design (Messiah is another claim) is another bifurcated gesture; yes, he included plants and landscape in his work, but so did the Ford Foundation of 1967 by Saarinen/Roche-Dinkeloo (Kevin Roche's birthday is tomorrow). It's a clever Emilio versus Ambasz proposition.

To remain in the public eye (a cynical observer might say), he donated ten million dollars to MoMA from the Legacy Emilio Ambasz Foundation (LEAF, get it?) for the Emilio Ambasz Institute for the Joint Study of the Built and the Natural Environment. Remarkable, but read the fine print and it's clear that MoMA will put on an exhibit cementing Ambasz as the Messiah of Green.

Still, ten million dollars is a remarkable gift from any architect! Bravo, Emilio and Ambasz, you've both done it again!

14 June
Kevin Roche

Kevin Roche with model of the Ford Foundation Building, 1960s

I'm not a fan of Kevin Roche's work, except two absolutely great projects done early in his career: the Ford Foundation Building and the Oakland Museum of California. I'd like to think that the early work was still in the shadow of Eero Saarinen, whose office Roche continued under his own name.

The genesis of the Ford Foundation is a bit fuzzy, as it was one of the buildings begun by Saarinen (with Roche the lead) but completed by the successor firm Roche-Dinkeloo (Roche apparently couldn't avoid colleagues with somewhat odd names).

Wherever it started, Roche finished it, and its prescience and timelessness are manifest. The Dan Kiley garden is a pure joy, and the social engineering (forgoing perimeter offices for execs and dark interiors for staff) still works. Even today (after a thorough restoration in its fiftieth year), walking in is a breathtaking experience. It fulfills the unrequited promise of John Portman's monstrous atria with a truly magical garden.

No less than Ada Louise Huxtable called it "an object lesson in the possibilities opened by fresh thought and a creative approach to the city's most important commercial building problem: the provision of ample and impressive headquarters for large corporations or equivalent organizations, in structures that have some civic conscience as well."

Roche's Oakland Museum is similarly unique and unequaled; museum as terraced garden, becoming both a park and a museum, eschewing the monumental tendencies of architecture in the 1960s (and Roche's architecture later).

The later work, as sometimes happens, veers from rethinking social issues toward making purely formal architectural games of little import. Vincent Scully opined that Roche's later works "all share a kind of paramilitary dandyism that seems especially disturbing at the present moment in American history."

This was ironic (and harsh) criticism about someone who early on managed to redefine, in the most nonmonumental way, the office and the museum. But, luckily, we still have Ford and Oakland to remember Kevin Roche by. Roche, in a transition that might not happen today, befriended Scully and even delivered a eulogy at his funeral, proving that both his and Scully's charisma could transcend their intellect.

15 June
Saul Steinberg

Saul Steinberg's Hand, 1978

I used to have a buddy, let's call him Buddy, who lived in East Hampton and was a carpenter, builder, motorcycle racer, etc., whose friend Saul Steinberg also lived in East Hampton. Buddy made little objects of wood for his friend: drawing tables, "books" that were two pieces of solid wood with hinges, briefcases (larger blocks of wood with hinges), and anything else Steinberg needed for his art. He also occasionally fixed his house.

These transactions were not like, say, Donald Judd handing a fabricator an idea to build (which was part of the idea of the art); it was an artist getting an assist from a pro. Steinberg told Buddy, "Don't make these things too well! It needs to look like I could have made it!" Steinberg took these constructions as raw material for his three-dimensional works. He painted them, carved them, and assembled them into larger works. Buddy wasn't making the painting; Buddy was stretching the canvas.

Calling Saul Steinberg a cartoonist (as he is usually considered) is like calling Barack Obama an author: a true but wholly inadequate description. Steinberg was an artist with a great sense of play and sense of humor. Like Bruno Munari's, his work ranged from actual cartoons to drawings to painted

constructions to just about anything that caught his fancy. His spirit was more Dada than Illustrator; his work was more play than labor. He was an artist with a truly riotous sense of humor, and humor doesn't downgrade art to commercial art (it just might elevate it!).

Steinberg left his home in Romania for Milan and studied architecture at the Polytechnic University. He graduated just as Jews in Italy were being rounded up (there is now a sobering plaque in the main rail station where they were loaded onto trains to deport), and he left for the US with a small, forged alteration to his papers. That talent (forgery) became a fascination with rubber stamps, documents, identity (his thumbprint portrait is genius).

"My purpose is to transform an idea that I had into a drawing. I am not so preoccupied by the outside world. I'm preoccupied with my own inside world," reveals how much his art is about his art. It's a meta-life, a self-created reality, a discussion of art via art.

That makes him, in my view, truly an artist. And a very funny cartoonist.

16 June
Lilly Reich

Villa Tugendhat, Brno, Czech Republic, designed with Mies van der Rohe, 1930

Charles Eames had Ray, Alvar Aalto had Aino, Le Corbusier had Charlotte Perriand, Robert Venturi had Denise Scott Brown, Josef Albers had Anni, and Mies van der Rohe had Lilly Reich as his unheralded collaborator. When she stayed behind in Berlin, while Mies emigrated to the US in 1938, she became an unwitting collaborator of a different sort.

What if (and I think you know the answer) some of the most famous designs in the history of modernism were actually designed by (gasp!) women whose contributions were erased from the icons' legacy? Shocking, I know. Lilly Reich worked with (intimate and professional partner) Mies for the thirteen years that included his most important early buildings and furniture, like the Barcelona Pavilion and the Barcelona chair (designed for the pavilion), the Tugendhat House, and the Brno chair, as well as a number of exhibitions.

Mies did not design any successful furniture after the thirteen years that he worked with Reich, making it pretty clear who designed the early furniture. He asked her to teach at the Bauhaus (interiors and furniture, not the male-dominated architecture or painting), and they were constant companions, but somehow that didn't translate into credit for their collaborative work.

Credit can be a tricky issue; there are so many criteria for judging contributions: competitions and prizes (like the Pritzker) often recognize only a single name, but the case of Mies and Reich is hardly like that of Venturi and Scott Brown. Reich was erased because Mies was ambitious and Reich's name was not seen as an asset to his reputation, though certainly her design work was an asset.

This was partially remedied with the 1996 MoMA exhibition *Lilly Reich: Designer and Architect* curated by Matilda McQuaid. But no exhibit, nor book, nor belated Pritzker, nor multivolume catalogue raisonné can undo decades of neglect and suppression of a reputation.

It's not unusual that collaboration can swallow up the independent cred of one of the parties, but it's unfortunate that Lilly wasn't able to regain her own outstanding recognition after they parted. Properly crediting Lilly Reich for her furniture would be a start to the rehabilitation of an enormous talent whose work is still part of the canon of early modernism.

Eames lounge chair and ottoman, 1956

I'm sitting in a vintage Eames fiberglass shell chair as I write this (not one of those new-fangled polypropylene ones), looking outside at a cluster of wire-frame Eames chairs; I have an Eames lounge chair in my bedroom (a gift from Herman Miller) and sit at an Eames aluminum group chair at my desk. An Eames surfboard table and little side table are in the living room, a vintage Hang-It-All graces my home, an Eames splint fills the coffin corner (the niches that allowed a casket to be carried out of the upstairs bedroom past the curved landing; I plan to use this one my last time out) in my brownstone, and I have liberally cribbed from the Eames House (and other Case Study Houses) my whole career. So, we're tight.

On one visit to the Eames House, I was walking across the living room, staring up at something interesting, and kicked over the famous wooden bird sculpture (luckily I didn't break it!), forever ending my invitations to privately tour the house (sigh). It really is a perpetually remarkable home, made of standard industrial parts assembled into a museum for living; the house displays its contents even better than it displays itself. It was redesigned using the same components, before actually being assembled. Rather than the Bridge House they originally planned,

they nestled a two-part linear affair against the hill. Good move.

On a less-destructive trip to the Eames House, I was lucky enough to observe Lucia Eames (Charles's daughter by his first wife), Pierre Koenig, Julius Shulman, and Eames Demetrios (grandson) at the small round table in the kitchen chatting about old times, surrounded by all the stuff Ray collected and displayed. For just a moment, the house seemed alive again as a home, not a shrine.

The finest, most enduring Eames creation is *Powers of Ten*. The 1977 film (after the 1968 sketch version) is, at once, a gorgeous graphic display of information, a heuristic device, and an illustration of math, physics, biology, and astronomy as parts of a simple scientific exercise. It's mesmerizing. As were they.

Charles Eames, and his design-partnership equal Ray, managed a balance of play and engineering, of fun and learning, and of humor and seriousness. Despite the enormous investment in new technology to fabricate their molded plywood furniture, their designs never became stilted or rigid (in either sense) but were always in service of the delight an object can induce. A heavy lift for two heavyweights in the American design canon.

18 June
Warren Platner

Platner side chairs, designed 1966 (with Saarinen & Knoll furniture)

Warren Platner is hard to understand. He was trained as an architect and worked for Raymond Loewy, I. M. Pei, and Eero Saarinen and won a Rome Prize in 1955 (and weirdly, if you Google him, a photo of Robert Venturi is likely to appear). He hired only architects for his own firm, claiming (in a rather Bauhausian declaration) that architects could design anything from buildings to interiors to furniture to lighting to, well, anything.

He's known for a suite of furniture that is so specifically of its time that it is virtually the only thing he is known for. That and Windows on the World, the restaurant that was destroyed on 9/11. Windows' lobby was slathered in mirrors at a time when white walls were in vogue; Platner's American Restaurant in St. Louis featured flowing wooden elements (it's hard to know what to call them) at a time when creating insane pastiche (like that at Tavern on the Green) was cool. He was defiantly out of step with the times ("skating on the edge of taste," as Alexandra Lange wrote of him).

He operated in the seams between eras, between styles, and between fads. He graduated from college as the US was about to enter World War II (educated prewar, practiced in a changed postwar world). He joined Eero Saarinen's office just before Saarinen died (working in the aftermath of Saarinen and the formative years of the successor firm, Roche-Dinkeloo). His own office, opened in 1965, worked on New York City projects while operating out of Connecticut. He used miles of brass at a time when brushed chrome and stainless steel were in vogue. And his furniture, designed in 1966, was produced the same year as Richard Schultz's iconic outdoor furniture (by the same company, Knoll).

The furniture, like Schultz's, is still made and still popular, but I haven't ever used it, and I couldn't say exactly why. It's clever, combining structure and seating in a swoop of skinny rods, which every description (now including this one) notes that it took up to one thousand welds to hold together. Like Platner himself, his furniture sits between the clarity of Charles and Ray Eames (or Schultz) and the sensuality of, say, Carlo Mollino, and maybe that's what is hard to understand. For me, anyway.

19 June
Charles Gwathmey

Whig Hall, Princeton University, Princeton, New Jersey, built 1895, renovated 1971

Charles Gwathmey became instantly famous at twenty-eight when he completed what is still his best work, the studio and home for his parents in Amagansett, New York. It was a perfect expression of where architecture, especially the variety that would soon crowd the Hamptons, was going. He never managed to achieve that level of concise perfection again, but then it may have been the smallest project of his career.

His houses became behemoths, and the clarity and proportions radically changed in these homes for the rich and famous. The tiny footprint of his parents' house and studio (and even though the studio was created after the house, kudos to Charlie for not attaching it to the house but turning a single object into a pair of objects in conversation) kept the proportions vertical and made the cube a primary reading. Large houses are inherently more horizontal, and Gwathmey never developed a rationale for managing those shapes.

He became known, some would say infamous, for his building annexes to great works of architecture: the Guggenheim Museum in New York and the Paul Rudolph–designed Yale Art and Architecture Building. Some said he

had no ego about these things, others thought him enormously charismatic with a substantial ego. Whatever it was, those works are neither sufficiently deferential nor sufficiently independent to make much sense.

In a third, earlier case, at Whig Hall at Princeton University, Gwathmey (still in his thirties) fully removed an entire side wall to reveal the innards of a classical revival building that had experienced a fire. It's a bold move that almost overcomes the somewhat clunky, but functional, plan. There were two matching classical temples, Whig and Clio, sitting opposite each other at the end of a quad. So even defiling one (it was not a popular redesign) still left the other intact!

Gwathmey was stylish and charismatic, and was even considered for TV by some network, but his screen test revealed a voice that was not ready for prime time. Gwathmey had much the same problem making the transition with his buildings (not the voice, in this case); he couldn't create large buildings with any of the clarity, power, or precision of his tiny ones. Too bad a screen test couldn't catch that issue earlier than some of his late buildings.

20 June
Kurt Schwitters

Merzdrawing 85 Zig Zag Red, 1920

Learning that Kurt Hermann Eduard Karl Julius Schwitters (pick a name, any name...) was rejected from membership in the Berlin Dada movement is like finding that Antifa has rented space in a Midtown office building; who knew that the most anarchistic movement could have an application process?! He eventually joined the Zurich Dada movement (their admissions committee obviously had lower standards or a beef with the Berlin branch office). This may all be apocryphal, but it's still an accurate portrait of just how deadly serious artists were about their affiliation in those early modern days in Europe.

Schwitters's bona fides include categorizing every single work of art he produced for ten years, every interior he decorated, and everything he wrote as "Merz" (or Merzbau, etc.) after an early collage that included a scrap of paper with the fragment "merz" on it (from the German word *commerz* in an ad). *That* is commitment.

Robert Rauschenberg said in 1959, after a Schwitters exhibition at the Janis Gallery in New York, that he thought that Schwitters "made it all just for me." For less esteemed artists, Schwitters's permission to make abstract collage has proved unfortunate. Anyone with scraps of ephemera and a decent glue can make what they all think are entirely original works.

Schwitters knew and worked with an assortment of famous Dada, de Stijl, and cubist artists, and because they were all making collages at the same time with some of the same raw material, their work is occasionally indistinguishable (see Picasso and Braque, for example).

The confusion among contemporaries has not only misidentified some work as Schwitters's but also has created an industry of Schwitters forgeries. His catalogue raisonné is paralleled by one of forgeries (catalogue faux?), one of which, *Bluebird*, appeared on the cover of a Tate exhibition catalog until it was identified as a fake.

Schwitters was one of the artists driven from Berlin by the rise of the Nazis and his inclusion in the infamous *Degenerate Art* exhibition. The diaspora was a boon to Paris, London, and New York but stripped Germany of some of its finest minds, even those rejected for membership in the local Dada chapter.

21 June
Pier Luigi Nervi

Staircase, Municipal Stadium, Florence, Italy, 1932

If you see an enormous concrete building that appears to be lacy, light, weightless, and elegant, it is probably by Pier Luigi Nervi. He didn't invent thin-shell concrete structures, but he did make them sing.

Just compare the Port Authority Bus Terminal in New York (any version you choose) to Nervi's 1963 George Washington Bridge Bus Station atop the Manhattan landing. Every version of the Midtown terminal I remember was a hellscape of the darkest and scariest kind. By contrast, the George Washington Bridge version (though called a "brutal assault on the senses" by some local critics) has a fluttering butterfly roof that makes this little oddity the best bus station ever.

Ada Louise Huxtable waxed poetic about the bus station when it was built and fifty years later, when she called it the equal to Santiago Calatrava's four-billion-dollar mall, the Oculus at the World Trade Center. I favor Nervi, who turned his engineering into art, over Calatrava, who turns his art into engineering. Nervi, who lived through two world wars (serving in the first) had no interest in the purely decorative; his sense of economy aggrandized the commonplace with efficiently derived and meaningful form. If only Calatrava embraced the same ethics.

Much of Nervi's work is in Italy, usually spanning huge spaces with thin concrete shells he says he learned to improve with ribs after studying Roman and medieval architecture. Like all the best structural engineers, he leaned on intuition as much as math. Just that small bit of intuition transformed what might be workaday structures into genuine works of genius.

Concrete is the only entirely plastic structural material (except, perhaps, plastic); it can take any form, and Nervi carved away all that was unnecessary or concealed the forces within the spans. Steel is additive (pieces shaped and connected), while concrete is practically subtractive (formwork describes the negative, and design is a process of removing all that is deadweight). Nervi found, within his forms, a trim yet expressive lattice of lines of force.

Pier Luigi Nervi essentially illustrated physics. He found the beauty of math, which is why his buildings sing.

22 June
Gordon Matta-Clark

Girouard, Goodden, and Matta-Clark at site of Food, New York, New York, 1971

If you ever ate in the legendary FOOD restaurant in SoHo (I can still picture the giant wedge of lemon poppyseed cake!), then you ate inside a Gordon Matta-Clark work. He started FOOD with artists Carol Goodden and Tina Girouard and staffed it with artists, making it the most authentically local, delicious, and inexpensive restaurant (along with the old standard Fanelli) in SoHo.

FOOD is gone, and sadly so is Matta-Clark, but his art persists in part due to his films, photos, and excised parts of his subtractive work. Matta-Clark made his art by cutting, splitting, chopping, and removing parts of (mostly decrepit, unused) buildings, occasionally (usually) without any formal permission. His work is supremely architectural (he called it anarchitecture), based in his schooling, ten years before mine, at Cornell University's architecture college. The architecture and art schools were intertwined then (as at Cooper Union and other schools), and it is unsurprising that Matta-Clark hopped back and forth across the dotted lines.

I never realized that I had a bit of Matta-Clark work at home, in the form of a Dennis Oppenheim silkscreen from the 1969 *Earth Art* show at Cornell. Matta-Clark helped Oppenheim cut a

slot in the ice on Beebe Lake, near the architecture school, starting his career of removal as interpretation. He went on to slice a New Jersey house in two, opening the split into a narrow V with hydraulic jacks. He cut cones into a pair of Paris houses before their demolition for the Centre Pompidou, and a side wall oculus into a rusting New York City Hudson River pier.

The excised elements became paintings or sculpture even as the source material was demolished. Filming it all, documenting it with photos, and writing about it preserved what was often fugitive art, disappearing as the world moved on.

My favorite Matta-Clark series was his purchase of tiny, unusable slivers of New York City property, left in the incremental process of land division, at auction for negligible amounts (twenty-five to seventy-five dollars). They were useless as building sites but not as commentary on the nature of the most fundamental, if artificial, aspects of human culture. And it made sense that Matta-Clark would find the empty spaces, the fault lines, between the structured world of property ownership and its urban actuality.

23 June
Cipe Pineles

Cipe Pineles, circa 1950

Every biography (or obituary) that starts with "the first woman to," like virtually every description of Cipe Pineles, seems to bury the lede. She wasn't just a first, she was among the best. She had to be to succeed in a world that today is 60 percent female but in her time was essentially 99 percent male. It's the Ginger Rogers syndrome ("backward and in heels"), and we may have a hard time believing it today, but every woman in design was dancing backward in high heels.

In the end, it's the work that defines these extraordinary designers, and Pineles was defined by her work as she redefined every publication she joined. She's credited with filling magazines with work by artists (Andy Warhol, Ad Reinhardt, Ben Shahn, etc.) and transforming *Glamour*, *Vogue*, *Seventeen*, *Vanity Fair*, and *Mademoiselle* along the way.

Pineles cemented the dual role later designers would adopt: practicing and teaching simultaneously. At Parsons School of Design she shepherded a book on bread, *Parsons Bread Book,* put together by her students, and that love of food (and food illustration) became a legacy project when an unpublished folio of her work on a recipe book was discovered and finally

published by a group of admirers as *Leave Me Alone with the Recipes*. In the design world, it's the equivalent of finding an unpublished manuscript by a famous writer.

Like a lot of designers, she was attracted to designers, especially good ones (and in her case, ones named William), and married (and outlived) two of them: William Golden and Will Burtin. That has always seemed to me to be a fraught coupling; one or the other partner will inevitably be having a better moment in their career than the other. I managed to skirt that head-to-head competition by marrying (and partnering) into graphic design rather than architecture. I think our kid learned the same lesson (he is in fashion, not in the graphic or architectural worlds).

While the work defined Cipe Pineles, it would be (despite the above) remiss not to mention that she was the first woman in Alliance Graphique Internationale (AGI) and the only woman from 1955 to 1968, and she was the first woman in the Art Directors Club (after being nominated for ten consecutive years). But, really, it's the work that defines her.

24 June
Gerrit Rietveld

Red Blue chair, 1917, photographed in Schröder House, Utrecht, Netherlands, 1924

The first time I traveled to Europe, my first stop was Amsterdam, and my first encounter was with Dutch architect Frits Tupker, who had me stay in his architect brother Hans's house in the center of town. It was, of course, filled with Rietveld furniture not just because Hans was Dutch, but because he had befriended Rietveld's longtime cabinetmaker, Gerard van de Groenekan, and was commissioning work as fast as it could be made, which was very slow indeed.

The most impressive piece was the sideboard that van de Groenekan was reluctant to make. But finally, in his eighties (and in the 1980s), he relented. Hans was very persuasive.

Rietveld was unique in being self-taught and designing the first de Stijl house, the Rietveld-Schröder House in Utrecht. It's one of the truly funny constructions of the early modern era, added, as it was, to the end of a row of typical Dutch houses, like a frozen explosion, or like a drawing of a house rather than an actual house, but definitely funny.

What is true of the house, and nearly all of Rietveld's work, is the implication that its geometry extends to, and organizes, the entire world. It's embedded in the x-y-z construction axes; the lines and

planes seem more about suggesting an expanding orientation (with the house, chair, etc. as the origin point) for the mathematical geometry of the universe, more than as any self-contained object. The house manages to be both a sui generis object and one that is open to, and perhaps even absorbs, the world around it. That's a big deal.

The same is true of Rietveld's most famous furniture, built more as a scaffold for users than a womb (chair) to sink into. The scaffold is all about the joinery, and it's no wonder that Rietveld's father was a cabinetmaker, whose shop Gerrit joined at age eleven. And no wonder that van de Groenekan, who is pictured working with Rietveld at age thirteen, became the official producer of nearly all of Rietveld's furniture even long after Rietveld's death.

Gerrit Rietveld never stopped being a cabinetmaker, and even though some of his pieces were eventually mass produced, his work was always a handmade gift to friends and colleagues, even as the pieces attempted to include the entire world.

25 June
Antoni Gaudí

Casa Milà (La Predrera), Barcelona, Spain, 1912

Antoni Gaudí y Cornet isn't like Frank Gehry simply because of some vague similarity of form (or names); they are alike in the seriousness below the surface, the ingenious way they each created a system to assure that their design, no matter how complex, would be sound and even efficient when stripped of its flowing garments. Like Michelangelo's sculpture (always good to invoke Mike A), their architecture works because the unseen skeleton supports the visible flesh.

That may be a particularly flowery way to describe two architects separated by generations and continents, but their seriousness is part of the ethical and technological framework each embraced to make their work real.

Gaudí admired Gothic works but considered them flawed and not fully resolved. The fact that Gothic cathedrals required huge systems of external buttresses proved to him that they were not the end point of that line of inquiry. He sought to develop structures free of the additional baggage caused by the trade-off of soaring interiors and heavily fortified exterior structures. And he did it with string, watch fobs, bird shot, and photographs based on catenary shapes and complex hyperbolic paraboloids.

A catenary is the shape a chain (*catenary* comes from the Latin for chain, *catenaria*) takes if you support the ends and let it hang. It's a perfect shape, one entirely formed by tension (as opposed to the opposite, compression) because that's all the links can do; hang on to each other! The trick is, when a catenary shape is flipped upside down it forms a perfect arch, one with only compression, which eliminates the horizontal thrust that Gothic flying buttresses counteract. These are pure shapes with pure structural integrity, automatically generated by hanging chains, which Gaudí photographed and then turned the image upside down, *et voilà*: a very fucking cool building like La Sagrada Familia Church in Barcelona.

As a process, Gaudí fastened a wooden panel with the floor plan to a ceiling and hung watch fobs from the column locations. He shaped the curves with bags of bird shot, resulting in immense and immensely complex models that were, when flipped upside down, inherently structurally sound.

Not just cool, but genius.

26 June
Milton Glaser

Furniture as I ♥ NY logo, Times Square, New York, New York, 2020

I have to assume that Seymour Chwast, Milton Glaser's equally talented but much shorter former Push Pin Studios partner, gets pretty tired of being asked, "What was it like to be Milton's partner?!"

Somehow, and this is not to take anything away from a gifted designer, Glaser got all the press. Maybe it was his photogenic, articulately verbal nature (his website starts with ten quotable quotes, each a gem, with some appearing below). Maybe it was his three absolutely iconic designs; I ♥ NY, the Bob Dylan poster, and *New York Magazine* (which he cofounded). Maybe it was fifty years of teaching at the School of Visual Arts. Maybe it was that F. Murray Abraham would play him in his biopic. I'm not sure, but like for all iconic figures, his repute is a mix of love and hate, talent and promotion, generosity and ego, living long and prospering. Whatever it was, it applied to Milton.

"You can only work for people you like."
Milton, as he was known (like Ralph in the fashion world), wasn't without missteps, like his rather elegant design for Trump Vodka packaging (how a lifelong New York liberal worked for that scumbag I simply don't understand) or the giant pear outside the Grand Union on East Eighty-Sixth Street that was a

hazard for the blind, but he never doubled down on those errors, just admitted his mistakes and moved on.

"Tell the truth."
He was honest about the sources of his cribbing, from the Marcel Duchamp self-portrait for his Bob Dylan poster to Robert Indiana's *Love* sculpture for his I ♥ NY logo, something designers are loathe to do.

"Less is not necessarily more."
Milton was a maximalist in a minimalist world, even after he spent time studying in Bologna with Giorgio Morandi (a factoid that I find astounding and highly enviable). He was an illustrator as least as much as a graphic designer.

"Doubt is better than certainty."
If you know the name of one architect, it is likely Frank Lloyd Wright, and if you know just one graphic designer, it is Milton Glaser. That doesn't mean you have to love all their work.

"Logic is not as powerful as intuition."
In a final act of design, Milton died on his birthday at 91.

27 June
Paul Colin

Josephine Baker, Paris, France, circa 1920

Paul Colin produced more than one thousand posters, even opening a school for poster artists, and was responsible for evolving poster art into a modern idiom. His work on most subjects is charming, but for his most famous subject, Josephine Baker, the work is a bit hard to look at these days.

He helped make Baker and her revue famous but couldn't seem to help himself from promoting some ugly caricatures along the way. Baker's fame derived from her remarkable talent, a leering male gaze, and the use of black talent in the 1920s as a kind of token of sophistication. Colin created the graphic imagery that supported this view.

Baker, who started her Paris career at nineteen, was much more effective, brilliant, worldly, and politically savvy than her image, but it is hard to compete with the images created by Colin. It's difficult to reconcile, especially as Colin and Baker were lovers and remained lifelong friends. One could even say that if not for Colin and his advertising, it's possible that Baker may not have succeeded as quickly as she did.

Unlike Colin's caricatured imagery of her, Baker was a revolutionary. She refused to work in segregated clubs or venues (and, because she was so in demand, changed the policies of famous locales). She was a resistance figure in World War II, working for the French equivalent of MI5, and received the Croix de Guerre and the Rosette de la Résistance. She was made a chevalier of the Legion of Honour by General Charles de Gaulle. She was even asked by Coretta Scott King to assume Martin Luther King's place as the leader of the Civil Rights movement after his assassination, but she declined out of worry for her twelve adopted children (who were of every race, religion, and nationality).

That's the modern dilemma: how to treat the complex history of art done by well-meaning artists that furthered an intolerant society's racist (or misogynist or homophobic or anti-Semitic or...) views.

There is plenty of other work by Paul Colin to like, just as we can skirt around Le Corbusier's virulent anti-Semitism or Mies van der Rohe's unsuccessful flirtation with the Nazi regime or the ancient Romans' enslavement of entire cultures. We can't avert our gaze from it all, but at least we now cringe at what were once routine expressions of hate.

28 June
Peter Paul Rubens

Palazzo del Augustino Palavicino in Strada Nuova, Genoa, Italy, drawn 1622

Peter Paul Rubens was a very successful artist with an enormous workshop (of unpaid interns), producing paintings that were either 1) painted by him, let's call them full Rubens, or 2) sometimes half Rubens (where he would paint only the hands and faces), or 3) occasionally just the workshop's work from his sketch (no Rubens?). He traveled widely, was sent on diplomatic missions, was knighted by two kings in two countries, and was an artist with access to the upper echelons of society. He was his clients' equal, not their servant, with a library and art collection rivaling theirs.

Rubens spent years in Italy, studying and copying paintings in Venice, then Florence and Rome. After a year in Spain, he returned to Mantua and Genoa as well as Rome, in all an eight-year trip carrying him through his thirties. The voyage transformed his painting, and he produced a pair of folios detailing the newest street in Genoa (the Strada Nuova, of course) lined with individual palazzos only recently built by the city's elite families.

Strada Nuova was the first place where power was concentrated in a single street. It was the beginning of a pattern of urban cohesion that ultimately produced Fifth Avenue and every other city street or piazza densely populated

with the rich and famous. Before the Strada Nuova, cities were balkanized with differing (often warring) families attempting to control areas, much like in Italy, which was then a series of competing city-states. Rubens's folios (pure architectural porn for those of us who get excited about carefully drawn plans and sections) are unique in the history of art, where an accomplished painter documented a new urban assemblage of grand houses planned in close confrontation with each other.

His documentation was part homage to the powerful and part pattern book for those following their lead. He predated the extraordinarily detailed Letarouilly *Edifices de Rome moderne* by more than two hundred years and followed Andrea Palladio's *Four Books on Architecture* by a mere fifty years.

Peter Paul Rubens documented the architectural wealth of Genoa on the Strada Nuova and painted the Rubenesque aristocrats who built them as one of their own.

29 June
John M. Johansen

John Johansen's House #2 (Plastic Tent House), Stanfordville, New York, 1974

Friends live nearby in the nutty little house that John M. Johansen built in our nutty little upstate town; it's a truncated pyramid of translucent fiberglass (he called it the Tent House) adjacent to a small rectangular structure that housed his office. Sadly, I never met him or his wife, Ati (Walter Gropius's daughter), but I do know some who did. Our friend Aki was there for dinner and dared to use the word *modernism* before Ati leaped at her, saying, "There is no modernism or modernistic, there is only *modern*!" That must have been a fun dinner.

I admire the Tent House (having built a few corrugated fiberglass buildings myself), but much of Johansen's work falls into the camp that Klaus Herdeg (former teacher of mine and author) described in *The Decorated Diagram*: that the Gropius-educated generation of architects mostly degraded the intellectual thrust of architecture with functional diagrams turned into buildings (harsh words, but beautifully supported by Herdeg). Johansen was one of those architects, though he was never famous enough to mess things up on a grand scale the way, say, I. M. Pei or Philip Johnson did. I guess we are lucky for that, because he was one of the fringier members of the group.

Take his Bridge House of 1956, the same year Le Corbusier built the Maisons Jaoul. Both seem to employ vaults as a structural leitmotif. But with Corbusier the structure defines the nature of space and provokes a discussion (between the two separate pieces of the house) about vaults, masonry, and spatial types (flat versus deep, for example), while Johansen imposes a supposedly Palladian plan with bilateral symmetry as a bridge over a stream. The Bridge House ignores the entire notion of directionality (which way a bridge spans), as evidenced by the vaults on the center module that run in the direction of the stream. It's a mess of a house because, in my humble opinion, it demotes everything spatial in favor of the meaningless symmetry of the plan.

All the architects Gropius wrought are gone now, Johansen among the last. Occasionally a decorated diagram, like the Tent House, is just interesting enough to be a charming relic of the time.

30 June
Jane Thompson

Cover of *Design Research* by Alexandra Lange and Jane Thompson, 2010

Among the worst dinners I've ever had was sitting next to Jane Thompson. She was simply the loudest, most overbearing person imaginable. As a designer once said to Ralph Caplan (an editor at *ID*, the magazine Thompson cofounded), "Unlike Jane, you never ask me things that are none of your business!"

Had I known that Thompson and I grew up in the same New York City suburb, we might have had something to talk about (other than herself), but I only learned that much later. Or had I thought to talk to her about Design Research (DR), the amazing store she and her husband started in Cambridge and brought to East Fifty-Seventh Street in New York, where I fell in love with it. Or maybe I could have verified the story that when DR started selling the Aalto stool in the 1950s, it didn't move at its original price tag of five dollars but really took off once the price was raised to twenty-five dollars.

I didn't think of any of that to talk about, but, really, that's my fault.

Jane Thompson was an amazing (if very loud) proponent of modern living at a time when my family had adopted her style; the dinner should have been like meeting a celebrity. Our house was filled with the things that Jane selected, and I can even remember my father letting me know that Marimekko translated to "Mary's little dress," a thoroughly useless tidbit that I can't seem to dislodge from my memory.

I can't be certain, but my father's bachelor pad, after his 1964 divorce, must have been filled with visits to DR. The tall Isamu Noguchi lamp in the corner, the cool dinnerware and furniture must have made the trek from East Fifty-Seventh Street to East Sixty-Fourth Street not long after the New York City store opened. It makes sense that DR was founded the year I was born and even more sense that my newly single father would shop there a decade later.

DR, it seems, was the measure of my own life's modernity, as it was for many others. And many of those others went on to create the next generation of modern design retailing: Crate & Barrel, Design Within Reach (founder Rob Forbes even pondered reviving the DR name), Pottery Barn, Williams-Sonoma, and many more who may not even realize the debt they owe to DR and Jane Thompson.

01 July
H. Craig Severance

40 Wall Street, New York, New York, 1930

Virtually no one has heard of H. Craig Severance and even fewer have heard of Chazy, the upstate New York town in which he was born. But nearly everyone has heard of the competition for the tallest building in the world, which around 1930 was entirely in and entirely about New York City (and male ego and money, of course). Everyone with an interest in building as sport knows the fantastical tale of William Van Alen and the Chrysler Building's spire; Severance was the reason for Van Alen's subterfuge and the target of his competitive angst.

Severance had been partners with William Van Alen for more than a decade when they split acrimoniously. It's not clear why, but a *New York Times* article a couple of years later had Severance instructing his wife to run over a police captain who was trying to ticket her for speeding and driving without a license, so it is possible that Craig (who his wife said had been "drinking a lot of highballs") had an anger management or drinking problem, or both.

Anyhoo...Severance was commissioned to design 40 Wall Street for the Manhattan Company at the same time that Van Alen was designing what would become the Chrysler Building.

Competition seemed historically inevitable, as 40 Wall Street was the site of Aaron Burr's Manhattan Company competing with Alexander Hamilton's nearby Bank of New York. There was some other kerfuffle between Burr and Hamilton, but I forget exactly what.

Each architect, upon hearing that the other had raised the height of their building (at first to surpass the Woolworth Building, then to surpass each other) upped the ante. Eventually, Severance was convinced he had won, and for about a week that may have been true, but for Van Alen's quarterback sneak; he built the slender spire inside the building and raised it one night as a surprise, exceeding 40 Wall by an unsurmountable 119 feet.

The whole idea that buildings can be considered the tallest on the basis of a spire is patently ridiculous; I am not taller than Usain Bolt (six feet five inches/two meters) because I am wearing an updo (or tiara or hat), nor am I faster than him because I drive a car.

But buildings play by different rules, and H. Craig learned that the hard way.

02 July
Hamilton Harwell Harris

The Box on Cox, Harris home/office at 122 Cox Avenue, Raleigh, North Carolina, 1970

Harwell Hamilton Harris may be responsible, indirectly, for my own architectural education; while he was dean at the University of Texas School of Architecture, he hired a bunch of relatively unknown teachers who became known as the Texas Rangers. Colin Rowe, Werner Seligmann, John Hejduk, Robert Slutzky, Lee Hodgden, Jerry Wells, John Shaw, and Bernard Hoesli (half of whom were later my teachers) and a few others developed a curriculum "that encouraged the development of a workable, useful body of architectural theory derived from a continuous critique of significant works across history and cultures. The curriculum discouraged the sculpting and shaping of a building's mass in favor of the visualization and organization of architectural space."

Couldn't have said it better myself. Harris eventually moved on to Raleigh, North Carolina, to teach, and there he built a little gem of a house and studio dubbed the Box on Cox (Avenue).

He started his career on the West Coast working for Richard Neutra (on the miraculous Lovell House) and for Rudolph Schindler, leaving to design a house for John Entenza, who later initiated the Case Study House program (which HHH never participated in,

weirdly). The Entenza House was pure Neutra (at Entenza's insistence); it clocked in at 850 square feet/79 square meters and is included with another Harris house in Berkeley, the Weston Havens House, in the 2020 essay "Queering California Modernism" as examples of the art of building for a gay single man.

Much of Harris's output exhibits the confusion, or hybridization, of his irreconcilable influences: Neutra and Frank Lloyd Wright and craftsman modern. His best work stays in one lane or another, but when you combine the three it often equals just slightly better-designed conventional homes. Not true to any of their main influences, these houses try to find the Venn diagram of his influences, often unsuccessfully.

It's interesting to consider how Harris ended his career with the Box on Cox. Its blank wall facing the street is a gesture akin to the Villa Schwob by Charles-Édouard Jeanneret (Le Corbusier) in La Chaux des Fonds (an obsession of Rowe and others at UT). But inside it is pure Eames House, Harris's attempt to finally reconcile the competing loves of his life.

03 July
Dankmar Adler

Guaranty Building, Buffalo, New York, 1896

Dankmar Adler, employer then partner to Louis Sullivan, might be the Margo Channing of architecture. Adler actually hired Sullivan (and later Frank Lloyd Wright) before making him a partner, parting after fifteen years of working together. Adler faded from view as Sullivan's star ascended, but not before the two produced some of the truly great buildings of their time. In the end, their successes worked when the pair collaborated, and each was a bit less famous on their own. Sullivan was even supported financially by the Adler family after Dankmar's death and his own destitute decline.

The Auditorium Building in Chicago, Adler and Sullivan's most complex complex, is a remarkable hybrid, containing a 4,300-seat opera house (Adler was an accomplished engineer, including acoustics; he even consulted on Carnegie Hall), a hotel, offices, and retail sitting on a technologically advanced floating mat foundation. In fact, most of the engineering modernity in Adler and Sullivan's work, including their early use of the steel frame, the gateway drug to the skyscraper, was due to Adler.

The Charnley House (which Wright claimed was mostly his work) was a crisply delineated and punctured solid

with a lovely push-pull balcony on the second floor; in Google Street View there is always a scrum of architecture students with open sketchbooks out front. It is more Wrightian inside, with a beautiful moment of light, space, and stairs slotting down through the center section.

Adler and Sullivan more or less invented the facade verticality of early tall buildings and imposed the three-part classical composition of base, shaft, and capital (or rusticated base, piano nobile, and attic story, depending on the precedent) onto the skyscraper's developing formal language. These ideas were not obvious at the time but continue to have some relevance, even when the pattern is barely visible (as at the original World Trade Center towers, where the three parts were barely expressed in the widened gaps between perimeter columns).

Adler, Sullivan, and Wright barely spoke after a while, and resentment abounded, but, after all, these were architects. If you put more than one master builder in a room, there are bound to be sparks.

04 July
Nuccio Bertone

Alfa Romeo Carabo concept car, 1968

Giuseppe Bertone (known as Nuccio) designed (mostly) Italian cars after World War II and helped define what the future would look like, though it never looked quite as cool as Nuccio projected.

Car design is an odd, insular world. The education of a car designer happens at a small number of highly specialized design and art schools in Italy, the US, the UK, and Germany. And, as in fashion, there are (at least) two tiers of design realization: concept and racing (couture) and mass-produced (ready-to-wear), with cross-fertilization and trickle-down style. Nuccio made both, not just on paper but in steel in his family's Carrozzeria Bertone.

I admit to being seduced by it all: the ideas and the reality. As I was growing up, my father came home with a series of outré autos, including a hearse (my mother was really pleased showing up at dinner parties in that), a 1959 Porsche 356 he bought in Stuttgart for my art teacher (an amazing, single, gay woman who loved that car), an MG TD (which the entire family and dog would pile into, despite being a microscopic two-seater sports car), a Renault Dauphine, a late 1960s Thunderbird convertible (whose top would fold into the trunk in the precise amount of time of the light change at the Willis Avenue Bridge), a

1960 Mercedes 190SL (utterly fucking cool), and a gold Rolls-Royce (he was not immune to some questionable taste).

Nuccio was an utter genius in shaping sheets of steel (and aluminum) into forms so evocative they seem to be speeding along even when parked. His designs grace mass production and concepts for companies as different as Fiat and Lamborghini, Lambretta scooters and Alfa Romeo, and Ford and Ferrari (a surprisingly good movie, by the way). Until Italians like Nuccio Bertone started designing internationally, there was a cultural consistency to a nation's car design history.

More than any nation, Italy has shaped cars into what we covet, even if the reputation of Italian cars for mechanical reliability is less than sterling. There will always be a stripe of human who will tolerate a less-than-comfortable chair for its design and a less-than-perfect car for the same reason, and you can't drive a chair.

05 July
Teddy Millington-Drake

Teddy Millington-Drake in the studio of his farmhouse, Tuscany, Italy, circa late 1970s

I didn't know Teddy Millington-Drake, but I did spend a somewhat inebriated night at his beautiful Tuscan farmhouse, Poggio al Pozzo, near Siena.

Four of us, living in Florence in 1977, took a Sunday drive in the countryside in my Citroën 2CV, the world's most underpowered car (an architect, an art historian, a writer, and a painter walk into a trattoria...): 1) me, 2) H. Travers Newton (an art historian and art restorer, and the one who spearheaded the search for the lost Leonardo painting *The Battle of Anghiari*), 3) Robert Minkoff (a classmate, co-op housemate, and writer who introduced me to the lot of them), and 4) Andreas Orsini-Rosenberg (an Austrian painter who did actually know Teddy Millington-Drake, I assume because everyone with hyphenated last names knows each other?).

We were driving around, drinking, eating, and sightseeing (and occasionally pushing my car up hills it couldn't manage with all four of us inside) until it started to get very dark very quickly, and we were getting fairly drunk almost as quickly.

Luckily, Orsini-Rosenberg said he knew a painter, Millington-Drake, a good friend of Cy Twombly who had a villa nearby. We found it, amazingly with only paper

maps and memory, and the lights were on! The four of us, and we must have looked a bit of a mess, knocked on the door, and some writer guy named Bruce Chatwin answered the door. He was there alone (not for long), having borrowed the house from his friend. His book *In Patagonia* had just come out a few months earlier, but of course none of us knew that. Chatwin was neither happy to see us nor happy to put us up for the night, nor did he want to spend time with us, but he was a reasonably well-mannered host.

The house was filled with what I thought were Twomblys but were Teddy's less-interesting approximations. But what a house and garden and pool. Millington-Drake had decorated some of the walls with scribblings, but it was mostly a style that later would be called Tuscan Farmhouse Modern. At the time, he was probably in Greece in his house in Patmos, where he spent the last thirty years of his life.

Belated thanks for a lovely evening, Teddy Millington-Drake. Thanks for taking us in, Bruce Chatwin. And of course, thanks Bob, Travers, and Andreas!

06 July
Tibor Kalman

Tibor Kalman: Perverse Optimist, designed by Michael Bierut, 2000

It seems like half of all the graphic designers I really like worked for Tibor Kalman at M&Co, and the other half were publicly excoriated by him. He had that effect on virtually everything, cleaving one world from the other.

Still, the work from M&Co, the firm he ran with his wife, Maira Kalman, and his output before and after it, was among the coolest, most iconoclastic, irreverent, provocative, intelligent, and funniest of its time. I think (here comes my theory of the case in 350 words) it can all be explained by the fact that Kalman was a member of Students for a Democratic Society (SDS) and spent the rest of his life figuring out how to integrate those tenets into a life beyond student-hood. It's the Tom Hayden problem, played out through design.

The problem with Switzerland (and by extension Helvetica) is that it is *all* so consistently polite, well designed, crisp, neat, and efficient. It's tough to appreciate all that perfection without some amount of ugly, bad, tasteless, or sloppy design. That's what Tibor provided, but it only works when most of society conforms to the orthodoxy; a nation of iconoclasts is, by definition, not iconoclastic.

Tibor tried a number of approaches: irony, radical transparency, humor (my fave), shock, and, along the way, a healthy dose of dogma, all to remain a dissident in a changing world. For him there were always some Port Huron Statement rules and complaints (see Tom Hayden and *The Big Lebowski*).

Hayden (whom the FBI placed on the Rabble Rouser Index) married Jane Fonda and had to deal with the dichotomy of a student's anger while being rich and successful. Tibor had to adapt to success, fame, and a world that was imitating a style he helped propagate.

His occasional self-immolation was his way of maintaining his difference, his unique role, his unassailable position. The problem with proselytizing is that once you've converted everyone you're out of a job (and it's being the contrarian, not just promoting a manifesto, that inspires the evangelist).

Fortunately, for Tibor Kalman and for us, the world wasn't transformed, and he always had a stage.

07 July
Grosvenor Atterbury

The Dunes, Wiborg estate, East Hampton, New York, circa 1895

Today we think of Grosvenor Atterbury as the architect of spectacular houses for the spectacularly rich in the Hamptons, for the Rockefellers at Kykuit, and in New York City, but his 1958 obituary in the *New York Times* focused almost entirely on his housing in Forest Hills Gardens and his early innovations in prefabrication.

These alone are interesting, but so is the fact that virtually no one knows of him today. He was, at the time, an extraordinary talent and one with enough social conscience (or noblesse oblige) to devote himself to housing not just the very rich but the middle class as well.

I, for one, miss that bifurcated approach: designing both houses and housing, both for fame and money and for the greater good too. For someone of Atterbury's pedigree (raised amid wealth, attending Yale and Columbia and École des Beaux-Arts, working for McKim, Mead & White), his interest in housing was admirable. He created, at Forest Hills Gardens, a system of prefabrication and construction that was revolutionary then and remarkable even today.

The system was an assembly of precast concrete panels, complete with internal cavities for insulation, for every element of the buildings' walls, floors, and roofs.

Even the wall molding and exterior decorative elements were cast into the panels. His wasn't the first attempt at low-cost concrete fabrication; Thomas Edison patented a system to pour an entire house (including stairs, bathtubs, and fireplaces) in a single pour into an enormous (and enormously complicated) mold. Let's just say it had issues.

So did Atterbury's, but his was far closer to economic feasibility than Edison's. And just as Edison is more famous now for other ventures, so is Atterbury. For example, the East Hampton community formerly part of the Frank Bestow Wiborg estate, the Dunes, that Atterbury built in 1910 on six hundred acres. Now all that is left is the rebuilt Pink House that was once the chauffeur's home but became the home of art and culture icons Gerald and Sara Murphy (née Wiborg), who had it torched in 1941 to avoid its costs. I suppose Grosvenor Atterbury might have regretted not developing his concrete house system a bit earlier.

08 July
Philip Johnson

New York State Pavilion, 1964 World's Fair, Queens, New York, opened 1964

It's fashionable, and entirely appropriate, to reject Philip Johnson these days. He was a young (well, thirty years old), worldly, gay man who attended two of the gargantuan Nuremburg rallies that Adolf Hitler held (one celebrating the annexation of Austria), designed a stage set for Father Coughlin, and attended a Nazi party rally at Madison Square Garden (guess he really liked rallies).

Seriously, these are pretty much unforgivable.

While I was never a fan of his work (except parts of his own Glass House compound, and of course the Four Seasons in New York and maybe the house in Cambridge he built as his thesis), I did participate in polishing his legacy at the Glass House; I designed the visitors' center waiting area that included an exhibition of his life after his death. Sorry for that. But it wasn't until Mark Lamster's remarkable biography that I fully understood the depths of his depravity. Hardly an excuse, but it's all I have.

As for Johnson's work, it was consistently the work of a man with no fixed ideas of his own, but a keen eye for the next big thing. His compound is a pastiche of things of the moment, from his cribbing of Mies van der Rohe in the

Glass House (underwhelming compared to the Farnsworth House) to the I. M. Pei–like sculpture gallery; the Frank Gehry–lite, sculptural Da Monsta; and the Aldo Rossi–themed study.

Johnson collected people and ideas the way he collected artwork, and his home was a salon for the best creative minds (and some of the best art) of his time. And what a collection: he donated 2,200 works to MoMA, an astonishing payload of art that the museum doesn't seem to be interested in giving up although it's been willing to remove his name from galleries and curator positions.

The question that has no satisfying answer is: are we better off with Philip Johnson's art, his intellectual output (like the International Style show or *Machine Art* show at MoMA), his handpicked set of the next generation of architects, his compound in the hands of the National Trust for Historic Preservation, and his clever quips that seem to show up whenever architecture is discussed?

As I said, no answer is satisfying.

09 July
Michael Graves

Benacerraf House addition, Princeton, New Jersey, 1969

A friend tells a story about taking Michael Graves on his first visit to the Villa Savoye. In those days (the mid-1960s) it was in partial ruin, unguarded and mostly ignored. As they were on their self-guided tour, my friend turned around and saw Graves unscrewing some door hardware to appropriate (steal). That is how he began and ended his career, appropriating the things he loved. But in between he was a fiercely brilliant architect, a very good painter, and someone with an incredible ability to draw the most seductive versions of some (occasionally) very bad ideas.

He was one of the New York Five who Judith Turner photographed into collective fame; Graves, Richard Meier, Peter Eisenman, John Hejduk, and Charles Gwathmey were a set based on a color, white, and maybe on their admiration for the same architects and buildings. To describe the work (and forgive the shorthand) Meier's was a bit doctrinaire, Eisenman's intellectually complicated, Hejduk's a poetic fantasy, and Gwathmey's a bit ham-handed, while Graves seemed like the smartest, most talented, and most visionary of all. He was a Rome Prize fellow, and a drawing of his still hangs in the large sitting room in that McKim-designed palazzo. His drawings there are truly gorgeous, though the rare-book room

he designed for the academy is less impressive.

While it was not cool to build when he started teaching at Princeton University, he managed to construct a few backyard machines: the slightly crazy and fantastic additions or renovations he built in the backyards of a few fellow professors' suburban homes. But things changed.

Graves began to build his sketches (his sketches that, I was told, his students would save after a crit, understanding the value they began to have). In full color. At full, or some might say enormously oversized, scale. He was convinced by his own talent that his buildings would be as charming as his drawings, but that turned out to be nearly impossible. We all (well, mostly) loved his drawings, and all (well, mostly) hated the built results.

The world at large did not agree with us, and Michael Graves became ubiquitous not only in the built environment but also in the aisles of Target and the catalogs of Alessi. And, of course, he designed door hardware as well.

10 July
Harvey Ball

Smiley face, designed 1964

Harvey Ball, in 1963 (in about ten minutes and for about forty-five dollars) designed the most-used icon of the twenty-first century: the smiley face. This is like the story of the Nike Swoosh, designed in 1971 by Carolyn Davidson, who was paid only thirty-five dollars (and was being paid two dollars an hour, so she must have spent more than ten minutes on it). Given the male/female pay differential, that seems about right. (Davidson was later paid a reported one million dollars, probably because Nike needed the good press and at that point one million dollars to Nike was like five minutes of net profit.)

Ball said he really didn't care that he had never copyrighted the mark, but later some dudes added "Have a Happy Day" and later "Have a Nice Day" (can you even think that without it being ironic?) and copyrighted the face and slogan together.

But now every text and email (and millions of other applications) use this mark, or its variations, amounting to billions of uses daily. Harvey always maintained it didn't matter, but we all know the story of Stephen Sondheim and the *West Side Story* lyrics credit; originally it was shared with Leonard Bernstein (he wrote the music and had the international profile) but was

later given, by Bernstein, entirely to Sondheim, at Sondheim's request. Lenny offered Steve his share of the royalties as well, but Sondheim, in a moment of largesse he later regretted, demurred, saying that full credit was enough. The money he forfeited is incalculable (though I imagine he had a number in mind).

On an artistic level, the smiley face has real and specific character: a perfect circle in a pure, sunny yellow; two different-size, hand-drawn oval eyeballs; and a crooked smile Ball likened to that of the *Mona Lisa* (at least he didn't have any delusions of grandeur). It is, of course, different from the emoticons we all use, but the yellow color, the circle, and the attitude all started with Ball.

More than a flag, rivaling a currency symbol, and maybe exceeded by only @ and #, the smiley face is a pretty remarkable ripple in culture created by a dude with a Magic Marker, in minutes, more than fifty years ago. Bravo, Harvey Ball, for giving away the best (or at least the most popular) art of our time!

11 July
James McNeill Whistler

Arrangement in Grey and Black No. 1, adapted as a US postage stamp, 1934

James McNeill Whistler is mostly known for the iconic portrait of his stern-looking (though only sixty-two-year-old!) mother: *Arrangement in Grey and Black No. 1* or, as everyone everywhere (at least those who watched cartoons as kids) knows it, *Whistler's Mother.*

What a scamp Whistler was; some have written that he was a deft manager of his brand. His obituary in the *Times of London*, although fairly complimentary about his talent, called him an "extremely irritating conversationalist" (his *obit!*) and noted that Whistler considered the public "an idiot or worse" if they failed to appreciate his work, or him. Whistler's memoir, *The Gentle Art of Making Enemies*, pretty much sums him up. But for all he could spew venom at others, he was quick to claim foul if anyone dared reciprocate.

The most famous example was his 1878 claim of libel against John Ruskin for calling his painting *Nocturne* "a pot of paint thrown in the public face," during which Whistler claimed not to have been born in lowly Lowell, Massachusetts, but in Saint Petersburg, Russia, saying: "I shall be born when and where I want, and I do not choose to be born in Lowell." Whistler won the case but was awarded a fraction of a penny in damages. Bankrupt, he

moved to Venice to make a series of commissioned prints.

He was, until their falling out, friends with fellow wit Oscar Wilde, who said, following a bon mot by Whistler, "I wish I'd said that," to which Whistler retorted, "You will, Oscar, you will!"

His most famous portrait came about as a model failed to appear and his mother stood for a portrait in her stead. Anna McNeill Whistler couldn't stand standing for the interminable process, so she sat, becoming part of the most famous (and most parodied) painting Whistler made. This picture of unyielding authoritarianism became, somehow, a symbol of beneficent motherhood, with no less than President Franklin D. Roosevelt sending a doodle to then postmaster general James A. Farley for a Mother's Day stamp. The stamp is cropped, with an added bouquet of flowers, but still manages to be more *Psycho* than what we now consider an approving portrait of motherhood.

I'm still waiting for James McNeill Whistler's clever rejoinder to that slight.

12 July
R. Buckminster Fuller

Geodesic dome enclosure, USA Pavilion, Expo 67, Montreal, Canada, 1967

Once a mythology has been constructed around a subject, it is very hard to deconstruct it. R. Buckminster Fuller constructed a mythos (first with his name: he had been Richard B. Fuller at birth, nicknamed Bucky) based on a combination of an extraordinarily complex mathematical mind, ambition, appropriation, and obsession. He was quite brilliant, but not quite as brilliant in all the ways he claimed: twice expelled from Harvard for partying and idleness, he constructed a tale of genius unable to be contained by the university. He "invented" and patented the geodesic dome more than twenty-five years after it had been created, built, and patented in Germany. His Dymaxion car and house failed not because of their brilliance but for lack of it in a world he thought he could bend to his vision. He became (understandably) depressed and alcoholic after the death of his daughter but invented a tale of his own attempted suicide and a redemptive vision to remake his persona. *Dymaxion* is a term created by a department store and copyrighted in his name by them.

Fuller did see things differently and was incredibly facile in transforming and combining observations into new ideas. That is a kind of genius, but one based as much on his mathematical mind (he could remain at an abstract level where these kinds of manipulations are free of the confines of reality) as on insight into the world the rest of us live in.

His gravestone includes the epitaph "Call Me Trimtab," a reference to how a small change can propel a larger one; taken from his time in the Navy where he observed how huge rudders on enormous ships could be easily moved with a trimtab, a small rudder on the larger rudder. That seems his most appropriate self-proclamation; his enthusiasm and ideas seeded the motivation of others. Not all the ideas were his, not all worked, not all were understandable, and not all changed the world, but all of them were inspiration to others who would, in the end, change the world.

R. Buckminster Fuller embodied, in totality, what we want a genius to be: committed, arcane, eccentric, compelling, articulate, and a fount of ideas that seem new and exciting.

13 July
Otto Wagner

Postsparkasse (Austrian Postal Savings Bank), Vienna, Austria, 1905

Otto Wagner was one of those figures through whom the rest of architectural history flowed.

He was mentor to Josef Hoffmann, Joseph Maria Olbrich, Jože Plečnik, and even Rudolph Schindler. Richard Neutra writes about how affected he was by growing up in Vienna and constantly traveling on the rail system through all the stations Wagner designed. And if Wagner had designed only the Vienna Stadtbahn stations, he would be considered a giant of architecture. But there was much more.

Everyone's favorite is the Austrian Postal Savings Bank (Postsparkasse or PSK), and it's my favorite for all those reasons plus its location on a street with my name, Biber Street (Biberstrasse). It's an obligatory portrait for me every time I'm in Vienna.

The main banking hall at the PSK, slathered in glass and with a glass floor to send light to the level below, is one of the greatest spaces ever created. It includes a set of aluminum (Wagner loved to use this new material) ventilation tubes that I used as inspiration (well, stole) for the USA Pavilion at the 2015 Expo in Milan.

To understand its modernity, just compare it with McKim, Mead & White's Penn Station in New York City, built at the same time with precisely the same idea of a skylit hall with a glass floor (in this case to light the tracks below). The PSK vs. Penn Station is *The Jetsons* vs. *The Flintstones*, or *Star Wars* vs. *Spaceballs*, created in the years just before the First World War. It's a triumph of the modern over classical, particularly ironic given that the Old World was home to modernity while the New World was still leaning on the past. One hundred years ago both these buildings awed their audiences, but sadly only one remains.

The PSK appears to be held together with rivets: on top of its steel structure, rivets fasten the marble panels to the exterior walls, patterning the exterior of the building. These details declare the stone facade is a non-load-bearing veneer pinned to a steel frame. I stole this detail for Gotham Bar and Grill (now just Gotham), where the riveted columns were a nod to Wagner's bank.

Designing bridges, dams, railways, buildings, churches, furniture, and city plans, Otto Wagner was, and continues to be, an inspiration and a marvel.

14 July
Ann Tyng

Anne Tyng with Tyng Toy, a modular building set designed for children, 1950

If you watched *My Architect*, Nathaniel Kahn's documentary about his father, Louis Kahn, and the three families Kahn propagated, then you saw Anne Tyng revisit the Trenton Bath Houses, a design she created in Kahn's office. She was the woman in the middle family (between his wife and Nathaniel's mother). Her daughter, Alexandra, was born during Anne's exile in Rome to avoid whatever scandal might arise from her long affair with Kahn. It's amazing the lengths she and others went to avoid causing Lou any discomfort, though she did publish *Louis Kahn to Anne Tyng: The Rome Letters, 1953–1954* after his death.

Tyng was a partner in Kahn's firm, an architect trained by Walter Gropius & Co. at Harvard, the only woman registered as an architect in Pennsylvania in 1949 (a proctor at her licensing exam turned his back, refusing to acknowledge her), and a brilliant mind obsessed with geometry. She worked for Konrad Wachsmann, her PhD thesis was titled "Simultaneousness, Randomness, and Order," and Buckminster Fuller called her "Kahn's geometrical strategist." Tyng was a gifted, insightful, influential, and disciplined woman who was ignored by history because she was a woman and eventually by Kahn because he could ignore her without consequence.

We see Kahn as an architect obsessed with geometry, and it is hard to know just how much of that obsession was Tyng's before it was Kahn's. It's exhausting to see this story of erased genius over and over as I write these birthday bios, and somehow it never seems to be a man who is both integral to an icon's success and overlooked or written out of history (I'm looking at you, Pritzker Prize). But it always seems to be a man (Leni Riefenstahl excepted) whose misdeeds eventually destroy their status as design masters, often after their death (see Philip Johnson, birthday six days ago).

MoMA is trying to address these inequities; the museum is facing the Johnson issue and has at least added Tyng's name to Kahn's City Tower sketch in its collection. Anne Tyng had the great good fortune to outlive Louis Kahn (as most of these collaborating women seem to: Charlotte Perriand, Denise Scott Brown, Ray Eames, Florence Knoll, etc.), but that's hardly compensation for a career erased.

15 July
Josef Frank

Cabinet 2192, also called the Corrugated Cabinet, 1954

Josef Frank, a decidedly modern architect born in Vienna, had a kind of backward career. He started with his most mature built work and ended with a series of rendered fantasies that seem more like the work of a novice than someone who had weathered the Secession and the International Style. In between these movements, he was so at odds with the prevailing design movements that he called steel tubular furniture a "threat to humanity"!

Yet he built a small, utterly white, and conforming modern housing block at the 1927 Stuttgart Weissenhofsiedlung and a number of increasingly crisp homes in Vienna. It was, predictably, his religion (care to guess which?) that drove him from Austria in 1933 to Sweden, his wife's home country, then to New York City, where he spent the war years teaching at the New School and trying to get commissions to build a house there. He returned in 1946, not to Austria but to Sweden, where he focused on the textiles and furniture he had become famous for in Sweden, and a series of fantasy houses he sketched and watercolored.

He became so famous in Sweden because of an enterprising design-oriented shop, not unlike Alvar and Aino Aalto did in Finland. In the Aaltos'

case it was Artek; in Frank's case it was Svenskt Tenn. Maire Gullichsen was Artek's cofounder and funder and later commissioned the Villa Mairea. Estrid Ericson founded Svenskt Tenn and encouraged Frank to produce literally thousands of designs for fabric, furniture, lighting, glasswork, and myriad domestic appurtenances that made him famous for creating a Swedish style (long after he helped found the Vienna Werkbund), much of it still made today.

In a late-life fit of identity crisis, Josef Frank felt he had lost his ability to build and sent thirteen letters, each with an illustrated house, to his wife's cousin. It's unclear if he was pitching for a commission or simply exercising long-atrophied muscles, but his retreat into a kind of naive art is fascinating. Rather than revert to the past, he was an architect reinventing himself in his sixties. While we might consider it a remarkable coda, Frank wrote a friend that he was sad to fall so short of his desires.

Ah, the life of an architect!

16 July
Adalberto Libera

Casa Malaparte, Capri, Italy, designed 1937

It must be posthumously frustrating to have one's most famous building subject to an endless dispute about attribution. We will never know how to divide the precise design credit for the Casa Malaparte, but it is consistent with (and originally attributed as) Adalberto Libera's work. Whatever part he played in it, it is one of those buildings that is impossible to photograph badly; every image is seductive, surreal, suggestive, and sublime. It is endlessly fascinating to architects, but Libera produced an astonishing number of other buildings whose reality similarly conforms to his surreal renderings. That alone is an achievement worth noting.

His work helped define Italian Rationalism, a convenient euphemism for Fascist architecture, which thrived in the thirties. Italian architects of the period were required to join the party, as did Libera, but he worked hard for the regime, designing exhibitions celebrating their anniversaries and including the fasces symbol (from whence Fascism was born) in monumental form on his buildings. The symbol, a bundle of sticks with a protruding axe head, was used from ancient Rome (and earlier) to the 1876 Emancipation Memorial of Abraham Lincoln.

It's interesting how tolerant (and admiring) we are of Italian Fascist architecture. We see it as the kinder, gentler Fascism, and Italians as being more charmed by the art of Fascism than by its oppressive tendencies. We aren't quite as forgiving of Albert Speer or German Fascist architecture; Germany is not Italy and Speer is not Libera, but the distinction is worth unpacking (elsewhere), though Eddie Izzard pretty much summed it up.

The only Libera building I've visited is the amazing Aventino Post Office in Rome, which he designed in 1935. It could have been built last year, yet it's still in use, and looking precisely as it did during the war. No doubt it's as frustrating to use as ever. Post offices may seem simple, but every bureaucratic institution in Italy is a bit of a nightmare. At Libera's version, at least you get to hang out in a gorgeous space while you are waiting endlessly.

17 July
Kenneth Grange

Clock, thermometer, hygrometer, and barometer for Taylor Instruments, 1971

Ken (Sir Kenneth, to you) Grange was a partner of mine at Pentagram for the first six years I was there and is a charming, funny, and gracious chap in personal life, while being a bit of a curmudgeon in business. He and fellow founder Colin Forbes seemed to be in a longevity contest, but he recently won with Forbes's death at age ninety-four. It was that competitive friction that prompted Forbes to move to New York and to open the office I later joined (thanks, Ken).

Ken can be riotously funny, as when he wrote an elaborate letter of complaint to OshKosh about the problem of things falling out of his overall pockets when using the toilet (and got back an equally comical response), or his minute of silence for the recently departed Theo Crosby, which he stopped after about fifteen seconds, saying, "Turns out a minute is a very long time." Maybe you had to be there.

It was Grange who turned me onto the corps of World War II artists and designers who fabricated an entire Ghost Army out of inflatable tanks, muslin airplanes (or aeroplanes), and tank tracks made with jeeps pulling trailers. It was a spot of pure genius and cleverness you would expect him to admire.

He has an absolutely sure sense of himself, once recounting how at some document signing he pushed aside another's pen and, pulling a Parker ballpoint he designed out of his pocket, said, "Now *this* is a pen"! His confidence paid off in business, where he excelled at wringing his real worth out of virtually every client. Royalties are a mainstay of the design world, but one really needs a collection of items to make an actual living (like authors need multiple books). Ken is so beguiling that return work is the norm for him; he designs suites of appliances or speakers or lamps for the same clients.

Ken Grange also, indirectly, prompted the name Pentagram; when Crosby/Fletcher/Forbes asked him to join, he wanted his name added to the masthead. As Mervyn Kurlansky had joined just before him, everyone realized that they might be mistaken for lawyers if they continued to add all who joined. "Pentagram" solved that problem (for five designers) as it has for every subsequent designer who joined. Sometimes curmudgeons are right.

18 July
Valerio Olgiati

Yellow House cultural center, Flim, Switzerland, renovation 1999

Books are really a miracle. It routinely takes more time to conceive, write, design, and publish a book than to design and build a building. The book that is most like a building must be Valerio Olgiati's monograph; it is so big, so heavy, so unephemeral that it might just be a building (a very white building).

Every page is as thick as ten ordinary pages and as stiff as a board, but the book opens and lays flat perfectly. The graphics are impeccable. The buildings are amazing. And it's even better if you don't understand the German text; there's nothing to slow you down.

I'd never heard of Olgiati when I visited two of his projects in Switzerland. Yellow House is, of course, all white, and a perfect punctured cube defining the exact center of Flim (and no, that's not a misspelling of Film).

His school building in Paspels, Switzerland, rendered in concrete, has an elementary but skewed plan. Its open cruciform circulation fills with sounds as classes let out, and its classrooms are clad in larch wood, the only material with any color in the whole school. It's a study in distorted clarity.

Each project for Olgiati is sui generis, seemingly the work of a variety of architects and surprising as the output of one man. They are related by their apparent perversity, like his own office, raised on four columns (not in the corners) and adjacent to (but not touching) a wall that could easily support the hovering box of an office. His Swiss Cardiac Center in Abu Dhabi takes a single facade and structural motif and plays it out in every imaginable way. He reuses the motif at the Perm Museum in Russia as a stack of floors looking as unstable as a kid's pile of presents. The Plantahof Auditorium in Landquart, Switzerland, is a perfect triangular prism but with one odd bit of structure poking out of it; inside, a pair of mirrored stairs diverge, forcing a choice between equal alternatives.

These are the work of an architect in full control of both the architecture and the behavior it permits. In that sense they are perfectly Swiss. But their perversity is entirely Olgiati's own.

19 July
John Hejduk

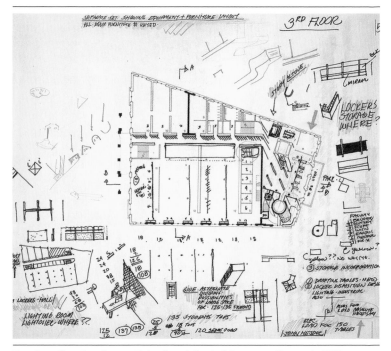

Drawing with notes, Cooper Union foundation building renovation, early 1970s

I once got a seemingly nice note from a young architect who won, on a bet, a copy of John Hejduk's *Mask of Medusa* and discovered my name in it. That was because it was mine, stolen from my office and sold (the lowest of petty crimes?). That wasn't the answer the writer may have hoped for. The book is now worth hundreds of dollars (used), so I won't be restocking my own bookshelf any time soon.

That's a shame, because John Hejduk may have built less and influenced more than any twentieth-century architect, and *Mask* was a trove of his musings. He spent a quarter of that century heading the Cooper Union, shepherding (and attracting) a litany of the most important architects of the following century. And that was his second rodeo, after his University of Texas stint as a Texas Ranger, helping define the most important modern architecture didactics for the next fifty years.

If that seems outsized, it is, just as he was.

What seems surprising is that he was able to build a few of his ideas (beyond his renovation of Cooper's Foundation Building in 1975, just as he rose to the dean's office), and they are just as

smart, evocative, well built, and abstract as his drawings.

The unbuilt work is pure poetry, an unlikely evolution from the rigorous nine-square-grid variations that he religiously explored in his early days. Those highly spatial, almost mathematical permutations operated within highly restrained limits, while his later works were exercises in poetic metaphor. Big evolution for Hejduk, but both efforts (and everything in between) were the products of a deeply contemplative mind.

He was, in the 1970s, part of the group variously called the New York Five, Five Architects, and the Whites. It's ironic, as he was later part of the informal group labeled the Blacks, not based on the color of the work but on the darkly pessimistic and bleak ideas he shared with Daniel Libeskind, Raimund Abraham, and Lebbeus Woods. He gave permission to others to create work that eschewed the sunny optimism popular then (and now).

It's why Hejduk's work is best left unbuilt and why it still inspires; we love the dark side but prefer to live in the light.

20 July
László Moholy-Nagy

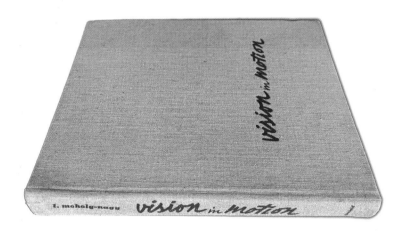

The author's mother's copy of *Vision in Motion,* László Moholy-Nagy, 1947

László Moholy-Nagy followed the route so many other burgeoning modernists did. He was first attracted to Germany as the center of modern design; landed at the Bauhaus, where he taught; was ejected from Germany as a nonnational (and a Jew); moved to London hoping to establish (with Walter Gropius) a London-based Bauhaus (while working at Simpsons of Piccadilly department store and living in the Isokon Building filled with similar expats); failed at that and moved to the US; and established the School of Design in Chicago, now part of the Mies-shaped Illinois Institute of Technology [IIT] campus). The peripatetic artist/educator/modernist wore, as a badge of honor, his inclusion in the *Degenerate Art* show in Germany in 1937, years after he fled the country.

The early modern artistic diaspora is a remarkably consistent story, with the US being the unwitting recipient of members of that diaspora, as Moholy-Nagy's Bauhaus colleagues (Gropius, Marcel Breuer, Josef Albers, Herbert Bayer, etc.) landed nearby.

For the next American generation of designers, architects, and artists, this flood of design dignitaries was a windfall; they taught at Harvard and Yale and Black Mountain College and IIT and the New School and just about every other serious design school. They published books on design that seemed especially relevant to the New World after World War II. That was the world my own parents became parents in, and therefore the world in which I grew up. On the shelf with various MoMA publications and issues of *Portfolio* was always Moholy-Nagy's *Vision in Motion*, a book published by his wife, Sybil Moholy-Nagy, just after his death in 1946.

These books, especially when they were collections of work sorted in some didactic framework (with the author's own work liberally dotted throughout), were as much hagiographies as textbooks. They created a legacy as much as they informed, especially in cases like Moholy-Nagy, following his death.

But as much as these books attempted to paint a world of cutting-edge modernity, they were created in a world that had not yet arrived there. And that is what is so captivating about them: the naive aspiration to a new, better, purer modern world told from a world still steeped in the past.

21 July
Louise Blanchard Bethune

Lafayette Hotel, Buffalo, New York, 1904

Even though women had been practicing architecture for literally centuries before Louise Blanchard Bethune, she is considered the first woman in the US to be a professional architect. And the first woman admitted to the American Institute of Architects (AIA). And the first woman to become a fellow of the AIA (FAIA). And the first woman to buy a woman's bicycle in Buffalo, New York. She might have been the first woman to attend Cornell University's architecture school, but was hired as a draftswoman by a Buffalo firm and entered the professional world directly, as was the norm in those days.

Bethune's firsts happened about 150 years ago, although Katherine Briçonnet in France designed the Chenonceau Tower at the remarkable Château de Chenonceau (which is built as a bridge crossing the River Cher and is my personal favorite) in the early 1500s. A century later, Lady Elizabeth Wilbraham studied Andrea Palladio, tutored Christopher Wren, and designed (it has been suggested) eighteen churches attributed to him and some four hundred buildings over her lifetime.

It was another 250 years before Bethune would be christened the first woman in the US to practice architecture professionally and work on some 150

buildings during her career. While Daniel Burnham and Louis Sullivan endorsed her membership in the nascent AIA and other local professional organizations seemingly with open arms, those same architects didn't seem to think that she deserved equal compensation for her work.

When asked to submit designs for the Woman's Building at the 1893 World's Columbian Exposition in Chicago, Bethune declined; men were paid ten thousand dollars for their designs while women's fees were only one thousand dollars. Even now a differential of 1,000 percent seems insane, and it is hard to see how it was justified then, especially as Daniel Burnham was the director of the works and essentially set the architectural standards. In the end, Sophia Hayden, the first woman to graduate from MIT's architecture school, designed the Woman's Building.

By the time Bethune retired, there were fifty women practicing architects in the US; this was still a pittance, but a slightly larger pittance, in part thanks to Bethune.

22 July
Jacques-Germain Soufflot

Interior of the Pantheon, Paris, France, building completed 1790

The thing about classical architecture is that it can be used for almost anything. Not just for a Treasury Building, a Supreme Court, a Capitol, or a White House, but also to accommodate a multitude of uses over time, as did the Pantheon in Paris, which changed from a church to a secular funerary monument, to a church, to a monument, to a church, to a monument (I'll stop, but you get the idea). At every change, the pediment sculpture was recarved and a new slogan added, but it's the architecture that makes it so convincing in any role. And it was Jacques-Germain Soufflot who designed it and promoted classicism to the French.

Soufflot spent a few years at the French Academy in Rome, though his Paris Pantheon is not as singularly monumental as the Roman Pantheon; it's more a mash-up of classical motifs. The pedimented temple front, dome (though more like the US Capitol in style), and cruciform plan seem routine, and the interior tries hard to be the Roman baths (Soufflot had certainly seen Michelangelo's church set into the Baths of Diocletian while in Rome).

The Pantheon is more a perfect vehicle for France's ambivalent relationship to religion than an attempt to universalize classicism. And sitting across from the Sainte-Geneviève Library designed by Henri Labrouste, the first public reading room, they together create a neighborhood establishing a historical-emotional foundation for France as a post-Enlightenment nation. On the one side of the square is every book ever written by anyone French or in France or for France; on the other side are the remains of every modern human who defined France as a free intellectual state of ideas.

It's a neat trick, and one we could use in the US. In our sometimes ridiculously democratic (as opposed to meritocratic) state, the closest thing to the Pantheon is the sculpture hall at the Capitol, which suffers from an overly distributed sense of devotion (two statues per state) rather than an actual unifying idea. Confederate traitors sit alongside founding fathers. Will Rogers, Ronald Reagan, Helen Keller, Thomas Hart Benton, Jefferson Davis, George Clinton (no, not that George Clinton), Robert E. Lee, George Washington, Thomas Edison, and Daniel Webster sharing a rotunda is more a brawl than a devotional space.

Jacques-Germain Soufflot would be horrified, though he might really like the space.

23 July
Raimund Abraham

Austrian Cultural Forum, New York, New York, 2002

There are (at least) three significant things about Raimund Abraham.

He was born at the run-up to World War II and until he was twelve knew no other world but a world at war. "I had horrifying experiences that shaped my aesthetics," he once told an interviewer. "I saw buildings disappear that were supposed to be permanent. I saw the entire sky covered with airplanes. But do you have any idea what a beautiful sight that is – an iron sky? It was magnificent."

He believed that architecture is not (necessarily) buildings and buildings are not (necessarily) architecture. He grew up and taught at a time when the act of drawing was, for him, sufficient, saying, "I don't need a building to validate my ideas." He believed, "The drawing itself is the final statement. I construct with my pencil, anticipating the structure."

His major opus, the Austrian Cultural Forum, a sliver of drama on East Fifty-Second Street, was and is a remarkable vision. What makes it so remarkable, in part, is the extraordinary level of detail and intention brought to it at every point. Abraham was a man who could build (extraordinarily) but chose most often not to. The mere fact that

he could validates, for me, everything else. "Architecture is not a profession, it is a discipline," he said. "I'm not a genius, I'm a laborer. I labor on my ideas."

It was once axiomatic that architects who taught were architects who were unable or unwilling to build. They wore an air of bitterness; their ideas, their critical faculties, and their insight were unsurpassed, but they were passed over for actual buildings. The client as the ruination of good architecture was the credo of that crowd.

But Raimund Abraham was different. While he could be quite dark, he was not in the bitter camp; he proudly drew ideas and built only when conditions were right. As he once said about his House with Curtains, if he built it rather then drew it, the wind would never keep the curtains as he wanted them. It would be a failure as a building. Later, Shigeru Ban, a Cooper Union student when Abraham was teaching, built the Curtain Wall House in Japan. I would love to know what Abraham thought!

24 July
Quinlan Terry

Drawing of Kings Walden Bury, Hertfordshire, England, completed 1971

A couple days ago was Jacques Germain Soufflot's birthday, an architect who helped bring classical architecture to France in 1750. What am I to make of an Englishman who is attempting to do the same thing in England in the twenty-first century? Quinlan Terry is that architect, and it is hard to fully support or fully reject his work, though many are aligned on both sides to do just that.

Embracing classical architecture not as a heuristic device or a way to understand the past to imagine the future puts one in the company of King Charles III, a decidedly retrograde individual of questionable taste. He actually offered praise to the Nazis, saying, "You have to give this much to the Luftwaffe: when it knocked down our buildings it didn't replace them with anything more offensive than rubble. We did that."

It's a tone-deaf display of ignorance, and it is hardly surprising that a man in his seventies who has never actually lived in our common reality would believe such a thing. Classical clothes do not make better buildings, but better ideas do. Pretending that the last two hundred years or so did not happen and that the answer to all architecture is found purely in the past is absurd. But pretending that the past is irrelevant is equally absurd.

In a small town near me, a fellow named Geoffrey B. Carter has been building a house for the last thirty years or so, more or less by himself and more or less using only nineteenth-century techniques, materials, and forms. It's a stunning little Palladian folly near Montgomery Place, the Hudson River mansion where he worked restoring the building and learning his craft. It makes perfect sense for him, as a craftsman, to undertake this personal challenge, and it is lovely to see. But it is not an intellectual pursuit; it is an intensely personal challenge, neither a critical reaction to modernism nor prescriptive as a solution for our times.

And that is the problem with Terry (and Raymond Erith, his mentor): they see classicism as prescriptive.

Quinlan Terry and futurist engineer Cecil Balmond received their honors the same year from Queen Elizabeth II, but instructively, Terry was awarded a Commander of the Most Excellent Order of the British Empire while Balmond had to settle for an Officer of the Most Excellent Order of the British Empire (a difference perhaps lost on the rest of the world, but Terry now officially outranks Balmond, if you believe in that nonsense). Like mother, like son, or possibly vice versa.

25 July
Maxfield Parrish

Daybreak, 1922

Mel Gibson must be the only person ever to lose money on high-end artwork; he purchased Maxfield Parrish's reputed masterpiece *Daybreak* for $7.6 million and sold it for a whopping $5.2 million. *Daybreak* is the most reproduced painting of the twentieth century, surpassing even Leonardo da Vinci's *Last Supper* and Andy Warhol's *Campbell's Soup Cans*; it has sold enough to furnish a copy in one out of four US homes. How one could lose money on that is a mystery.

In the 1980s, working in Midtown New York, I used to seek out formerly elegant bars, often at hotels, that had entered, shall we say, a period of decline. I would join friends at the Algonquin (Dorothy Parker, Robert Benchley, and Alexander Woollcott were regulars), the Monkey Bar (Tennessee Williams), the Cordial Bar (*Saturday Night Live* cast plus Jackie Gleason and Ed Sullivan), and, of course, the King Cole Bar at the St. Regis, which was dominated by the Maxfield Parrish mural of, you know, Old King Cole. All these places had a fair share of camp, but the King Cole Bar was the campiest.

I don't know what it is about Parrish (and Norman Rockwell and N. C. Wyeth) that is so seductive and repulsive at the same time. Technically, their works are marvels. Parrish invented a system of pigments separated by layers of glaze that makes the paintings look internally illuminated. And the hyperreal accuracy is astonishing. But the subjects, especially before he gave up "girls on rocks" (as he put it) for landscapes, are so loaded with barely concealed eroticism (and pedophilia) that Michael Jackson found them arousing enough to use *Daybreak* as the model for a music video.

Even George Lucas admits to using Max's paintings for *Star Wars* imagery, though not for the eroticism, I would guess.

For art that was so popular and admired (and made Parrish so rich and famous), it is hard to put into words what is, at the same time, so totally wrong about it, but I will try.

It is too easy. It is illustration, not fine art. It is too popular. It is too melodramatic. It appeals to the laziest of art appreciators. It is too good technically paired with too contrived in content.

Maxfield Parrish's paintings are the fast food of art; at some point we all eat fast food, usually when we're growing up, but most of us outgrow it.

26 July
Cesare Cattaneo

Monumental fountain of Camerata, Italy, 1936, rebuilt 1960

That Cesare Cattaneo died at thirty-one makes it incredible that he completed any built work at all, much less any significant built work. But like the prodigious output of Georges Seurat, who died at the same age, that of Cattaneo matters more than the brief window in which it was produced. I. M. Pei, who died at 102, liked to say that a long life creates its own fame, but so, it seems, does dying young.

Early work, and that is all we get from Cattaneo, has the advantage of not being habitual, routine, or trite (by definition). There is something about the first of anything one designs (the first house, the first building, the first museum); these projects contain all the ideas and none of the experience you gather with age.

That can be refreshing. I lightly redesigned the first restaurant I designed (Gotham Bar and Grill) for a reopening and at the same time visited some houses I designed from the same period (basically Cattaneo's age at death). Let's call it Kinder-Biber-Werk.

While there are a few details I cringe at, they are normatively okay even though I would *never* again design them that way. They are of their time (and of my own) and maybe get by on that, but for Cattaneo the few things he realized are not just of their time, but also seriously great icons of their time.

His work is also pretty much intact, which is a testament to both its quality and its appropriateness. My favorite project, and one that is timeless, is the Camerata Fountain. Cattaneo designed it for a traffic circle in Como, but it was first built at the Sixth Milan Triennial in 1936. Its story from that point on has many mutually exclusive paths: it was disassembled after the triennial; or it was bombed by the Allies, who mistook it for an antiaircraft installation; or it was moved to Como in 1961, or possibly 1962; or it was rebuilt in Como in 1961 or 1962; it was supposed to be built in marble but was rendered in cement, or it was always intended to be concrete (this is really my personal evaluation, so ignore it).

Whatever the truth, it hardly matters. The fountain was and is truly fantastic. And Cattaneo might even be remembered forever because of it.

27 July
Ludwig Hohlwein

Prisoner of Love, circa 1928

Oh, Ludwig. We were really with you, even through your nationalistic World War I posters (they seem so tame today). But, really, you lost us at Nazism.

Hohlwein started his career as an architect, designing interiors and decorating ocean liners (that was a job?), but he gave it up for the much more lucrative world of poster design (!). Poster design then *was* the advertising industry; there was no modern media like radio or television, just newspapers, magazines, billboards, the sides of buildings, trucks, etc. Posters were a large part of advertising in the public realm.

Hohlwein designed thousands of posters for dozens of companies and places. He established a style that had, in addition to large, hand-drawn type, a cleverly modern combination of flatness and modeling. These define a style beyond Hohlwein; they define an attitude about who matters and who the audience was (as does all advertising).

His reductive style turned everyone into an icon. The posters seem to reveal the underpinnings of what was to become the lionizing of certain common *Volk* as the chosen people (and by exclusion, villainizing others). He didn't need to change much as he began

working with Joseph Goebbels in the National Ministry for Public Enlightenment and Propaganda; he carried on in his style, but with a slightly different, um, brief.

Disappointingly (some might say fortunately), when Hohlwein was offered a chance to emigrate to the US, he declined. Instead he joined the Nazi Party and urged his artist colleagues to do the same. Is it worse to build monumental buildings for the Reich, or design the propaganda? Is there an expiration date on an artist's sins? Hugo Boss manufactured uniforms through World War II. The BMW logo references the airplane propellers of fighter engines it made. And don't get me started on Volkswagen (or the forced labor most German companies used during the war). What are we to do with all of them?

Hating the sin but loving the sinner may be the Christian thing to do, and, after all, 99 percent of the population of 1930s Germany was Christian. But hating the sinner and loving the sin seems inadequate as well. I am searching for ways to continue to admire Ludwig Hohlwein (and all the others) through the fog of disgust that envelops them.

28 July
Santiago Calatrava

Quadricci Pavilion, Milwaukee Art Museum, Milwaukee, Wisconsin, 2001

Is there an architect alive more admired and more hated than Santiago Calatrava? I'm struggling to think of one, but Calatrava gives us plenty of fodder to consider him the acme of adulation and antipathy. Neither extreme is entirely undeserved.

Calatrava claims to be most influenced by Swiss engineer and bridge builder Robert Maillart, but he seems to have missed half the message. Maillart created gorgeous bridges of great formal and emotional power, but he won those commissions with the extreme economy of his work. He was nearly always the low bidder; the artistic element of his work was a product of his search for the minimalist solution to any problem. He was always trimming away bulk, weight, and fat.

Calatrava's projects have become notorious for cost overruns (the Oculus in downtown New York City cost four billion dollars, twice the estimate), gargantuan scale, and unconsidered aspects of the designs that injure users (like the glass treads on his Constitution Bridge in Venice). He may be the world's most-sued architect, yet he keeps getting hired for bigger and bigger work.

When my firm was building the Harley-Davidson Museum, he was building his addition to the Milwaukee Museum of Art (MMA, originally by Eero Saarinen). The story of his getting the commission is legendary; he walked into the presentation with nothing but a bit of charcoal and an easel of drawing paper and proceeded to draw his design while talking the rapt audience through his thinking. It was a bit of remarkable theater (the drawings are now framed and hung in the completed museum), but the rest of his process was not so simple.

The MMA addition is an attraction, but holds no art. Much more expensive than anticipated, it has overwhelmed the actual museum (you know, where the art is). It is called The Calatrava as the final step in his takeover of the entire identity of a venerable museum. While this was happening, I was quoted in a local paper saying that the Harley-Davidson Museum would never be referred to as The Biber, which my client misunderstood as my disappointment but was actually my way of saying that the MMA should not become a subsidiary of the Calatrava brand.

Still, he and his brand persist.

29 July
Sigurd Lewerentz

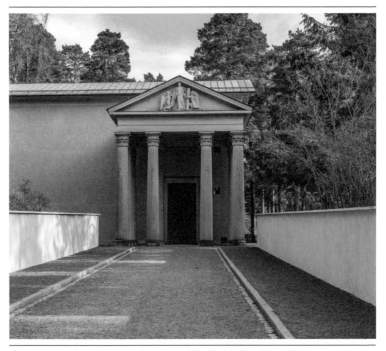

Resurrection Chapel Skogskyrkogarden, Stockholm, Sweden, 1925

Having watched all four seasons of *The Restaurant* (*Our Time Is Now* in Swedish), I feel perfectly qualified to opine on all things Swedish, including Sigurd Lewerentz. His villas, summer houses, and summer restaurant projects seem to be the stuff of *The Restaurant's* luscious (nonurban) locations. These vertically attenuated spaces (transitional from the Nordic classicism Lewerentz started with to the Swedish modern he ended up defining) are the perfect backgrounds for Nina, Calle, Helga, and the whole extended Löwander clan. Even the summer episodes on Gällno look like Lewerentz's early work.

If that's all there was, we might not have ever heard of Lewerentz. His first big splash was winning with Erik Gunnar Asplund a competition to design the Woodland Cemetery in Stockholm, the first of many, many cemeteries he designed. In fact, the definitive monograph, published around his 136th birthday, is titled *Architect of Death and Life*.

This raises so many questions. First, why was Sweden building *so* many cemeteries? The Woodland one that started him on this road to death was built in 1915, and Sweden was neutral during World War I, so it wasn't to bury war casualties.

And why did Sigurd design so many? I count more than forty (including tombs, cemeteries, and chapels) in his chronology of work, including the design of his own and his wife's tomb in 1929, when he was still in his forties! Clearly something was going on there.

Plus, competitions for everything? Siggy spent half his career chasing work doing competitions, even for private houses. And he was famous!

Gunnar is buried in Woodland, the cemetery he designed with Sig; Siggy is interred at Eastern Cemetery in Malmö, a cemetery he designed alone. Is this a sign of a rift? Possibly, but while they were born the same year, Lewerentz died thirty-five years after Asplund, so maybe they just grew apart.

But I digress. The last thing to know about Sigurd Lewerentz? At age fifty-five he gave up architecture and ran a window and hardware factory, producing his own designs. Maybe he was just biding his time, waiting for his chance to use that cool tomb design.

30 July
Giorgio Vasari

Uffizi, Florence, Italy, 1581

If Giorgio Vasari, in his magnum opus *The Lives of the Most Excellent Painters, Sculptors, and Architects*, published in 1550, invented the serial biography of artists (and therefore, perhaps, art history itself), then let this little bio (as part of a series of bios of the most excellent...) be my thanks to him.

It's clever to realize that the best way to become immortal (like the geniuses of art) is to write about those geniuses of art. *Hamilton* (the show, not the man) has as its coda, "Who Lives, Who Dies, Who Tells Your Story?" The history of war may be written by the victors, but who writes the history of art? Vasari, it turns out.

He first used the word *Renaissance* to describe that period in art, *Gothic*, too. He told the stories that became legends: Giotto winning a commission by drawing a perfect circle in red without moving his arm (don't ask) or painting a fly on Cimabue's canvas that the painter tried to brush away. Or his friend Michelangelo, for whom his chapter in *Lives* was the first of a living artist; eventually Vasari designed Mike Angel's tomb.

Vasari, usually considered a middling artist and architect, was anything but.

His Uffizi is a genuine invention: a building that is a street, and one connecting the seat of power and culture to the river (and ultimately to the Palazzo Pitti via the elevated Corridorio Vasari, a way for the Medici to safely commute from home to office).

His reworking of the Salone dei Cinquecento in the Palazzo Vecchio produced a fine, and quite enormous, room, and his heroic paintings, while not Leo or Mike's work, are quite powerful.

At Villa Giulia in Rome, he designed the garden court between the main villa and the nymphaeum, connecting two more elaborate (and more famous) works, but doing it rather nobly. It is a great outdoor room.

In fact, most of his work was about connections: the Uffizi connecting the Piazza della Signoria to the Arno; the elevated corridor; and *Lives*, connecting society to its artists. The Vasari Loggia in his hometown of Arezzo is, like every loggia, a connector.

Vasari recognized that what he lacked in genius he more than made up for in guile. Thanks, Giorgio. If this book is dedicated to anyone, it should be you.

31 July
George Franklin Barber

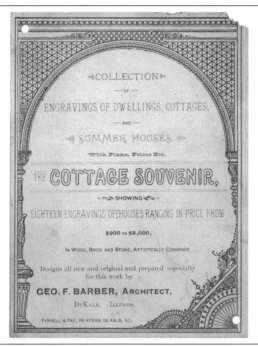

The Cottage Souvenir: Eighteen Engravings of Houses..., 1887

George Franklin Barber learned architecture from pattern books like Palliser's *American Cottage Homes*, then went on to create more than eight hundred house designs that he sold through catalogs and magazines, amounting to an estimated twenty thousand sets of plans sold. Barber's office eventually employed thirty draftsmen and twenty others, an interesting balance of technical and sales force.

These houses, mostly a kind of Victorian, Queen Anne, gingerbread variety, were built all over the country. Hundreds of them still stand, and they are just the kind of house you might admire in your small town; they really are lovely.

This kind of mass custom depends on an infrastructure of builders who could build well and adapt plans to the specifics of the site. Today we might consider this approach bound to fail, but it was hardly a new idea.

Vitruvius (Rome, first century BCE) published his *Ten Books on Architecture*, including all sorts of building prescriptions. Andrea Palladio (big V. fan) did the same with his *Four Books on Architecture*, recognizing that the attention span over the

intervening millennia and a half had been reduced considerably!

In Barber's time, a growing middle class needed homes, and there were vast areas underserved by architects. With Barber, the pattern book would become a mail-order magazine with detailed plans available for a fee. The houses they tendered included both those that could be cheaply built in wood and more luxe models in stone and brick, sometimes on the same page and sometimes in the same model. A wood version would be priced at X dollars and a brick and stone version of the same house at 4X dollars. The Sears, Roebuck evolution of Barber's idea was shipping house kits across the country or selling the parts and trimmings to accessorize your own home.

The generic quality of the houses was the point. At home nearly anywhere, they would all fit together nicely in suburbs or stand alone as farmhouses.

Barber's entire concept was, of course, yet another step in the demotion of the architect from master builder to annoying-but-necessary player, but that downgrade goes well beyond his success.

01 August
Raphael Soriano

Lipetz House, Raphael Soriano's first house commission, 1936

There's a story about Julius Shulman (the West Coast chronicler of virtually every midcentury modern house by virtually every West Coast midcentury modern architect) having the idea of hiring a different architect to each design a different room in the new Hollywood Hills house he wanted to build. It's a funny idea from a knowledgeable fellow creative and legendary photographer, but it may be that he thought of houses the way he recorded them: room by room, shot by shot. He may have thought of a house as a photo album of great moments. Like a decorator show house. Or a world's fair.

To hear Raphael Soriano tell it, "Julius wanted to invite different architects to each design a room. I said 'Julius, that will never be, because nobody will do that. That's not going to work any more than to have ten chefs do one meal.' He came to me and said, 'Soriano, I think I'll select you to do the..' And I said, 'Fine, thank you.' And I did."

Even though I think Soriano's analogy is flawed (given potluck, restaurants...), he made the point. And Shulman probably wanted to keep his stable of architects all happy (he was shrewd) but saw the light. Soriano was probably easier to work with (and much younger) than, say, Richard Neutra or Rudolph

Schindler, both of whom Soriano had worked for and for whom Shulman had photographed projects.

Shulman's house is fantastic, and a photo of Soriano sitting on a hillside in Los Angeles with two dogs and a shepherd hung in the entrance. Julius and Raphael were close throughout their lives.

Soriano once lived on the same street as Charlie Chaplin, Man Ray (who did two portraits of him), and Agnès Varda, all of whom he befriended. And architects like Pierre Koenig and Craig Ellwood worked for Soriano. His life nearly ended when he was hit by a runaway car; he spent six months in the hospital and wasn't expected to recover. He did recover and went on to do some of his best work.

Loyal clients stuck with Soriano, but many fled after his accident. After some complaint filed against him by a Bel Air client, he was censured in Los Angeles and moved to San Francisco. He left a legacy of fifty buildings, only twelve of which remain, which turns out to be enough to cement his reputation.

02 August
Pierre Charles L'Enfant

"Plan of the City of Washington," Andrew Ellicott's revision of L'Enfant's plan, 1792

If you dislike Washington, DC (the physical, urban reality of the place), as much as I do, then blame Pierre Charles L'Enfant. If it's the business of politics in DC you dislike, then look elsewhere; L'Enfant is blameless for that particular tragedy.

L'Enfant was one of those French aristocrats (like the Marquis de Lafayette, under whom he served) who came to America to fight against the English. Though he attended France's Royal Academy of Painting and Sculpture, L'Enfant became a military engineer. After being wounded and held prisoner, he was exchanged and served on Washington's staff thereafter.

Naturally, he was a friend of Alexander Hamilton (like, who wasn't? except for that one guy, what's-his-name) and opened an engineering firm in New York City after the Revolutionary War, where he renovated the City Hall into Federal Hall for the earliest capitol in the nation's first capital.

His big moment was the plan for the new capital, Federal City, which would become the City of Washington, and finally Washington, District of Columbia.

The plan was remarkably sophisticated; we think of it as very Parisian (urban fabric organized by diagonals, boulevards, round points, and other typically French geometry), but Paris's transformation by Baron Haussmann in fact followed L'Enfant's DC plan by more than fifty years. His DC idea is more a transposition of the landscape ideas of André Le Nôtre onto a new city (for a new nation).

Although his plan was ultimately realized by others (he might have been a tad difficult to work with), it makes manifest a set of precise relationships between the parts of government and its more memorializing, cultural, and mnemonic moments. The city plan was a diagram of the nation itself, a kind of constitution in three-dimensional form.

Its faults, in my view, are ones of scale; DC is too horizontal and not vertical enough. Its spaces are too flabby for my taste, but apparently not for Pierre Charles L'Enfant, or George Washington, or Thomas Jefferson. But that has always been the American fulcrum: the urban versus the rural, the dense versus the sparse, government as the solution versus government as the problem. In L'Enfant's creation, we have the promise of both sides of the equation.

03 August
Joseph Paxton

Side hall, Crystal Palace, London, England, 1851

If I had to save one book from my burning library (just planning...) it might well be the 1971 paperback I bought at the V&A for six pounds; *The Building Erected in Hyde Park for the Great Exhibition 1851* is a reprint of Joseph Paxton's entire set of drawings of the Crystal Palace.

What this set represents (without due credit) is the first truly modern building, the first truly demountable building, the first entirely prefabricated building, and the most technologically advanced building of its time. The book is a self-contained education (including mine) in architecture, construction, and engineering, all for six pounds.

Prince Albert (conveniently, the A of the V&A) came up with the idea of an exposition (the Great Exhibition of 1851) that would dwarf the French Industrial Exposition in Paris in 1844 and demonstrate the technological and artistic advances of international industry and culture. It was a giant trade show, with something like fourteen thousand exhibits in a glass-and-iron building that was the largest building of any kind on Earth.

The profits (yes, profits) from the venture paid to move the building to another site and to seed the building

of the museums on Exhibition Road opposite its original site in Hyde Park. You can still see the ghost of the space the Crystal Palace occupied, a vast, treeless plain to the east of the Albert Memorial. The building was enormous and, as a cute gesture, was 1,851 feet long.

The competition for its design attracted 245 entries; only two were remotely realistic. Joseph Paxton, a greenhouse designer, submitted a design he assembled in just weeks. It was entirely sheathed in glass (possible, in part, because the glass tax had recently been dropped), and its cast-iron frame was bolted together and glazed with the help of clever trolleys he designed to carry glass and men while rolling in the wooden gutters. A man could glaze over a hundred panels a day: helpful, as the building had close to three hundred thousand large panes.

From the start of design to the completed building took less than nine months. It covered more than eighteen acres (Bucky Fuller, eat your heart out) and enclosed ten elm trees already on the site. It was moved to Sydenham and burned down in 1936. Winston Churchill called it "the end of an age," but really it was the beginning of a new one: modernism.

04 August
Pierre Chareau

Courtyard facades, Maison de Verre, Paris, France, 1932

The first time I saw the Maison de Verre was the best.

Visiting Paris in 1977, I was staying with married classmates at their apartment in the banlieue. Caroline had an appointment with her ob-gyn, so Harry offered to drive us into the city so she could visit her doctor and I could spend my day, as usual, stalking architecture. When we arrived, Harry suggested I walk them to the office door. He rang the bell, opened the courtyard door, we stepped in, and my jaw dropped, just as Harry began to roar with laughter in his full-bodied way. Caroline's doctor was the son in-law of Pierre Chareau's client, Dr. Jean Dalsace, and her appointment was *in* Maison de Verre. Unfuckingbelievable.

I was actually a bit shaken coming upon this insanely wonderful building, casually entering it to wait for Caroline's appointment. We spent a half hour there just basking in the details. Harry and Caroline were both tickled that they could give me a chance to see one of the six or seven most amazing modern houses on the planet (which, since you asked, are Villa Savoye, Farnsworth House, Fallingwater, Kaufmann Desert House, Villa Mairea, Maison de Verre, and

possibly Casa Malaparte). You can make your own list, but it had better include Maison de Verre!

I've seen the Maison de Verre many more times since, but none of these visits were as earth-shattering as the first. The most recent time was on a tour with a graduate student studying the house's sanitary system for her thesis; she gave an unforgettable tour that included every single bathroom, toilet, sink, and bath in the house! And the rest too.

All praise to Pierre Chareau (and collaborators Bernard Bijvoet and Louis Dalbet), who, in 1928 moved their drafting tables into the demolition site and designed the home while working right there. It is an unequaled, idiosyncratic, and masterful work and the only reason we still know who Chareau is. Hardly a one-hit-wonder, his other work is interesting, especially his alabaster lighting, furniture, and mechanized designs, but these only to help complete the picture of the Maison de Verre's designer.

It is hard for buildings to sneak up on us, but endless thanks to Harry and Caroline for an unparalleled architectural experience.

05 August
Mart Stam

S34 cantilever chair by Thonet, produced 1920–1929

Mart Stam isn't as famous as Marcel Breuer, but he did invent the furniture that Breuer is famous for. Winning a court case in 1932, Stam was granted authorship of not just the famous steel tube cantilever chair, but every chair using that principle. Thonet, then producing the Breuer chair as B33, had to change its name to the Stam chair S33, but somehow it didn't stick (probably because Stam was granted the European patent, but not a worldwide one).

Stam, at twenty-eight, built a very sweet little housing block at the 1927 Stuttgart Weissenhofsiedlung, which showcased every modern architect of note at the time. Stam's has one rather fetching detail: the line of ribbon windows (pretty much ubiquitous at the time) continues as a freestanding screen past the solid part of the building, creating a kind of ghosted building made of fragmentary parts. It wouldn't be the last time he played that game.

In Prague from 1929 to 1932, he built the Villa Palička. The house presents to the street a fairly typical modern facade of its day: solid, cubic, slotted with ribbon windows, formally composed. But Stam carved out the rear to create a defined outdoor room,

transforming the house into a sectional drawing, a fragmentary house. It is unlike anything I have seen short of the Villa Savoye's carved-out roof terrace, but Villa Palička is upside down, carved out below and built above.

Stam seemed interested in what wasn't there as much as what was. The cantilever S33 chair was unique and patentable because it was the first (or at least the first in tubular steel) to eliminate the rear legs entirely. The chair, when sitting in it, sort of disappears, leaving the sitter floating in a seated shape without (if you squint) visible supports.

My own logo, created by Tony Brook of Spin Studio, plays a similarly reductivist game: it is missing the *i* in Biber, except for the square dot over the missing vertical. The stroke is implied by the space between the letters, and the design actually helps explain how to pronounce the name, as in b + ber = bee-ber.

Mart Stam's name isn't quite a palindrome or even a paired anagram, but it does seem almost as reductivist as a name could be. Just like his work.

06 August
Stefan Sagmeister

CD cover of *Feelings* by David Byrne, 1997

Stefan Sagmeister reaffirms my notion that 50 percent of the graphic designers I really like worked for Tibor Kalman (as did Stef, briefly) while the other 50 percent were publicly excoriated by Tibor (and who knows, he might fit there too).

Sagmeister has managed to make his own life a work of art, or at least a work of design, possibly a performance. That was particularly evident in his movie *The Happy Film*, where he tried a kind of "Five Obstructions" experiment on his own varied search for, you know, happiness. For someone who seems supremely confident (as when he interviewed the Rolling Stones, not the other way around, to see if he would take on an album cover for them, and asked them, "What's your favorite Stones album cover?" to which they answered, correctly, "The one Andy did"), it is a work of supreme vulnerability.

But, and this question arises whenever artists jump media lanes, is Sagmeister approaching art as a designer? Or is his design work really art in disguise? Or is the whole thing a performance? Kurt Schwitters famously said, "I am an artist, and when I spit it is art" but substitute "designer" and it sounds absurd. (Note, Piero Manzoni substituted an *h* for the *p* in *spit* and made *that* his art.)

We makers think what we make is *our* art, but is it art? Art historian Ernst Gombrich (forgive the college-bound reference) says that pleasing the untutored crowds is a violation of the fundamental ethics of Western artists since, well, at least Giotto. Art is not there to please but to poke, challenge, disturb, alienate, etc. the unwashed. But design is virtually there only to please; it exists to communicate, to identify, and to connect, and is (so Gombrich says) the opposite of art.

Stef is a brilliant designer. That he uses his own face, body, psyche, and life as part of his work gives it the look of art, but not exactly the ethic of art. He is also a brilliant speaker and performer, and his work in the sullied world of design is among the most effective of his generation; he has won every award possible and was even voted Austrian of the Year in 2018.

But true artists don't really get awards; they get hate mail.

07 August
Giorgetto Giugiaro

Ferrari 250 GT Berlinetta SWB Speciale, designed by Giugiaro at twenty-one, 1959

Once someone is declared the car designer of the century (awarded December 18, 1999, by the Global Automotive Elections Foundation), it doesn't leave much room for anyone else (like, for example, Nuccio Bertone, for whom Giorgetto Giugiaro worked for as a young designer) and it's a long time until the next will be named. Giugiaro was that designer, and it's no wonder; his work (like his design for the Volkswagen Rabbit) includes more than unaffordable Italian supercars.

A VW Rabbit with a five-speed manual transmission was my first new car, and it was a marvel: fun to drive, crisp and cool looking. Plus, it could hold an insane amount of cargo. A contractor friend told me he fit an entire set of kitchen cabinets in his; it may have been the original clown car (capacity wise).

Giugiaro went through a svelte phase, a boxy phase, a wedge phase, and probably eleven other phases, and each one produced a memorable design; the DeLorean (*Back to the Future*), the submarine Lotus Esprit (*The Spy Who Loved Me*), the VW Karmann Ghia (*Kill Bill*), plus, like, a thousand Lamborghinis, Ferraris, Maseratis, Alfa Romeos, Lotuses, and BMWs, each amazing in its own way.

But wait, there's more.

Giugiaro designed a Nikon camera (OK, not earth-shattering), a Seiko watch (cool, chunky, asymmetrical), the Siemens Rialto phone (a wildly colorful reference to the Rialto Bridge in Venice), a bicycle (smart, elemental), a taxi concept (for a MoMA show), a motorcycle (just okay), and, best of all, pasta (engineered to hold as much sauce as possible, but less than successful, as it took a bit longer to cook).

Elon Musk bought the submarine Lotus Esprit and said it influenced the Tesla pickup truck design; Giugiaro's taxi concept and his earlier Lancia Megagamma are said to have influenced the minivan explosion, so maybe, yeah, car designer of the century!

08 August
Charles Bulfinch

US Capitol Building with original dome by Charles Bullfinch, completed in 1824

Charles Bulfinch's life is really the stuff of movies. He was born into wealth and class in Boston, watching, at twelve, the Battle of Bunker Hill from his home. This was a year before the Declaration of Independence and was, ultimately, a loss for the colonists.

After attending Harvard, he took his grand tour of Europe in his twenties, and his travel itinerary was directed by Thomas Jefferson, his mentor. Upon his return, he got married at twenty-five to his first cousin and designed his first building. I am not sure of the connection, but it's a good plot point.

Bulfinch returned from his tour in time to see the US Constitution ratified. Over the next ten years, he worked on a variety of churches and public buildings in the classical style. He was quite good, in a staid, governmental, classicist kind of way (which he promoted).

He's considered to be the first American-born architect practicing professionally in the US. For years he worked as a gentleman architect (that is, without fees, you know, like interns, but forever) but after financial disaster(s) he began a paying professional practice. It's an interesting problem, how to value a discipline that was once done just for sport.

As an unpaid Boston selectman (does he never learn?!), he struggled and had several bouts of insolvency. He was paid all of fourteen hundred dollars for creating the Massachusetts State House, so it is no surprise.

He was briefly jailed for debt in a prison he himself designed (in another age, in another movie, this would be the key to his breaking out of prison)! When President James Monroe spent a week in Boston, he adopted Bulfinch as his constant companion, and he later appointed him as Architect of the Capitol.

In DC, Bulfinch completed the Capitol after decades of controversy; he designed parts of it, including the temporary wood dome (later replaced by the cast-iron one we see today). Triumphant, he used his DC work to establish himself as a major cultural figure and kept himself solvent through the end of his long life.

And scene.

Note: His work really is remarkable: he designed the Boston Commons, Faneuil Hall, India Wharf, Harvard's University Hall, the Massachusetts State House, the west front and temporary dome of the Capitol, and more.

09 August
Eileen Gray

E-1027 Villa, Roquebrune-Cap-Martin, France, 1929

Eileen Gray may be famous for the wrong reasons. Everyone knows that Le Corbusier defiled her Roquebrune-Cap-Martin home and masterpiece, E-1027, with murals that so offended her that she never returned. Everyone knows that she designed a chrome-and-glass adjustable side table that, because of its ubiquity, seems a bit trite (it is not). Most think of her work as essentially art deco (which she despised). And some of us know what E-1027 stands for (if not, Google it).

The flip side of these easy factoids is that E-1027 may have been saved due more to Le Corbusier's work on it than hers (though now she is famous enough). And the ubiquity of her designs is because it still looks so damned good. The infamy and ubiquity and misclassification worked; her revived fame came at a time when she was no longer under the shadow of her contemporaries, proving that late recognition can work.

In 2010, before the completed restoration of E-1027 (and the forty-fifth anniversary of Le Corbusier's drowning in the sea below the villa), I scaled the wall (architects as cat burglars?) with then-partner William Russell to prowl around the utterly remarkable apparition. There is

something so finely wrought about the house that separates it from the almost entirely male history of early modern architecture.

Most heroic early modern houses (with which the history of modern architecture seems to begin) are just that: heroic. Male, forceful, muscular, and acrobatic, these houses (and you know who you are) are entirely different from each other but connected by that genderization. They tend to stand erect, with chests puffed out, while Gray's villa reclines in a languorous pose. Where they exaggerate, E-1027 understates just a bit. Where they use a chain saw, Gray uses a scalpel.

True, it is a tiny house (1,400 square feet/130 square meters), though that is palatial next to (and it is next to) Le Corbusier's minuscule Cabanon, which clocks in at one tenth that size. But E-1027 has a jewelry-like attention to tiny details and efficiency, and yet manages to be elegant and feel grand. It is not intellectualized or a slave to a single idea, but is a house of moments, views, vistas, and spaces within spaces.

It's no wonder Le Corbusier was so jealous of it.

10 August
William Van Alen

Midtown Manhattan, with Chrysler Building towering above its neighbors, 1932

Everyone knows the story of William Van Alen's Chrysler Building surpassing the height of its competitor (40 Wall Street, designed by Van Alen's former partner, Craig Severance) with a dramatic reveal of the spire and mast that was built inside it, hidden until the moment when it was clear that its competition was topped out. It's a great tale, a worthy deception, and a parable of relations between architects: fierce competition occasionally tempered by resourceful cleverness.

Van Alen's career was both made and unmade by the project; it made him famous and uniquely valuable, but in suing Walter Chrysler to collect his fee (a suit he won), he became unemployable, essentially blackballed by the client class. This goes back to the old idea of architecture as a gentlemen's avocation: you shouldn't need to be paid for your work; the work is its own reward. And if you insist on being paid, you may well pay in the end.

The Chrysler Building, in 1930, ended the Woolworth Building's seventeen-year reign as the tallest on earth, but its status lasted only a year, until the Empire State Building was completed. It may have lost its record for height, but for the design of lobbies Chrysler has never been surpassed; the ceiling mural

by Edward Turnbull is a particularly meta element of the lobby (though much else is self-referential). The ceiling is dominated by a view of the building itself (an elevation laid flat) and surrounded by illustrations of the workers building the building. It's a dizzying spectacle; airplanes fly overhead, machinery and power are celebrated, and hardly a car in sight (the car references are all external).

Then there's that ubiquitous picture of a costume ball with architects dressed as their buildings, including Van Alen as the Chrysler Building. Until Michael Dukakis rode in the tank, there hadn't been a more fatuous dressing up for a photo op. Van Alen stands out in the photo not just for his crown but also for his patterned suit; the other architects have generic outfits with some very sad hats. Of the two on the right, one is unidentified (early photo bombing?) while the other has the Museum of the City of New York on his head. *Sad.*

We all have group photos we regret (hurts to think about it). Van Alen may never have lived this one down; he went on to teach sculpture and, after the Chrysler Building, never built again.

11 August
Peter Eisenman

Memorial to the Murdered Jews of Europe, Berlin, Germany, 2005

Peter Eisenman is a difficult one, in many ways. He is undeniably smart, very smart, and capable of producing profoundly affecting work. His Memorial to the Murdered Jews of Europe in Berlin is simply devastating to experience. His football stadium in Arizona (where I worked designing its private suites) is a fine example of a new stadium, though its best feature is a real grass field that rolls out to enjoy the sun when not in play.

Other examples of his work tend to slide down the spectrum from disappointment to absolute horror. His House VI is legendary, prompting a book from the owners in rebuttal to any of the scant praise. The glass slot in the bedroom floor that forced the owners to use a pair of twin beds (à la *I Love Lucy* or *The Dick Van Dyke Show*) rather than a larger bed is the apex of inanity.

But, really, who is to blame for that kind of insane intrusion? Eisenman, of course, whose justification is that the house is more a record of a process than an object conceived in service of the clients (I will spare you the bullshit language of that contorted defense). But the clients are hardly blameless; these are very smart people (one with a PhD) allowing themselves to be used by an artist, willingly submitting to his torturous imposition. A process is continuous. A house is not. What pair of deluded, highly educated fools couldn't sort out that elementary conundrum? We know the answer.

Unfortunately, this type of abusive architect-client relationship (like the idea that a project should cost twice the budget and take twice the time planned) colors architects' reputations for the rest of us.

There is a tendency, with Peter at the forefront, for architects to attempt to recapture the esteem in which we were once held with arcane language, obfuscation, and overintellectualization to create an aura of grandeur. If mere clients can't understand their work, this stratagem goes, then it must be great!

My favorite image of Eisenman is from the 1984 documentary *Beyond Utopia*, where he is interviewed while getting his hair washed and cut at his barbershop (sorry, salon). In the same film Philip Johnson admits to not understanding a word Peter says, and that lets most of us off the hook as well.

12 August
Ron Herron

Competition entry for Trondelag Theater, Trondheim, Norway, 1975

Ron Herron cofounded Archigram in London around 1960; by about 1974, the group had changed everything and changed nothing. Herron joined Pentagram (and no wonder that name seemed right to him) in 1977 and left a few years later to design the Imagination Headquarters in London. Had he stayed at Pentagram, he would likely have still been there when I joined a decade later.

What I didn't know then was that Theo Crosby (called by the biographer Simon Sadler the "hidden hand" behind Archigram) promoted, employed, published, and collaborated with the group since its founding, so it makes sense that he invited Herron to join Pentagram. Herron worked on a retractable roof for the Globe Theater reconstruction, which Crosby would conceive in the mid-1970s and realize decades later.

Herron's most famous work, *Walking Cities* (1964), is a touchstone of brilliance and provocation even today, and it clearly influenced not just architects but also movies like *Star Wars*. But it was influenced by the Maunsell Forts, insect-like defense structures that appeared in the River Thames and elsewhere to protect England during World War II.

Peter Cook (not that Peter Cook, but another Archigram founder) once challenged a journalist by saying, "Name one Archigram project that couldn't be built." When the journalist suggested the Walking Cities, Cook responded, "Why not; we can build ocean liners." Perhaps, but aren't Archigram projects immeasurably better as ideas than as reality?

Centre Pompidou is the building most faithful to the ideas of Archigram, (Richard Rogers was at school at the Architectural Association in London just as Peter Cook arrived), and some Archigrammers consider it theft (of form without content). The museum does celebrate its technology à la Archigram, but it can't walk.

Ron Herron used collage in architectural drawings in ways virtually never done before; the whole graphic style of Archigram is part of its brand. And if you're not actually building your drawings, then your drawings better be pretty fucking great (and they are).

It's too bad I never met Ron, but I am only one degree away. Thanks (again), to Theo Crosby.

13 August
Tony Garnier

Proposal for "Cité Industrielle," published 1917

"Tony Garnier" sounds more like the name of a mobster, as in "Have Tony G make him a pair of concrete overshoes," than of a Prix de Rome–winning architect. Or maybe it could be a hair product.

And then there is bassist Tony Garnier, who performed with Bob Dylan in the Halle Tony Garnier, a former slaughterhouse/livestock market (maybe Satriale's in France?) that the architect Tony G designed in Lyon.

And let's not confuse Tony Garnier with Charles Garnier, architect of the Paris Opera (now called Palais Garnier). Chuck is referred to as Tony's father somewhere on the internet, but that's not so.

Our Tony Garnier was an architect who worked in that "not still classical, not yet modern" world that others like Auguste Perret occupied. Tony G's big moment was his Cité Industrielle, an urban plan exhibited in 1901 and 1904 but not published until 1917. He worked on it while on his Prix de Rome fellowship, to the dismay of the academy. It was an extremely detailed, quite specific design for a new city of thirty-five thousand people, with separate zones devoted to work, housing, health, and leisure. Interestingly,

Garnier did not include any religious or law enforcement zones, as he believed the citizens would rule themselves (!). Ah, socialism.

Cité Industrielle was a remarkable conception that influenced virtually everything that followed in urban design, town planning, and architecture, but barely moved the needle on Garnier's fame. Sad, because despite what we might now think of his ideas of separating the functional parts of a city, it made enormous sense when (and this is hard to imagine now) cities were the home of heavy industry; zoning it out of urban centers would preserve a decent residential life.

Garnier's thing was light, air, space, and greenery: a healthy living environment but definitely not a suburb. His work was dense and highly spatial, and it combined a classical sense of axiality with a modern, concrete materiality. It was so detailed that it managed to operate at a scale that still makes sense, unlike Le Corbusier's Ville Radieuse of giant towers and featureless public spaces.

Tony G had it right, but louder voices prevailed.

14 August
Sverre Fehn

Nordic Pavilion, Giardini della Biennale, Venice, Italy, 1962

There's one pavilion at the Venice Biennale Gardens that has always seemed not just the best idea, but also the best expression of a region: the Nordic Pavilion by Sverre Fehn. For places as cold and occasionally bleak as Finland, Norway, and Sweden, the pavilion is as open, light, airy, and cool as any of the pavilions there. Trees grow inside and through its roof, though *roof* might be the wrong word; it's more of a lattice just barely keeping out the rain and diffusing the light into a cool, ethereal wash. Compared to the nearby USA Pavilion, which was admittedly built more than twenty-five years earlier and by a private collaborative rather than a government, the Nordic Pavilion is simply sublime. But then nearly every pavilion is sublime compared to the US one.

The whole Venice Biennale Gardens, where both the Architecture Biennale and Art Biennale happen, is quite a supermarket of architecture and architects: Alvar Aalto designed the Finland Pavilion (and it may be why some felt the need for a Nordic one) as an oddball exercise in wood and triangles; across from the Nordic Pavilion is the Carlo Scarpa–designed Venezuela Pavilion, and he also designed the little garden in the main pavilion; Gerrit Rietveld designed the

Dutch Pavilion in the 1950s; BBPR (the Italian firm founded by Richard Rogers's father's cousin, among others) designed the Canada Pavilion; James Stirling designed the bookstore, now called the Stirling Pavilion (I guess when you die...); Josef Hoffmann designed the Austria Pavilion; his second attempt was built and is as modern today as it was in 1934.

The biennale grounds are like an expo that never changes; national pavilions are occasionally made over but manage to stay just a few steps behind the times. Except the US, which was more than a bit behind from the beginning.

Sverre Fehn demonstrates that a pavilion need not be a compromised, flabby, or retrograde exercise but can be both quietly startling and peacefully revolutionary.

The Pritzker Prize committee agreed, and even Fehn declared that as much as he tried to run from Scandinavian style, he found that he was running from himself, as one of the founders and practitioners of the style.

15 August
Paul Rand

Lobby sign carved with Yale University Press logo, New Haven, Connecticut, 1985

Rand Paul is the most obstructionist, hypocritical US senator (and doctor) who ever occupied a place in the Capitol, except possibly for his father Ron...wait, sorry, wrong dude.

Paul Rand was the most admired and sharply critical graphic designer in the history of twentieth-century US modernism. He is legendary for his corporate identities, like those for (drumroll...) IBM, Westinghouse, ABC, NeXT, Borzoi, Cummins, Enron (nobody's perfect), UPS, Yale, and I could go on.

His first rebranding was his own name (and I believe that Rand Paul is skating dangerously close to copyright infringement) from Peretz Rosenbaum to the less Jewish, more ethnically indeterminate Paul Rand, neatly choosing a four letters plus four letters name that was a designer's dream. (Note: my own name stacks five over five, something pointed out to me by my wife, Carin Goldberg, when she designed my first office logo; Spin Studio cleverly reduced that to four letters, and I believe I could go to three over three with JMS/BBR, but I digress...)

By sheer force of his personality and talent, Rand dignified and transformed the discipline once called commercial art into graphic design. He could change his name but not, perhaps intentionally, his Brooklyn accent, like John Hejduk, the similarly wicked-smart (though much taller) genius who kept his confounding Bronx accent to the end. It's a clever ploy (if it is a ploy) to feign provinciality while far outpacing one's competition.

Rand and Hejduk read a lot, not just about their craft but also about the ideas that surrounded them. Being a public intellectual with a strong accent (like Shelby Foote and his viscous Mississippi accent) seems to work best in Ken Burns's documentaries. Then again, I could listen to Robert Caro's New York accent forever.

Paul Rand's later work, and attitude, has been criticized for being overly cranky (even reactionary), as when he resigned from Yale because Sheila Levrant de Bretteville was appointed to head graphic design there. De Bretteville, similarly, was born in Brooklyn, is seriously smart, and retains her local accent, so I'm surprised they didn't bond.

Maybe too many letters in her name.

16 August
Alessandro Mendini

Poltrona di Proust (Proust chair), first version, 1978

Alessandro Mendini started out in the studio of Marcello Nizzoli, who famously designed the Lettera 22 typewriter and other serious (and seriously beautiful) appliances. Those works did not foretell Mendini's future, which became more decorated, variegated, and blazingly colorful as time progressed.

He joined Studio Alchimia in 1979 with Ettore Sottsass Jr., Andrea Branzi, and Michele De Lucchi, all of whom became even more famous in their next incarnations, Memphis and beyond. Their work, like that of the futurists, attempted to fracture current design orthodoxy with radical design, and like futurism it lasted for only a short, brilliant moment.

Memphis was the next incarnation for Sottsass (who founded it in 1980) and where Alchimia members landed next. Mendini was included in the group that continued and expanded Alchimia's explosively colorful and iconoclastic output. Memphis was, in a sense, the end of Italian modernism and the apex of Italian postmodernism, though that is not a very precise description of what was happening.

Through it all, Mendini produced work that was bolder, and occasionally much larger, than that of his colleagues. His

Groninger Museum is a pastiche, a collage on a giant scale. This was a guy who, sometimes quite skillfully, assembled objects, buildings, and ideas out of a grab bag of ingredients.

The issue (for me) isn't that Mendini went through a phase, but that he never left it. He is, ironically, not unlike Tom Wolfe (a promoter of all things nonmodern-orthodoxy), who dressed like a superannuated pimp as a young man and never seemed to outgrow it. We all eat fast food as kids, but a diet of it as adults will kill you. Mendini seemed to thrive on that diet, even as it became increasingly hard to swallow.

Take his Proust chair, which he designed when he was at Alchimia; it's a readymade baroque chair painted in pointillist style and revised over and over and over again his whole life. Most recently, he created a plastic outdoor version of it. He milked one idea (a chair Marcel Proust might have sat in) for the rest of his years.

It was dazzling the first time, charming the next, and irritating for the rest of time.

17 August
O. H. W. Hadank

Logo for Gutmann & Weinberg, 1921

Oskar Hermann Werner Hadank, O. H. W. Hadank, as he was known (though his first name is listed variously as Oskar, Otto, and Werner, sometimes in the same article), was one of those proto-modern design figures whose work manages to be neither traditional (he rarely used Fractur type) nor definitively modern (he invoked heraldry on occasion). Trying to find an analogous figure in architecture, I am still searching; it's not quite Edwin Lutyens, and though he overlapped with Le Corbusier and Mies van der Rohe, he never found the attraction of startlingly new design. Maybe it's Auguste Perret, though he embraced new technology, which seems to have no analogy in graphics at the time. Maybe T. H. Robsjohn-Gibbings, who designed modern furniture that was equally at home in less-than-modern settings.

Or maybe there is no analogy, and Hadank was a unique character in design. His work managed to fall just on the "correct" side of the traditional and modern divide for the Third Reich, though he apparently evaded doing any Nazi propaganda. He was seen as a captain of industry, professionalizing the graphic design profession and allying it to the commercial and industrial sources of commissions. And he consciously (and sometimes literally) ennobled his clients with his work, walking an interesting line between disappearing behind the work and becoming so famous that his own brand was seen as added value.

Apparently Paul Rand really admired this guy, and in some of Hadank's work you can see why. From his start in the nineteenth century, he managed to produce some very modern work, almost unwittingly, along with work that seemed more at home in premodern times. He had the heart of a modernist but the hand and vocabulary of a traditional designer.

Maybe he is most like the Swedish architect Erik Gunnar Asplund (nearly the same age), who produced work that almost always seemed modern but would not shy away from using referential elements when appropriate, which was almost always. Asplund created designs of the right scale, the right image, and the right attitude to both advance the art and mark its moment in time.

Seem like a good pair, these two.

18 August
Seymour Chwast

The Protagonists, published in the *New York Times,* 2019

You have to admire Seymour Chwast; at more than ninety, he is still the same lefty (both politics and handed) he always was; is still working and producing new, thoughtful work; and is still (albeit for the second time) married to Paula Scher. But despite that consistency, he isn't in the least stuck. We all hope to be as flexible as he is at whatever age we can manage.

Seymour has genetics on his side; his mother lived to be like one hundred plus and for all I know is still alive, driving her son crazy. Many of his original Push Pin Studios partners are gone (Reynold Ruffins dying recently and Milton Glaser passing on his ninety-first birthday), and Seymour seems to be in a race to outlive Ed Sorel.

Maybe it's what Stephen Jay Gould proposed forty years ago: that every living thing is allotted approximately the same number of heartbeats (about one billion, though humans, the outliers, somehow manage to max out at three billion). I have never seen Seymour run, nor talk at a New Yorker's clip, nor catch flies with his hand (à la Obama); he lives at a pace that I imagine will allow him to outlive us all. Not so much Type A as Type C, he keeps at it, not knowing anything other than working every day as an artist.

While some may live long out of spite, Seymour seems to do it out of humor. His work never fails to be funny, except when it is political and deadly serious; if it amuses him he seems certain it will amuse us too. He is usually right.

When you Google anyone, there is always that list of most-asked questions, one of which is always, "What is x's net worth?" (which I refuse to believe is always among the most queried). Seymour's are: What does Seymour Chwast do? What does Paula Scher's husband do for a living? What was the importance of the work of Push Pin Studios? How do you pronounce Chwast? (It's "Kwast," btw.)

"What was it like to work with Milton Glaser" is not one among them, though I imagine he is asked that all the time (and usually answers with equanimity). When Seymour Chwast outlives us all, it will simply be the end of an age of graphic design he defined over the course of sixty-five (and counting) years.

Happy birthday, Seymour (and happy hundredth, in case I miss it).

19 August
Coco Chanel

Chanel logo, designed by Coco Chanel, 1925

"The best things in life are free. The second-best are very, very expensive." It's quips like this that define the wit and wisdom of Coco Chanel, but her life was anything but as blithe as they suggest. She was a fierce survivor and a determined promoter of all things Chanel and luxurious. Mostly Chanel.

"My life didn't please me, so I created my life." Gabrielle Chanel was born into poverty and raised in a nun-run orphanage, a past she rewrote and ran from her entire life. Her birth certificate mistakenly spelled her name Chasnel; to avoid highlighting her illegitimate birth, she never officially altered it.

"As long as you know men are like children, you know everything!" Chanel used men to achieve her ends. They financed her original millinery shop and eventually her fashion boutiques. She succeeded on her own, but the field was leveled by others.

"I don't do fashion. I am fashion." Coco transformed women's fashion, using the relative comfort of menswear to create a new, more powerful, less constricting way to dress. And she controlled her entire brand, including designing the linked Cs logo.

"I don't care what you think of me. I don't think of you at all." Her choices in men were occasionally questionable: she consorted with a German spy during World War II. It was no casual affair; he installed her at the Ritz and introduced her to the Abwehr (Nazi intelligence, the ultimate oxymoron), and she was tasked with carrying a proposal to Churchill from German officers. She was barely allowed to escape to Switzerland after the war, reportedly with Churchill's help.

"In order to be irreplaceable, one must always be different." She returned a decade later to Paris to revive her fashion house and her reputation. It worked, especially in the US, where her collaboration was less offensive.

"A woman who doesn't wear perfume has no future." Chanel No. 5 manages to do the impossible: remain the most admired and purchased perfume for a hundred years. No other fashion item has that longevity and ubiquity.

"I only drink Champagne on two occasions, when I am in love and when I am not."

Ah, Coco.

20 August
Eliel Saarinen and Eero Saarinen

TWA Flight Center, John F. Kennedy International Airport, New York, New York, 1962

The most telling story (in addition to having the same birthday) about the Saarinens, father Eliel and son Eero, concerns the announcement of the winner of the St. Louis Gateway Competition. A telegram was sent to Cranbrook Academy of Art (where Eliel ruled and Eero lived) congratulating the winner, E. Saarinen, whereupon a celebration ensued...for Eliel Saarinen. It was just assumed (and Eero failed to question) that Eliel won. It was, of course, Eero who actually won, and when that was made clear a couple of days later, the family started the party all over again. I would love to read Eliel's diary from that day. And Eero's, for that matter.

Growing up under that level of dominance must have been crippling for Eero, but he managed (with the Gateway Arch) to slide out from under Eliel's thumb. The arch was genius in conception (Eliel's entry was more like the optical illusion of the impossible trident) and in actuality. In the short thirteen years of his life that followed, Eero produced an astonishing set of buildings, furniture, and entire campuses.

It's not just the quality of each building, but the range of design vocabularies they explored: everything from the entirely curvaceous TWA Flight Center to the orthogonal rigor of Bell Labs and the entire spectrum between. The breadth of design is supplemented by the range of iconic US companies and institutions Eero built for: Bell, GM, Deere, MIT, CBS, Lincoln Center, IBM, TWA, Yale, Tanglewood, and many more. Plus his furniture for Knoll, which is still utterly modern and utterly cool. I grew up with a Womb chair, knowing what it was before I knew what a womb was, and I remember passing by the CBS Building under construction with my grandmother, admiring it and nabbing a piece of the granite as a souvenir.

Eero Saarinen's curved work is especially impressive; without computers for design, without parametric design tools, 3D printers, or analytical structural programs, Eero used only paper and pencil, T square, and French curves. He worked in models of increasing scale, figuring it all out in three-dimensional mockups so large he could place himself inside them.

Impressively, in his greatly abridged career, he surpassed his father in fame, in impact, and in genius.

21 August
Friz Freleng

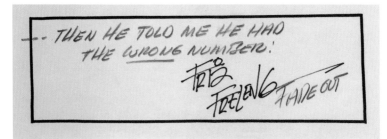

Note and signature on back of storyboard for *20 Second Bridge,* undated

I grew up watching and loving cartoons, and, while it never occurred to me then, I was bemused (which, by the way, does not mean slightly amused, but rather confused or puzzled) when I realized these things were made for kids by adults. The exceptions, the ones that seemed more meta than others, the ones that broke the fourth wall and acted like they were sophisticated beyond their natural audience, were often invented, drawn, scored, and directed by Friz Freleng and the Warner Bros. Studio.

Looney Tunes and *Merrie Melodies* were the Rolling Stones to the Disney Studio's Beatles: Bugs Bunny was Mick (the coolest and smartest wabbit), Daffy Duck (created by Tex Avery) was Keith, Elmer Fudd was Charlie Watts (though way fatter), and Marvin the Martian (drawn by Chuck Jones) was Bill Wyman (kind of stoic, kind of scary). I'm not sure who was Ronnie Wood (Tweety Bird?). You can assign your own roles, but it's only possible because these were very edgy creations.

Cartoons have forever warped certain pieces of classical music for people my age (especially Wagner). Nineteen-forties cartoons were our history teachers; one, "Herr Meets Hare" features Fatso Hermann Göring, Bugs disguised as Hitler and Stalin, and copious wartime jokes. "Bacall to Arms" is a movie parody (*To Have and Have Not*) within a cartoon, a metacartoon! All of these forced us kids to figure out what the hell was going on; they were our point of entry for some otherwise inappropriate content.

Freleng was a classical violinist and timed his cartoons on musical score sheets, accounting for his supremely precise comic timing and the musical quality of the dialog. But the extraordinary level of sophistication (aiming the dialog high enough for adults, recognizing the actual news of the day, and writing and directing with precision) were what defined Warner Bros. cartoons. Disney was technically superior, but Warner Bros. had what nearly all cartoons today have: intelligence and attitude.

We owe that to Friz and company.

That's all, folks!

22 August
Leni Riefenstahl

Filming *Olympia,* 1936 Olympics, Berlin, 1936

You know the scene in *Inglourious Basterds* when Michael Fassbender tries to convince a suspicious German officer that his weird accent is indeed German, but from Piz Palü? He claims to be in the 1929 Riefenstahl movie *Die weiße Hölle vom Piz Palü* (*The White Hell of Piz Palü*), skiing with his entire fabricated family. It almost works, until he orders three whiskeys using his three middle fingers rather than the thumb and two fingers, and it goes downhill from there.

Viewers had already seen the film within the film and the title on the marquee; it was playing as they watched Shosanna execute a perfect reel change in the Paris movie theater she operates. *Die weiße Hölle vom Piz Palü* was (and is, with context) actually an admired film and made Riefenstahl famous as an actor. In 1932 she directed and starred in her own *Das blaue Licht* (*The Blue Light*), which won a Silver Medal at the Venice Film Festival and impressed Hitler enough to hire her to make propaganda films, the second being *Triumph des Willens* (*Triumph of the Will*).

Leni admitted (proudly) that she was utterly enthralled hearing Adolf Hitler speak but claims she resisted making *Triumph* ("no, Adolf, no...") before relenting. The film is an astonishing achievement, if you can put aside all concerns about morality, history, memory, genocide, world war, dictators, the Holocaust, etc. (which apparently Riefenstahl did, for the rest of her very long life) and just think of it as revolutionary filmmaking, but with Aryans.

If Leni had demonstrated, at any point during her 101 years on Earth, any remorse or shame, we might see *Triumph* as (gorgeous) reportage. She didn't and we don't: her own guilt is inseparable from the assembled masses she pictures in the film. She wasn't an official Nazi party member (which probably kept her from prison after the war), and the fact that she used forced labor (literally people on their way to Auschwitz) in her films was probably just the casting director's fault (!). Poor Leni, she is really the victim in all this looking-backward stuff.

Or so she would have you believe. The unrepentant Leni Riefenstahl makes it impossible to see her films as anything but a beautiful crime, one more case of "What are we to do with art made by monsters?"

23 August
Laurinda Spear

Pink House, Miami Shores, Florida, 1978

There is a *New Yorker* article on polychromy in classical sculpture that focuses on the horror we Westerners feel when forced to confront the fact of painted marble, rather than pure whiteness. It's the same feeling we once got when considering the architecture of Arquitectonica, the firm Laurinda Spear cofounded in Miami.

It's the form-versus-surface conundrum; we want to believe that form and space reign supreme, but we are overly distracted by color and surface. When we imagine that a sculpture of a Greek archer was rendered wearing harlequin patterned leggings and a riot of other colors, it seems gauche and kitschy, when it is, in fact, the historical truth. It challenges how we think of the Western canon, Western art, Western purity, and race. Much of Greek and Roman polychromy (and writing) points to the populace including a wide range of skin colors, least of all white.

The Pink House, which Spear designed for her parents, doesn't necessarily explicitly raise the issue of race, though it does favor a vernacular that some consider a bit vulgar (the critical uproar nearly caused Spear to paint the house white). It may be okay for Luis Barragán to paint houses pink in Mexico, but here in the US? How can we like this house

so much, even forty-five years later, when we are trained to believe that sophistication comes wrapped in monochrome (neutral) packages? At least there is black-and-white photography to spare us the vulgarity!

Building for one's parents is a tradition among architects. It reinforces the assumption that architects hail from the upper classes, another misconception helping to explain why the profession is so overwhelmingly white. Charles Gwathmey built a pair of adorable little (whitish) buildings for his parents, but he relented from his orthodoxy in 1995, when he built the Museum of Contemporary Art North Miami; it is a collage of colors, no doubt due in part to Spear's erasing that white line in the sand.

The Pink House is not just pink; it is a spectacular design in any color. Layered, carved, and inverted (with the pool in front), it's a serious piece of architecture in a lovely painted package.

In 1970s architecture, there were the Whites (New York Five), the Grays (Robert Venturi and the rest), and at least one Pink, thanks to Laurinda Spear.

24 August
Charles Follen McKim

Main Concourse, Pennsylvania Station, New York, New York, 1910

We think of Stanford White as the progenitor of all things McKim, Mead & White because he (the flamboyant, red-haired, giant, mustachioed drama queen who was shot to death in the rooftop restaurant at his own Madison Square Garden by the husband of his former mistress) captured headlines and imaginations. In truth, Charles Follen McKim produced much of what we admire of their work.

New York's University Club and Century Association buildings are McKim's work. The former is a robust corner palazzo on Fifth Avenue, enlarged to New York scale. It hides six floors within its three-tiered facade except where the reading room (no talking allowed, or aloud), library (most beautiful outside Trinity College Dublin), and dining room (the third of the triumvirate) are stacked up, each with a magnificent height and running the full one hundred feet of Fifth Avenue frontage.

The Century Association, a few blocks south, is more restrained and less ostentatiously grand, sporting a flattened facade that, without the corner lot location of the University Club, feels more two-dimensional than three-dimensional. It's the Palazzo Rucellai versus Palazzo Strozzi, to put it (pedantically) in Florentine terms.

In Rome, McKim got to design a real palazzo in the land of palazzos, the American Academy in Rome. Perched on the Gianicolo, above Trastevere, it includes color (gasp!) on the facade, the terracotta hue that seems ubiquitous in Rome. McKim was so invested in the academy that he made up for its financial losses personally in the early years of its founding.

Back in New York, McKim designed the Morgan Library, exquisitely understated on the outside with a lavishly appointed interior.

His master oeuvre was Penn Station, an American version of the Roman Baths of Diocletian and Caracalla; it had a sequence of remarkable spaces, including a 150-foot-high stone version of Caracalla as a waiting room, and ended in a skeletal rendering in steel and glass, almost a line drawing of the Diocletian baths, as a gigantic train shed. It was one of the greatest rooms ever created.

As Vincent Scully said of McKim's masterwork, through Penn Station, "one entered the city like a god. One scuttles in now like a rat."

25 August
Astra Zarina

Astra Zarina in Rome, Italy, circa 1968

Astra Zarina is a name that's so cool it sounds like it had to be written for the screen, but in fact it belongs to a renowned architect and teacher at the University of Washington.

In 1960, Zarina was the first woman to receive a Rome Prize in architecture (a mere seventy-five years after the first Rome Fellow), which would shape the rest of her life. Ten years later, teaching at the University of Washington, she created the UW Rome Program, where students like Steven Holl were inspired to become the luminaries they later became.

But her passion was Civita di Bagnoregio, a small Italian hilltop town sixty miles north of Rome. During a visit, while waiting out a rainstorm in a single-room house, she chatted with its owner and agreed on the spot to buy it. During the two-year renovation, she and her architect husband, Anthony Costa Heywood, installed the first indoor bathroom in town and began slowly renovating other local structures.

They established a second Italian program for UW in Civita, documenting and renovating buildings in a village that had twelve residents when Zarina first arrived. The program continues after her death as a model for addressing threatened architectural and urban historical masterpieces. Other models are much more top-down than Zarina's.

Before he was ambassador to Italy, John R. Phillips bought a small village, Borgo Finocchieto, and restored the entire town as a place for his family and for weddings and business meetings. While utterly authentic, it is an island of extreme gentrification.

Pleasant Rowland (founder of American Girl) did something similar in Aurora, New York, home of her alma mater, Wells College. She couldn't buy the whole town, but her various renovations are tinged with a Disney feel, not surprising given her American Girl background.

These efforts sponsored by individual rich Americans are entirely unlike Civita di Bagnoregio; Astra Zarina helped define the way talent, rather than money, can transform the world.

26 August
Balkrishna V. Doshi

Le Corbusier with B. V. Doshi at Shodhan House, Ahmedabad, India, 1955

B. V. Doshi was lucky enough to work for Le Corbusier in Paris in the early 1950s before work had started at Chandigarh. Doshi returned to India to work on the buildings and houses in Chandigarh and eventually established his own Corb-influenced office. It's a pattern we have seen before: the exportation of Western ideas (or Western ideas about other cultures) to entirely independent cultures.

I've taken to noticing the suggested searches provided by Google when searching a name; Doshi's suggested searches expose a different, less respectful view than accorded Western practitioners or those from outside who remain in the West. The first (most popular) search is, "Is BV Doshi a qualified architect?" an odd question for a Pritzker Prize–winning architect, one of fewer than fifty architects worldwide who have been awarded the honor. Seems hard to believe that anyone would ask that of José Luis Sert or of any other architect who worked (often for no pay) for Le Corbusier.

For Le Corbusier, Doshi worked on the Villa Sarabhai, probably the only of his houses to include a second floor water slide into a swimming pool (I didn't notice one at the Villa Savoye).

Doshi also worked with Louis Kahn, just to complete the dynamic-duo dance card of modern architects building in India.

It's always interesting to see how acolytes filter or distort or attempt to reproduce their mentor's oeuvre. It's never better than the master's work, and often it's much, much worse. I worked for an architect who was an (unpaid) acolyte of Frank Lloyd Wright, and his work was not even close to Wright's (though it had its own character). While Doshi created his own style, the influences on it are obvious.

In some ways, he lived up to the original social tenets of Western modernism more than the original architects; he committed his life to providing decent and authentic buildings for all Indians. He has done that and is among the last living connections to Le Corbusier, Kahn, and other modernists. It's one answer to the question of whether working for famous architects is a good decision; for B. V. Doshi, the answer is a resounding yes.

27 August
André Lurçat

Villa Bomsel, Versailles, France, 1925

There's a class of early modern architects (André Lurçat included) that managed to create some lovely sculptural objects, but somehow never seemed to make it into the immortal class. They didn't lack the skill, but they probably lacked the insane marketing drive the ones we remember had. In some cases, they were good at style but less so at the intellectual backdrop.

It seems they didn't have the enormous egos of the masters (for example, Le Corbusier saved every single scrap of paper he ever touched, just to document what he knew would be his legacy). Though Lurçat built extensively (and some of his projects, like Casa Guggenbühl in Paris from 1926, compete successfully with any of its contemporaries), there is more to his lack of fame than lack of marketing prowess.

In the early 1930s, there was a rush to work in the relatively new Soviet Union. Le Corbusier, despite his decidedly right-wing leanings, went there to build and left in disgust, never to see his one Soviet building. Albert Kahn lasted longer but eventually left when payment changed to rubles. But Lurçat was a committed communist and went to live and work in Moscow for more than three years. Unlike his more famous colleagues, Andy's crime was not rejecting Stalin, etc. and not storming out of the Soviet Union disillusioned, never to return.

Lurçat finally left in 1937 and did no work during World War II with the Vichy government in France, unlike Le Corbusier, who was anxious to work for whomever would hire him.

While it may seem transgressive, it is no different than architects' rush to build in China just as the recession was ramping up. Expo 2010 Shanghai alone was a starchitect-fest. Architects turn decidedly apolitical when faced with the choice between building and not building. Somehow we ignore their (our) lapses when convenient.

Lurçat never got the benefit of that doubt. At a time when every modern architect proclaimed the benefit of modern architecture to the masses and embraced the socialist ideal of the right to healthy, dignified housing (and schools, and offices) it was Lurçat who actually built dignified housing (not just houses for the wealthy) and was a true believer.

André Lurçat seems to be lost to that confusing history, but luckily not to all of us.

28 August
Roger Tory Peterson

Flickers, 1973

Roger Tory Peterson was, as a kid, saving up to be able to buy his first camera when it was suggested that he take up drawing. That turned out to be a very good idea. As I sit writing this, a copy of Peterson's *Eastern Birds* is a few feet away (and a copy of David Allen Sibley's guide is underneath it).

Before Peterson, there were finely rendered, gorgeous drawings and lithographs of birds by, for instance, John James Audubon, but they were made for entirely scientific classification and documentation.

Peterson aimed for something different from a phylogenic catalog: bird identification in the field by people like you and me. He was an information architect, organizing the visuals on the page to clarify the visuals in the field. He invented an identification methodology that is still in use, still being refined (as of his 1980 edition, the one I have), and still the bible for birders since its 1934 first edition (which sold out in a week).

It's ironic that he was saving for a camera when he took up drawing; there are photographic bird guides but, as he wrote, they catch a bird in only one position, one context, under one lighting source. They represent a moment in time, not necessarily a tool for identification or learning. His admittedly filtered drawings highlight the markings and characteristics that distinguish bird from bird.

His guide is so densely packed with information, so perfectly laid out, and so refined that it is the most compact, most useful guide ever. The size alone declares its usefulness in the field (compared to a Sibley guide that is twice the size and three times the weight).

I admit to being utterly enchanted by Peterson's field guides; I live these days on a twenty-plus-acre landscape with a broad wetland running through it. Today a great blue heron has been wading in the ponds and flying from one to the other (they are truly dinosaurs). Mergansers and wood ducks waddle about, woodpeckers are busy drilling holes, and orioles and cardinals flit by. Bluebirds are everywhere, and a family of phoebes has hatched and occasionally returns to poop on my porch. And with luck I occasionally get to see ospreys, bald eagles, kestrels, and red-shouldered hawks.

Roger Tory Peterson has made it all especially joyful.

29 August
Michael Bierut

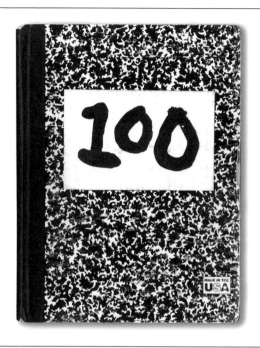

Sketchbook #100, composition book, National Blank Book Company, 26 August 2013

I've learned more just by working near and with Michael Bierut than I might have in decades of postgraduate work. We designed projects together, gave talks together, ran Pentagram together, assembled presentations together, and had a very good time doing it all. And the book you are holding is not only designed by Michael but also exists because he was good enough to suggest it as a book, and to shepherd it through a process that seemed entirely opaque to me.

His intuitive grasp, fueled by a fiercely idea-driven mind, of issues of both design and the actual making (and selling) of design is fairly awesome. His range of knowledge (and photographic memory) has produced some jaw-dropping impromptu performances, like the time that he started to reel off, in detail, Elvis Presley's early work and life when first meeting the folks from Graceland. Or the time he discussed the vagaries of Coca-Cola's history (and secret formula) when Coke's folks stopped by.

When we met with possible clients, I would wait for the moment that he, seeming utterly disinterested or bored or doodling in one of those standard grade-school composition books he adopted, would lift his head and pause before pouring forth a stream of staggering insights. He often led with, "Maybe the problem isn't…" before he reframed the entire brief in front of our eyes.

Once, on board a jet waiting for takeoff at LaGuardia Airport, we heard over the intercom, repeated twice, "easy victor forward wing," code (we now know) for "evacuate via the middle and front exits." As we sat in the exit row, the flight attendant ran by (now I get the sensible heels) shouting to open the exit doors and get the fuck out! Michael pulled open the door and (rather than the directions we were supposed to read, Michael) handed it to me (it's quite light, by the way) before disappearing through the hole in the plane. I followed him out onto the wing, jumped to the tarmac (a much longer drop than expected), and ran across the runways, expecting one of those action movie explosions to blow us up (it didn't).

The punch line is that hours after all that, after the adrenaline subsided, Bierut looked at his watch and said, "I think we can still make the 12:30 flight" (we did).

That relentless optimism, unflagging drive, and occasional fearlessness is why Michael Bierut still, after decades of doing what he does, continues to amaze.

30 August
Theo van Doesburg

"The square is to us what the cross was to the early Christians."

Theo van Doesburg on symbolism in the new religion of modernism

I was designing a restaurant for Bobby Flay, his second in New York, when graphic designer Alexander Isley covered the walls with collaged images in a kind of explosion of sniped posters. One had a bullfighter and bull; Bobby saw it and said the restaurant should be absolutely "bull free." Isley cut out a circle of some color and pasted it over the bull, leaving the toreador (and some toro legs sticking out), to which Flay said, "Well, now you're just mocking me."

That's how I feel about the (possibly apocryphal) story of Theo van Doesburg and Piet Mondrian's split; Piet simply couldn't abide a diagonal, so Theo created paintings taunting Mondrian in every possible permutation. Van Doesburg, outgoing and flamboyant, relentlessly mocked the shy and introverted Mondrian, in painting after painting, occasionally seeming to deconstruct Piet's paintings into his own, with diagonals! In one he left all the rectangles and lines orthogonal but rotated the canvas forty-five degrees into a diamond! Talk about mocking...

Imagine a time when an international artistic brawl, and the end of a productive friendship, would involve whether to introduce diagonals into modern abstract painting! Mondrian had the last laugh, living to seventy-one,

while his nemesis van Doesburg died at forty-seven. Ah, good times.

Van Doesburg was actually quite accomplished at appropriating the work of others and crafting his paintings to become critiques of his idols (or antiheroes). It was as much (I am assuming) an intellectual as a passive-aggressive pastime.

Van Doesburg, like so many other poseur artists of his time (and sometimes now), changed his identity by changing his name. He was born Christian Emil Marie Küpper and became Theo Doesburg, then Theo van Doesburg. In this persona he formed (with Mondrian) *De Stijl* as a magazine and then a movement. He dabbled in Dada (onstage in Weimar, with Kurt Schwitters barking in the rear of the theater). He confronted suprematism with diagonal versions of Kasimir Malevich's ruminations on a square.

His architectural work was often quite successful in expanding the canvas to three dimensions and was remarkably prescient.

Theo van Doesburg was a provocateur, a critic, an artist, and (happily) a ridiculer of the first order.

31 August
Landis Gores

Kerson House, Port Washington, New York, 1954

Landis Gores and Philip Johnson, who opened an office together after World War II and worked together for six years, are a parable of talent and success, luck and money.

Landis Gores was brilliant, attending Princeton and Harvard, becoming part of the Harvard 5, and, during the war, working on the British Ultra decoding program, where Alan Turing and others broke the Enigma and other German cipher machines. He was awarded an Order of the British Empire and a Legion of Merit and left the US Army as a major (at twenty-six years old), having contributed to perhaps the most significant noncombat effort of World War II.

Philip Johnson, on the other hand, had more than flirted with Nazism for years leading up to World War II but cleverly retreated from his Fascism as he assessed the political situation. Brilliant as well, but in quite different ways, he attended Harvard and enlisted in the US Army at age thirty-three as a private in 1942 (but only after being cleared by the FBI, who suspected he might be a German agent) and spent the war in the US.

They formed an office in New York City together, Johnson the idea man, Gores

the one who would make the ideas into buildable architecture. Together they worked on the Rockefeller Townhouse, the MoMA Sculpture Garden, and Philip Johnson's Glass House before parting in 1951.

Philip Johnson went on to be, well, Philip Johnson. Landis Gores sadly contracted polio in 1954, just a year before the Salk vaccine was available, and spent the rest of his life in a wheelchair. At first, clients were reluctant to engage Gores, but enough eventually did to keep him working on increasingly energy-conscious homes.

The truth is that Gores may have bested Johnson's talent but not his verve. His work never exceeded the work he did with (or for) PJ.

Gores was clearly a better person than Johnson (though the bar was fairly low), but Private Johnson was much better at attracting the best work (pays to be wealthy and well positioned), conceiving the best work (the three projects they did together are among Johnson's best), and convincing clients to buy what he was selling.

Johnson always had a version of Gores as he went on through life, but Landis never had another Philip.

01 September
Charles Correa

Jawahar Kala Kendra Arts Center, Jaipur, India, 1993

Charles Correa was not the jazz pianist, but if architecture is frozen music (Goethe said that), then maybe he was a bit of a jazz musician (I said that). He was, despite his name (Charles Mark Correa) India's premier modern architect.

Most surprising, for an architect whose MIT thesis was a series of animated films about participatory urban design, is his Champalimaud Centre for the Unknown, home of a Lisbon-based research institute. It was our Portuguese doctor who first mentioned the place and its amazing architecture. I'd never heard of it, but even more surprising than its mission (advanced neuroscience research, applied research, and lots of other things I don't quite understand) is who designed it, sitting at the spot that Vasco da Gama and others launched their ships into the, well, unknown: Charles Correa.

Champalimaud may be Correa's version of the Salk Institute, or it may be a riff on Oscar Niemeyer, but whatever its inspiration, it is an entirely unexpected project. Louis Kahn's Salk Institute, whose geometry is entirely the opposite of Champalimaud, creates a public space between buildings that is focused on the sea, as does Correa's. But Champalimaud's buildings are almost

entirely curved and made of stone; they are soft where the Salk is crystalline, rounded where Salk is sharp and crisp. It wouldn't be his first building that referenced Kahn; his memorial to Mahatma Gandhi recalls Kahn's Trenton Bath House. It's unclear if Correa knew Kahn, but he certainly knew his work, given how much Kahn built in India. In a film about Champalimaud, Correa quotes Kahn, which is an indication of the closeness of Kahn to his project.

But the two architects couldn't have been more different in most ways. Correa was genuinely committed to the urban realities of his projects and the people they served. Kahn was utterly involved in the architectonics of his work, but the masses (except those of concrete) hardly played into his thinking. Correa's genius was to absorb the work of others and transform it into his own voice: "In an era dominated by the 'starchitects' and their iconic structures, architecture cannot be mere adjectives and exclamation marks. Cities need grammar."

Very nicely put, Charles.

02 September
Dan Kiley

Currier Farm, Danby, Vermont, 1959

Before doing independent landscape work, Daniel Urban Kiley had one remarkable job while he was the Army Director of Design Services for the Office of Strategic Services (and how does one even get that job?). After World War II, he designed the courtroom for the Nuremberg trials. Not for the movie set, *Judgment at Nuremberg*, for the actual trials! Luckily, during this work he saw the places that inspired him later in life; the gardens of André Le Nôtre and the French approach to landscape. Strange combination of experiences...

Daniel Urban Kiley's middle name says a lot. He treated landscapes more like urban spaces with controlled geometry and structure than flower gardens or other contrived naturalistic places.

Landscape architecture is a bit inscrutable for a few reasons: it constantly changes; it uses a set of elements that resist control; it doesn't become itself until years have passed; it often has no brief other than to be wonderful; it is hard to judge; and it is everywhere, even when undesigned.

It's like what Massimo Vignelli said about graphic design (when asked if he really uses only three typefaces),

"It's not the typeface, it's the typography." For me, landscape architecture is as impossible to do as graphic design. It's not about inventing a new flora or using plants in unsustainable ways. It is about arranging elements that are often ubiquitous and often familiar in unfamiliar and affecting ways.

Dan Kiley, like only a few others, managed to turn the same elements others used into startling compositions. There was really no such thing as modern landscape when he started; there were some small cubist gardens and some surreal rooftop terraces, but nothing as expansive as a modern landscape. While he was studying at Harvard, landscape architecture was taught in the Beaux-Arts model, despite the presence of Walter Gropius. Kiley never finished his education there.

Starting with organizing a space for the worst people on Earth and ending with the creation of places that can live almost forever is the sort of range one might have expected from Daniel Urban Kiley.

03 September
Louis Sullivan

Carrie Eliza Getty tomb, Graceland Cemetery, Chicago, Illinois, 1890

Maybe I'm just obtuse, but I don't really see how Louis Sullivan, despite his often interesting, and occasionally sublime, work, was the "father of modernism" in the US. Or, as some claim, the "father of the skyscraper." It might be his obsession with distracting decoration that puts me off. Or maybe that there are other contenders like Daniel Burnham (whose birthday is tomorrow and who hired Sullivan for his 1893 Columbian Exposition in Chicago) for creating the first steel frame, first tall building, and first plate glass in a facade.

Claims to be the first aside, Sullivan designed some seriously great buildings. His Charnley House (which Frank Lloyd Wright, his draftsman, claimed as his own) is that moment before Louis started to slather on the decoration (there is a bit on the balcony), and it is seemingly carved out of a single solid. Inside there is a fantastic slot up to the skylight that illuminates what would otherwise be a darkened interior.

Despite what he did later, he said then, "We should refrain entirely from the use of ornament for a period of years, in order that our thought might concentrate acutely upon the production of buildings well-formed and comely in the nude."

Even more famously, Sullivan said, "Form ever follows function," something he said he cribbed from Vitruvius, writing in the first century BCE. He was, apparently, not one to follow his own advice.

Later Lou became obsessed with the arch, especially really, really large ones. But before that, he and his partner Dankmar Adler designed a spectacular hybrid in Chicago, the Auditorium Building, with a forty-three-hundred-seat theater (Radio City Music Hall holds six thousand) embedded and wrapped in a hotel, offices, retail, and restaurant; it was then the largest building in the world.

Sullivan went from begging for naked buildings to documenting a methodology for his system of decoration at the very end of his life. His late work is, in effect, American art nouveau applied to some otherwise very naked, very beautiful, buildings.

I guess function, to Louis Sullivan, included decoration.

04 September
Daniel Burnham

Flatiron (Fuller) Building under construction, New York, New York, completed 1902

The book *The Devil in the White City* by Erik Larson is about the 1893 World's Columbian Exposition in Chicago and the first modern serial killer (the devil gets top billing). Its true story revolves around Daniel Burnham and Frederick Law Olmsted Sr.'s creation of the White City and H. H. Holmes's horrific murders at the same time. What's so bizarre, and unexpected, is that the boring part (the architecture) is really the most fascinating read, and the murders are just, well, background.

That design could trigger such high drama is, in large part, due to Burnham's personality, but was as much about how design, as a public activity, can move a populace. Deeply. As we are by Larson's book.

Burnham was famous for his "Make no little plans. They have no magic to stir men's blood..." quote, but the coda that usually gets left out is "...and probably will not themselves be realized." So, the quote was Burnham's practical business policy as much as his lofty philosophy. In his days, one (even one unschooled in architecture like Burnham and Frank Lloyd Wright and lots of others) could not only design buildings but also get commissions to design cities. Whole fucking cities like, say, Chicago or San Francisco or Manila or

parts of Washington, DC. And even pick up a few little building commissions along the way, like Union Station. Of course, that was when entire cities, like Chicago, could be destroyed by a single fire, as in, "Nice city, too bad if something should happen to it."

When Colin Forbes moved to New York to open the second Pentagram office, he landed at George Nelson's office (for a while Nelson was described as a Pentagram partner) and somehow was considering buying the Flatiron Building for $100,000 a floor! (This was considerably less than Pentagram paid twenty years later for a tiny building nearby.) Burnham's Flatiron Building, the local landmark near the Pentagram offices when they were on Madison Square, is still his best. No, it was never the tallest building in the world or even in New York City, but it looked like the tallest, and kind of still does.

Daniel H. Burnham undeservedly gets less respect than, say, McKim, Mead & White, but when he died his was the largest architectural firm in the world. Make no small plans indeed.

05 September
Claudio Silvestrin

P Apartment, Milan, Italy, 2009

Back in the 1980s in New York City, there was a fashion designer, Zoran, whose loft was so minimal it barely existed; entirely white (walls, floors, ceiling), the loft's only visible elements were a mattress (white, on the floor) and a long line of a few steps leading to a lowered area with a grate in the floor. It was the shower. That was it. Everything else was hidden behind a wall. I sometimes get that feeling when looking at Claudio Silvestrin's work, especially his work for Ye (then known as Kanye West).

Silvestrin's promo includes this very odd claim: "Considered a master of contemporary minimalism, Silvestrin is admired by international architects and designers, such as Giorgio Armani, Terence Conran and Kanye West." So, two clients and a dead person?

Silvestrin was briefly partners with John Pawson, whose minimalist cred is pretty much uncontested. Silvestrin's work can be a bit more robust, but of course the English and the Italian versions of minimalism are born of different cultures; for the English it's an expression of modesty, for Italians it's more like the luxury of less.

I first encountered Silvestrin's work at Princi, a bakery and café created in Milan and appearing these days, it seems, everywhere. It's like a modern forge lined in limestone, rough, smooth, and everything in between, with a fire at the back and finished product popping through the glass at the street, connected by a stone counter that seems a mile (sorry, kilometer) long. But the star is the bread, the pizza in a hundred variations and cut to size by servers with a pair of ordinary scissors, plus the coffee.

If a project has rough-hewn vertical limestone monoliths or a rough-edged thick slab of limestone as a (massively heavy) coffee table or even a bed-sized hewn slab of stone looking rather soft and cushy, it is likely that Silvestrin had a hand in it.

His projects can be seductive and beautifully executed, but his accompanying philosophy is one more attempt to elevate work with words rather than deeds. Unless there is a guidebook to every building or a docent narrating the architect's intent, architecture must stand on its own. Silvestrin's work does stand on its own, despite his words.

06 September
Niels Diffrient

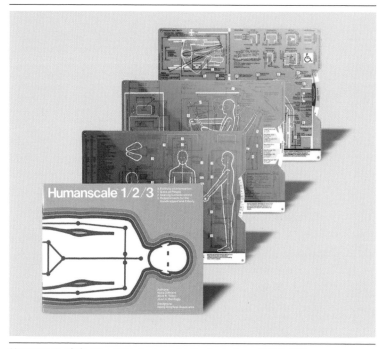

Humanscale 1/2/3 adjustable design guideline tools, issued 1974–1981

If Niels Diffrient had designed only three things in his life, he would be a star (which, neatly, is also the name of the town where he was born): the Princess phone, the Polaroid SX-70, and the Humanscale 1/2/3 ergonomics series. There is genius and cultural import in each, and these are only a small part of his impact.

Even though I met him, I somehow assumed he was from Scandinavia; he was decidedly not, unless Mississippi is in Denmark (you know, like the Louisiana Museum of Modern Art). He grew up in Detroit and landed eventually at Cranbrook Academy of Art. That's how he came to work for Eero Saarinen, helping him with the chairs he designed for Knoll.

A winning student, Diffrient was awarded a Fulbright scholarship and went to Italy, where he worked with Marco Zanuso. He returned to spend twenty-five years at Henry Dreyfuss's design office in Pasadena (where he designed the three iconic pieces above). From that point on, he became engrossed in ergonomics, shifting design, slowly but inexorably, toward things humans can use without ending up hobbled.

Before the ADA (Americans with Disabilities Act, which should probably be DAAA: Differently Abled Americans Act), my office used the *Humanscale 1/2/3 Manual*, with its clever dials and charts. Because of Niels we learned to fit our work to those who actually use it (shocking!), though, full disclosure, I still make things too tall for some (one) family members. File that under "better to ask for forgiveness than permission."

Diffrient quietly worked into his eighties designing chairs that worked in new and newly comfortable ways, without the thirty-nine adjustments and 652-page instruction manual that some modern chairs seem to have. His chairs are the analog version of invisible technology; we don't want to be constantly adjusting the brightness of our phones or changing the time on all our devices for daylight saving, etc., so why would we want chairs that need engineering degrees to operate?

Niels Diffrient set the agenda for us all, quietly, inventively, and beautifully.

07 September
Daniel Weil

Clock for an Architect, gift to James Biber upon leaving Pentagram, 2011

Daniel Weil is obsessed with time. And now, unwittingly (but not unwillingly!), so am I.

It's not just the myriad clocks he has designed, each one an argument about some aspect of life, but also how time finds its way into everything he does. His Pentagram Papers issue 40 was called *Time Signatures* (it features his mother's collection of signed opera programs), and the latest exhibit of his work at London's Design Museum was *Time Machines*. His earliest published design is the Bag radio, but its lesser-known partner is a similarly bagged electronic clock.

"Motion is the physical analog of time" was a bit of Weil wisdom tossed off while we were working on the Swatch store in New York City. It helped explain why the store was lined in miles of exposed glass pipe that revealed watches shooting around the shop, powered by pneumatic tubes, an ancient technology that was used in banks and department stores for at least a hundred years.

That's a typical Weil move: repurposing the familiar as the new, crashing out of one context into the next (the future?). He has taken cake pans and turned them into light fixtures and used a Pirelli floor tile pattern as a CD cover.

The other Weil leitmotif is play; he is unrelentingly playful, and even his drawings look like some genius baby drew them (and maybe one did). His children's book about chess (yes, chess) again references time and uses a day/night differentiation of the pieces rather than the typical black/white.

But any attempt to wrangle this polymath's oeuvre into a neat package (like "time") will ultimately omit half his thinking. His unbridled enthusiasm is not just his fibrillating design metabolism, but also his process of unburdening himself of his excess of ideas. Watching him attempt to empty his fount can be exhausting (for us and him).

Danny was the first three-dimensional design partner to join Pentagram after I did, and it's hard to express what a joy and relief it was to have someone (exactly) my age as a colleague and eventually a friend. That joy continued until my last moment there, when Danny designed the parting gift, a "clock for an architect" that still graces my shelf.

Good times, Danny, good times.

08 September
Denys Lasdun

32 Newton Road House, London, England, 1938

Brutalism looks pretty good now (or at least it does on Fuck Yeah Brutalism), but somehow that doesn't include the work of Denys Lasdun. Brutalism always looked better in the buildingless void of the countryside, or a completely sympathetic context like Chandigarh, or an edge condition. Lasdun's work is often embedded in an urban condition, where it can do the most harm.

Edge conditions (like Central Park for the Guggenheim Museum) are incredibly forgiving; nearly anything can work at boundaries between density and openness. In Lasdun's case, that's the National Theatre on the South Bank in London, of which King Charles III (that paragon of open-minded thought) said, "It seems like a clever way of building a nuclear power station in the middle of London." (Such a way with words, like "monstrous carbuncle.")

There are exceptions to the no-brutalism-in-an-urban-condition rule; Marcel Breuer's Whitney Museum (currently housing the Frick collection) somehow works while breaking the "edge" rule, and Lasdun's Royal College of Physicians fails despite it. The RCP sits on Regent's Park at the end of a long row of terrace houses by John Nash, architect of all things Georgian in London, and Lasdun thought they really worked well together (!). They don't, but it's exactly the kind of 1960s rationale architects could convince themselves of.

Lasdun said, "It is a sort of sculpture that you can only do with reinforced concrete, but you need to work to a certain scale....It is not a cosy little material." No, maybe not, but concrete stills needs a relatable scale, texture, and materiality that buildings like the RCP don't possess. Have a look at the Rietveld-Schröder House for guidance.

The difficulty in supporting good architecture is that sometimes (maybe often?) bad architecture wears the same clothes. Brutalism can be so spectacularly successful and so spectacularly awful. It's not the typeface, it's the typography, as Massimo Vignelli said (and as I find myself repeating repeatedly). Terrible buildings and great buildings are often made of the same stuff.

King Charles III doesn't help when he rages against architecture rather than acknowledging we don't (all) live in the eighteenth century; and we don't help our argument when we laud any modern architecture just because it's modern.

09 September
Poul Henningsen

PH Artichoke lamp, 1958

You say artichoke, I say lamp. Poul Henningsen, known as PH, was the incredible polymath who designed all those layered lamps we love, and they were almost a side hustle for him.

He was the illegitimate son of well-known writer Agnes Henningsen and satirist Carl Ewald, and he became famous for his leftist screeds and veiled resistance-supporting songs, especially anti-Nazi ones. He designed a self-pumping bicycle, a glass-topped grand piano, and light fixtures that shielded exposed filament bulbs to produce glare-free light. Oh, and he made a film about Denmark, in his spare time. And that was just pre–World War I.

Henningsen's anti-Fascist writing was so provocative he was scheduled for assassination by the Danish Nazi leader and deportation to a concentration camp by the Nazis themselves, in a kind of "belt and suspenders" death order. So thorough, these Fascists. He escaped certain death (maybe twice!) by rowing to neutral Sweden with Arne Jacobsen and their wives. Really, why isn't this a movie yet? Or at least a heroic painting, *Designers Crossing the Sound*?

Back in Denmark after the war, Henningsen rejected both Fascists and communists and became an antiestablishment figure in the 1960s. He wrote about architecture and design, calling a Bang & Olufsen radio "a monster with a bloated belly, an insult to people who like modern furniture." It prompted B&O to reconsider its production and hire designers for the first time.

But his light fixtures are why we know his name. They are magnificent (and pricey) for a couple of reasons: they are perfectly engineered to shade the bulb (even though now we have frosted ones), and they comprise a system of sizes and layers while occasionally breaking out and doing nutty things like the Artichoke lamp or Spiral lamp or Snowball lamp or Louvre lamp.

Beyond lamps, Henningsen designed the Axe table (legs are axe handles), a perfectly lighted mirror, more and more pianos, chairs (including the Pope chair), and probably, who knows, the iPhone. He was unstoppable.

Every night I gaze at one of his bits of genius, a PH5, before nodding off.

G'night, Poul Henningsen. And thanks.

10 September
Rudolph Schindler

Lovell Beach House, Newport Beach, California, 1926

I once toured California modern houses with clients, having dinners, lunches, or drinks at many of them. I toasted Pierre Koenig and Julius Shulman at Case Study House 22 and lunched at the Eames House with Lucia Eames and Eames Demetrios. And I dined at Rudolph Schindler's Kings Road House, in the courtyard with the outdoor fireplace, in what was a magical morphing of an occasionally perverse communal home to a place of serene beauty; spending time there, using it as intended, was transformational.

It's true of architecture: drawings offer just a taste, photos a tease, and a visit a start. But spending real time at a building is an experience. People sit in front of a Mark Rothko painting for literally hours to fully experience it; a piece of architecture, especially something as challenging as a Schindler house, deserves at least that.

Reyner Banham said Schindler designed houses "as if there had never been houses before." That is either high praise or throwing shade, but it's true.

Schindler was omitted from the 1932 MoMA International Style show that Philip Johnson assembled, though his fellow Austrian and frenemy Richard Neutra was included. Both had designed houses for Dr. Philip Lovell (born Morris Saperstein), a health guru in Los Angeles; the Lovell Health House, Neutra's first masterpiece (it's the house in *LA Confidential* where Pierce Patchett lives, and dies) and the Lovell Beach House by Schindler (born Schlesinger). It's hard to see why both weren't included in Johnson's show, except that it is possible that Schindler was an asshole. When someone is described as a "curmudgeon" or "not quite a misanthrope," it's pretty clear who they are.

Johnson also slighted Frank Lloyd Wright (Schindler and Neutra had both worked for Wright and both had quit) in the same show and had to appease him with a solo show.

Schindler and Neutra, his one-time housemate at Kings Road, split and didn't speak for decades. Schindler and his wife split as well, sharing the divided house (see "misanthrope" above). When Neutra was admitted to the hospital, he ended up in the same room as Schindler (this actually happened), who was dying of cancer. They reconciled in the end (Schindler's end, that is; Neutra's came seventeen years later).

Rudolph Schindler's houses have a cult following, which would suit him perfectly.

11 September
Cedric Price

Snowdon Aviary, London Zoo, London, England, 1965

If you want to see a Cedric Price building, well, structure, still standing, you'd better hurry. The London Zoo aviary he designed for Lord Snowdon and Princess Margaret is about to be altered. It's the only existing built work by Price, yet he has been enormously influential.

The aviary, an ephemeral, transparent scrim containing a slice of the biome nearly indistinguishable from its surroundings, is a perfect building to remain. It is less a building and more a drawing or outline or bit of geometry to operate within. It's more idea than building.

Price was all about change, indeterminacy, flexibility, adaptability, movement, and lots of other ideas that tend not to be buildings. But his explorations, especially the Fun Palace of 1961, had and have impact. That building is constantly being referenced as a timely concept and has, for the last sixty years, stood for a kind of possibility that ended up being the Centre Pompidou. Even the Shed in Hudson Yards has its foundation in the Fun Palace.

But these and other buildings that reflect the Fun Palace mostly reference its form; Price's ideas behind the building were instead about social engineering, reshaping society, and exercising power at the decentralized mass level, not the centralized level that the Centre Pompidou and the Shed address.

Indeterminate structures, those that can truly change form in response to changes in needs, are shibboleths that seem perfectly attuned to the 1960s. Archigram's walking cities, instant cities, and pop-up cities; Superstudio's conceptually gridded landscapes permitting anyone to plug in and exist anywhere; Le Corbusier's Venice Hospital project, an extendable grid anchored on the island but capable of growth into the sea; and Candilis, Josic, Woods, and Schiedhelm's Free University of Berlin (more system than object, yet the only actual building of all these progeny) all play in the same sandbox. The problem, of course, is once responsive structures are built, they instantly become the opposite of their original intent.

Cedric Price pursued actual buildings, built a few, and even supported one's demolition. It was demolished the same year Price died, neatly ending both his and his building's life.

12 September
Richard Howard Hunt

Freeform, State of Illinois Building, Chicago, Illinois, 1993

Without attempting a full psycho-biography of Richard Howard Hunt, I will note that he was the son of a librarian/artist and a barbershop owner, which exposed him to both the worldly academic and the local neighborhood cultural founts in Chicago before World War II. He attended the School of the Art Institute of Chicago; he sold a piece to MoMA before he graduated. In 1960 he became, while wearing his US Army uniform, the first Black man in Austin, Texas, to be served at a segregated lunch counter (without apparent incident). He served on the National Endowment for the Arts governing board and several Smithsonian boards. And he placed more public sculpture in sites across the US than any other artist.

This is a man seemingly comfortable in virtually any context, from the boardrooms of the Smithsonian to his 150-foot-/45.7-meter-high studio in an abandoned power substation to the Woolworth lunch counter sitting among an entirely white crowd to the opera houses he visited with his mother to the basement below the barbershop where he set up a welding shop.

Hunt did his European tour in a Citroën 2CV, spending most of his time in Florence. I did the same, exactly twenty years later, touring Europe in a red 2CV

and spending months in Florence. Hunt learned metal casting at the famed Ferdinando Marinelli Artistic Foundry there, while I mostly learned about the antipasto at Trattoria del Pennello. A useful education for both of us.

If Hunt is comfortable anywhere, one might say the same about his art, because it's mostly plop art (in the UK, plonk art) that could be anywhere (or nowhere). James Wines coined the phrase plop art, a play on pop art and a pejorative about sculpture that is simply plopped (plonked) down in front of any building or in any public space.

"Percent for art" programs have mandated much of the "we need something" art in front of thousands of new buildings. We don't (always) need something; the reductio ad absurdum is the Vessel in Hudson Yards, a much reviled (with good reason) waste of two hundred million dollars that even violates the "first, do no harm" tenet of public works.

Richard Howard Hunt doesn't offend, or harm, viewers, which is why he holds the record for most-placed sculpture. But he also doesn't challenge or enlighten viewers, which explains his works' ubiquity.

13 September
Ralph Rapson

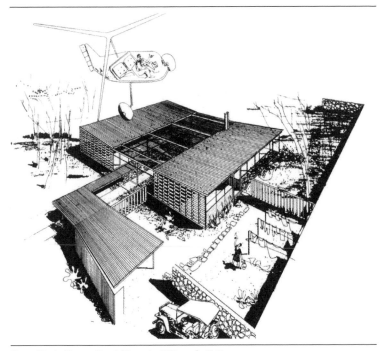

Case Study House No. 4 (Greenbelt House), 1941

Ralph Rapson once said he "felt sorry for anyone who wasn't an architect," eight words that express the wonderfully naive optimism, the unbridled joy, and the limitless pride in the profession that Rapson, as the thirty-year dean of the University of Minnesota School of Architecture, imbued in thousands of students.

I struggle to understand how he constructed the iconic renderings that made him famous; he lost his right arm as a child and drew with only his left. Whatever his technique, Rapson famously took drafting to an extraordinary level. His 1945 rendering of Case Study House 4 shows the husband arriving home by helicopter while the wife hangs laundry to dry on a line. As Esther McCoy pointed out, Rapson focused on the wrong machine (and we are all still waiting for our flying cars!).

Today computer-aided design (CAD) is easily done with one hand, as is freehand drawing. At Cornell University's Department of Architecture, the first-year studio is still taught with mechanical and freehand, not computer, drawing. It's not mere sentimentality; drawing with a direct, physical connection forces a critical

consideration of the drawing. When scale changes (going from easily manipulated size to enlarged scales that can provide detailed information), hand drafting requires an entirely new drawing set; CAD never requires this reconsideration when changing scales, leaving out critical steps in the development of designs.

Drawing by hand, without tools, is a disappearing art (I don't draft these days, but I do draw). The hand-eye-brain connection is critical to architects, just as the idea-word-composition is to writers. The ability to express a thought gets muddied if drawing is not an available skill There are writers who compose longhand and others who type, and it's hard to see a difference in the result; but architects who don't draw are at a disadvantage.

Ralph Rapson worked in his office until the day before he died at ninety-three, producing work of lasting value and consistent formulation. And the quality of his work, like that of others differently equipped, completely erases any thought about how he drew it.

14 September
Ettore Sottsass Jr.

Olivetti Valentine typewriter, 1969

Traveling in Italy in 1982, my wife and I saw the absolutely gorgeous Callimaco floor lamp (I know, but it was) designed by Ettore Sottsass Jr. right at the start of the Memphis moment and not yet available in the US. We simply had to have it. We bought it and carried it on the plane (which is hard to believe, given that it is more than six feet/two meters high) back home. That lamp we loved is, nearly forty years later, still loved.

The Callimaco lamp is still in production. It sells for only two times the original price and now is much improved, with LED bulbs that don't fry insects as ours does.

Memphis has been having its moment for the past few years, right on time based on the thirty-five-to-forty-year recycling periodicity of fashion. It's hard to explain why it looks so good now (maybe the need to shock is gone, but the basic design ideas remain?), but it's easy to explain why it was so influential the first time around. It liberated design. It validated collage. It enlivened dead surfaces. It defined the moment when architecture became fashion.

We returned from Italy with our lamp just a bit before I designed Gotham Bar and Grill, hardly a Memphis concoction but still a collage of sorts. And, right

on time, it is being revived with a slightly updated design, reopening after its closing (at an astonishing thirty-six years) at the start of the pandemic. Revisiting one's work after a generation is design time travel: equally cringey and prideful, with a chance to fix the cringes and enjoy the rest.

Sottsass designed, at around the same time Gotham opened, the Fiorucci store in New York City. I walked in one day (I worked just around the corner) to find Andy Warhol and Fran Lebowitz sitting at a table, hawking books or something and looking rather glum. It wasn't Ettore's fault; everything he designed brought a smile to your face (well, most people's faces).

That includes the Valentine typewriter; designed in 1969 (way earlier than I had imagined), it still looks like no other and is, in my view, one of only three modern typewriters still worth having.

But then nearly all of what Ettore Sottsass Jr. designed is still worth having.

15 September
Myron Goldsmith

McMath-Pierce Solar Telescope, Kit Peak National Observatory, Arizona, 1962

Myron Goldsmith studied under and worked for Mies van der Rohe in Chicago before getting a Fulbright scholarship to work with Pier Luigi Nervi in Italy. That's a bit like apprenticing for Piet Mondrian before going to work for Alexander Calder; it would be hard to imagine two more oppositional generators of form. But this helps explain Goldsmith's output while working at Skidmore, Owings & Merrill for nearly thirty years, which ranged from ridiculously understated to gorgeously expressive.

Myron worked on the Farnsworth House while at Mies's office; this is documented with pics of Edith Farnsworth at his drawing board, with him in his regulation white lab coat. His next gig was at Nervi's, Italian for "right angles are not sexy." He spent his career careening between those two mentors.

It's interesting to sort out what pushed Goldsmith toward the elegant (but often excruciatingly boring) box or some truly powerful sculpture. It might be the program; given a truly demanding program, he could conjure an appropriately spectacular formal response.

His McMath-Pierce (and is there a better name for a big scientific thing?) Solar Telescope is a great building, more like a gargantuan Barnett Newman sculpture (*Broken Obelisk* is from the same year; must have been in the air). I don't pretend to understand how an immovable telescope makes sense, but I do see how a 285-foot-/87-meter-long empty tube of light, half belowground and half above, set at a rakish angle could turn into a giant sculpture. It's the best thing Goldsmith ever designed. My only question is why the two tubes don't meet at a perfect geometric intersection (I mean, come on, would Mies approve?).

Then there's the unbuilt curved Ruck-a-Chucky Bridge (and really, did he just make up these names?) that is as elegant and inventive as anything Nervi or Robert Maillart or Santiago Calatrava ever made (actually, much more elegant than Calatrava). And it's all because the road had to curve as it crossed the gorge, and it was nearly impossible to put supports in the river. And voilà.

Myron Goldsmith, this man I'd hardly heard of, created works of true genius powered by weird geometry and a pair of mentors, neither of whom, alone, could have dreamed these beauties up.

16 September
Jean Arp

"Ever since my childhood, I was haunted by the search for perfection. An imperfectly cut paper literally made me ill."

Jean Arp, from *Jours effeuillés: Poèmes, essaies, souvenirs*

I love the era when artists were insanely dogmatic, making declarations and joining or rejecting groups with names like der Blaue Reiter, Abstraction-Création, der Moderne Bund, de Stijl, Vorticism, and Dada many of which Jean Arp belonged to at one point or another.

Arp wrote in October 1921, "I hereby declare that on February 8th, 1916, Tristan Tzara discovered the word Dada. I was present with my twelve children, and I wore a brioche in my left nostril. I am convinced that this word has no importance and that only imbeciles and Spanish professors can be interested in dates."

His pre-Dada Dada-like performances included acting mentally ill when called to be drafted in the German Army. He filled out his date of birth on the first line of the form, then every line following, then added up all the dates (inaccurately) at the bottom. Apparently it worked; he avoided military service in World War I and lived to write such gems as, "The morality of idiots and their belief in geniuses makes me shit."

From that stridency came a life of painting, collage, and sculpture in his signature style: curves, blobs, squiggles, and shapes of every kind but that somehow could only have been made by Arp. From Dada to a formal language of shapes is a long walk, but maybe dogma is for youth and vaguely sensual shapes are for one's later years? Arp grew to enormous fame with large-scale commissions, and eventually three separate foundations preserved his legacy.

Had Arp's first wife, Sophie Taeuber-Arp, not died accidentally of carbon monoxide poisoning in 1943 at designer Max Bill's home, she might have competed for the most famous Arp. Her death left Arp in a decade-long depression, but, determined to promote her reputation, he put together her catalogue raisonné and re-created some of her sculptures.

Jean Arp's shapes are Arp's alone; even when simply a black-and-white graphic piece, they are like a signature. No one can make them quite as well, even today. He moved from flat drawings and paintings to cutout shallow reliefs and finally to fully three-dimensional sculpture, bringing his own distinctive vocabulary to all his endeavors.

News (Hot Milk Is Too Hot), 2018

David Shrigley's art is very funny. Not just funny, it is comically drawn in the crudest manner that seems to mock itself. It dares you to call it art as it appears to have no craft, no high level of skill. It's not trying to impress you with its difficulty or precision or artfulness; it seems like just a thoughtful gag (at least). But it's always funny.

For example, *News (Hot Milk Is Too Hot)* (and every other piece in the series) under a red "NEWS" banner is part *Onion* headline, part *Forrest Gump,* and part Lawrence Weiner (or Ed Ruscha or Ray Johnson or Jim Nutt).

If Shrigs was doing cartoons in a weekly paper (and he did, actually), he might be a cartoonist or illustrator. But somehow he transcends those labels, especially when one of his ideas becomes memorialized, as in his shopping list made into a massive memorial-styled monument at Art Omi. Or his thumbs-up sculpture in Trafalgar Square.

Unbelievably prolific, he has set thirty drawings a day, every day, as his workload. That's ten thousand drawings a year. I'm not sure that I will have ten thousand things to say in my entire life, much less in a year. Shrigley is a fount of ideas, words, phrases, and images. He deserves the artist label (and the Order of the British Empire) just for his output.

And it's not just drawings, but also paintings, woodcuts, collage, and etchings, and not just on paper but also on walls, objects, products (I have an olive oil can with his work on it), and sculpture.

Shrigley obviously subscribes to the Kurt Schwitters declaration, "Everything an artist spits is art." Whatever he makes (and he says he throws away most of what he makes) is art because 1) he is an artist, and he says it is art; 2) he makes his work for himself, not for others; 3) it has no other purpose but to stimulate, amuse, entertain, and challenge; 4) he makes art every day; and 5) it hangs in galleries and museums

Any of the above criteria could be challenged (making work for himself is what *Se7en*-style lunatics do too), but I say if you get three out of five you're an artist. I also say you get extra points for being funny. And it helps if you didn't do commercial (perish the thought) art before becoming a fine artist. That transition is a tough one David Shrigley didn't have to make.

18 September
Paul Segal

Offices for *Rolling Stone* magazine, New York, New York, 1977

When I met Paul Segal, he was a beard-wearing, motorcycle-riding, Dakota-living (the building, not the state), Volvo-driving, Princeton-trained architect designing the offices for *Rolling Stone* magazine in New York City and a bit of work for another resident of the Dakota who needed a white room for his white piano (yes, that resident). It really didn't get any cooler than that.

I've only worked for two architects: Kaneji Domoto, who interned with Frank Lloyd Wright (after he was released from a Japanese internment camp), for summers while I was still in school, and Paul Segal, after I graduated. Segal's office was a tiny maid's room in the Dakota (eventually sold to that client with the piano). It was so small that, as the fifth person in the office, I didn't fit (insert size joke here). I helped a carpenter build the new office at the very top of 730 Fifth Avenue, under the pointy gilded roof, just to have a desk. It ruined me for working in dull spaces, which I've never since had to endure.

Paul was lucky enough to spend his childhood summers in Paris and was even luckier to lunch one day with Samuel Beckett. Beckett offered to introduce him to Le Corbusier, which Paul declined ("What was I going to say to him beyond 'I'm a big fan of your

work'?"!). (Check out the punctuation lineup back there; six in a row!) I get that, but what a story it would have been (when Paul tells it, he starts with "I was having lunch in Paris one day..." and only then adds, "Okay, it was with Samuel Beckett"). He's filled with stories like that, which he always told in a non-braggadocian way, if that is possible with stories like that.

Paul Segal's talent is managing a slightly unstable stable of highly creative, highly demanding architects. Not an easy task, and I say that as one of those he managed to manage! His other talents are generosity (and again, I say that as the recipient of his largesse) along with the loyalty he always modeled. He always refers to his staff, after they move on to open their own offices (overwhelmingly the case) as "alumni." It's a nice touch and is still appreciated, but it's also a perfect expression of how he feels about all of us, and how we still feel about him.

19 September
Martta Martikainen-Ypyä

Motorized Company Barracks, Helsinki, Finland, 1938

In 1930 Finland, 30 percent of the architects belonging to the Finnish Association of Architects were women. Today, nearly a hundred years later, 18 percent of American Institute of Architects members are women.

In 1942 the sheer numbers of Finnish women architects prompted them to create their own organization, Architecta, the Finnish Association of Women Architects. Martta Martikainen-Ypyä was one of the successful architects who helped found Architecta.

That year, Aino Marsio Aalto, architect and wife of Alvar Aalto, gave a rousing speech, so rousing, in fact, that many assumed Alvar had a hand in writing it. That pretty much sums up the dilemma of women in architecture.

Martikainen-Ypyä's buildings always exhibit a kind of thoughtfulness that precludes showy glitz in favor of more contextually appropriate buildings. Her work could be heroic when called for or much more about quietly defining an optimistic future in other circumstances. She seems to have embodied the cultural ethos of harmony in her work.

One heroic example is the 1936 Motorized Company Barracks that is her answer to Aalto's Paimio Sanatorium. Or her Starckjohann Building, one of the first self-service retail stores in Finland, which includes a majestic wall of glass wrapping the lofty ground floor to invite shoppers in, yet manages to be monumental and diminutive at the same time.

With her husband, Martikainen-Ypyä opened a firm that produced a series of very fine buildings that are virtually unknown outside of Finland. Architecture, except that of a few marketing geniuses, was essentially a regional discipline in her day, and it was (and I would say still is) a noble pursuit to create buildings for a local, not international, audience.

It is almost as though every country had only one world-renowned architect: Finland, Alvar Aalto; Germany, Mies van der Rohe; France, Le Corbusier; US, Frank Lloyd Wright; Spain, Antoni Gaudí; Brazil, Oscar Niemeyer (plus every other self-exiled). None of these famous architects are women, but half had a barely acknowledged woman architect doing the work on famous endeavors.

Finland was, of course, a paradise compared to the US (and most of Europe), and Martta Martikainen-Ypyä thrived in that paradise.

20 September
Hans Scharoun

Berlin Philharmonic Hall, Berlin, Germany, 1963

While famous modern architects built their signature houses for captains of industry, the wealthy noble class, or even families of retail conglomerates, Hans Scharoun built his Schminke House (and the name should be the first clue) for a local pasta factory owner in Löbau, Saxony. It is suitably nutty, exuberant, and eccentric, especially when compared to the crisp white constructions of his contemporaries.

Scharoun was among the very few International Style architects who remained in Germany during World War II (others left in haste or were "assisted" by the Nazis), and while the Schminkes were regarded as war criminals for providing the Wehrmacht with (I guess) pasta, Scharoun was lionized as an architectural master. Not sure how that works.

His nuttiness is most apparent at the Berlin Philharmonic, completed after his death and clad in gold anodized panels, making it perhaps the gaudiest of an early modern architect's later works. It sat for years with unclad concrete walls, so it must have created quite a local stir when it was finished.

We should have seen this coming: Scharoun's single-family house in the 1927 Weissenhofsiedlung exhibition was among the wildest items there, and the Schminkes hired him after seeing that house. Critics hang a lot of praise on their observation that the craziness is accompanied by a rational, efficient plan. Like Frank Gehry (the two architects were recently exhibited together, due to their similarities), he was capable of elaborating a rational core with highly personal flourishes. The work produces a similar effect: either you love this stuff or hate it.

I both love and hate these things, whether from Scharoun or Gehry. They are clearly animated with the eccentric extravagances we have come to expect, but like a waiter who is constantly performing his other career, they can get tiring. The world is not a world's fair (yet), and a city filled with these highly effusive gestures would be unbearable. They rely on the rest of the city obeying the unspoken rules to be the sole "artist" among the dregs. Yes, that is as self-obsessed as it sounds.

We can enjoy Hans Scharoun, and his progeny, as long as we can escape their ubiquitous sphere of influence.

21 September
Sara Little Turnbull

Sara Little painting at her desk, 1940s

What is the word for human onomatopoeia, when a person is a version of their name? Like someone named Baker becoming, well, you know, a baker?

Or vice versa, as when was Sara Finkelstein (who stood under five feet) adopted the name Little as her professional name. She adopted a large asterisk as her mark to denote a person with much more than her name suggested.

And she was much, much more. She's been called "Corporate America's Secret Weapon," the consultant who represented the user.

Sara Little was one of those whirlwinds who, from an early age until her death at ninety-seven, never stopped. She appeared in Yiddish theater as a child, gained a scholarship to Parsons School of Design, worked at Macy's precursor, and was a *House Beautiful* editor (and much, much more) all before she was twenty-five.

She left that world at age forty-eight to open her independent consulting firm and for twenty years operated out of her 400-square-foot/37.2-square-meter hotel room. She married for the first time (just halfway through her very

long life) at age forty-eight, adding Turnbull to her adopted name. She was just getting started.

She worked for a long list of the largest US corporations, taught at Stanford University, opened a research institute, created the model for the N95 mask, lived at the Watergate Hotel during the infamous break-in (which has given every scandal the -gate suffix), and invented (or predicted) the family room.

The famous stories about her reveal someone intensely observing the world and delighting in finding application for its wonders. She suggested matte makeup (after discovering geishas), a pot lid holder (based on the way she saw a cheetah grip its prey), rope twist soy candy (to make protein attractive to children), and a better pick-proof lock (after discussions with the experts, convicted felons in prison).

Sara Little Turnbull used the term *cultural anthropologist* to describe what she did; her interest in design was rooted in her curiosity, her daily absorption of masses of press, her extensive travel, her need to make things (anything and everything) better, her belief that design was seminal to society, and her need to help everyone understand it.

22 September
Erik Gunnar Asplund

Skogskyrkogården (Woodland Chapel), Stockholm, Sweden, 1920

Based on Colin Rowe's dictum, "If a building's windows are either too large or too small, you can be sure an architect was involved," Erik Gunnar Asplund is surely an architect. He may have been two different architects, judging by the poles his work occupied.

Asplund could be startlingly modern or comfortably classical, sometimes at the same time in the same project. It's as though Erik was the modernist and his alter ego Gunnar stayed, in a Nordic kind of way, classical.

On the one hand he designs the Lister County Courthouse; it has windows that are too small but serve to aggrandize the visual scale of a small building. He embeds a circular courtroom (and judge's bench) on an axis that continues all the way through town to the train station. But it's the building's circular courtroom, bulging out the back of the building, that alludes (bizarrely) to pregnancy and childbirth, as do the insanely bloated balusters.

This is right around the time of Sigmund Freud's and Otto Rank's theories and debate about "birth trauma." The courtroom appears to be emerging from the rear of the building in what may have been a gesture (seriously) of rebirth, or trauma, or simply the pressure one feels within the heightened space of the courtroom.

The circular space, with or without a dome, is a constant recurring theme with Gunnar's work (Erik seems a lot less obsessed with centering a project around it). The Stockholm Library, everyone's favorite, has a giant cylinder thrusting upward. And Gunnar's unbelievably lovely Woodland Cemetery Chapel is a gorgeous reassemblage of portico, pyramidal roof, and domed circular room. It needs only a large oculus to make the veiled, miniature reference to the Pantheon even clearer. Erik's other work at Woodland is as modern as imaginable: strict, orthogonal, and utterly without decorative elaboration. It's almost a dare to relinquish sentimentality.

At the Stockholm Exhibition, it's all Erik; the huge advertising mast is magnificent, the best built version of a modern trope. And the exhibition halls are pure steel-and-glass modernism at its best.

With Asplund you get to choose; Erik and Gunnar are both remarkable in their own ways!

23 September
Louise Nevelson

Shadows and Flags, Louise Nevelson Plaza, New York, New York, 1977

Louise Nevelson and Louise Bourgeois both emigrated to America and lived in New York City; both attended the Art Students League; both had to contend with the masculine abstract expressionist movement; both made sculpture from scraps found on the street; and both lived long lives making art. Apparently Bourgeois was very much aware of "the other Louise," as she called her, but it doesn't appear that they were close, or even friendly. Art is pretty competitive, even more so if you are nearly the sole woman (though perhaps not the sole Louise) in an art community.

Nevelson moved to Mount Vernon, New York, at precisely the time that my mother was born and grew up in Mount Vernon (it was, apparently, an enclave of middle-class Jewish families that had moved from New York City). My mother knew Nevelson's art but not her personally, though she did attend the Art Students League.

Nevelson divorced her husband, left Mount Vernon, and started working as an assistant to Diego Rivera while he was painting his Rockefeller Center mural, *Man at the Crossroads.* She had an affair with Rivera, coming between him and Frida Kahlo for a while.

While her Kips Bay neighborhood in New York was being demolished for urban renewal, Nevelson and her son ranged the streets collecting wood left by her evicted neighbors. The wood fed her fireplace for warmth, but clearly the exercise in gathering it had an impact on her art that eventually evolved into the monumental wood pieces she would become famous for.

Nevelson was often at the edge of poverty; it was late in life that she finally sold pieces to museums and became the powerhouse we consider her today. She was in her sixties when the Whitney Museum bought its first Nevelson. This was just a couple of years after she was included in the MoMA *Sixteen Americans* show that included Robert Rauschenberg, Jasper Johns, and others; she was one of only two female artists in the show, curated by Dorothy C. Miller. The room of her white-painted wood constructions undoubtedly catapulted her into the fame she now has.

Her outdoor work (in metal, not wood) graces Nevelson Plaza in New York City, the first public space in New York to be named after an artist of any gender, or any Louise.

24 September
Henry P. Glass

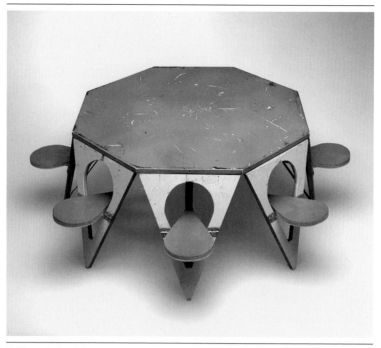

Folding picnic table, 1961

Henry P. Glass survived Dachau and Buchenwald and went on to design some cheery and playful furniture, something it is hard to wrap one's mind around. When released from the camps in 1939, due to his wife's persistence, he left Germany and moved to New York City, where he worked with Gilbert Rohde and Russel Wright on the 1939 New York World's Fair. That alone should have given him professional whiplash.

To assist the Allies, he reconstructed from memory the plans of the camps he "visited." I have often said (though I am beginning to doubt) that I could draw a plan of every room I was ever in, so I get it. It's a weird visual memory thing. Mimi Sheraton said she remembered every meal she ever ate (including some at the 1939 World's Fair!).

From New York City he moved to Chicago to work and study under László Moholy-Nagy and György Kepes, before opening his own design office in the Merchandise Mart.

Glass went on to invent the hairpin leg, perhaps the most singular icon of midcentury furniture design. He held fifty-two patents and convinced the School of the Art Institute of Chicago

to develop an industrial design program; he then taught there for the next twenty years.

There is a level of joy in his work that seems, given his personal history, a particular triumph. It's serious, in the sense of being highly efficient, well-thought-out, and inventive. But the manifestation of all that seriousness is work that can make you smile.

Glass's folding picnic table, with eight triangular legs and cute little "pin-drop" (as we might call them today, in the age of Google) seats, is adorable, clever, and efficient. His collapsible chairs, in every configuration imaginable, are similarly inventive. And his folding, cabana-like campsite units are almost at the level of Italian design of the 1970s.

It's interesting how much of his work is based on portability or foldability. This is a man who understood what it meant to need to depart in haste! Or possibly to live in the minimal and rationed way he did. But, either way, he managed to convert his trauma-induced tendencies into productive avenues.

Henry P. Glass did it with a sense of humor and a love of play, a personal and professional success.

25 September
Francesco Borromini

San Carlo alle Quattro Fontane, Rome, Italy, 1641

It's amazing how many of the greatest Italian, mostly Roman, architects (who were, of course, also sculptors, painters, and humanists) had last names beginning with *b*. Francesco Borromini, Filippo Brunelleschi, Donato Bramante, Gian Lorenzo Bernini, and even a certain Buonarotti (you may know him as Michelangelo) weren't just participants, they were the defining geniuses of their moments, from barely Renaissance to definitely baroque.

We can love them all (and of course I love all the architects whose last names begin with *b*!), but Borromini may be the least well known of a distinguished group. The rest are monumentally famous; Borromini is more of an acquired taste. Disregarded for centuries as flashy and possibly insane, his reputation was resurrected only in the 1940s.

He worshipped Michelangelo (his spare quarters had a bust of Mike) and was used (some say exploited) by Bernini, his utter opposite, who lived in palatial homes and was as outgoing and womanizing as Francesco was strict and ascetic. He worked with a single assistant, drew his work himself, never married or had children, had a housekeeper and a library of a thousand or so books: an architect monk.

To visit just a few of his works in Rome (like Sant'Ivo alla Sapienza, San Carlo alle Quattro Fontane, San Giovanni in Laterano, Palazzo Spada, with its little forced perspective, and the Oratorio dei Filippini) is to see work so rich, so layered, and so voluptuous it is hard to imagine they were made alone by the architect monk. They range from tiny and intimate to grand and even bombastic, but each one is an utter gem.

People get pretty emotional about Borromini. It's hard to deny and harder to explain. He seems to provoke us to religiosity, making us believe that work like this must be inspired by a higher being (as an atheist, I'm more than a bit disconcerted to be so moved). Even with a space full of tourists, his buildings inspire silence. Just watching the light move through one of his spaces is a study in celestial architecture.

Of course, it had to end in tragedy. His suicide, running himself through with a sword, is a shocking end to a life that left us more than we need to consider Francesco Borromini divine.

Really more saint than monk.

26 September
Margaret Macdonald Casson

"It's never been anything but absolutely super."

Sir Hugh Casson on sharing an office with Margaret Macdonald Casson

Margaret Macdonald Troup, a rare woman graduate from the Bartlett School of Architecture in London, joined Christopher (Kit) Nicholson's office. Kit, brother of painter Ben Nicholson, was an aspiring modernist who (assisted by Troup and Hugh Casson) designed some impressive buildings, including the London Gliding Club with its 88.5-foot/ 27-meter horizontal viewing window. Kit was a gliding enthusiast and died at age forty-four in a gliding competition in Switzerland (at least it wasn't at his own club).

By then Margaret and Hugh Casson had married. Ret (as she was known) opened an architecture office in South Africa (her homeland), then returned to London at the start of World War II. She did the thing that wise spouses often do: she dodged a head-to-head competition with her spouse and began to design interiors and products (while her husband designed buildings) and take photographs (while he was a prolific watercolor artist).

It's a familiar pattern; creative types, when faced with talented parents or spouses, find the seams between their skills and become expert where the idols aren't. That's what Ret seems to have done.

It seems like a sensible approach, but the result was that Margaret Macdonald Casson was virtually written out of history. Hugh Casson, in one online publication, is pictured alone, as it was unable "to find a picture of Margaret" (!). This omission is true of her art and design as well; she is barely visible online, while Hugh's prolific watercolors and sketches (which are very good, if you like that kind of thing) are everywhere. Margaret is described as making photograms she called sciagrams; they are both fascinating and impossible to find.

The V&A holds the archives of both Margaret Macdonald Casson and Hugh Casson, and it would be a worthwhile undertaking for the museum to digitize her work and make it available. Online images are the things a reputation is made of.

27 September
Alan Fletcher

Logo, Victoria and Albert Museum, 1989

Alan Fletcher's first words to me were, "Colin [Forbes] thinks I'd really like you, any idea why?" It's a perfect Alan Fletcher question; it has no good answer. It's more a riddle than an inquiry (and really a challenge to defend myself), and he later claimed not to understand why I found it so funny (and revealing). He had a sense of humor (but possibly not about himself), and everything with Alan was a fucking arm wrestle.

Alan left Pentagram, the firm he had founded and named, less than a year after that opening line. He said, when a corporate shrink was retained to run the very first partner meeting I attended, that if we needed that kind of help to get along, it was no longer worth it. His twenty years of design leading up to Pentagram and twenty years building Pentagram ended because we needed therapy!

It may be that Fletcher was addicted to the fight as an integral part of creative work and that the thought of everyone hugging all the time was simply abhorrent (and maybe it is). I sat in on a London office meeting before I joined Pentagram; it was the most contentious fray among colleagues I had ever witnessed, and it was just a normal weekly meeting! I decided that,

as I was joining the New York City office, I could ignore it. Ironic that reputationally brash New Yorkers were better mannered than polite English types!

Despite the description above, Fletcher was incredibly inclusive (I guess you can't arm wrestle alone), incredibly generous, and incredibly talented and very smart and very verbal (I can't understand why he didn't simply *love* therapy). And he was visually adept in ways that connect dots you can barely see. He was a remarkable talent.

He spent a lot of time, after those forty years, on "personal" work: drawings, watercolors, collages, and books that, for me, never had the crisp, singular punch of his "commercial" work. Commercial work is solving other people's problems. Personal work is about solving problems of your own making. It seems he was better at others' problems; on his own his works were a bit flaccid, a bit dated, a bit derivative, a bit self-indulgent, all things Alan Fletcher would hate.

Maybe he had no one to arm wrestle with.

28 September
Wallace K. Harrison

Metropolitan Opera House, Lincoln Center, New York, New York, 1966

Wallace K. Harrison is the kind of architect who might be easy to ignore. He wasn't inherently heroic, though he designed some incredibly heroic buildings. He wasn't an iconoclast; he once said that "an opera house should look like an opera house." He wasn't a media whore, though he appeared on the cover of *Time* and the list of people who frequented his home would all be boldface.

But he was a manager of great ideas. And he was part of some of the most sublime New York architecture and some of the most absurd as well.

Harrison survived working with the most enormous and contentious egos in the architectural world: Le Corbusier on the United Nations Headquarters in New York City, Philip Johnson (and others) on Lincoln Center, Raymond Hood on Rockefeller Center, Robert Moses on both New York City world's fairs, and Nelson Rockefeller on virtually all of the above, plus the Rockefeller Apartments and Empire State Plaza.

Harrison began at McKim, Mead & White, so he understood massive egos. He partnered with Harvey Wiley Corbett to design, among other things, the still remarkable Master Apartments (where I once happily lived).

Rockefeller Center is the height of urbanity, playing with scale (at both ends of the spectrum) while respecting the city grid. Its Fifth Avenue buildings halve the block in scale and rhythm (Atlas sits in a recess that reads as a street) with the four "empire" buildings representing France, Italy, Britain, and (before that unfortunateness with the Nazis) Germany. It's now the International Building. The entrance between the French and British buildings was cleverly christened the Channel Gardens.

He was one of those rare architects who took pleasure in supporting other architects. His Long Island estate was one of the five sites of the Aluminaire House designed by Albert Frey and Lawrence Kocher, which he bought for $1,000 after it was exhibited at MoMA as part of the International Style show. It may be the most peripatetic home ever built. The next (and hopefully final) site will be at the Palm Springs Art Museum.

What might have been Harrison's best work turned into his worst. The Empire State Plaza in Albany was one of Governor Nelson Rockefeller's attempts at immortality (as was, ironically, the World Trade Center). Today it just confirms that the Rockefellers were not always icons of taste.

29 September
Monica Pidgeon

Piazza di Spagna, Rome: climbing the Spanish Steps, 1960s

Monica Pidgeon, with Pentagram cofounder architect Theo Crosby, edited and transformed the journal *Architectural Design* (*AD*) from a free trade magazine into an international publication of the first order. Among the first to publish the work of James Stirling, Norman Foster, Richard Rogers, and Ove Arup; an enthusiast for Archigram; and a promoter of all things Architectural Association (AA, London's then equivalent of today's Sci-Arc), *AD* defined British architectural radicalism.

Pidgeon and Crosby also collaborated on the book *An Anthology of Houses* (1960), featuring the 1950s work of a huge assortment of international modern architects. And Crosby curated *This Is Tomorrow*, the influential 1956 exhibition at the Whitechapel Gallery.

Pidgeon was the rare female in the male-dominated profession of architecture who was present at, or at the center of, every important national and international congress: Congrès International d'Architecture Moderne (CIAM), International Union of Architects (UIA), Modern Architectural Research Group (MARS Group), etc. She was, as well, an extraordinary photographer, and her work is included in the Royal Institute

of British Architects (RIBA)–published *Rome: Eternal City*.

Starting in 1946, she continued to produce *AD* through 1975, cleverly converting it to an advertisement-free journal sustained by issue sales. She briefly edited the *RIBA Journal* before establishing Pidgeon Audio Visual (PAV) in 1979. A prescient enterprise, PAV collected the images and recorded presentations of architects to distribute to colleges and others. Now available at PidgeonDigital.com, this early foray into "podcasting" was Pidgeon's passion until her death.

I was obsessed with *AD*, as were most students in those days; it was the only source of a certain iconoclasm. Monica Pidgeon was an educator of the highest order, disseminating a range of ideas, images, iconic individuals, and provocative issues that continue to resonate in the world of design, architecture, and art. Luckily she left us with an invaluable archive of architectural thought, curated with the benefit of her insightful editorial eye.

30 September
Decimus Burton

The Palm House at Kew Gardens, Royal Botanic Gardens, Richmond, England, 1848

I can't find a longer Wikipedia page for an architect than that for Decimus Burton. It's longer than Frank Lloyd Wright's, Le Corbusier's, and Frank Gehry's; it's also longer than Pablo Picasso's, slightly longer than Queen Elizabeth II's, and much longer than Burton's friend Queen Victoria's; it's longer than Tom Hanks's (but not Meryl Streep's), but only half the length of Jesus's (everyone has a Wiki page).

So who the fuck is this Decimus Burton (this towering genius of...whatever he did)? He was the tenth child born to James Burton (get it? And just ask his brother Septimus, the seventh; though the twelfth was named Jessy...I guess Duodecimus was a step too far?).

Decimus was tutored in the classical style by both Sir John Soane and John Nash; both are much more famous but still have nowhere near Burton's Wiki-weight. Decimus's father, James Burton, an architect and wealthy developer and builder, could finance projects for architects like Nash in exchange for tutoring his tenth child, starting at fifteen years old. No matter, as Decimus was a bit of a prodigy.

His hagiographer, Guy Williams, said Decimus was "rich, cool, well-dressed, apparently celibate, the designer and

prime member of the Athenaeum, one of London's grandest gentlemen's clubs." So...a gay architect? What a shock.

Burton's nemesis was Augustus Charles Pugin, the preeminent promoter of the Gothic style in England and the architect of the tower containing Big Ben (which it turns out is a bell, not a clock). His obsession with Burton's coolly classical work was legendary, but Pugin died at forty in a state of insanity. Burton outlived the younger Pugin by nearly forty years, so he had plenty of time to repudiate the vituperations.

Burton's work is pretty fantastic. A number of terraces at Regents Park, Marble Arch, the Palm House and Temperate House at Kew Gardens (both remarkable greenhouses), and even one work by Joseph Paxton (who later built the Crystal Palace) are attributed by Guy to Burton. But Williams wants to attribute everything to Burton, despite being in conflict with Burton's own Royal Society obituary.

Whatever. What good is a hagiographer if they don't fawn over and attribute every possible credit to the object of their affection? Guy ♥ Decimus!

01 October
Jacopo da Vignola

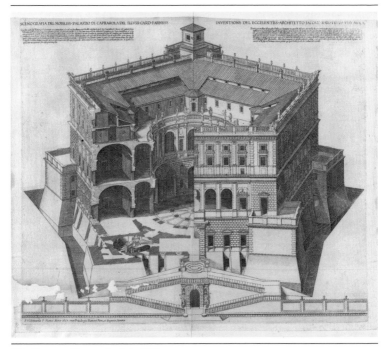

Villa Farnese, Caprarola, Italy, 1575

Before there was Vignelli or Viñoly, there was Vignola, a remarkable architect who is remembered (unfairly) more for his books than for his buildings. Jacopo da Vignola did write two seminal texts of the day. *Regola delli cinque ordini d'architettura*, on classical Roman architecture, focused more on the practicality of how than on the academic why. It was the most widely read, published, and acquired book on architecture, possibly for centuries (popular architecture books being an admittedly low bar).

Vignola's other seminal book, *Le due regole della prospettiva pratica*, codified, with mathematical precision, and made accessible the not-fully-understood art of constructing two-dimensional perspectives out of three-dimensional imaginings. Encountering this book must have been like me seeing, for the first time, a computer-generated three-dimensional rendering of the building a few yards from my student studio on the cover of *Scientific American* in 1974. The book was nothing short of revolutionary and, for Vignola's audience of architects, a way to communicate evolving designs short of building gigantic models.

His first book was about how to build, his second was about how to

see. Together they helped define the direction architecture would take for hundreds of years. No small thing, but Vignola left a legacy of buildings that were themselves critical steps in the progress of that art.

His Villa Farnese in Caprarola is an enormous, five-sided pile about thirty miles from Rome. Vignola may have inherited the pentagon, but the circular courtyard is all his and may be the first complete one in the Renaissance (he built the half-courtyard version at the Villa Giulia in Rome some years earlier). The villa sits impossibly high and large at the end of a road slicing through Caprarola that Vignola created to assure an imposing view of his work. You keep approaching it and it keeps getting larger! Once you actually arrive, it has an amazing underground entrance and a carriage turnaround under the circular courtyard, so when the Renaissance equivalent of, say, Lady Gaga arrived, she could be whisked past the paparazzi.

I wish even one of the amazing cutaway drawings of Villa Farnese was created by Vignola, just to promote his book on perspective, but they came later, based on the foundation of his seminal text.

02 October
Bjarke Ingels

Gift to students based on Experimental Jetset Beatles T-shirt, James Biber, 2008

Googling Bjarke Ingels, the first question suggested under "People Also Ask" is, "Is Bjarke Ingels the best architect?" I didn't bother to check the answer, but the question is a testament to his incredible marketing prowess more than to his architectural talents. Take the name of his office, BIG (Bjarke Ingels Group); it's really genius, especially compared to his first office's name, PLOT. BIG was the aspiration, and it has now become reality.

If Jacopo da Vignola (birthday yesterday) mastered the art of perspective to sell his work to his clients, like the Pope, Bjarke has mastered the art of animation to sell his ideas. There is a direct line connecting the two, architectural animation being a sequence of perspectives using the same math Vignola clarified five hundred years earlier, with each frame of BIG's presentation rendered at an inconceivable speed by computers. "Inconceivable speed" could also describe BIG's ascent.

Watching Ingels present an idea is a thing of beauty, often far surpassing the beauty of the thing presented. I watched him build the case for the VIA 57 West apartment building, his first large (big!) New York City project at the entrance to the West Side Highway. He

created an argument for the inevitability of the building's form as a hybrid of a tower and a courtyard, the two models he said were synonymous with New York apartments (which is a questionable claim). He then manipulated the courtyard by pulling up one corner (you know, to make a tower), and voilà! The hybridized form of the building appeared.

It was such a mesmerizing presentation, and Bjarke, who has the studied insouciance of the supremely confident, is the perfect presenter. At thirty-eight (then), with his dark suit and open-collar white shirt (unbuttoned a bit too far), unshaven, sprightly, comfortable on stage and in English, he was the perfect vehicle to sell the New World to the Old World.

The results, though highly photogenic and legible, are less satisfying than the presentation; VIA 57 West is a great signature but a questionable building. Bjarke Ingels is often beyond clever, but clever is not necessarily the goal of permanent urban objects.

To paraphrase Mies van der Rohe, "I don't want to be interesting; I want to be good" (or big!).

03 October
Denise Scott Brown

Franklin Court, Philadelphia, Pennsylvania, 1976

Denise, as Denise Scott Brown was happy to be called by the more than twenty thousand petitioners clamoring for her to be given the Pritzker Prize (that she was denied) with Robert Venturi, her husband and professional partner, is a powerhouse. Brilliant, inventive, insightful, and vocal, she helped define an approach to architecture that has been as important as any in my lifetime. The picture of her, arms akimbo (and how I have waited patiently to use that phrase) in front of the fragmentary Las Vegas skyline, is more well-known than the one of him, with his back to the camera (her Colossus of Rhodes pose compared to his René Magritte pose.)

It would be interesting to hear what Scott Brown thinks of Las Vegas today. *Learning from Las Vegas* was coauthored by Venturi, Scott Brown, and Steven Izenour; published by MIT Press in 1972; and designed by another legend, Muriel Cooper. With its original cover intact, a copy can fetch five thousand dollars; so the book's value has changed almost as much as Las Vegas itself!

On a theoretical level, the book (and others by Venturi and Scott Brown) purports to critique modernism and propose an alternative to it. Critiques

of modernism are easy, though credit to Bob and Denise (and Steven) for a clever way of positing that critique.

The authors coined the terms "ducks versus decorated sheds" to differentiate highly "articulate" and integrated forms (or "ducks," which they say are a trapping of modernism) from a more generalized approach (sheds) with surface decoration that can be disassociated from the form.

This distinction may be blurred in the Sainsbury Wing of the National Portrait Gallery in London and their Franklin Court project, both arguably ducks and both my faves.

Scott Brown has suffered the indignities of being ignored for the Pritzker, and wrote, "In mid-career, I married a colleague and we joined our professional lives....I watched as he was manufactured into an architectural guru before my eyes and, to some extent, on the basis of the joint work and the work of our firm." She is a vocal proponent of collaborative work and the inclusion of teams in the creation of architecture, but one has to wonder how much of that enthusiasm is defensive after being repeatedly subjected to erasure.

04 October
Giovanni Battista Piranesi

Pyramid of Gaius Cestius, from *Vedute di Roma (Roman Views)*, circa 1756

If Giovanni Battista Piranesi were art directing a movie, it would be *Blade Runner*, or maybe Tim Burton's *Batman*. Everything Piranesi drew had the dark look of decay, even though he artificially reassembled a lot of the ruins he documented to better explain them.

By the end of his life, he created more than two thousand prints, mostly as archaeological records of the past, to ennoble classical architecture and make it more accessible and influential. It was also convenient that Rome had become the center of the grand tour. Piranesi's *Views of Rome* were suitable "postcards" to collect and bring home, proving one's sophistication and wealth.

The plates, giant sheets of copper that Piranesi drew upon, are still being used to issue prints, and they have been subject to multiple reprintings. Others, in the intervening centuries, have added overwork to highlight faded areas and occasional redrawing or even rededicating the folios to others. Reprints became an industry long after Piranesi's death, first at the hands of his children, who were summoned to Paris by Napoleon I, and later by Firmin-Didot. The plates were eventually repatriated, and prints are now issued in Italy, but still...

The quality of the prints and the reputation of Piranesi have gone up and down over the centuries. His originals were extremely precise, with highly developed line work, but subsequent prints can be muddy and dark. He may not have foreseen the degradation of his life's work at the hands of future generations of publishers riding his coattails, and we can reasonably ask whether the impression of brooding, dark work is really Piranesi or just bad prints.

It's like Lenny Bruce's plea to the judge at one of his trials. A cop had written down his act, word for word (almost), and recited it on the witness stand to the judge and jury. His flat delivery (imagine Sergeant Joe Friday doing Lenny Bruce) and occasional flubbed lines ("It was lost wages for Las Vegas, not las wages") prompted Lenny to tell the judge, "He's dying up there, and I'm goin' to jail!"

Giovanni Battista Piranesi had already drawn his own prisons, maybe just to make the point.

05 October
Maya Lin

The Wave Field, Ann Arbor, Michigan, 1995

I met Maya Lin only once; she was in a big fancy gown, and her high heels were killing her. She was perched on one of those delicate little chairs at about 2:00 a.m. in the White House Green Room (wearing a green dress that worked well in the room) on January 1, 2000, the first day of the new millennium. We chatted about a contractor (a word that really doesn't do him justice) we had in common and some other pleasantries, and then I was off to say hello to a bunch of other people I only knew from a very long distance.

I was at the White House New Year's Eve party because I had designed the National Millennium Time Capsule; Maya Lin was there because she was, you know, Maya Lin.

Lin really changed things in the memorial business. Every single memorial after her 1982 Vietnam Veterans Memorial in Washington has had to position itself relative to that singular display. It really is an overwhelming experience to see, especially if you served, or if you avoided serving but were affected by the Vietnam War during your entire youth. I was the latter (lottery number 222 helped me avoid the draft), and, back when fifty-five thousand American deaths was a significant number (unlike during the COVID-19 pandemic, when

twenty times that number is barely acknowledged), it was harrowing to see it enumerated into stone.

The chronological arrangement of names has never seemed quite right to me; they start and end in the middle of the V-shaped walls, the deepest point. It would have made more sense (to me) if they started at the left and ended at the right, with the deepest section being the period of highest losses, of overwhelming grief. But it turns out that, after the design of these things, the ordering of names is a critical decision. The 9/11 Memorial had to develop an algorithm just to order the names.

Lin went on to do some sublime, and some less-than-sublime, work. Her own early success and fame is a hard act to follow. She has had the well-deserved luxury to follow her own interests, producing work that is not quite architecture (in the strictest sense) and not quite pure fine art, but rather, when it works, a very successful hybrid of the two.

06 October
Le Corbusier

Chapelle Notre-Dame-du-Haut, Ronchamp, France, 1955

You either believe that Le Corbusier was the single most important modern architect ever to live, or you don't. And, just to be clear, I do.

Le Corbusier was the most indefatigable, precisely intellectual, continuously reinventive, prodigiously productive architect who, perhaps, ever lived (and that is despite his misogyny, anti-Semitism, flirtation with Nazism, and insane urban planning ideas). Who else comes close? Frank Lloyd Wright? Please, don't even. LC's work was about the entire history of architecture; FLLW's was about himself. Michelangelo? Maybe, but he had some other talents beyond architecture. Ictinus and Callicrates? If you saw the Parthenon in its fully polychromed glory, you might withdraw this pair from consideration.

Happy to entertain suggestions, but really, he is it.

When I was in college, I had never been to Europe. It wasn't affordable, summer programs were rarer than they are now, and I worked summers to pay for the next year of school. But then I won a traveling fellowship and spent the next year driving all over Europe, in a red Citroën 2CV, to see, photograph, draw, and commit to memory every building I could get to. A lot of them were Le Corbusier's, and nearly every one was a revelation.

I kept collecting them even after that year. I knocked on the door of the Villa Schwob in La Chaux-de-Fonds and was admitted to the most delightful tour ever. My wife and I spent a night at La Tourette sleeping in separate monks' cells (there are no double beds in a monastery!) while recovering from food poisoning. I wandered the Salvation Army Building (Cité de Refuge), finding the kitchens to be the best part. Le Cabanon is the cutest 12-by-12-foot/3.6-by-3.6-meter space ever conceived. Ronchamp is unexpectedly spatial (as opposed to purely sculptural). And though it should seem tired and overrated, the Villa Savoye is anything but, even after several visits.

There may be singular pieces of architecture you like more (Maison de Verre, *par exemple, est magnifique*) but one-hit-wonders do not a GOAT make. There may be architects you like more, but nice isn't the point.

LC is the Beatles, if they were producing their very best for fifty fucking years.

Check and mate.

"I never thought my paintings were abstract."

Jean Paul Riopelle musing on the nature of his paintings, which were quite abstract

"The Second-Greatest Canadian Artist" is not an *Onion* headline or a joke about the world's thinnest book, but it does describe Jean Paul Riopelle, who was always just behind the main event ("We're number two!"). His work sells for millions (fetching the second-highest price ever paid for a Canadian artist! see what I mean?), but it's a bit like the John Updike quip, "The true New Yorker secretly believes that people living anywhere else have to be, in some sense, kidding."

Riopelle did Jackson Pollack just after Pollack, but he painted vertically and threw the paint. He tried to finish every painting in one session, so paint had to be at the ready to fling at the canvas. Part of the genius of Pollock (painting horizontally) was an invention that catalyzed his entire oeuvre. Somehow, you can walk right into a Pollock, but you would bounce off a Riopelle. There's no air in Riopelle's work, while Pollock's defies gravity.

Jean Paul gave up brushes for a palette knife and started building paintings, not just painting them. He traveled to East Hampton in 1960 (missing Pollock, who died there in 1956) and lived there for a year. Then took up with Joan Mitchell (insert Joni Mitchell joke here), with whom he lived for nearly twenty years, but in separate homes and studios in France. It was a made-for-TV relationship, "stormy" and "fueled by alcohol." He must have really thrown some paint then (rim shot)! When Mitchell died, he painted his most acclaimed work. And they put it on postage stamps.

In addition to stamps, Riopelle was lauded in every possible Canadian way: he became a Grand Officer of the National Order of Quebec, represented Canada at the Venice Biennale, and has a star on the Canadian Walk of Fame. Seriously, that's a thing; hopefully he's located between, say, Sandra Oh and Robbie Robertson and not too close to Guy Lombardo.

I do need to apologize to my many Canadian friends; the list of stars on the Walk of Fame is both surprising and reminds me how so many people I think are American are actually Canadian: Louis B. Mayer and Jack Warner, who knew? Alexander Graham Bell, hello? Kim Cattrall, really? And "where was Alex Trebek from"? Thanks, Canada.

08 October
Dion Neutra

VDL Research House II, Los Angeles, California, rebuilt 1964

One of the problems with a single daily birthday bio is that inevitably some serious players are left out. It's like the adage about your obit: don't die the same day as a celebrity; you'll be bumped to page fifty-seven. That's what happened to Richard Neutra; he had the misfortune to share a birthday with Jean Prouvé, who just edged him out (in my book). But his son Dion's birthday is a chance for redemption, though Dion is competing with Serge Chermayeff.

When renovating the Sten-Frenke House, a 1934 home in Santa Monica by Richard Neutra, we had to seek Dion's permission for access to the extensive Neutra archives at UCLA and Cal Poly Pomona. We secured it, but only after Dion got to complain about all sorts of extraneous issues. He was a real crank.

Being the virtually unknown son of a truly great architect is not easy. Dion even changed the name of the office (after his father died) to The Office of Richard and Dion Neutra and sold his talents with the pitch "Why not hire a real Neutra to renovate your Neutra house"! It's his way to claim as his own work that was, in the case of the Sten-Frenke House, done when he was just eight years old. Even his name was a hand-me-down; his mother was Dione, and she was a force of nature.

As a young architect, I visited the VDL House in Silver Lake, where the whole Neutra family lived in what was an architecture lab. It had a very 1950s vibe though it was designed twenty years earlier. When I was ready to leave, I thanked the older woman who had let us in and was sitting in the corner of the living room with her cello. As I started to leave, she said, "Look at the books" and pointed to a coffee table covered with Richard Neutra books. When I didn't immediately start flipping pages, she barked again, "Look at the books!" So I did.

That's when I saw the famous portrait of Richard Neutra with his wife, Dione, playing the cello. I looked up and realized it was Dione who had let me in.

I later met Dion's brother, Dr. Raymond Neutra, a research epidemiologist and physician. He was everything Dion was not: gracious, warm, open, and unpretentious.

It was hardly Dion's fault he became such a pill; it's never a good idea to join your parent's business!

09 October
Jacques Tati

Jacques Tati, 1961

At least two of Jacques Tati's films (and bits of others) are centered around extreme architecture that he created for comic effect and social commentary. He wrote, directed, acted in, produced, and probably lit and filmed these incredible architectural events.

In *Mon Oncle*, Tati creates Villa Arpel, a goofy, modern, suburban house replete with fatuous and bizarre residents to effectively play the house like a fine instrument. Round windows sport inhabitants' heads to become eyeballs following the action; a fish fountain is a movie in itself; clicking high heels and mumbling Tati are the treble and bass of the soundtrack; the scrupulously followed winding path becomes the metaphor that Tati's circuitous gags take to the punch line.

In *Playtime*, Tati's masterwork and the film that nearly bankrupted and ruined him, he creates an entire city (christened Tativille) of starkly modern office buildings. These gray worlds, and gray people, set the stage for Tati's antics; hilarity ensues. He constructed Tativille exteriors from scaled-down facades literally rolled into place, creating a Sixth Avenue–like land of glass towers. The interiors were full scale and hard edged, and they sounded, at turns, squeaky,

humming, echo-filled, and mechanical. Sound was always Monsieur Hulot's companion.

A landmark exhibition on Tati was held in 2009 at Cinémathèque française, which occupies the former American Center in Paris, designed by Frank Gehry. The combination of the show, including the architecture that nearly bankrupted Tati, in a building that bankrupted the organization that commissioned it, is ironically potent. The building was the perfect foil to the absurdist exposition inside. Buildings have been known to ruin institutions (think Cooper Union's Morphosis building that caused it to charge tuition for the first time since before the Civil War, or the American Folk Art Museum, whose gorgeous companion to MoMA has been dismantled and absorbed into the museum) and occasionally filmmakers.

In trying to convince my son to watch Jacques Tati's films, I realized they may not be funny on an iPhone. Just think what Tati could do with that!

10 October
Julius Shulman

Photo of Case Study House 22, Los Angeles, California, design, Pierre Koenig, 1960

Julius Shulman was well into his nineties when he photographed the Sten-Frenke House for us. (He started working with Richard Neutra in 1938 and so missed shooting the 1934 house that we renovated in the early 2000s.) He was assisted by his colleague, at whom he expressed his characteristic impatience; this was a man who worked fast, as time was running out. Architectural photographers are notoriously the opposite, incredibly patient and methodical.

It was a pure joy watching him use his tricks (arranging plates into a sculpture on a shelf) or selecting the books to leave in the shots ("not Schindler, he was a pill"). And the photos are perfect in the way only he could make them.

We celebrated his ninety-fourth birthday at Pentagram and hosted him at the Cooper Hewitt National Design Awards. The best ninety-plus company ever, he passed a note to my wife, Carin Goldberg, during a way-too-long acceptance speech with "Will she ever shut up?" scribbled on it. He was irrepressible.

His talent was finding the accidental photographs that defined his career; the most famous was at Case Study House 22, Pierre Koenig's aerie hanging over Los Angeles. In it, models waiting for their turn are seated, chatting, in the glass corner cantilever. Shulman moved to hide a light behind a window mullion, snapped, and caught his most memorable image. At the Kaufmann Desert House (one of the very best modern homes ever created, for the same family that commissioned Fallingwater), he asked Mrs. Kaufmann to lie by the pool to, again, block the light that would have flared the picture. It is the second-most-iconic image in his oeuvre.

Commissioning his own house and studio, he first wanted to ask ten different architects to each design a different room. He somehow imagined that he could compose, or collage, a home much the way his photos were assembled to create an editorial spread in architecture magazines. It would never have worked, and he ended up asking Raphael Soriano to design the entire house, the one he lived in until his death at ninety-eight.

As a quiet homage to Julius Shulman's birthday, I started my own studio on 10/10/10 (2010, of course). It was a nice way for me to remember a very nice, very gifted, and utterly unstoppable talent.

11 October
Emil Králiček

Cubist lamppost, Jungmannovo Square, Prague, now Czech Republic, 1913

Czech cubism lasted about fifteen minutes, but it seems to have defined Prague and Emil Králiček as well. His cubist lamppost predates Constantin Brancusi's similar *Endless Column*, version 1, though it is admittedly different in details and material. Still, it is a bit of a revolution that Králiček invented but, never one to boast, left unheralded. He was media shy or just didn't consider it part of his value as an architect.

Czech cubism seems like a misnamed movement. It was based on a crystalline geometry, maybe in reference to early Picasso and Braque cubism. Everything in Czech cubism is broken into triangles, rhomboids, trapezoids, and probably other geometries I have forgotten since taking high school math. No matter, as after just two years the movement gave way to rondocubism, permitting round shapes to make their way into the constructions.

Králiček moved on to rondocubism, but this was a time of movements that had strict rules about what exactly the formal language allowed. I've never understood this idea in politics and can't endorse it in art or design. It's micro-tribalism. And probably a way to validate in cultural terms what is really, utterly subjective.

Králiček worked for Joseph Maria Olbrich, a founder of the Vienna Secession movement (yet another movement!) who designed the Secession Building. So Králiček moved from movement to movement, from curves to fractures to circles to whatever movement came next. It's like architectural whiplash.

Architects tend to be optimists; we have to be in order to believe in projects that can take years to complete and are subject to devastating wrong turns at a thousand points during the process. This is not necessarily confirmed by suicide rates, which are not insignificant for architects (17.6 per 100,000) and are well ahead of the supposedly high rates of healthcare professionals but well behind rates of miners (something Joe Manchin hasn't mentioned). So, not *all* architects are optimists.

Emil Králiček's legacy was almost lost after his suicide because of his reticence about publicity, but he was rediscovered after the Velvet Revolution (which was not an interior design movement).

12 October
Richard Meier

Shamberg House, Chappaqua, New York, 1974

There are architects who approach every project as a unique and different challenge and who craft a response to the specifics of the situation. And there are architects who see each challenge through the lens of their own body of work and who look to advance and refine their oeuvre over time. Richard Meier, of course, belongs to the latter group, and once you accept that approach, his work becomes easier to understand and evaluate.

But that doesn't preclude a critical view of the whole idea of an overly consistent body of work and what it means to treat every project as just one more to be run through the mill that produces Meier buildings each time. And I haven't even gotten to the Charlie-Rose-level sexual harassment charges that caused him to retire, in disgrace, from his eponymous firm.

I visited the Shamberg House, an early Meier from 1974, with friends of the owners, and when I asked why a particular Frank Stella print was where it was, the owner answered breathlessly, "That's where Mr. Meier wanted it" (it turned out the print was also selected by the architect).

This is precisely the problem with these houses (and his approach): they ultimately belong to the architect. Owners are afraid to change anything, lest Mr. Meier be cross. It's infantilizing, and it's an attempt to invert the real power in the client/architect relationship. Richard Neutra was said to have an open invitation (of his own) to drop by any time, with anyone at whichever of his projects he desired to see. Mr. Meier doesn't even need to stop by to exert an everlasting influence on his enablers.

He's made some really lovely buildings; I am particularly fond of the Barcelona Museum of Contemporary Art that creates a plaza, and the Perry Street towers that, until he jumped the shark and built a third one, created a conceptual gateway to the West Village. But the Getty Center is a mess (just asking Richard Meier to use another material was like asking Franz Kline if he could color it up a bit for cheerfulness), and the Ara Pacis Museum is fucking awful.

Never varying from his signature approach is simply tiresome, but the behavior forcing him to leave the scene as he did is disgraceful, period. Fade to black.

13 October
Giorgio Massari

Santa Maria del Rosario, Venice, Italy, 1743

Venice (the original one, not the California version) is an essentially Gothic city. All those pointy arches, the stone tracery, the structured asymmetry, the typical Venetian palazzo with its water entrance and large halls above. But 250 years after the Ca' d'Oro, it was being built and rebuilt in a style more Palladian than Gothic by people like Giorgio Massari.

There's that odd thing that happens in Venetian buildings of almost any era: the facade is often built of lavish materials but barely wraps the corner before turning into a more workaday material. Even when the side is as visibly prominent as the facade: Massari's Palazzo Grassi privileges the Grand Canal face rather than the one commanding its own piazza. Maybe buildings were taxed/regulated based on the grandeur of the facade materials. Or maybe it's more about construction costs; limiting luxury to a single facade saves money.

Their "facadism" is more peculiar than our local example; New York City Hall was originally marble on its south face and brick on the north because the idea that the city would grow uptown and expose the "rear" seemed absurd at the time. Not so in Venice, where the sides of buildings are often visible; there it

seems more like a conscious effort to wear a mask, to declare fealty to the idea of one principal plane rather than the volume.

New York City is built on granite bedrock, and Venice is built on mud. Both use piles to provide support for buildings, but Venice is more apt to settle. Stone is much heavier than brick, and brick can accommodate more movement (smaller units) than large pieces of stone. So the restrained use of stone may be a strategy to limit settling and movement.

Massari is called, by none other than Rudolf Wittkower, the best Venetian architect of the first half of the eighteenth century, and I suppose he was. He helped normalize the modern classical style in a land of Gothic splendor. Modernization included regularization; the asymmetrical Venetian facade gave way to single repetitive modules. We're happy with that regularity when, say, the facades define the Piazza San Marco, but less happy when they grace the Grand Canal.

Blame Giorgio Massari, but no one appreciates progress in Venice.

14 October
Paul T. Frankl

Rattan furniture, 1940s

Paul T. Frankl was yet another Viennese architect and designer to depart Austria (World War I did it for him) and end up defining American modernism; Rudolph Schindler, Richard Neutra, Joseph Urban, and Frederick Kiesler, along with Frankl, settled on both coasts (often with Chicago interludes) to convince reluctant Americans to adopt modernism. It wasn't an easy sell; Americans seemed obsessed with traditional European design as a marker of wealth, class, and taste.

Frankl began to change that with his art deco designs (though he missed the 1925 Paris exhibition that gave it its name). Even before the Chrysler and Empire State buildings, he hit upon his design hook; Skyscraper Furniture (his name for the series) was a clever, simple, and legible reference to the coming age of skyscrapers. It worked, making his gallery and showroom in New York City a center of modern design during World War I and beyond.

At the same time, he bought a cabin in Woodstock, New York, and developed a range of more rustic trestle furniture for the exurban crowd. He even named it (he was clever with names) Woodstock.

Books, in Frankl's day, were incredibly influential design tools, and he wrote

several books that cemented his position as an arbiter of modern style. He even dedicated one in 1938 to Frank Lloyd Wright and asked him to write a preface. In it, Wright waffled about the meaning of "preface" (he landed on "apology"), and while dithering about definitions he made it clear he hadn't seen the book. Wright was endorsing it in the hopes he would, whenever he actually read it, like it.

Frankl moved to Los Angeles in 1934, hung with his fellow expats, and eventually opened another gallery on Rodeo Drive, which attracted Hollywood celebs like Fred Astaire, Cary Grant, Katharine Hepburn, Walter Huston, and Alfred Hitchcock. He LA-ified his furniture based on context, as he did in Woodstock. This time he used rattan, making it acceptable for interior furniture (as opposed to the poolside use it had at the time). The lightweight, casual look was perfect for the California lifestyle.

Paul T. Frankl used the best promotion available at the time, books and retail stores, to sell modern design to the public. That and his uncanny eye for adapting to local needs.

15 October
Brice Marden

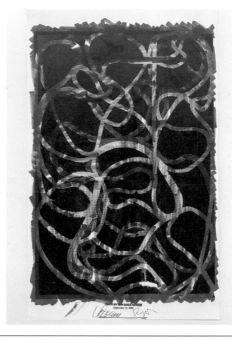

I Made My Own Brice Marden, Carin Goldberg/Brice Marden, Tivoli, New York, 2004

I'm not sure why the urge to join the hospitality industry is so strong among creative types, but Brice and Helen Marden could be the poster children for that sideline. They have at least two hotels with restaurants, one in Tivoli, New York, where they live just down the road in a Hudson River mansion.

I understand the prestige of always being able to get a table. (A Hollywood type once tried to impress me, saying, "I can get a table at ANY restaurant," as if that fully established his cred.) I understand wanting to dine in surroundings that don't hurt your eyes. And I understand how creating work in two dimensions seems to beg some artists to expand at least one more dimension into architectural work.

Marden's early paintings are almost three dimensional in that he would "build" his paintings by assembling separate canvases into larger wall assemblies. Some even referenced post-and-lintel construction (think Stonehenge). He later would paint on marble fragments, implying his paintings were torn from a more complete construction. Maybe hospitality was the next logical step, but restaurants and hotels are unrelenting work. Plus, restaurants tend to take on the personalities of their owners, and

an artist's disposition might be the precise opposite of the temperament of a host. Artists tend to make things for themselves, the public be damned. Hospitality (except in the mold of *Fawlty Towers*) is intended to please the public, even at the expense of the host.

On the other hand, the only time I met Marden, he was sitting at a little table at Tivoli's street fair offering, for some nominal donation to the local community, to create art for visitors, in real time, in front of them. And during the pandemic he offered to buy a local church building for an arts and community space, so maybe he is suited to hospitality!

Somehow, Marden, who started as a rather strict minimalist creating rectangular monochromatic panels, is now making paintings constructed of a tangle of meandering squiggles. In a kind of final resolution, he has assembled monochromatic panels and the calligraphic painting (as he calls the squiggles) together into massive, mural-scale constructions and in layered single-canvas paintings reconciling his early and late work.

We are now left with Marden's art, and the Mardens' hotel/restaurants. They pretty much address all the senses and seem like a complete picture to me.

16 October
Margaret Morton

Margaret Morton at her Leica Gallery retrospective, New York, New York, 2015

Margaret Morton was easy to like. She had a bright, positive countenance and was more interested in others than in telling others about herself. That worked perfectly for someone who photographed the unhoused people in New York City, people living in temporary digs in railway tunnels and on the street. She published not just their photos, but also their stories. She wasn't a voyeur (though that is part of what a photographer must be) as much as a reporter. Compared to Jacob Riis, she aimed to humanize the subjects rather than demonstrate their squalid contexts.

She didn't dwell on her work, but when I saw her show on Kyrgyzstan cemeteries, it was clear that she was much more ambitious, driven, and brave than her tiny frame seemed to indicate.

I was lucky enough to be at the American Academy in Rome for the same month that Margaret was there, and we traveled to some fantastic places near Rome, including the Bomarzo Park of Monsters and Villa Medici at Caprarola, as well as some architectural moments in Rome. She managed to be there and present, but faded just a bit into the background to avoid affecting the places she photographed.

Her work challenged, to some extent, the Observer Effect, whereby the mere observation of an event changes that event. She was engaged with her (animate) subjects, and her photos often acknowledge her own presence, as when people look directly at the lens, and her. But she was not there to judge, proselytize, or crusade, but to report. Her presence was intended to be spectral, visible but not of the same weight as her subjects. Quite a delicate dance.

She was excited to show me the Farley Post Office photos, displayed in the Farley Building, that she took before the building's transformation into a rail station. It was one of those rare metaopportunities to see the real thing and the photographs of the real thing in conversation with each other.

Margaret Morton spent decades teaching at Cooper Union, a place she loved and that loved her back. Her death from leukemia was a shock; it seems she didn't want anyone to worry about her, retreating into the spectral as she did as a photographer.

17 October
Pierre Koenig

Pierre Koenig in Case Study House 21 (Bailey House), Los Angeles, California, 1958

The single most iconic photograph of a modern American house must be the nighttime view of Pierre Koenig's Case Study House 22, the Stahl House above Los Angeles. I'm not sure that Pierre ever properly thanked photographer Julius Shulman or could have. The house is great, but the photograph is transformational.

While on a California modernism tour in 1999, I spent time with Koenig and Shulman and Mrs. Stahl (Mr. Stahl was feeling ill) at 22 while Julius recomposed his famous shot. It's legendary that the shot was accidentally framed when Shulman stepped out for a moment to admire the view. The women pictured were the girlfriends of the assistants, and the exposure was one of those layered things one did before Photoshop: seven minutes for the views of Los Angeles and, with all the house lights replaced with flashbulbs, fractions of a second for the interior.

Koenig's houses then were very tiny: 22 was 2,300 square feet/200 square meters and 21 was just 1,320 square feet/123 square meters. There is a resonance between Koenig, who believed in *steel-über-alles* as the most efficient material to build in, and these tiny, efficient houses. His own

first house, built while he was still a student, was just 800 square feet/75 square meters plus a carport and is truly fantastic.

As his houses got bigger, and as Koenig got older (he was thirty-five when Stahl was completed), the crystalline perfection of his designs was muddied. While showing me through his own second house, from 1985, he impatiently tried to get me to listen to his spiel about why it was so great, but it just wasn't.

By 1995, he designed a cube-twisted-within-a-cube house that is so contrived as to be unrecognizable as a Koenig. Same vocabulary, but not the same verve or clarity. It's true with these birthday biographies as well: editing them down to fit on a single page is an exercise in clarification, condensation, and compactness. Smaller is often much, much better.

Pierre Koenig spent a couple of days with me as I hung at the Stahl House, visited another Case Study House or two, and ended up with Julius and Lucia Eames (Charles's daughter) sitting around the cramped kitchen table at the Eames House (Case Study House 8), just like old times.

18 October
Albert Frey

Palm Springs City Hall, 1952

Albert Frey had a very good sense of humor. How else do you explain the dimmer he mounted directly on the gigantic boulder that he built his Palm Springs house around?! There's a convenient headboard nearby, but Frey went to a lot of trouble to chisel the wire into the stone and mount the dial right at eye level. Very droll.

The whole idea of a giant boulder intruding into the house is, I suppose, a tell that this is no ordinary house. It's quite compact, just eight hundred square feet/seventy-five square meters, and that includes the boulder! The pool is built over the carport (the least cool part of the house; it looks like a 1980s addition), and the whole thing was, at the time, the highest elevation that anyone had built a house in Palm Springs. The town thought he was a bit nuts (maybe they had no sense of humor) but approved his design anyway; it was completed in 1964, and Frey lived there until his death thirty-four years later.

Frey's provenance is impeccable; Swiss, he worked for Le Corbusier in the early days of the Villa Savoye when he, José Luis Sert, and Charlotte Perriand were the only employees of the office. He landed in New York City (the only architect then in America who had worked for Le Corbusier) and joined with Lawrence Kocher to design the Aluminaire House. The first all-metal house in the US was built in ten days for an exhibition; dismantled; exhibited again at the International Style show at MoMA in 1932; disassembled again; installed at Wallace K. Harrison's estate; disassembled again and moved to another location at Harrison's place as a guesthouse; disassembled (and saved) by moving it to New York Institute of Technology campus in Central Islip; dismantled again when that campus was closed; stored for years; and now in Palm Springs (to be near its brethren), ready to be reassembled, hopefully for the last time. Le Corbusier liked to say that his 1967 Heidi Weber Pavilion on Lake Zurich was the first fully demountable building, but Frey had him by thirty-five years (and John Paxton had him by 115 years).

Albert Frey built hundreds of buildings in Palm Springs, and not all are laugh riots. But the Palm Springs City Hall has an oversized canopy with a giant hole through which three palm trees grow, so it isn't all deadly serious, either.

19 October
Verna Cook Salomonsky

Rendering for *House and Garden* of ideal house, 1935

I grew up in the suburbs, which is not one singular thing. There are the "good" suburbs, built between the world wars, and then there are the postwar versions. The interwar suburbs tend to be larger, more varied, and better sited and landscaped (they were on the east side of the long spine running down my city), and the postwar ones (on the west side of my town) tend to be newer, smaller, and more repetitive.

Verna Cook Salomonsky was an architect of the "good" kind, mostly in Scarsdale and other tony communes in Westchester County, New York, where the likes of Rob and Laura Petrie (but in real life Carl and Estelle Reiner) lived. Cook Salomonsky and her husband (and fellow Columbia School of Architecture grad), Edgar Salomonsky, established an office in New York City that seemed to move around a lot during the 1920s (and why I know all this I am not sure), from Lexington Avenue to Madison Avenue to East Forty-Ninth Street and back to Madison.

Edgar committed suicide in the couple's Scarsdale kitchen in 1929, just two months after the stock market crash (no idea if that was the cause), but Verna persevered and built hundreds of homes in Westchester and, later, California. She was very successful and well-known in the profession. Verna even designed one of the model homes for the 1939 New York World's Fair; it was selected by *House and Garden* as the magazine's first "Ideal House." She was the only female member admitted to the Architectural League in 1936, just two years after it opened membership to women, which seems especially bizarre given how the body is now constituted. But architecture was a boys' club (and still is at the upper reaches of firm control).

She wrote extensively, my favorite being an article in the *Washington Post* titled "The Year-Round Service Porch, Half Indoors, Half Out, a Constant Delight." Indeed.

She left the United States for France after eye strain forced her to close her practice, but hurried back as World War II began, marrying an engineer who eventually worked for the American Embassy in London after the war.

She marked her passport application with her profession, "architect," only to have it crossed out by an administrator who inserted "housewife." She wryly suggested that she wasn't quite sure if she was up to that particular profession.

20 October
Christopher Wren

Cathedral Church of St. Paul's, London, England, 1710

Christopher Wren was more like his friend Sir Isaac Newton, or even Leonardo da Vinci, than any other architect one can conjure. The man was a genius and a polymath. For his architectural career, it didn't hurt that he came of age as the 1666 fire destroyed much of London and was appointed to build fifty-plus churches as part of its reconstruction, not to mention St. Paul's Cathedral, his magnum opus.

Wren was the sickly son of another Christopher Wren who nevertheless managed to live ninety years at a time when the life expectancy was thirty-seven years. He was no dilettante; he made significant contributions in the fields of anatomy, physics, mathematics, astronomy, optics, mechanical devices, and, of course, architecture. He was, no surprise, quite rich, inheriting his mother's considerable fortune upon her death. The best way to make a small fortune at architecture, like at raising horses, is to start with a large fortune. So, he had that.

He had some very smart friends in addition to Newton, and they all chatted after Wren's lectures in London. They eventually got a royal charter for what became the Royal Society of London for Improving Natural Knowledge, what we know today as just the Royal Society. It comprised the most important collection of people like Wren from every field. He even had a role in provoking Newton to write *The Mathematical Principles of Natural Philosophy* (1729), the most important work on motion prior to Einstein's.

Wren had already designed a couple of buildings as a student at Oxford when he visited Paris (his only trip abroad) and encountered Gian Lorenzo Bernini (yes, that Bernini), who further schooled him in the arts of drawing and architecture. Returning to London, he competed for the design of St. Paul's a week before most of the city burned to the ground. Nice timing, because he was appointed King's Surveyor of the Works, where his official position led to him becoming the reigning architectural influencer of his time.

Famously, under the dome at St. Paul's is a black disk set in the floor and engraved in Latin that says, "Should you seek his monument, look about you." Fair enough, but outside the confines of St. Paul's, London is filled with Christopher Wren's monuments. If we include his nonarchitectural works, he may be the most influential architect who ever lived.

"I hope I haven't grown up."

Catherine Hardwicke on the value of thinking young

After a tour of twenty-five modern homes in California, ranging from those by Irving Gill to Rudolf Schindler, from Richard Neutra to Pierre Koenig, from John Lautner to Albert Frey, my friends (and clients) bought an early Neutra house in Santa Monica. While we were waiting for permits to renovate it (it was a registered landmark and took a lot of time), the client used the house as a film set for his movie *Laurel Canyon*. Lisa Cholodenko directed it, and Catherine Hardwicke was the set designer. Hardwicke went on to make more movies as director and designer, including, with our friend, *Thirteen*.

Turning a 1934 International Style house by Neutra into a casual Laurel Canyon aerie is precisely the kind of transformation that Hardwicke excels at; and turning a script into a movie is, I suppose, a similar kind of alchemy. The transformation of the house took some clever surgery by Hardwicke, who studied architecture at the University of Texas at Austin. More than one person I know has gone from "serious" architecture to production design or art direction of movies (all of them women, not surprisingly).

If you want to insult a set designer, just dismiss the movie work as "easy" due to lack of "real life constraints." The truth is the opposite; sets have to do all sorts of things that real buildings don't, like break down for storage, have movable walls for shooting positions, create age and patina in new construction, and include lighting and other "real life" items in constructions that are prefabricated and movable. It's like comedic acting: it's acting plus comedy, not less than acting.

Hardwicke's movies began as personal stories, as with *Thirteen*; she and thirteen-year-old friend Nikki Reed wrote the screenplay in six days over Christmas break. Reed played the lead at fourteen years old, in part because Hardwicke wanted to avoid an older actor playing a much younger part (and in part because it was her story).

Catherine Hardwicke has gone on to direct blockbusters like *Twilight* and their opposite, movies like *Lords of Dogtown* (critically appreciated, but with very low box office sales), proving that alchemy is not driven by box office, and nor is she.

22 October
Peter Cook

Kunsthaus Graz, Graz, Austria, 2003

He's not the Peter Cook of Peter Cook and Dudley Moore, but seeing him lecture, you might be understandably confused. There's a lot of histrionics, leaping, wearing interesting eyeglasses, and being architecturally cheeky. He is a bit outlandish, recently calling UK architects "biscuit boys" (whatever that means, I'm pretty sure he could be canceled for it). But the man has serious cred; he founded, with others, Archigram in London in the early 1960s. It was the first real revolution in British architecture since, possibly, the Crystal Palace a hundred years earlier.

Peter Cook is not unlike the other Peter Cook in a few ways: tall and thin, clever and witty, sharp tongued and committed. Both Cooks were part of very influential groups; however, our Sir Peter is still alive, giving him the added benefit of age (his slightly younger doppelganger died in 1995 at fifty-seven).

And our Peter could really draw. His images (and those of other Archigrammers) were a jolt to an otherwise staid (perhaps biscuity) state of architecture in the 1960s and '70s. My former partner Theo Crosby was a big supporter of Archigram and managed to publish its work long before he founded his own "gram" (Pentagram).

The two men would surely hate each other's architecture today, but in the heady years of swinging London they found each other as forecasters of a brave new world. Cook's was a fantasy of plug-in cities and Theo's was...well, I'm not quite sure.

There are, it turns out, lots of Peter Cooks (the name, that is), including several architects. Christie Brinkley was married to one of them (who is now married to a woman one third his age). Another is a design principal at HGA and just appointed to the US Commission of Fine Arts. Yet another is a teaching assistant at Cornell University.

But there is only one Sir Peter Cook, and he is still, in his late eighties, making trouble, acting the iconoclast, irritating nearly everyone, and standing for the complete overhaul of nearly everything. It's refreshing (and pretty impressive) to see him continuing the role he created nearly sixty years ago.

23 October
Paul Rudolph

Yale Art and Architecture Building (Rudolph Hall), New Haven, Connecticut, 1963

It's hard not to like Paul Rudolph's work, because, with all the phases he went through, there's something for every taste. He emulated Frank Lloyd Wright early on (and referenced him throughout his career), followed by Mies van der Rohe, then a de Stijl thing started to creep in, followed by the concrete brutalist stuff that is part Le Corbusier, part Marcel Breuer. Am I leaving anything out? Oh, right, Rudolph's Japanese Metabolist work. And his Louis Kahn–like urban megastructures. What's not to like?

A lot, actually. From the exquisite small residential work of his first guesthouse, with its operable flaps counterbalanced with cannonballs, it's a long walk to the later brutalist extravaganzas. The interesting part is watching him change, devouring history while at the same time propelling it forward.

At Yale, where Rudolph held sway for six years, there seems to be a tradition of the dean designing a campus building; Rudolph may have started that nepotistic tradition by designing the Yale Art and Architecture Building while he was in charge. It's a building that people love to hate and love to love. It's a building that fights against its users, that forces people to confront it, that isn't the slightest bit neutral or accommodating.

Maybe that's why students set it on fire. It was 1969, and professors had been fired, so maybe it wasn't just the building that provoked the arson. The building has been hated by so many for so long that most haters didn't even realize that the thing they hated was really the result of years of purposefully ruinous interventions that destroyed the original.

The restoration of the building in 2008 was really a backhanded compliment; Charles Gwathmey, a student of Rudolph, cleared out the added partitions and floors while adding a thoroughly awful extension. It's hard to understand how Gwathmey, who apparently worked on the drawings for the original building, could promote Rudolph while embarrassing himself by his own design; the only explanation that makes sense is that he didn't realize how bad the good would make him look.

Paul Rudolph might be happy that the argument continues, but likely unhappy with his debate partner.

24 October
Charlotte Perriand

Nuage cabinet/shelving, designed 1952

Charlotte Perriand seems preter-naturally joyous for someone whose design credit had been forgotten (to put it politely) by Le Corbusier (who originally replied to her application for a job in his office with, "We don't embroider cushions here"). She outlived him by thirty years and resurrected her reputation as the true genius and author behind much of his furniture.

She famously was the only woman in the picture: the woman reclining on the famous lounge, the one triumphantly flashing the alps topless, the one behind whom Le Corbusier holds a plate to imply a halo. I've never seen a photograph of her when she wasn't smiling.

Her work, thanks to gallerist Patrick Seguin, now fetches the same astronomical prices that Jean Prouvé's and Le Corbusier's do; they are all close relatives in their period and design approach, and occasionally in their designs. Of course, Perriand worked closely with Prouvé and Le Corbusier to their benefit, just as they worked together for their own.

One look at Le Corbusier's built interiors prior to her arrival at age twenty-four says it all; they have no truly modern furniture, and therefore present an

incomplete vision of modernity. Marcel Breuer's furniture had not yet arrived (it was developed at the same time Perriand was inventing furniture in Le Corbusier's studio), and Le Corbusier used either his beloved Thonet Prague chair or a few stuffed easy chairs. Perriand changed all that, finally making the designs true Gesamtkunstwerk (and, yes, love that word).

I am still in awe of the extraordinarily simple genius of a set of tiny wall sconces that she designed for a Japanese hotel; pivoting flaps cover the bulbs. Two folded pieces of metal, the bare minimum of electrical gear, and voilà, a light fixture!

If there is any doubt about provenance, just flip through her sketchbooks; she chronicled, in extraordinary detail, every step forward. The drawings dimensioning the entire contents of a home, from clothes to dinnerware (to account for storage units), give a sense of the detail and comprehensiveness of her research.

Charlotte Perriand's furniture has the clarity, singularity, and materiality (and some other -ities I can't conjure) that makes it uncomplicated to love her work and, equally, to love her.

25 October
Sven Markelius

Collective housing, Stockholm, Sweden, 1935

Back in 2012, I wrote an article for *Design Observer* in which (almost as an aside) I gratuitously dismissed Sven Markelius, who was awarded the RIBA Gold Medal in 1962, as an unknown and undeserving recipient (ouch). To be fair, it was the same year the AIA Gold Medal went to Eero Saarinen, someone who, despite his shared Scandinavian heritage, seemed a tiny bit more deserving. I was (fairly) criticized for the slight, and here is my atonement.

Sven Markelius built, in 1930, the first International Style (Swedes called it functionalist) house for himself in Sweden. At a time when Erik Gunnar Asplund had already built the Stockholm Library, Sven's Villa Markelius and the 1930 Stockholm Exhibition trumpeted modernism in Sweden.

Markelius was among the authors of the manifesto *acceptera* (accept!), a bit of propaganda selling modernism to the Swedish public. The sales pitch presented an either/or paradigm: either you were "A-Europe" (industrialized, modern, functional, connected, and evolving) or you were "B-Europe" (agricultural, isolated, disorganized, unchanging). It was a common pitch: look forward or look backward. And in 1930, as the world appeared to be capable of radical modernization,

it would be Neanderthal to resist. So, accept!

Swedes bought it. A wave of functionalist architecture ensued. Markelius built not only his own house but also the 1935 Collective House in Stockholm, a communal living arrangement he moved into and never moved out of (until he died, that is). He ended up being the unofficial handyman of the complex, a cautionary tale for any architect occupying, or visiting, their own design.

He was Sweden's representative at the design sessions of the United Nations, though the idea of this nearly invisible man competing with marketing dynamos like Le Corbusier, Oscar Niemeyer, and Wallace K. Harrison is probably why we (I) hadn't heard of him.

Honestly, I still don't see why Sven Markelius was considered so deserving of the RIBA medal, following Mies van der Rohe, Pier Luigi Nervi, and Lewis Mumford the three previous years. But this is supposed to be my apologia for dissing him, so, congratulations, Sven! Well deserved!

26 October
Hilma af Klint

"The pictures were painted directly through me, without any preliminary drawings, and with great force. I had no idea what the paintings were supposed to depict; nevertheless I worked swiftly and surely, without changing a single brush stroke."

From the notebooks of Hilma af Klint

One of the delusions of living in New York is the notion that you can always get to landmark art exhibitions (and plays and dances and concerts) after the fuss has died down. Plenty of time to see these things! After all, I live here.

That's how I missed the Hilma af Klint exhibition at the Guggenheim, and I still regret it (not that it's taught me to be more timely).

Her work is an astonishing revelation. She started "automatic painting" in 1896, and that is not a typo. Her nonobjective *Temple* series began in 1906 (again, not a typo), years before Wassily Kandinsky, Piet Mondrian, Kasimir Malevich, or anyone else came even close to her level of pure abstraction. It's like finding a photograph of Mozart, except she actually did paint these before World War I.

If not for her secrecy about the paintings, she would be the most famous early abstract painter in every art history book. Instead, she insisted that her paintings not be shown until twenty years after her death. I can understand why Richard Nixon wanted to keep his tapes out of circulation for decades and why Jackie Kennedy's pink Chanel suit will be kept from public view for another eighty

years (kinda) and why an author would want to hide an unfinished manuscript, but one's fully completed intentional creations?

These were spectacular works, a series of enormous paintings, both cohesive and meaningful. Why keep them from public exposure, not even to be seen upon her death? It's a "tree falls in the forest" kind of question; if a painting remains unseen, does it even exist? Obviously, in the literal sense, yes, but isn't the whole idea of art to be shown, read, seen, heard, or inhabited?

Showing artworks is not only about becoming part of the zeitgeist or history or fashion; these pieces of art (or design) don't seem complete until seen. If Hilma hated the paintings, she would have destroyed them. Instead, she set up a twenty-years-after-death timer before the vault opened. Was it a time capsule (and to what end)?

While I'm sorry I will miss Jackie's dress (not really) and technically I missed Hilma af Klint's show, I'm happy to live in a time when her paintings have come out of hiding. Not seeing them would be an unrealized loss for all (or most) of us.

27 October
Roy Lichtenstein

Entrance hall, Tel Aviv Museum of Art, Tel Aviv, Israel

The top ten list of pop-art artists would have Roy Lichtenstein as number two (we all know who number one is). There are lots of other contenders, but they all seem to tie for third; they were making much more complicated, painterly art. Maybe Claes Oldenburg would be third. But after that...

Lichtenstein was born in 1923, grew up on the Upper West Side, attended the Art Students League of New York, and had two sons in the early 1950s, exactly as my mother did (the similarity ends there). He was drafted (unlike my mother) and planned to attend the Sorbonne but returned to the US when his father was near death. He bounced around teaching while he worked his way through the Western canon of art, landing on abstract expressionism a bit too late.

It may be apocryphal, but Lichtenstein's discovery of comic book–style imagery came when his son was reading a Mickey Mouse comic and said, "Bet you can't paint as good as that, eh Dad?" *Look Mickey* was his first real pop-art painting. He continued exploring, and the rest is pop-art history.

There's a much deeper and more interesting intellectual underbed to Roy's work beyond the appropriation

of the "worst" of American public artwork (advertisements, gum wrappers, cartoons, comic books, etc.). The flatness of the surface is a dematerializing technique, as well as a way to remove all the "expressionism" from his work. He moved to paintings of brushstrokes as a nod to the lack of them in his art and to their primal masculinity in abstract expressionism.

The paintings are almost deadpan, seemingly cropped from quotidian sources and hung without frames. They show snippets of life, celebrating the uncelebrated art of the unheralded. His work was like *Saturday Night Live*'s fake commercials that turn real commercials into parodies. His was art about art that changed the way we see all art.

While he made it too easy to mock pop art, there is real emotion in these uninflected works. They reach into a viewer's own comic-strewn past while they arrive at the vanguard of ironic art. Critics say he found a hook and never moved on. Lovers say he discovered a seminal aspect of culture and would never finish plumbing its variety.

I say Roy Lichtenstein was a genius, and the world would be a less interesting place without him.

28 October
Charlotte Posenenske

Posenenske installation in 2010, Haus Konstruktiv, Zurich

It's amazing we (well, I) don't know more about Charlotte Posenenske; she was a landmark minimalist sculptor who, in the 1960s, produced work as interesting as Donald Judd's while upending the capitalist value proposition of art.

Maybe that is why she is not more celebrated. It may also be because she produced art for just twelve years at a time when men were dominant in modern art (and I am still looking for the era when they aren't). She moved on to become a sociologist and industrial-work consultant, saying, "I find it difficult to come to terms with the fact that art can contribute nothing to the solution of pressing social problems." After 1968, she never made, exhibited, or participated in the art world again, and she died at fifty-four, a brief flash of light.

She not only had her work fabricated industrially, she made series (not editions) that could be infinitely reproduced and sold at the cost of the material (no artist's or gallery fee). To really upend the artist-patron (she called them consumers) relationship, she encouraged consumers to rearrange the modules of her sculptures at will. She democratized art while producing some really remarkable work.

Her life was often tortured in ways that shaped her dual careers: art plus social worker (not even sure that's the right word). Her Jewish pharmacist father committed suicide for fear of being sent to the concentration camps; though she was raised Protestant, she was considered a "half-caste" and had to be hidden until the end of World War II. Because she was not permitted to go to school, she finished late, as the oldest in the school, always the other.

Somehow all of this, and many more equally affecting difficulties, combined to produce her strictly ordered view of life. Once having found the perfect drinking glass, she not only used it exclusively but also thought all of society should do the same. When she found the perfect wall plug, she showed up at the Siemens factory to get five of them. Art was not to be made for exclusive consumers, but for all.

The sad and happy ending is that, while dying of cancer, Charlotte Posenenske reversed herself and allowed her series to be put back into production. Thankfully. Sadly.

29 October
Kazuyo Sejima

21st Century Museum of Contemporary Art (bookmark), Kanazawa, Japan, 2004

Kazuyo Sejima is sublime, and her work (I never can tell which is hers and which is her SANAA partner Ryue Nishizawa's, and maybe it doesn't matter) is refined at a rare and remarkable level. Her projects seem almost Platonic (in the Platonic solid polyhedron sense of the word) in their absolute self-contained perfection and crystalline nature. It is hard to image adding anything to or removing anything from these projects; they would conceptually collapse. The clarity and balance they achieve is as remarkable in person as it is in plans, photos, etc.

Seeing her work the first time made me consider giving up architecture; she had somehow redefined the art, leaving us all in her wake. It's like an athletic performance that eclipses all others. Or a piece of music that is so perfect it seems divine.

The work depends on a very high level of execution quality, of precision and exquisite details, and that is why I know of only one of her projects that disappoints. The cheap construction of the New Museum in New York City reveals just how much compromise can compromise a promising building.

In opposition is the 21st Century Museum of Contemporary Art,

Kanazawa; exquisitely conceived and beautifully built, it offers a perfectly shaped gallery for each artwork or artist arranged as volumes of different plans and heights within a circular glass-walled enclosure. It is breathtaking and transformative.

Sejima's curation of the 2010 Venice Biennale was masterful despite what seemed, at first, to be an insipid premise: "People Meet in Architecture." The show opened with a continuous three-dimensional looped movie by Wim Wenders of the Rolex Learning Center that included a scene with Sejima and Nishizawa gliding by on Segways. Sometimes an organizing statement need not be complicated (or pretentious) to produce complex results, and this simple truth was perfect.

SANAA's Kunstlinie in Almere, the Netherlands, manages to incorporate water as a design element without sacrificing the efficiency or crisp geometry of the spaces.

It's ironic that the one SANAA building I haven't seen is the one closest to me: Grace Farms in New Canaan, Connecticut. Maybe I'm just saving it the way I don't binge some streamed TV series; seeing it won't leave much SANAA to look forward to!

30 October
Simone de Pollaiolo

SIMONE D°. IL CRONACA ARCHIT.
P. Vasari T. II.   FIORENTINO   *J. Batt. Cecchi fc.*
68.

Portrait of Il Cronaca, circa 1769–1775

Making it into Giorgio Vasari's *The Lives of the Most Excellent Painters, Sculptors, and Architects*, the first Italian art history book and still the best biography of the Italian Renaissance, was like making it into the Bible, and the book was about as accurate as the Bible. I feel for Vasari; putting together more than two hundred comprehensive biographies is exhausting, even if not exhaustive. At this point in my year of biographies (which became this book), I had written more than three hundred of these mini bios. I have Google (and a strict character limit!), while Vasari had to invent a lot of his info (none of his subjects, except Michelangelo, were alive when he wrote their chapter) and was less than scrupulous about fact-checking, except perhaps in the final forty-two-page bio of himself.

Why did Vasari call Simone Del Pollaiolo, profiled in part 3, volume 2, Il Cronaca (The Chronicle)? Vasari tells us that in Del Pollaiolo's excruciatingly detailed descriptions of his travels to Rome, he sounded like a chronicle. Bit of projection when Vasari, chronicler of the entire Renaissance, calls Del Pollaiolo Il Cronaca.

Il Cronaca finished what was the largest palazzo in Florence (and a model for the University Club in New York City), the Palazzo Strozzi. But more interesting is the Palazzo Guadagni, his attempt to break the tripartite model of the Renaissance palazzo (rusticated base plus piano nobile plus attic story). He added a fourth story of open colonnade, floating the roof above what looked like a roof terrace but is just a perimeter balcony. It's a cool variation on an established pattern.

Il Cronaca had a hand in Florence's Hall of the Five Hundred in the Palazzo Vecchio, a room that Vasari eventually enlarged and decorated with his own heroic murals. The room once held the famous disappearing murals by Leonardo da Vinci opposite a never-executed one by Michelangelo: dueling geniuses across the seventy-five-foot/twenty-three meter width of the vast hall, whose work is lost to history.

Il Cronaca isn't lost, thanks to Vasari's bible of the Renaissance.

31 October
Zaha Hadid

Afragola High-Speed Train Station, Naples, Italy, 2017

Zaha Hadid was one of those rare visionaries to create a machine capable of executing their ideas. What started as a painting-based, perspective-shifting, seemingly unbuildable, winning competition entry for a private club at Hong Kong's Peak has become a portfolio of remarkable depth and breadth. That can only be attributed to Dame Hadid's intelligence, persistence, talent, and passion. She died suddenly at sixty-five in 2016, and her loss (our loss really) was even more terrible because the profession lost a role model, and not just for women.

Even given the level of admiration I have for her and her work, I'm not sure I like it. From the admittedly small selection (and relatively early work) I have visited, I can feel the force of Hadid concentrating on making an explosive building rather than a fully usable one. That is certainly true at MAXXI, her Rome museum of twenty-first-century art. Its interior (and that is where the art is) is practically hostile to art. While it may be more interesting to shape space dramatically, it results in a building that competes with the art rather than provides a space to let the art dominate. It's great empty (not unlike Daniel Libeskind's Jewish Museum in Berlin), but when it's full of art it feels like sitting next to an annoyingly loud theatergoer; the distraction of the building can be overwhelming. Hadid's Vitra Fire Station is similarly a tough building to use (it's not fit for purpose, as they would say on *The Great Pottery Throw Down*). But it's lovely today, converted into an exhibition space for an enormous wall grid of chairs used to chronicle the history of the art of the chair. It takes a focused and vision-filled array like this to compete successfully with Dame Hadid's building. Having found its new purpose, it's a welcome exploration.

Among the stable of starchitects, Hadid had a definitive style that one either bought or didn't. Like Frank Gehry's work, her buildings are easily identifiable, and that worked to her advantage. Her offering was demonstrated in her portfolio, begging the question of how such a personal vision can continue after her death. If the works were truly hers, how can they persist in her absence?

As Zaha Hadid fine-tuned her studio and its technology and as her catalog of completed buildings grew, she grew too, and made more and more workable, usable, and therefore better buildings. It's what we will miss in her absence: all her next buildings.

01 November
James Renwick Jr.

St. Patrick's Cathedral, New York, New York, 1879

You probably don't know the architect who designed St. Patrick's Cathedral in New York City. Or Grace Church. Or the Smithsonian Castle in Washington, DC. Or that he was in his twenties when he won the competitions to design these icons. James Renwick Jr. was that architect. He entered Columbia University at age twelve (no matter how much I read that that was a "normal" age for a certain class to begin their professional education, it makes no sense to me given what I know about twelve-year-olds, including myself), and by the time he entered and won the Grace Church competition he was a wizened twenty-five years of age.

The Grace site was omitted from the gridding of Manhattan (Eleventh Street doesn't continue through it), some say because of the powerful family, the Brevoorts, who owned it and had their favorite orchard there. It's still a staggering idea; in 1843, when the land was sold to Grace Church, there was an orchard in the West Village.

Renwick's uncle Henry Brevoort sold the land to Grace Church, and it seems a stretch to believe his twenty-five-year-old nephew simply won the competition for the most fashionable church in New York. It was a classic case of nepotism; nevertheless,

Renwick did a bang-up job with the design, and Grace Church is still an elegant gray lady.

Gray because of the Sing Sing marble it used, as in the Sing Sing Correctional Facility, which was built at the location of a quarry so that inmates could provide labor for quarrying and cutting the stone. When Alexander Hamilton (in the musical, of course) chastises Thomas Jefferson for bragging about how they actually produce things in the South (with free labor), Hamilton may have conveniently forgotten how the North conscripted its own enslaved labor.

Renwick's best-known work is St. Patrick's Cathedral; Grace Church was farmland, so imagine that the St. Patrick's site, two miles north, was wilderness. The archbishop realized it would one day be the center of a great city, an amazing leap of faith.

James Renwick Jr. was all of forty when the cathedral's first stone was laid and sixty when it was completed. Still a young(ish) man to have built a cathedral, but if you start your professional career at twelve it's amazing what you can get done!

02 November
Battista Pininfarina

Pininfarina logo

Ever since Mrs. Robinson hitched a ride home and asked, "What kind of car is this?" Dustin Hoffman's car in *The Graduate* has been an icon, practically a character in the film, and the envy of anyone of a certain age. The red 1966 Alfa Romeo Duetto Spider 1600 was simply the coolest car we had seen in an age of some very cool cars. Plus, you know, Dustin Hoffman. And Anne Bancroft.

Battista Pininfarina was born Battista Farina; nicknamed Pinin for being the smallest child in his family, he later officially changed his name to Pininfarina. He designed that car, and a few hundred others. It's no accident that a red Farina-designed 1946 Cisitalia was the central design of the Automania show at MoMA. In the twenty years between these two red cars, Pininfarina shaped the automotive epitome of cool.

Those twenty years began with Italy going from being a monarchy to a republic, and from a postwar catastrophe to the "Italian economic miracle"; the era began with 3 percent of households owning a refrigerator and ended with 94 percent owning one and 66 percent owning a car. Italian auto design tracked that expansion, and Pininfarina rose with the tide.

The era of 1946–1966, powered by the explosion of the suburbs, was when cars became the affordable luxury that marked people's socioeconomic status. All the General Motors brands (now mostly gone) were a carefully dimensioned step stool of aspirational mobility. Pininfarina played a role in nearly all those steps, designing for everyone from Fiat to Ferrari (but not Ford, though it tried to recruit him).

The array of his cars is simply astonishing; in addition to designing hundreds (mostly produced as one-offs) of muscular, sleek, aerodynamic cars for Ferrari, Farina penciled (as they say) and built humble, often boxy cars for Fiat, Austin, Lancia, Chevrolet, Cadillac, Nash, and, of course, Alfa Romeo.

Battista Pininfarina designed small, sporty, two-seater cars that appeared postwar, leaving behind the giant prewar saloons, as the British would say. Affordable (well, except for the Ferraris) and cute, these elfin autos used less gas, were easier to park and drive, and projected an image of a carefree, fun life. They were an essential part of bringing Italy, and the rest of the world, back from the dire years and into the bright auto-filled future.

Good times, Pinin, good times.

03 November
Annibale Carracci

Corpse of Christ, 1583–1585

It sometimes seems like the subjects of mannerist painters were all bodybuilders. They were beefed up, slightly inflated (except their genitals, which were always subject to shrinkage, so maybe steroided up?), and muscular to the extreme (even their toes look muscular). Just think of *The Creation of Adam* in the Sistine Chapel; Adam hasn't even been animated yet, but his outstretched arm is almost a Popeye cartoon of swole bulk.

Annibale Carracci set out to change all that with realistically proportioned (if still quite fit) humans and natural backgrounds; he shifted painting back to a more plausible, if still quite baroque, representation. His work is almost like moving from operas to documentaries, or from Calvin Klein ads to those for Dove, or from the Marvel Universe back to early Superman movies.

The paintings lost none of their spatial illusion or their drama but acquired a kind of precision and fidelity to reality that must have been refreshing for those tired of the exaggeration and hyper-drama of mannerism. My favorite is his *Corpse of Christ*, an attenuated view of Christ's body from feet to head, a remarkable rendering at a dramatic angle, and an homage to Andrea Mantegna's *Lamentation of Christ* of a hundred years earlier.

Carracci also began the dissolution of real architectural space: his illusionistic combination of statuary, frames, sky, and figures that (like the Sistine Chapel) structured the space more convincingly than the architecture itself.

The Carraccis (Annibale with his brother Agostino and cousin Ludovico) opened a painting academy in Bologna to proselytize the new naturalism. When his brother became unbearably wordy and pretentious, spouting a philosophy of painting, Annibale countered, "Those of us who are painters have to do our talking with our hands."

His crowning work in the Palazzo Farnese in Rome is a ceiling cycle that was hailed as equal to any produced before it (including the Sistine ceiling). Cardinal Farnese, dismissive of Annibale's personal style and looking for a final insult, deducted the supposed cost of Carracci's meals for the six years he spent painting, resulting in a pittance left to the painter at the end of the project.

In part due to his treatment by Farnese, Annibale Carracci fell into a depression, vowed never to paint again, suffered a stroke, and died at forty-eight.

04 November
James Earle Fraser

Indian head nickel / Buffalo nickel, first issued 1913

When I was a kid, I collected coins, which really meant looking through my parents' change for cool shit. In the way I occasionally get a two-dollar bill in my change these days (and really, isn't it a thrill?), I would occasionally find an Indian head penny (from, like, the 1800s!) and tons of Buffalo nickels (mostly worn smooth) and some steel Lincoln pennies (made during World War II when copper was, I guess, needed more than steel?). I would also find Mercury dimes, before Franklin D. Roosevelt founded the March of Dimes and his own head replaced Mercury's.

So, it was a real déjà vu thrill when just the other day I got a Buffalo nickel in my change, and that is due almost entirely to James Earle Fraser, the sculptor who fashioned and fought for it. There were lots of reasons it almost didn't happen, and lots of reasons its meaning is entirely different today.

Fraser's nickel with a Native American in profile (a composite of several individuals, more a type than a portrait) on the front and a bison on the reverse looks appalling today. What once looked like a dignified tribute now reads as a token of genocide, both for people of the First Nation and the bison slaughtered to reduce Native populations. The coin neatly packages expressions of oppression in portable form.

There's an even more disturbing sculpture from Fraser: his most famous, called *End of the Trail*. Fraser (who grew up near tribal areas in the Dakota Territory) claimed it was a call to protect the vanishing First Nations and their land, but, like his nickel design, it seems to do the opposite.

James Earle Fraser apprenticed with Augustus Saint-Gaudens, whose remarkable work (and you've seen it everywhere) manages to instill every carefully chosen subject with dignity and resolve. Fraser may have thought he learned that lesson, and perhaps he did but only applied it to white men, as with the now removed Theodore Roosevelt sculpture group at the Museum of Natural History in New York. Whether a personal or cultural failing, the work of heroicizing some and marginalizing others can't continue without comment or contextualization.

While it's still exciting to find a Buffalo nickel in my change, it is no longer an untainted thrill.

05 November
Raymond Loewy

Streamlined pencil sharpener, patented 1934

When Trump called for a redesign of Air Force One, he probably thought he was insulting Obama or Clinton or some other recent president; actually, he was insulting John F. Kennedy but mostly dissing Raymond Loewy.

Loewy designed the livery for Air Force One in 1962, during the same period he designed the Studebaker Avanti, the coolest American car of its day. He designed, or rather styled, steam locomotives and pencil sharpeners to be streamlined; refrigerators and copy machines to be soft and seductive; and logos for TWA, Exxon, and, my favorite, Lu cookies, to be as modern as possible. He famously restyled the Lucky Strike package, betting his fee that sales would increase (they did).

Loewy was a magnificent salesman; he developed the acronym MAYA for "most advanced yet accepted" to describe the ideal product redesign. He was interested in change but not too much change, certainly not more than the public would accept. He was a stylist more than an engineer; he reworked the skin but not so much the guts of products. This is epitomized by his streamlined pencil sharpener; it appears on a US postage stamp despite its lovely absurdity.

I have a charming set of pastel renderings for a TV show called *Make Up Your Mind* with host Jack Sterling. They all have a not-so-hidden leitmotif from the sponsor, Wonder Bread, that includes multicolor balloons and other subtle clues that match the bread packaging. (Game shows, and in fact most radio and TV shows in Loewy's day, were sponsored and even produced by a single advertiser.) Loewy's office drew these renderings around 1953, though even with 150 on staff he liked the illusion, the myth, really, that he designed everything himself.

He succeeded at making everything he redesigned better, more stylish, and definitely swoopier. Refrigerators had nicely rounded corners, trains adopted aerodynamic cowls, and everything looked just a bit faster. Faster, cleaner, and smoother felt like the future.

Raymond Loewy's idea was to make products that were more beautiful than they were when he found them, and that simple idea was elaborated into a philosophy, a style, a sales pitch, and ultimately into a whole world created in that image.

06 November
Charles Garnier

Opera Garnier (Paris Opera House), Paris, France, 1875

Charles Garnier was a doppelgänger of Tom Hayden (of the Chicago Seven and Jane Fonda's second husband fame) on Hayden's worst day. Garnier was not an attractive guy, but he managed some very attractive additions to his era, and not just to the Paris Opera, or, sorry, the Palais Garnier.

A new French national opera house was triggered by an assassination attempt on Napoleon III; it was intended to create a more secure entrance for the emperor. It is stunning that today the building built for Napoleon bears the name of the then thirty-six-year-old architect who won the 1861 design.

Garnier was in seventh place at the end of the competition's first round but rose to the top upon the second. His scheme is, and was likely recognized as, a bit of social engineering for the upper classes, not just in the protected side entrance (grand though it was) for Napoleon III. The enormous stairs, hall, balconies, and loggias were social mixing spaces; the opera was not simply a performance to watch, but also a scene to be seen performing in. Garnier, on opening night, received an ovation as he stood upon the stair landing, priming the social pump, as it were, by demonstrating that performances were not limited to the stage.

The plan explains the hierarchy of the entire construction; it is a diagram of social status and social interaction. The theater, the emperor's entrance, and the broad access hall make up only one-fifth and the seating only about one-tenth of the total building area. Equal, and equally enormous, amounts of space are devoted to the stage (even larger than the seating area) and back of house, while the loggia, stairs, and grand foyer are equal in size to the performance spaces.

The design says, quite clearly, that the performance of (and by) the attendees and the performance of the actors, dancers, singers, and cast are of equal value. The salute to Charles Garnier was really a celebration of his creation: Paris's new salon for the top of society.

While the society for which it was created has vanished, it manages, like so many paragons of architecture, to work equally well today.

07 November
Platt Rogers Spencer

Coca-Cola logo, based on Spencerian script, first used 1887

I think @DudeWithSign (and really you should look him up) is right when he broadcast: "I learned cursive for absolutely no reason!" As any architect, cue card writer, or script-challenged kid will tell you, cursive is whack (and just as an aside, why are cue cards handwritten? Wouldn't large printouts be better/faster/easier?).

I'm not even sure what cursive is for these days. Cursive is the landline of writing today; useless, but somehow you think you should have one, just in case.

Platt Rogers Spencer defined the cultural high point of cursive writing; he invented, or rather hybridized and codified, penmanship as the necessary artistry of writing. My grandfather had amazing Spencerian script, my father had a slightly degraded version, my own script is pitiful, and my son's children will be required to learn only what is necessary to fill out forms by hand, that is, block letters.

Add to the perfect ovals and loops, the flairs and the flourishes, the fact that all this writing was done with pens dipped in ink (and later with fountain pens), and the whole enterprise seems an impossibility.

Spencer's penmanship defines a nineteenth-century elegance and articulateness that is entirely absent from handwriting today. Everything written in Spencerian script looks and sounds like Alexander Hamilton wrote it. Spencer's educational schools were called Business and Penmanship schools, somehow implying that if you could write it elegantly it would ipso facto be professional and business-worthy, perhaps the start of the "fake it till you make it" ethos!

Typewriters began to supplant fancy script in the 1920s, when the Palmer Method overtook Spencerian script as the handwriting of choice at schools. It's what I (supposedly) learned sitting at those flip-top desks that used to be the elementary school standard.

Those desks still had recesses for inkwells, and some even had glass bottles with dried black ink. Ours were in the top center of the desks, equally accessible for the right- and left-handed, but others were all the way in the upper right corner, just to make it clear that if you wanted to stay a lefty, life was not going to be easy.

Now all that's left of Platt Rogers Spencer are a lot of lovely letters in antique shops and the Coca-Cola logo.

08 November
Michele De Lucchi

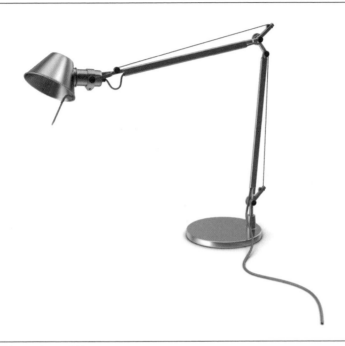

Tolomeo lamp, 1986

One big difference between product design and architecture (besides the obvious difference in scale) is the singularity of architecture (generally made once, for one place only) versus the multiplicity of products (made to be reproduced in large numbers for everyone, everywhere). This difference is reflected in the way these two types of designers are paid: a single (often inadequate) fee for architects, and a fee (also often inadequate) plus royalties on each item made or sold for designers. It's a front-end versus back-end deal, and the back end is the only place to make serious money over a serious amount of time.

The Tolomeo lamp is what made and sustained Michele De Lucchi since he designed it in 1987, making him rich enough to work in what amounts to a palazzo in Milan (the whole ground floor is a gallery) and to do pretty much as he pleases. It's a point of envy among architects that the rare but highly successful product is the gift that keeps on giving. It would be the equivalent of the architect getting a percentage of the profit every time a building they designed was sold, if only.

A successful product may be rare, but when it happens, it is a goldmine. And like a successful drug, it is just the start

of variations: extra-large Tolomeos, extra-small Tolomeos, silver Tolomeos, Tolomeos in a rainbow of colors, with aluminum shades and fabric shades, with incandescent and LED bulbs, as desk lamps, wall sconces, ceiling fixtures, and on and on. It's Tolomeo's world, we just live in it.

De Lucchi's lamp is the second big windfall for Artemide, its manufacturer; they hit it earlier with the Tizio lamp by Richard Sapper. I never owned a Tizio, but I seem to have a lot of Tolomeos: desk lamps at the office, bedside lamps at home, and clipped to the bookshelves in my library. Mounted to weighted bases and clamps and in recessed sockets, they seem to adapt to any use, and the slim profile and slightly anonymous form and color seem to make them appropriate everywhere.

Michele De Lucchi, as part of Memphis, designed a lot of stylish but marginal items, and after he designed Tolomeo he has done a lot of idiosyncratic and not terribly interesting architecture, all under the design and financial umbrella of Tolomeo!

09 November
Stanford White

Stanford White and his mustache, undated

Stanford White is a poster child for the profligate architect, especially his soap-opera-worthy death on the rooftop of his magnificent Madison Square Garden (when it was actually on Madison Square) at the hands of his former mistress's husband, Harry Kendall Thaw.

He is also a poster child for men with frighteningly outsized mustaches, if we are to go by the photo of him at age thirty-nine by portraitist George Cox (which doesn't show his bright red hair). Simply stunning.

Because of the fame of his debauchery (or despite it), he was somehow considered the lead of his legendary firm, McKim, Mead & White. That must have been infuriating to the other partners, who had to bail him out of financial distress and endure his sullied reputation. It turns out that White was the Jeffrey Epstein of his day, something that became clear to everyone as the trial of his murderer unfolded (called "The Trial of the Century" by William Randolph Hearst's papers, though the century was a mere seven years old). Even his friend Mark Twain had nothing but scorn for the man White turned out to be.

Charles Follen McKim, by contrast, was a Quaker and a remarkable designer steeped in a classical architectural education; he deserves more credit than he is given for the work of the firm. Wherever there is a Roman scale and an academic approach to McKim, Mead & White's work (Penn Station, University Club, Farley Post Office, Boston Library, Columbia University, American Academy in Rome, Century Association), you can be sure McKim drove the design.

Stanford White was as careless in his professional life as in his personal one. An uninsured warehouse filled with his priceless collection of antiques and entire historic rooms (the ones he would sell at huge profit to his wealthy clients) burned to the ground, sealing his financial ruin. His lavish life barely skipped a beat as he accumulated debt that would be more than twenty million dollars in today's currency.

Frank Lloyd Wright, never one to miss a chance to disparage another architect, said, "Thaw killed White for the wrong reason." Defiling architecture, to Wright, trumped White's more personal foibles.

10 November
William Hogarth

A Rake's Progress, Plate 1, etching from Hogarth painting of 1734, created in 1735

There used to be a guard (a docent, really), at John Soane's famous house in Lincoln's Inn Fields in London, who, if you were persistent, would open the hinged panels in the picture room to talk you through William Hogarth's eight paintings of *A Rake's Progress* or the four of *The Humours of an Election*, picture by picture, scene by scene, with a patterned banter, almost a rap, essentially reading the paintings like pages of a children's book.

That's because William Hogarth was, in addition to being quite an extraordinary artist, perhaps the king of narrative paintings (and engravings, and cartoons, etc.). An early-nineteenth-century critic, Charles Lamb (who considered Hogarth's works to be essentially books), said, "Other pictures we look at; his pictures we read."

I am not a fan of the narrative interpretation of painting; it is a way of imbuing artwork with ideas, emotions, and tales outside the frame. It is often a way to ignore the quality or painterly ideas in favor of literature. Hogarth's work is different; narrative was his intention. He created satirical images that read like frames in a graphic novel, and there is even an occasional likeness to Rube Goldberg (the other narrative

artist I love) in the numbered, funny, linked causalities he created.

Hogarth was essentially a movie director (and writer and producer and editor) in an age long before cinema. And he was a politically motivated cartoonist 150 years before Thomas Nast. But it is his morality plays – the panelized stories of (mostly) ruinous ends wrought by being idle, a rake, a harlot, in an arranged marriage, a gin (rather than beer) drinker, or cruel to animals – that made him popular beyond measure. He managed to skewer the high and low and to document them both as well.

Because his paintings, reprised as etchings for mass distribution, were so popular, the inevitable forgeries caused him to push for the first copyright law (Hogarth's Law) protecting visual art from plagiarism in 1735.

William Hogarth, nearly three hundred years later, is still relevant, still legible, and still inspiring; somehow hypocrisy has not gone out of style!

Plus, he was very funny, and that always helps.

11 November
Paul Signac

Place des Lices, St. Tropez, 1893

Georges Seurat gets all the credit for inventing pointillism (as well as credit for inspiring the musical *Sunday in the Park with George*) and has been lauded with solo exhibitions at MoMA, but Georges died at thirty-two, while his friend and colleague Paul Signac lasted another half century. That alone should have given Paul an edge, but Georges might have been a better artist, and sometimes talent wins.

Signac hung with van Gogh, painting with him in Paris and visiting him in Arles. With Seurat and others, he formed the Salon des Indépendants, a group of artists who sponsored a yearly exhibition promoting younger artists, like Henri Matisse (whose paintings Signac was the first to purchase). The salon eschewed juries and awards, trying to both democratize art and give artists a chance to present their work to the public unfiltered by outside curation.

Pointillism, and divisionism, and chronoluminarism all were developed by Seurat, Signac, and friends and suggest more than just a stylistic tendency. They are about how we see, and they attempt to interject science into painting by separating out complex colors into discrete single-color dots, patches, or cubes (which drifted into cubism) that would combine in the viewers' eyes to reconstitute the color complexity of reality.

It's essentially what Chuck Close did with later paintings, and it has resonance with pixels and color as displayed on modern monitors and television screens. All this, in the nineteenth century, predicted a very modern way of understanding "seeing" and using that understanding to create art. That resonant modernity is, I would guess, one reason why Sondheim's musical was so successful (especially with cute references like naming Georges's mistress Dot!).

It's no coincidence that the workings of the retina were being discovered just before the time of pointillism and other light- and form-shattering art. Receptors in the retina do resemble pixels, with images reconstituted in the brain, just as pointillism demonstrated outside the eyeball. Imagine how for millennia painting had been a quest to perfect the smooth, pixel-less transitions from light to dark, color to color, and near to far, only to be upended by fracturing the whole idea of painting with dots of single discrete color. It was that revolutionary, a banner Paul Signac carried well into the twentieth century.

12 November
Frank Furness

Pennsylvania Academy of the Fine Arts, Philadelphia, Pennsylvania, 1876

While most of the history of architecture, especially modern architecture, has been the evolution from thick, heavy, solid structures to light, thin, and transparent ones, Frank Furness never got that memo. His work was muscular, bold, heavy, thick, and solid, much like the gruff, mustachioed man himself. Louis Sullivan, who worked for Furness, described him as sporting plaid suits, a giant fan of a red beard, a scowl, and a dismissive manner toward nearly everything.

Yet somehow this seeming misanthrope built more than six hundred buildings; the remaining ones (many were demolished in the 1950s and 1960s, before he garnered the appreciation of people like Robert Venturi and Louis Kahn) are much beloved.

Venturi elaborated on his fondness for Furness, calling his Clearing House building "an almost insane short story of a castle on a city street," but Venturi liked anything boldly iconoclastic. Lewis Mumford called his work "bold, unabashed, ugly, and yet somehow healthily pregnant architecture," while Martin Filler said, "Frank Furness, one of those unruly creative prodigies for whom there will never be any rational explanation."

The rational explanation may be that he managed to convert Victoriana, which could tend toward lace and frilliness, into a particularly masculine style without losing any of its eccentricity. Furness's clients, like the railroad heads for whom he did nearly a third of his work, tended to be male, and maybe his own supermasculinity (he was awarded a Medal of Honor for his bravery in the Civil War) paired with the supermasculinity of his buildings may have been reassuring to them.

Whatever it was, he was among the highest paid architects of his time and one of the most popular; he founded the Philadelphia chapter of the American Institute of Architects and designed a monument for his regiment at Gettysburg, where he had fought.

Frank Furness may be one of those architects who is less famous than the architects he influenced; he started with Richard Morris Hunt who led to Louis Sullivan who led to Frank Lloyd Wright who led to...well, you get it.

I love his work (with all of its signs of a creative struggle), though I would have likely hated him.

13 November
Georg Olden

1863-1963 UNITED STATES 5 CENTS

EMANCIPATION PROCLAMATION

Emancipation Proclamation commemorative stamp, US Postal Service, issued 1963

Georg Olden might seem like an alter ego or anagram for William Golden (with whom he worked at CBS for fifteen years) but was his own man; the grandson of a slave and son of a Baptist preacher, he became an important part of the design of all the early TV some of us remember: *I Love Lucy*, *I've Got a Secret*, *Lassie*, *Gunsmoke*, etc.

He was a graphic designer in the Office of Strategic Services (OSS, the precursor of the CIA), where he enlisted after Pearl Harbor. What the graphic design department at OSS did, exactly, is kind of fun to imagine. His department head became head of communications at CBS, which led to Olden being hired, at twenty-five, to lead a staff of fourteen in designing sixty CBS shows.

His work is exactly what I love about early TV: it's graphic, black-and-white (as was TV in those days; when I showed my very young son an old movie, he asked, "Was everything black-and-white in those days?" Yeah, kind of), and perfectly of the design moment. As Olden said, "The door is open for artists on TV."

He left CBS for Madison Avenue, first at BBDO and ultimately McCann Erickson, who he sued when he was laid off for suspiciously racial reasons (Olden was one of five Black employees at McCann; the other four were porters).

Before his departure, he became the first Black designer of a postage stamp. The 1963 stamp celebrated the hundredth anniversary of the Emancipation Proclamation, and it was unveiled by John F. Kennedy in the Oval Office, with Olden in attendance, on a stand with a very corny parting-curtain device. Four years later, Olden designed a Voice of America postage stamp, something less obvious to commission a Black man to design.

He designed the Clio Award itself, then proceeded to win seven of them, and was generally celebrated by the ad industry, though now he is occasionally criticized as not doing enough for other Black designers. Somehow setting an example of excellence was/is not enough, an attitude he rejected.

Georg Olden's ascendance ended when he was shot to death by his companion, Irene Mikolajczyk, in Los Angeles, at age fifty-four. She was later acquitted of the killing of the man who, in large part, defined the graphic style of early TV.

14 November
Sonia Delaunay

"Color is the skin of the world."

Sonia Delaunay on the ubiquity and meaning of color

It took Sarah Stern several name changes, marriages, and adoptions to become Sonia Delaunay, but that name was the least dramatic of her transformations. Her father worked at a nail factory in Odesa, Ukraine; she moved to Saint Petersburg to live with the Terks, her uncle and aunt; was eventually adopted by them and sent to Karlsruhe and Paris for a traditional art education; married a gay gallery owner (as cover for him and for access to her dowry); and met Comtesse Berthe Félicie de Rose and her son Robert Delaunay at her husband's gallery. Soon Sonia was pregnant with Robert's child, and, after dissolving her marriage to the gallerist, they married.

While making a quilt for their son, she discovered abstraction. She moved back to Paris and made clothes in abstract blocks of color for actors and the wealthy (like Gloria Swanson), which led to her designing costumes for movies. In 1927, after the International Exhibition of Modern Decorative and Industrial Arts that gave art deco its name, she lectured on painting and its effect on fashion at the Sorbonne. During the Great Depression she closed her clothing business, Casa Sonia, and concentrated on painting, which she had already redefined fifteen

years earlier when she cofounded with Robert the art movement Orphism.

While Le Corbusier was working on his Pavillon des Temps Nouveaux for the 1937 Exposition Internationale des Arts et Techniques dans la Vie Modern in Paris, Delaunay was decorating, with her husband, pavilions for the train and air industries. Their murals rival Diego Rivera's for Rockefeller Center; they look like Diego's if they had been painted by Gerald and Sara Murphy (if that makes any sense). Except the Delaunay murals were not destroyed by a reactionary Rockefeller.

She was right at the leading edge of the avant-garde, painting in 1913 abstractions that are every bit as revolutionary (and way more colorful) than any cubist painting. Sonia and Robert called them Simultanism, perhaps a better way to describe the ideas embedded in cubism, but without the marketing genius that Picasso and friends had.

Sonia Delaunay sublimated her own legend to her husband's, but living until age ninety-four, almost forty years after Robert's death, gave her time to resurrect and supplement her own.

We're doubly lucky for her long life.

15 November
E. Stewart Williams

Sinatra's Twin Palms estate, with piano-shaped pool, Palm Springs, California, 1947

E. Stewart Williams looked beyond sheepish the only time we met.

I was visiting his home in Palm Springs after he had sold it to Dale and Leslie Chihuly, and he was nearly in tears at what he saw: the living room was a collection of "notable" designer chairs, lined up in an arc, and the house had none of the signs of life he must have seen for the forty or so years he lived in it. He just kept shaking his head and looking down while making excuses for the changes he saw.

Williams was ninety at that point, and it's not hard to imagine him tearing up, even if the house was exactly as he left it, so no shade on the Chihulys.

The pain on Williams's face is part of an inevitable truth for architects' work, even one's own home: no matter how much control we think we have, it ends abruptly, and that loss is a feature, not a bug, of making architecture. I wrote a piece for the *Cornell Journal of Architecture* (volume 12) about this very issue, prompted in part by my visit with Williams.

Despite his reaction at age ninety, he must have been an optimistic guy in his youth (I think all architects who are not institutionalized are inherently optimists;

it takes too long and is too hard to make good buildings without the belief that they are worth it). His works exhibit none of the angst he felt that day.

The legendary beginning of his legendary career was Frank Sinatra (variously described as wearing a sailor hat and/or licking an ice cream cone, maybe both?!) walking into his office in 1947 and asking for a Georgian style house in Palms Springs to be completed in six months for a Christmas party. Williams, then in practice with his architect father and brother (Williams, Williams and Williams) persuaded Frank to forgo Georgian and finished the house in time for New Years, 1948, amazingly.

The piano-shaped pool may seem a bit hokey, but the house is terrific and set a pattern for desert modern, luckily not Georgian. It wasn't the first example, but it was owned by Palm Springs' most famous resident, and that set the bar for cool in the city.

If E. Stewart Williams was disappointed in his own house, he need only go to see Sinatra's (maintained in perfect period condition) or the dozens of other lovingly cared for buildings he designed. Those might provoke tears of joy!

16 November
Alexander Isley

Wall collages at Bolo restaurant, New York, New York, 1993

Alex Isley has two things about him that always endear graphic designers to me: he worked for Tibor Kalman at M&Co (and I seem to like most people that came out of that studio), and, related to that, he has a great sense of humor that he uses in design. Oh, and he is very talented, smart, clever, and personable, but those are just extras.

Most graphic designers don't get to work with a lot of other graphic designers, but as an architect (especially when at Pentagram) I've collaborated with dozens of them, Alex included. When it works, there is nothing more fun, and it always works with Isley.

We started at Mesa Grill, Bobby Flay's first restaurant. Alex's solution was so spare, so smart, and so perfect; he took the word *mesa*, set it in all caps, and trimmed off the top. Like a real mesa. The sloped M and A helped make a perfect typographic, flat-topped mesa.

From that minimal beginning, we designed Bolo, Bobby's second restaurant. I honestly don't remember whose idea its collage was (that's the sign of a great collaboration; no one remembers whose idea it was), but it was Alex who created the wall decoration, by hand, with colored

paper, glue, and a few copier images. I followed with sandwiched glass and metal light fixtures and enough color to support his bold wall coverings.

Alex is famous for his holiday gifts, which from most design studios are some utterly useless object with way too much plastic or personalized printing to use without embarrassment or, worse, a calendar, which is about as useful these days as a subway token. Not so Isley's gifts; he has steadily supplied his friends with a stream of useful objects (stapler, scissors, flyswatter, cheese grater, hammer and single nail) that some have said they don't know whether to hang on the wall or use (Alex opts for use).

Isley does one more thing that is endearing to all who know him: he hasn't adopted the look of cool urban graphic designers or architects, sporting interesting glasses or a fair amount of Japanese fashion. Nor is he normcore, though he is disarmingly normal.

If you ask anyone who knows Alexander Isley, they all do the same thing: smile, tell you how much they like him, and say something like, "Alex is great." Not Alexander the Great, just great, and just a pleasure to know.

17 November
Isamu Noguchi

Bust of R. Buckminster Fuller, chrome-plated bronze, 1929

For decades, before becoming the Isamu Noguchi we know, Sam Gilmour (as he named himself when young) traveled extensively, interned for artists like Constantin Brancusi, and made abstract art, but never really clicked with the art, design, furniture, or landscape world. During all those years, he created portrait busts to make a living. They were good; the chrome busts of R. Buckminster Fuller and others that stripped everything unessential are especially good, but even Noguchi's more traditional ones are remarkably accomplished. He was in his twenties when he started these busts, after apprenticing with Gutzon Borglum, the sculptor who carved Mount Rushmore.

He clearly succeeded doing the busts (he seems to have done hundreds), and they are primarily of the famous, the talented, and the powerful. He produced, at the same time, hundreds of abstract sculptures as well. If the "never get too good at something you don't want to do" adage is true, Noguchi was, for a moment, trapped by his own talent.

He was so good at portraiture that his abstract work was his side hustle until he voluntarily entered a confinement camp during World War II (as a protest,

but for much longer than he had expected). For seven months, before he was able to return to New York City (where, as a resident he could legally reside outside a camp), he produced purely abstract sculpture, much of it salvaged and scrounged from the bleak Arizona landscape where he was interned.

It might have been like a "pandemic pause" for Noguchi; he went into the camp hoping to establish an arts program and left with a new focus for his work. The world finally caught up with him, and nearly halfway through his creative life he began the one we recognize him for.

The range and quantity of his work is stunning: furniture, lighting, sculpture, landscapes, memorials, playgrounds. Any one of these efforts would be a lifetime of work; his Akari lamps, his Herman Miller and Knoll furniture, and his monumental sculptures are each industries in their own right.

We're lucky; Isamu Noguchi's studio in New York became a museum that is still cataloging, displaying, researching, and disseminating his work.

18 November
Gio Ponti

Ceramic tiles, originally designed for Hotel Parco dei Principi, Sorrento, Italy, 1962

Late in the last century (and I am still deciding whether I like the sound of that), I stayed in Sorrento, at Parco dei Principi, a hotel designed by Gio Ponti in 1960 and opened in 1962. It was a museum of Ponti: his custom beds and headboards with their built-in radios and vintage telephones were in every room, his sofas lined the wide, tiled hallways, and his fantastic tile (where he started his career) was everywhere in every imaginable form.

While the rooms were being cleaned and all the doors were open, and I realized that every room had a different pattern of the blue-and-white custom floor tiles! I snapped pictures of every single room and have been obsessed with the patterns ever since.

I was working on a new oceanfront house and his tiles seemed perfect for the main bedroom, so I got samples of custom tiles from a dozen tile-ists (?). None came close to the originals until someone suggested one final attempt, and it was perfect. How was that possible, after so many bad versions, I asked? "We did the originals for Gio" was the manufacturer Bardelli's answer!

Milan, Ponti's home, is filled with his work: the 1956 Pirelli Tower is still the most elegant modern tower (slab, really) ever; 1930s office buildings (where the US consulate was housed) are startlingly modern; and his residential buildings dot the city. There he taught for decades at the Polytechnic University of Milan, published *Domus*, and said, "The most resistant element is neither cement, nor wood, nor stone, nor steel, nor glass. The most resistant material in construction is art." Amen, Gio.

Except for his enthusiasm for Fascism during World War II (Italian Fascism being a stylish alternative to the Teutonic version), he managed to endear himself, and his quirky style, to nearly everyone, with the added benefit that his work is not yet a cliché (though just wait...).

His furniture's attitude is occasionally quite upright and sometimes quite relaxed. His Superleggera chair looks so fragile that a napkin might collapse it (it won't; it is surprisingly strong) while his D.153.1 lounge chair looks impossible to get out of.

Gio Ponti, the *supermassimo* of Italian design.

19 November
Louise Dahl-Wolf

Orson Welles and family, photographed by Louise Dahl-Wolf, 1940

It might seem that the photographer who influenced the generation-younger Richard Avedon and others would be at least as famous as them, but then she was a woman, so that might explain it.

And maybe the photographer who shot eighty-six covers for *Harper's Bazaar* under Diana Vreeland, Carmel Snow, and Alexey Brodovitch should be as famous as her colleagues, but somehow, um, no.

Louise Dahl-Wolfe completely changed fashion and portrait photography, but she doesn't get the same credit as, say, Avedon or Annie Leibovitz. She took fashion photography outside, where clothes actually live, and while her photos today may seem overly posed and a bit contrived, they still exude sexuality and are the stepping stones to what followed. As Avedon said, before Dahl-Wolfe, Vreeland, and Snow, American style did not exist.

Some images we know well, like the iconic portrait of Edward R. Murrow, are Dahl-Wolfe's, and she seems to have started the whole "women at the beach" genre. She famously rejected the fifteen-year-old model Carmen Dell'Orefice (as too young to be in the business), but Carmen just toddled over to *Vogue* and was on its cover in short order, and is today a legend.

Fifteen may have been too young, but seventeen seemed just right when Dahl-Wolfe discovered and shot Betty Joan Perske, which placed her before the public as well as a Warner brother, who turned her into Lauren Bacall.

Dahl-Wolfe was known to be a bit prickly, a bit demanding, and not at all tolerant of her competition. She tried to get Lillian Bassman fired and thought Dick Avedon had a "long way to go" to be a worthy photographer. It's not hard to imagine that even after working at *Harper's Bazaar* from 1936 to 1958, after her works were included in the first MoMA photography show in 1937, and after establishing herself as an industry icon, she was still concerned that her replacement was just a few feet behind her. Her 1989 *New York Times* obituary was just a couple of short paragraphs, so her concern may have been well founded.

It's interesting how many pioneering women in the arts were photographers. Maybe photography, as the newest art medium, was not yet dominated by men, as architecture was, or at least the world was open to the idea that women like Louise Dahl-Wolfe could photograph beautifully.

20 November
Corita Kent

Portrait, 1967

If Andy Warhol had been a nun (and in some ways he kind of was), he would have been (Sister) Corita Kent (formerly Sister Mary Corita and often known as just Corita).

The mid-1960s, when Corita began to make the work she is best known for, was a moment when religious figures were on the political left as often as they are now on the right. Her antiwar, pro-love artwork borrowed the visual language of supermarket price posters of the time, and it was silkscreened in the same out-of-the-can colors. She admired Warhol and was transformed by his 1962 exhibition at Ferus Gallery in Los Angeles; in 2015 the Andy Warhol Museum mounted a landmark show on Corita.

Warhol was looking to change the way we saw the world. As he said, "Once you got Pop you could never see a sign the same way again" and "once you thought Pop, you could never see America the same way again."

Corita used art as a social and activist canvas. She was inspired by the familiar vernacular of advertising and signs, using that appropriation in service of change, hope, justice, optimism, peace, and charity. She was Warhol with a conscience. Or a folk singer who sang

with art. But that kind of activism was not what the Catholic church would tolerate in the 1960s. She was denounced by her bishop and called a communist and worse. She left the church just as *The Flying Nun* hit TV and as "sisters" became more than women in habits.

Now, of course, religious protest tends to occur in the singular form of anti-choice rather than pro-peace or pro-freedom, but in the 1960s, with Martin Luther King Jr. as its most visible proponent (Corita's 1969 piece overlaid "The King is dead. Love your brother." on his image), many in the clergy agitated for equality, justice, peace, and unity.

Corita continued her artwork and activism after she left her convent and was asked in 1983 to design a US postage stamp. Her rainbow swash *Love* was the result, but Corita, furious, boycotted the unveiling because it was staged on *The Love Boat* TV show (she proposed the United Nations). She followed up with *Love Is Hard Work*, a poster of the same design, to make her point.

Corita Kent always had a point and always made it with art.

21 November
Wim Crouwel

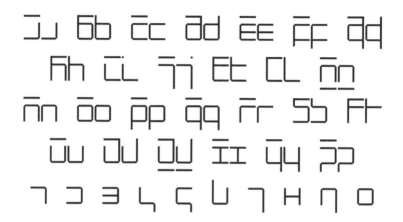

New Alphabet, 1967

How could you not love Wim Crouwel, just based on the photo of him in his *2001: A Space Odyssey* getup?!

Crouwel once said, "Akzidenz-Grotesk was not available in Holland....I would buy Swiss newspapers and cut the letters out and glue them in place, and then take photographs to use as artwork."

Ah, the analog world! Hard to imagine, but until about 1990 there was no way to digitally set type. But Crouwel working ransom-note style was particularly insane. So, it is rather remarkable that he was so ahead of the curve in digital style.

Wim spent enough time in Switzerland to adopt the name Gridnik (which he named one of his typefaces) and carried that grid tradition to the end, never wavering, never devolving into anything remotely handmade or personally quirky. He was occasionally pilloried for his immovable stance, but that only seemed to make him even more committed to it.

The paragon of Gridnik logic was the 1971 design of the Dutch PTT telephone book. Some may not even know what a phone book is, except perhaps as the pairing of two opposite words, like jumbo shrimp or Republican patriot. Those who can still remember a time before cell phones know they were thick, heavy volumes printed on thin newsprint that listed all of an area's citizens' and businesses' names, addresses, and telephone numbers (except those who preferred to be – at an additional charge – unlisted).

Crouwel stripped away capital letters and dotted leader lines from the listings, and, most controversially, he put the numbers before the names/addresses. This kept the grid working and allowed the variable (name/address length) to rag to the right rather sensibly. The uproar was instantaneous; people did not want to be known as numbers and asked, Why the numbers first, and no capital letters?! In fact, Crouwel's design was a brilliant piece of work, but, like Massimo Vignelli's New York City subway map, it was reversed a few years later.

It's surprising that the Dutch (who practically defined early modernism) couldn't accept it when it came to their own identities. It may be fun for us to see Wim Crouwel in his futuristic uniform, but actually wearing it is another thing altogether.

22 November
Dorothy Draper

Dorothy Draper, 1942

One client of mine ordered a whole living room full of furniture before she realized she needed cataract surgery. Postoperatively, when she could finally see clearly, she realized that the colors she selected were *insanely* bright, almost neon!

That was pretty much what a Dorothy Draper interior looked like. Intentionally.

"If I like it, it's right. If I don't, it isn't," is the utterance of the utterly confident, and Draper was utterly confident. She had to be to suggest such electric interiors. While it's possible that she had cataracts, there may be a different logic to her Technicolor compositions: more color can reset the saturation adjustment to seem more normalized than "neutral with accents." Nothing pops out because it all does.

Draper aimed toward a bath of color, an immersive environment, a place that's exciting even without people. For a recent restaurant redo, I took the interior's densely hued surfaces, dating from the 1980s, and warmly neutraled them out; the people and food are the color. Instead of a highly chromatic room, it's a bit of respite from the intensity of the exterior of New York City. In Hollywood and Palm Beach, where Draper worked, maybe the

relatively calm exteriors demanded a vibrating interior. Draper had an ulterior motive: she was interested in applying her ideas in the aspirational community of housewives everywhere, and paint was an available, inexpensive way to change their world. While she was making couture interiors, the world had access to the ready-to-wear version. Despite her client list, her intentionally democratic approach to an elite profession (a profession that Draper is sometimes credited with creating) is inspiring.

Even in black and white, there was a cinematic quality to Draper's work. It exuded drama and became the visual signature of not just films but the people who made them. Hollywood Regency was the perfect style for West Coast poseurs.

Starting in the 1920s, those who couldn't bear to embrace modernism could retain a soupçon of European tradition (signaling class) with Draper's overscaled and highly graphic elements (to signal new, bigger, better) and colors that were simply overwhelming (differentiating their iconoclast class).

With permission granted by Dorothy Draper.

23 November
El Lissitzky

Lenin Tribune, 1920

I am amazed that we know the exact birthday of someone born in, say, the fifth century but are not certain of someone's born much more recently. Partly it's just a matter of class; the lives of the royal and the rich are well documented, the poorer and less celebrated are less well documented.

But another part is the calendar. For whatever reason, when the Julian calendar grew out of favor and the Gregorian calendar was trending, different countries made the change at different times; the rollout was a mess. The change even reset the first day of the year from March 25 to January 1, so people could be born in different years, depending on the calendar in use. Weird.

El Lissitzky was born into that confusion. Russia was a bit behind with the calendar thing (by about two hundred years) but made up for it in other ways; when Lissitzky was twenty-seven, the Russian Revolution began. Eventually, the revolution had visual styles to go with it (suprematism, constructivism, etc.). Lissitzky (Jewish) was delighted to see the viciously anti-Semitic tsarist regime replaced, and his own view of the world expanded when he was appointed cultural ambassador to Weimar in Germany, where the Bauhaus was just getting underway.

The revolution, his friendship with Kasimir Malevich, exposure to European modernism, and a fiercely activist mind combined to produce the El Lissitzky we know. His *Beat the Whites with the Red Wedge* is a typical barely concealed anti-anti-communist piece that is almost (but not quite) ruined by its explicit name.

What he brought to the pure abstraction of suprematism was purpose beyond the confines of pure art, plus a third dimension. Suprematism was insistently flat; Lissitzky moved it toward constructivism (he called it *proun*) with three-dimensional constructions within the frame. And graphic design. And architecture. And social purpose. It was very much in the mold of communism as populism that rejected the elite, but actually was just as rarefied while it adopted a populous tone.

In his short life, no matter when he was actually born, El Lissitzky produced an astonishing variety and volume of astonishingly beautiful work.

24 November
Cass Gilbert

Woolworth Building, New York, New York, 1913, piercing clouds in 1935 photograph

I feel close to Cass Gilbert and equally close to the architect he is constantly confused with: CPH Gilbert. One of my studios was in Cass's best building, the Woolworth Building, and another was in CPH's least-known building at 204 Fifth Avenue. Both were great homes, when "office" still defined where we went to work.

Woolworth was especially icono-graphic; there were gargoyles in the lobby depicting Gilbert, Woolworth, the banker, the builder, the broker, the accountant, etc. The lobby was cruciform in plan, so patron saints were appropriate, and its mosaic-tiled, vaulted ceiling, murals to commerce, and elaborate Gothic exterior details added up to a genuinely American church, the Cathedral of Commerce (not my appellation, but exactly right).

He hated being known for just that building, but (sorry, Cass) it's the most important and most groundbreaking that he did. He designed the Supreme Court Building in Washington, DC, the US Customs House in New York City, and I could go on, but none come close to Woolworth. He was a star, important, a celebrity, even, and thoroughly looked the part: pince-nez, perfect attire, mustache, hat at the ready, and probably a pretentious accent (for which I have no proof; just seems right).

Gilbert's most famous nonbuilding is also his most famous incomplete project: the George Washington Bridge (or, as on highway signs, the Geo Wash Br, as I thought it was called when I was too young to figure it out). It is truly the work of Othmar Hermann Ammann, the structural engineer, who proposed Cass Gilbert to clad the towers in stone. Cost, time, and the Great Depression intervened, and we have our beloved steel lattice. Gilbert's loss was modernism's gain; the lack of decorative cladding was the very definition of 1930s modern architecture. Urban legend is that the pink granite cladding has been sitting in storage for the last hundred years.

It's a case where failing to finish a design, doing less (and eliminating what was then thought to be the architecture) results in a better piece of architecture. I'm not so sure that Cass Gilbert would agree, but as glad as I am for his excesses at Woolworth, I am equally happy for their elimination at the Geo Wash Br.

25 November
Morris Lapidus

Fontainebleau Hotel, Miami, Florida, 1955

When Morris Lapidus was in his nineties, a group of Pentagram partners had dinner with him at a Miami Beach restaurant. He was pretty frail, and his granddaughter accompanied him, got him seated with us, and ordered him a large vodka tonic. About halfway through his drink, he really came alive, and the conversation picked up. Somehow I mentioned Mies van der Rohe, and he rolled his eyes and said, "Oy, Mies, what a pill!" (it's still one of the funniest utterances about a famously unfunny architect I've heard). I didn't know their backstory (Lapidus had designed Seagram's offices and felt slighted that Mies later got its Park Avenue headquarters commission).

Mies was exactly who Lapidus, with his baroque modernism, was rebelling against. Lapidus absorbed the critics' accusations of vulgarity, of appealing to the unwashed masses, of camping up modernism. He decried the sterility of modernism and even accused Mies of trying to "pimp" the Seagram Building with bronze cladding. His autobiography, *Too Much Is Never Enough*, targets "less is more" as clearly as his buildings provided the counterpoint to doctrinaire modernism.

Philip Johnson, always ready with a bon mot (or snipe, or both together)

defended Lapidus with the back of one hand, saying his work was utterly appropriate for "a great mass of people who don't know the difference between architecture and Coney Island." Nice, Phil. A critic later wrote in *Art in America* that "Johnson is the Lapidus of good taste, just as Lapidus is the Johnson of bad taste."

Lapidus struggled with his outsider position as a Jew in a WASP world; architecture was notoriously anti-Semitic, and, rightly or not, he associated strict modernism with Germanic modernism. There was always an undercurrent, such as when he was criticized for (despite his "crass" work) having more projects on the boards than Mies, Le Corbusier, and Walter Gropius combined. Subtext: the deserved white (German and Swiss) Christians were being outclassed by this gaudy, kitschy, tasteless man who didn't deserve his success (and was making too much money at it!).

But Morris Lapidus was too good at public relations; he loved the accusations and proudly aimed his work to awe the unwashed. His early retail roots always governed; he simply sold architecture the way he had sold shoes and gloves in his retail innovations: extremely well.

335

26 November
Charles Schulz

Charles "Sparky" Schulz drawing Charlie Brown, 1956

I don't know what it is, but I simply love *Peanuts*, the comics (the flat, line-drawn version, not so much the increasingly three-dimensional color animation). They are imbued with a sense of deadpan irony, atomic age anxiety, and the pure unbridled joy of the 1960s. The four simple daily panels defined a cultural sense of humor (and timing) as much as any media did.

Peanuts started running in newspapers just before I was born and stopped when I was approaching midlife, so it was a constant narration for the first half of my life (the first half if I expect to live to one hundred, always a confusing aspect of midlife). It may be that everyone who grew up with the comic strip is in love with it, but I think that *Peanuts*, like the Beatles, is multigenerational (and in fact, my grown son has a Snoopy hat, though he may not love the whole gang as I do).

Peanuts (and *Peanuts* books like *Happiness Is a Warm Puppy*) was a craze for adults and children during its run, and it still had its psycho-comedic pace and depth to the end. Charles Schulz, its creator, died at seventy-seven in 2000, just hours before his last (pre-penned) strip was published. Maybe it was a reverse

Dorian Gray; Schulz grew old so that his alter egos could remain young.

Sparky (Schulz's very *Peanuts* nickname) was an odd dude, which might make sense given the depressive, dejected, lonely loser at the center of his work. He watched *Citizen Kane* forty times (and had Lucy spoil the ending for Linus). He joined World War II just after his mother died. He became famous for an attempted kidnapping of his wife.

Charles Schulz claimed, near his own death, that he would never allow Charlie Brown to actually kick the football (that Lucy always pulls away), as it would be a violation of the character's definition. But isn't an occasional win the random positive reinforcement that would keep Charlie Brown trying forever? Apparently not.

27 November
Manolo Blahnik

Hangisi blue satin jewel-buckle pumps, $1,200 at better stores everywhere

It is more than fifty years since Manolo Blahnik first made his signature stilettos, and it is hard to think of another fashion brand that has maintained its cachet over half a century: Chanel, perhaps; Levi's, probably; Borsalino, maybe; Ralph Lauren, of course; Prada, naturally. It's a small club.

And while Nike and Doc Martens are as old, how many fashion brands, at the highest level of the art, have outlasted Manolo Blahnik? The top ten shoe brands today are all sports brands, not fashion brands; they're what we wear. But among fashion brands, there are few more consistently admired, coveted, and more identified with luxury than Manolo Blahnik. and not just by Carrie Bradshaw in *Sex and the City* (but of course that didn't hurt). And while there may be older brands, none have been exclusively designed by their founder; Blahnik claims to make every single shoe prototype himself, and it may be that the lack of outsourcing or delegating the design has kept the brand at its high level.

In at least two episodes of *Sex and the City*, Carrie has her Manolos stolen: once in a mugging and once while attending a no-shoes baby shower. At that point, Manolos had become cultural currency; they were markers, symbols, signs (whatever) for the luxurious and rarefied life we imagined all celebrities led. Price was part of it, exclusivity and small production was another. But apparently these shoes are more than just decorative accessories; they are very light, extremely comfortable (within the genre), and remarkably engineered footwear.

They must be; the scenes of Carrie running in five-inch heels across the cobbled streets of Paris without a single misstep are mesmerizing. I can barely do that in Nikes, and she manages it on pointe. The level of skill it takes just to wear stilettos is underappreciated; it shouldn't be possible but is a learned trait for entire generations of women. Is there a single thing that scores of men do that requires a level of skill even close to wearing a pair of Manolos?

In 1980 there was a transit strike in New York, and suddenly "sneaker brigades" of women eschewing heels were everywhere. It seemed like the perfect opportunity to permanently forgo torturous footwear, but style, however uncomfortable, is not so easily relinquished. Just ask Carrie.

28 November
Henry Bacon

Construction of Lincoln Memorial, Washington, DC, building completed 1922

In Washington, DC (a city filled with some fairly terrible, or at least fairly inconsequential, buildings), the Lincoln Memorial is the perfect building in the perfect place. Why it took six attempts to pass a bill in Congress to establish the memorial is a mystery. The first five failed because of House Speaker Joseph Gurney Cannon (weirdly, a Republican from Illinois and the first person to grace the cover of *Time* magazine, vol. 1, no. 1, sporting a Lincoln-style beard). The bill finally passed in 1910.

It is not just the building itself, of course, but the sculpture, the engraved epitaphs, the site at the end of the mall, and the reflecting pool (built later) that help make it perfect. But this last building by Bacon was undoubtedly his best for its simplicity (a solid, tall volume surrounded by a colonnade of thirty-six Doric columns, one for each state of the union when Lincoln died); for its unusual orientation (the long side, rather than the customary short end, faces the mall); for its scale (so grand that the size of the sculpture had to be increased from ten feet to nineteen feet high); and for its foreground (a huge flight of stairs that climb an artificially created hill to the colonnade).

None of these elements can explain the extraordinary emotion experienced by a visit to the Lincoln Memorial. It is as sacred a space as exists in America. The stentorian silence of the colossus, lit from sunlight shining through translucent marble panels above; the inscribed texts from the Gettysburg Address and Lincoln's second inaugural address; the lack of doors or even a conditioned interior; the long climb in the sun to the cool, dark space inside; and the view back down the mall and reflecting pool as you leave add up to a poem to Lincoln.

We're fortunate to have this particular memorial; Bacon competed with John Russell Pope for the design. Pope went on to design the Jefferson Memorial, by comparison a perfectly ok, but fairly uninspiring building. It seems fitting that of the two monuments, one rectangular, the other round in plan, one for a president who freed enslaved people, one for a president who enslaved them, the former is by far the best, most visited, and most beloved.

We are all lucky that Henry Bacon prevailed, persisted, and designed his remarkable ode to Lincoln, proving that architecture can both ennoble its subjects and stir its visitors and achieving in marble what Lincoln achieved in words and deeds.

29 November
Gertrude Jekyll

Garden of 1 Strode House, Barrington Court, England, 1920s

Gertrude Jekyll's family unwittingly lent their surname – even though it pronounced it *jee-kul* – to Dr. Hyde's alter ego, Mr. Jekyll. But Gertrude Jekyll's alter ego was Edwin Lutyens, the prolific architect of English country homes of a certain proto-modern era. They met when he was twenty, and twenty-five years her junior, and her connections essentially propelled him into the world he would help define: large country houses in, ostensibly, an arts and crafts style.

Lutyens designed Munstead Wood with Jekyll, an early collaboration that she lived in until her death. The duo worked so well together because Lutyens created the outdoor architecture that acted as rooms, courts, terraces, lanes, and rotundas for Jekyll, who created the lush, colorful, hardy, and well-composed content for those architectural frames. The whole idea of English garden rooms started with them; there had, of course, been outdoor rooms for millennia, but filling them with informal, colorful, yet highly planned gardens was new. It was, and is, a compelling combination.

The English have a unique relationship with their gardens; the whole of the UK is a garden in some sense. The entire isle has been farmed, shaped, planted, hedgerowed, inhabited, and worked over for thousands of years; there is no virgin land in the UK. The garden somehow outranks views, the shore, and virtually every other landed asset, becoming the most desirable place to be. Brits even tend millions of small, shared, often remotely located plots as their own gardens. That would be a reality show if they could figure out how to make the plants grow overnight.

Jekyll was no mere hobbyist, but a garden theoretician, writer, and designer who documented and published the hundreds of gardens she made. She never married, and gardens were her only offspring. As a horticulturalist she created, saved, and propagated dozens of plant species; *Rosa* 'Gertrude Jekyll' is a gorgeous pink shrub rose.

On Thursday November 29, 1932, Gertrude Jekyll's eighty-ninth birthday, her brother Herbert (who had worked with Lutyens) died; she followed him only ten days later. Luckily garden design is a long game.

30 November
Andrea Palladio

Palazzo Chiericiati, Vicenza, Italy, designed 1550

When you visit a villa by Andrea Palladio (which is in some ways an even more religious experience than visiting his churches), you end up, unwittingly, doing the Palladio shuffle. The delicate floors require all visitors to don felt overshoes, enormous soft slippers that fall off every time you lift your foot, so you basically just shuffle around, polishing the marble mosaics in the floor as go. Visitors glide from room to room silently, hovercraft style, with an occasional *Risky Business* entrance. (My wife, Carin Goldberg, collected these "visitation slippers" for a *New York Times* article, and I like to think it was because we both did the shuffle.)

Each of these villas is conceived as a house of rooms. We are so accustomed to every room having an ideal shape and program for its use, but these houses are a set of idealized spaces with perfect proportions, perfect arrangement, and perfect decoration (murals, etc.) rather than custom made or fit for specific purpose. As a result, the rooms are fit for nearly any purpose, which sets up an ongoing negotiation between dwelling and dweller.

Palladio's Venetian churches display the complexity of simplicity he seemed to have engineered. Compared to later, more staid classical buildings,

these couple of beauties, San Giorgio Maggiore and Il Redentore (and I always mix them up; they are both across the lagoon and can be seen together from Piazza San Marco), have flattened facades of as many as five layers. The implication of three dimensions collapsed into two-dimensional compositions is that the mere passing through the facade is a grand spatial sequence compressed into an instant. The churches' interiors are sublime and understated; white spaces become celestial by virtue of their formal perfection rather than dissolved in decoration.

That modernity of crisp space over excessive decor is how Colin Rowe, in his essay "The Mathematics of the Ideal Villa," could compare a Corbusian and a Palladian villa. Pure heresy in 1947.

In addition to Palladio's greatest hits, my favorites are his Teatro Olympico (an indoor version of a Roman amphitheater with forced perspective views) and Palazzo Chiericati (so utterly modern it could be from the 1930s). So, maybe not so heretical after all.

01 December
Minoru Yamasaki

Minoru Yamasaki viewing model of World Trade Center, 1960s

The ignominiousness of having two of your most visible projects (comprising a score of actual buildings) destroyed on live TV must be a painful jolt to one's career. Minoru Yamasaki had died long before, and luckily missed seeing his World Trade Center destroyed (and the subsequent demolition of the US Constitution and a few Arab states) but had to endure the infamy of his Pruitt-Igoe housing projects blown up in a very public display of regret.

The World Trade Center towers were a pair of buildings that were hated (by architects) most of their lives but adored in their absence. I felt that way too; the oversimplified rectangles (the joke being that they were the packing boxes for the Empire State Building and the Chrysler Building), the dubious relationship in plan, the insanely small windows that had to be pried open at the plaza just to get into the buildings, and the stupidly blank plaza (stories above the ground) added up to a pair of really dumb buildings.

But those dumb buildings are sorely missed. I still see a dotted line in the sky where they once stood, and their replacement is actually a good deal dumber (Dumb and Dumber?). The simpleton shapes began to look rather elegant in their dotage, and of course

their downfall was horrifying and tragic. It's hard to imagine mere buildings, and not even federal ones, with that much emotion attached to them. Maybe the original Penn Station or Madison Square Garden, but none that are as modern as Yamasaki's.

Yamasaki moved to New York City to avoid internment during World War II (apparently it was a sanctuary city even then) and went to work at Shreve, Lamb and Harmon, the architects of the Empire State Building, just five years after it was completed. His towers would, forty-four years later, eclipse that building and hold the world title for tallest building for a mere two years. It's a record that is increasingly hard to sustain.

It's a bit surprising (to me) that Minoru Yamasaki achieved such stature and fame. His buildings are peculiar and idiosyncratic in ways that seem dated and off-putting. His Pruitt-Igoe housing project was deemed so harmful to its residents that it had to be dynamited, yet he continued to get big commissions.

Fame is fickle.

02 December
David Macaulay

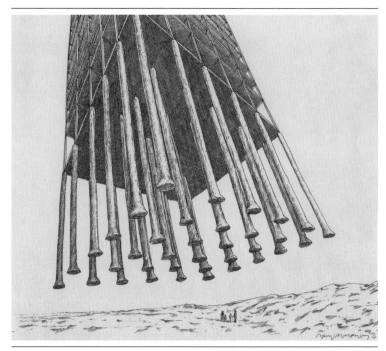

Building foundations as seen from below, *Underground,* 1976

Large built projects are almost inconceivable; how do you build the Roman aqueduct system, or the London Underground, or the Verrazano-Narrrows Bridge? We know they exist, but how they came to be is hard to picture. David Macaulay answers questions like that about pyramids, cathedrals, cities, and castles along with a myriad of tinier objects.

In my first year of architecture school, as the very first project, I was assigned a building or space on campus and told to draw it, by hand in ink. In plan, section, and axonometric. Again, and again, and again until the drawings looked like they were drafted, not freehand. The point was learning to be able to draw what I saw and eventually draw what I thought.

These drawings, as valuable (and extremely painful) as they were, documented only a finished existing structure; they were mute about how these complex constructions came to be. And that is the fulcrum upon which David Macaulay has based his entire career; using his enormous talent for drawing along with an abiding curiosity about how to make things, he has explored the process of making (and occasionally unmaking) monumental cultural icons.

Ken Follett explained how a cathedral came to be is his novel *The Pillars of the Earth.* It's a story (via individual characters) of the multigenerational, class-based, centrally organized society that could make culturally central, meaningful, and complex things over a very long period. Macaulay's explanation of that technology and system for assembling very large ideas into reality is like the illustrated companion of Follett's narrative. And for the visually inclined, it is every bit as fascinating.

Once Macaulay made his book about how to build a cathedral, he went on to the city, pyramid, underground, and castle, graphically unwinding each of these social constructions and showing the process over time. From there it was a short leap to *The Way Things Work,* the manual of quotidian technology that we live with but barely understand.

David Macaulay's books have been translated to PBS shows and BBC series, but the simplest tools (pen, ink, paper) are still the most powerful.

03 December
Gilbert Stuart

George Washington (The Athenaeum Portrait), original painted 1796

Is there a more famous unfinished painting than *The Athenaeum Portrait*, Gilbert Stuart's portrait of George Washington? I can think of Michelangelo's magnificently brutal unfinished sculptures, *Prisoners* (or *Slaves*), at the Accademia in Florence. They're a bit different; waiting to emerge from the marble blocks, they need more material removed to be revealed; Stuart's painting is waiting for the addition of everything but the face. Mike Angel's *Entombment* or Leo da Vinci's *Adoration of the Magi* paintings are both incomplete but are a tad more elaborate, much larger, and more complete. Plus, you know, they were Michelangelo and Leonardo. Because of them, unfinished (*non finito*) paintings became cool for a few hundred years.

But *The Athenaeum Portrait* isn't exactly as advertised. Gilbert Stuart (and don't you love people with two first names?) used his study of Washington's head as a model for dozens of subsequent completed paintings he sold, most for a hundred dollars each. And postage stamps. And the dollar bill. His was a media industry, and the market was hot. He even used the head for his full-length portrait of Washington, though the eyes have been refocused to a distant gaze rather than staring back at the viewer.

Stuart also did mirror images of the model head (looking right); David Rockefeller owned one, but it was supposedly earlier than the famous one (looking left). Washington sat three times for Stuart, and from those sittings he painted more than 130 paintings, most after Washington's death. Cottage industry indeed.

Stuart could have lived on GW paintings alone, but he managed a few other subjects, about a thousand other portrait clients. It was no accident; he was enormously talented, as his first famous image, *The Skater*, shows. There is incredible humanity and personal insight in his paintings; only Washington's detachment and impassiveness kept his portraits as inscrutable as he was. It was, for Washington, a cultivated deportment, an attempt to define an American attitude. Stuart may have perfectly captured that stance, but there are so few paintings (except his own) of GW that we have simply accepted his as the standard bearer.

That was exactly Gilbert Stuart's idea.

Arts & Architecture magazine, various dates in 1950s and 1960s

John Entenza's extraordinarily brief obituary in the *New York Times*, fewer than a hundred words, elides the influence he had on the history of modern architecture in the US. No one, not even Philip Johnson and his 1932 MoMA International Style exhibition, had the impact that Entenza and his *Arts & Architecture* magazine and Case Study House program wielded. They resound to this day, perhaps more potent than ever.

From Entenza's own first house, designed by Harwell Hamilton Harris in 1937, to his next, Case Study House 9, designed by his close friends Charles and Ray Eames and Eero Saarinen (next to the Eameses' own house), Entenza lived what he preached: a new type of American postwar modern house, which he portrayed in *Arts & Architecture.*

Was there ever a more fully American modern movement for private homes than the Case Study Houses? Frank Lloyd Wright's may count, but they were very much his personal style, not a widespread movement (and every imitation pales next to the master's work). Everything that originated at Harvard (by Gropius, Breuer, Johnson, and their colleagues) started with Bauhaus modernism,

not the homegrown version West Coast modernism established.

Case Study Houses weren't just reflecting the postwar moment, West Coast climate, enormous demand for low-cost housing, and the expansive US economy; they were the result of John Entenza reading the moment, buying the Californian magazine *Arts & Architecture,* stripping away the local focus, and realizing his idea for a new Weissenhofsiedlung experiment.

The effect of the Case Study Houses was far more than eight or thirty-six or thirty-six thousand houses; it was pitching affordable design as part of the burgeoning American dream. Compared to the influence of Mies van der Rohe, Johnson, MoMA, and the institutions of architecture, one could note that there are only two glass houses in America. Entenza did much more with much, much less (even making Mies's point in the process).

It's no accident that seventy-five years after the start of the Case Study Houses program, it still enthralls. It's not just because of the architects, extraordinary though they were. It never would have happened but for the writer, editor, publisher, and genius John Entenza.

05 December
Lina Bò Bardi

SESC Pompéia Factory, São Paulo, Brazil, 1982

Lina, Lina Bò Bina, Banana Fana Fo Fina...Lina Bò Bardi. Lina Bò Bardi is such a cool name, but that fucking jingle is stuck in my head every time I say it. So, apologies.

Lina (nickname of Achillina) Bò (until she married Bardi) was the coolest Italian Brazilian architect, designer, activist, and editor imaginable, and she hung out with the coolest people imaginable.

After graduating from architecture school at twenty-five, she moved from Rome to Milan and started an office with Carlo Pagani. They ended up with Gio Ponti and edited *Stile* magazine until 1943, when her office was bombed (you know, World War II), and later edited *Domus*. She and Pagani traveled Italy documenting the war damage and got involved in reconstruction, but apparently her earlier participation in the resistance made that difficult (hence her move to Brazil).

That is the story, in any case, but it doesn't add up. *Stile* was definitely a magazine about Fascism and design, and why would participating in the resistance make postwar work difficult? Seems like the opposite. But Bò Bardi did become an active member of the communist party (which is so mainstream in Italy that it doesn't seem to be the problem either) and spent her life combining social activism, architecture, and teaching in Brazil.

Though she designed a lot of projects, she is known for three buildings and a chair: her first (Casa de Vidro, her own glass house), her last (SESC Pompéia Factory), and one in the middle (São Paulo Museum of Art, MASP), plus the Bowl chair. They are all remarkable, shocking, fantastic, and really smart.

Her house is a floating glass box in the rainforest, the museum is raised above the ground on huge red beams, and the SESC is an incredible social project with a renowned concrete cube, tower, and bridges with roughly shaped punched windows that look like renovations but are all-new buildings. The Bowl chair (now reissued) is a bit of genius that should have been in every Julius Shulman photo.

Lina Bò Bardi's career was resurrected with an exhibition at SESC Pompéia three years before her death, and after that she seems to have snuck into our consciousness. I'm not sure when I first noticed her, but she seems to grow in esteem with every passing year.

06 December
Phyllis Birkby

Phyllis Birkby at work, 1998

"Well, Miss Birkby, it appears that if you were a man, you should be studying architecture." It's hard (for me) to imagine how utterly condescending, upsetting, and wrong this statement was from the guidance counselor (the name guidance counselor is the only funny thing about them) to the sixteen-year-old Phyllis Birkby. Fortunately, Birkby was motivated by its idiocy rather than cowed by it.

No wonder she eventually started a school of architecture for women (Women's School of Planning and Architecture, WSPA), became a seminal feminist (which I just realized is not cool to say; this'll be my last time), coined the moniker "patritecture," lectured, wrote, and actively fought the ways architecture embodied (with unfortunate permanence) the same violence to women that laws, authorities, and men perpetrated. That seems either obvious or oddly archaic, but still familiar. And it hasn't changed all that much (see "unfortunate permanence" above). Like Confederate statues, Hillary Clinton's long bathroom walk in the middle of the US presidential debate was structurally demeaning and subjugating. Extraordinary as half the population is affected, but a small fraction of the other half even cares.

As Birkby said, "I am troubled that no matter how much rhetoric is expounded about equal rights and the full humanity of women, if the physical world we build does not reflect this, we speak in empty phrases."

In the 1970s, Birkby made films documenting gay life; they are so evocative of a time when a march could include signs reading "Crush Phallic Imperialism" next to "Lesbians for Nixon" (my wife, Carin Goldberg, said maybe it should have said "Lesbian for Nixon"). This was when 1.2 percent of registered architects were women.

Birkby's career in practice included Waterside Plaza, when she was at Davis Brody, and dozens of other buildings and spaces while in her own firm. She taught at, in addition to WSPA, Pratt Institute, New York Institute of Technology, City University of New York, Southern California Institute of Architecture, and University of Southern California. She formed the Alliance of Women in Architecture with Judith Edelman.

She saw, fifty years ago, that architecture can be a tool of repression or of freedom. Thank you, Phyllis Birkby, for starting that conversation.

07 December
Gian Lorenzo Bernini

St. Peter's Square, Vatican City, Rome, Italy, 1667

Gian Lorenzo Bernini was all about spectacle.

His greatest hits are the two spectacular fountains in the Piazza Navona and the remarkable piazza defined by curved colonnades in front of St. Peter's Basilica. Not much else would be needed to seal his fame, but Bernini wasn't about to stop there. He was fiercely competitive, looking to dominate and/or humiliate his rivals; he must have understood that though he was richer and had more staff and lived in a palazzo worthy of nobility, he was less talented than, say, Francesco Borromini and certainly forever subservient to Michelangelo (who died thirty-four years before Bernini was born) except in terms of his Wikipedia entry, which is 50 percent larger than Mike Angel's (for those who count those things, and he would have). As he said, "Those who never dare to break the rules never surpass them."

His best is very, very good, but it can be overly melodramatic (for my taste); it is like comparing earlier superhero films with the current CGI-boosted ones. The tech embellishments don't make the quality of the films better, but they are louder, flashier, more visually packed, and awesome. As I said, spectacle.

The Bernini and Borromini rivalry has been played out in both true and apocryphal tales, but they all illustrate Bernini's competitive nature (and his extroversion versus Borromini's introversion). It's in part the arrogance of the rich and well-born versus the humble yet innately talented. Bernini had enormous skill, was born to an accomplished sculptor, and at age eight was understood to be a prodigy. Borromini was born to a mason, lived like a monk, and basically was a sole practitioner, working with only an assistant. Bernini had a huge studio and staff and was rich and well-connected, yet he lost commissions to Borromini (which must have really driven him mad).

There's a level of entitlement (almost forgivable, given his genuine talent) to Gian Lorenzo Bernini that is nonetheless irritating. But to many he is the very definition of the baroque and a worthy successor to Michelangelo.

Maybe, possibly, if you like that baroque kind of thing. And spectacle.

08 December
Georges Méliès

Still from *A Trip to the Moon,* 1903

My grandfather was born in 1888 in Brooklyn, a city not yet electrified, into a world without automobiles, airplanes, or movies (actually, that year the first movie was created; it was less than two seconds long). When he died, men had landed on the moon, everyone jetted everywhere, and we had seen two installments of *The Godfather* (the second clocking in at three hours, twenty minutes!) I don't think anyone has ever lived through more change.

To get from the 1.66-second British thriller *Roundhay Garden Scene* to *The Godfather* (not even Francis Ford Coppola's longest film!), the remarkable Georges Méliès and his brothers were indispensable. Film, like photography, was first seen as a tool of documentation, recording the world as it was. Méliès, who had a background as a magician and owned a theater, transformed the scientific use of film into staged illusions and eventually narratives of increasing length. In 1902 he made *A Trip to the Moon* (fourteen minutes) and in 1904 *The Impossible Voyage* (twenty-four minutes). Both were huge hits, presaging what film would eventually become.

But, as everyone who has seen Martin Scorsese's *Hugo* knows, Méliès fell from grace, lost his glass-encased studio in Montreuil and his Paris theater, and ended up selling candy and toys in a small store at the Gare Montparnasse. His career was eventually celebrated, but only after he had destroyed hundreds of his films along with their sets and costumes. During World War I, the French confiscated four hundred of his films, melting them down to recover the silver and celluloid (for shoe heels!). His decline was precipitous, and his bitterness was palpable, until he was finally recognized by everyone who ever made a film.

What they recognized was a man playing with an entirely new technology, advancing it from documentation to entertainment, from entertainment to art. Even Walt Disney, not one to easily praise others, said Méliès "discovered the means of placing poetry within the reach of the man in the street."

Georges Méliès was far from the only magician to transform film, but he was the first. Magic and film are both about invention and the disappearance of technology to leave us with pure art and emotion – a remarkable trick.

09 December
Steven Holl

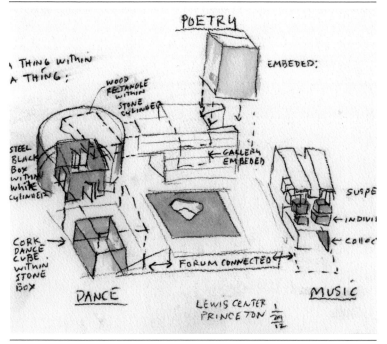

Sketch of the Lewis Arts Complex, Princeton, New Jersey, completed 2017

Making architecture is both an intensely personal act and a thoroughly public one. It can also be both an artistic and a technical endeavor. Finding balance is rare, and Steven Holl is what that balance looks like.

Colin Rowe once asked whether Le Corbusier was "rather more a painter than an architect," and we can ask that of Holl. It's not a criticism of either's architecture, but a way to explain how that architecture is made. How Holl draws and paints is central to how he makes buildings.

Holl talks about a transformation in his thinking that he ascribes to various philosophical texts and other personal realizations. That's fine, but the proof (or all that matters to everyone else) is in the buildings, and there are only two ways to experience a building: in person or not. A building's photogenic qualities are about two-dimensional representations of three-dimensional environments. An actual space/time experience is the ultimate litmus test, and I am divided in the few Holl buildings I have visited.

His first transformative building, St. Ignatius Chapel in Seattle, is my favorite. It may be the scale, it may be my own taste, and it may be the collection of meaningful moments, details, and sequences, but it is a place that makes me smile. It is obviously a repository of a great deal of emotion, thought, and concentrated ideas.

Less successful are places like Simmons Hall at the Massachusetts Institute of Technology, which seem essentially designed as externally determined objects with everything else subservient to those images. The difference may be that as buildings grow in scale (and include some very large collections of very large buildings), Holl's methodology is both determinative and limiting.

His watercolors are where everything starts, and the cute, cartoony quality of the drawings is often translated into buildings that still embrace that cartoon-iness. They have become much more sculptural, much more uniform in surface (in fact, he has come to cover everything, including windows, in the same cast glass frosted channels) until the scale becomes hard to fix.

But it's hard to quibble with a practice that has so successfully balanced the personal and the public.

10 December
Adolf Loos

Competition entry, Chicago Tribune Tower, 1922

There's the *Seinfeld* episode where George has a job interview that ends well but ambiguously, so George just decides to inhabit the position. Bold move. Later, he invents Vandelay Industries to keep unemployment insurance. (Note: across the street from the real J. Peterman in Blue Ash, Ohio, is the actual Vandelay Industries, whence the name.) Sometimes you have to creatively misunderstand things!

Like Adolf Loos. He met Josephine Baker (she taught him the Charleston), and she expressed her unhappiness with her architect. Loos (nearly deaf and aging) understood that he had been commissioned to design a house for her. Apparently not, but he designed one for her anyway. The black-and-white striped exterior seems an obvious reference to her race, but it is the swimming pool, complete with several underwater windows, that seems more like Loos's fantasy than Baker's request. Loos was jailed for pedophilia a year later. He was a strident motherfucker.

Briefly a part of the Secessionists, Loos later was highly critical of them in his essay "Ornament and Crime" (not ornament is a crime), claiming the advance of civilization was paralleled by the reduction in ornament on utilitarian objects. It was, therefore, a crime to insist that craftsmen adorn objects that would go out of style as a result. Later, he mocked the idea of Gesamtkunstwerk with tales of clients who were frozen in their perfectly designed worlds, unable to add or remove even a single object. He was relentless and dogmatic, and likely unbearable.

The interiors of his built projects told a different story; the level of luxury of their materials (admittedly used in relatively undecorated states) is astonishing. We sometimes forget that the earliest modern houses were for wealthy clients who expected luxury no matter the style, and Loos provided. For Loos, the apotheosis of refinement was the English bespoke suit; custom made and perfectly constructed of luxurious materials, it was a rather perfect analogy to his work.

Despite all that was wrong with Adolf Loos, his adamance created some spectacular buildings and interiors, from the tiny Kärntner Bar to Villa Moller (and Villa Müller).

If, that is, we can forgive his faults.

11 December
Ferdinand A. Porsche

Butzi at work, 1968

Ferdinand Alexander Porsche is not to be confused with his grandfather Ferdinand Porsche (who seems to have been intimately involved in both World War I and II; he was Austrian, chauffeur to Archduke Franz Ferdinand, and designed the Panzer and Tiger tanks, weapons, and ultimately the Volkswagen Beetle for his friend Adolf), nor with his father, Ferdinand Anton Ernst Porsche (called Ferry, he took over while his father was jailed in France for war crimes; he designed the Porsche 356, the bulbous beauties that included the Speedster that James Dean died in).

Ferdinand Alexander (nicknamed Butzi) was the first Porsche not to help Germany in a world war! He designed the Porsche 911, the coolest fucking car since the 356; more than a million have been made since 1964.

Ever since my father brought home a silver 356 from Stuttgart (bought for my art teacher) in the late 1950s, I have wanted one (I know this is a cliché, but clichés exist for a reason). He had a white 1963 version and later a 911 T (sadly, in gold), and they were all enviable autos. I know they are impractical, expensive, and possibly dangerous (the earlier ones), but that hasn't blunted my desire for one.

Even becoming a walking, driving cliché has only slightly dampened my enthusiasm. But enough about me.

The 911 is (was, really, as the car seems to have been progressively bulked up over the years, much as some of us have, and has lost its edge) a remarkably trim car. The engine in the back (originally a VW idea) leaves the front flexible enough to flatten for aerodynamic and visual reasons. It's a dramatic and deliberate departure from Porsche's grandfather's beautifully inflated 356. The latest models feel steroid-y or muscle-bound or just a bit flabby.

Porsche left the car biz when the management structure changed and started Porsche Design, among the first brand expansions that actually worked. Butzi understood, earlier than most, that the essence of a brand can be extended if one is careful about how, what, when, etc. (Cadbury's instant mashed potatoes, Smash, being an example of the opposite).

It's nice when the progeny doesn't fuck up the brand. And it's especially nice when they can avoid becoming Nazis in the process!

12 December
John Lloyd Wright

Construction made with Lincoln Logs

Titling a book about one's father *My Father Who Is on Earth* may be all we need to know about that relationship. And that the author's middle name was originally Kenneth, later changed to Lloyd.

John Lloyd Wright was Frank Lloyd Wright's second son, whose on-again, off-again relationship with his father seems utterly understandable. FLLW was not just a renowned narcissist, but also (like most fathers, even the best intentioned) really hard to work under, and under is where John would remain.

John was raised in Wright's famous Oak Park home, with the amazing vaulted children's playroom. Frank left John's mother for a client's wife (a trope John would later reprise) and moved to Taliesin with her (where she was later murdered by an insane staff member). John tried, but failed, to resist following in his father's profession; when he attempted to apprentice with Otto Wagner in Vienna, Frank lured him to work in his own office.

John worked for Frank in Chicago on the remarkable Midway Gardens and in Japan on the Imperial Hotel. A salary spat split them again; FLLW was not financially stable and never paid John a steady salary, preferring to dole out

money irregularly, treating him as you might a child.

John left Japan and went home to invent a toy that has become vastly more famous than he would ever be: Lincoln Logs. The toy was based on a detail for constructing the Imperial Hotel; notched beams lock them together for earthquake resistance.

JLLW went on to design hundreds of houses but was always fighting the impression (not entirely undeserved) that he was simply reproducing his father's work. It's a problem with FLLW's work: only he could do it. Everything else seems like an inferior copy, especially if your name ends in Lloyd Wright.

Among the lessons never learned by JLLW are: 1) don't work for your father; 2) don't take up a profession that competes with a famous father; 3) don't marry your client's wife; 4) don't sell your patents; 5) don't send your father the manuscript of your book about him.

John Lloyd Wright cleverly published his book, including all the annotations FLLW added, printed as annotations added by FLLW.

Touché.

13 December
Mary Wright

Photo from Mary and Russel Wright, *The Guide for Easier Living,* 1950

In some ways this book followed the observation that Marcel Breuer, Walter Gropius, and Florence Knoll all had birthdays within the same week (and had all worked closely together in various ways). Though she is unrelated to John Lloyd Wright (whose birthday was yesterday), Mary Small Einstein Wright was related to Albert Einstein, which is way cooler.

The birthday adjacency didn't seem to extend to physical places until I realized that Mary Wright lived (and died) on the same block of East Forty-Eighth Street where E. B. White and Kurt Vonnegut also lived. I worked on a project on that block and used to see Vonnegut sitting on his stoop, though I doubt Mary Wright, Russel Wright's collaborator and wife, would be caught sitting on hers. Good block.

Sadly, Mary Wright died young, at forty-seven, before I was born, but I did meet her daughter Annie at their home, Dragon Rock at Manitoga. She was living there twenty-five years after her father's death (and fifty after her mother's) as it was in the process of becoming a landmark owned and run by a nonprofit. It's an amazing house, perched on a quarry on a piece of land Mary and Russel bought together but never built upon until after Mary's death.

It's hard to know how successful Russel would have been without Mary. He was involved in stage set design and stage production; she pushed him toward the domestic objects we know him for. She innately understood marketing, and their extraordinary fame was due to her intelligence.

Mary was an artist as well, drawing since she was a child. Having traveled in Europe among literary circles, studied sculpture with Alexander Archipenko, and attended Cornell University's architecture department, she knew her way around art. But her instincts in integrating modern design into a lifestyle that privileged leisure in a postwar America were flawless.

Her book with Russel, *Guide to Easier Living*, proposes a modern, efficient, casual, and comfortable lifestyle that was an entirely new idea to my parent's generation yet was inherited by mine.

14 December
Berthold Lubetkin

Penguin Pool, London Zoo, London, England, 1934

When an architect's most famous early buildings were all designed for various British zoos, one has to ask if they start to see all their clients as, well, zoo animals? If the penguins and polar bears seem OK with it (though I'm pretty sure no one asked them), why not people? And does that imply that all occupants of modern architecture are on display? That is almost certainly how a certain class of the English population treated 1930s modernism: not fit for evolved species.

But if Berthold Lubetkin and his firm Tecton (set up in 1932 after he emigrated to London) considered their work to be only for the most exotic of mammals, then Lubetkin included himself in that species; he lived atop his Highpoint housing block for more than twenty years, in what was thought to be the highest residence in London (Highpoint was named for its very high elevation).

It was much admired in 1932 as "worker housing." Lubetkin said, "Nothing is too good for the common man," but of course Highpoint was, and has been since it was built, home to the upper middle class and above. A friend who just moved in is anything but a common man! And that's a common problem; socialists and other left-leaning designers (as Lubetkin was) may think their work is for the *Volk* when it is actually for a wealthier clientele. I have no particular gripe with that, but I do with the project's utter lack of any spatial or urban reference to its context. This must be part of why Le Corbusier praised Highpoint so highly; it subscribed to his own anti-urban notions. This is especially true of Lubetkin's later Bevin Court, a three-armed extrusion replacing a bombed-out square connected to Percy Circus, a lovely, still-existing, round square. It would have been *so* easy to use Bevin Court as a modern connection to the past, but that just wasn't done in the 1950s.

Berthold Lubetkin designed a few sensitively modern housing projects, like the four houses on London's Genesta Road; they are insistently modern but at least maintain a consistent facade alignment with the adjacent houses and a height that doesn't overwhelm them. The infill situation made it harder to violate the unspoken rules of decorum.

But that might be too much to ask for someone whose primary model was a zoo!

15 December
Oscar Niemeyer

Mondadori editorial headquarters, Milan, Italy

Oscar, Oscar, Oscar (to quote Felix Unger). Oscar Ribeiro de Almeida Niemeyer Soares Filho made it to 104 years old (remarried at ninety-nine) and managed to cover the entire twentieth century and part of the twenty-first. He led a prodigious practice for seventy-eight years (as long as two careers) and designed a pile of milestone works along the way that redefined Brazilian modernism. If Lina Bò Bardi represented one direction, Oscar pursued the opposite: the rational versus the emotional, the user-based versus the architect-defined, the spatial versus the sculptural.

If you live long enough, it all looks like genius. Niemeyer was once a fringe figure, an eccentric stylist of mostly local significance, until he outlasted all his critics.

He and Le Corbusier (whom he worked with on Brazil's first tower in the late 1930s) both designed capital cities from scratch at precisely the same time; both were monumental exercises and both rendered in concrete, but with two very different formal results. Today, Niemeyer's Brasília looks much less cartoonish than it once did, and Le Corbusier's Chandigarh much more, well, distressed. Neither led us in very productive directions urbanistically.

And no one ever described Chandigarh as "whimsical" (as they do Brasília)!

Brasília style begat Lincoln Center's skewed modernism and the Empire State Plaza. It provoked responses like Skidmore, Owings & Merrill's Air Force Academy Cadet Chapel. Niemeyer's work pops up in the oddest places: Le Havre, France (cultural center); Segrate, Italy (Mondadori headquarters); Los Angeles (Strick House); Paris (Communist Party headquarters), and these are just the ones I've visited!

Oscar deserves an Oscar™ for his performative buildings. They are, indeed, sculptural extravaganzas, but always with an interesting conceptual hook. The Cathedral of Brasília rests on the impossibly small points of its ribs. Same with the Alvorada Palace, which looks like Herman Miller stole for its logo (or vice versa). Itamaraty Palace is a crisp glass box within sculpted arches that seems to float on reflecting ponds, visually weightless.

The monumental scale of these works is hard to appreciate in photos, but the theatricality is not. Oscar Niemeyer never lost that scale, no matter his age.

16 December
Ed Ruscha

Merchandise from *Ed Ruscha / Now Then,* MoMA, New York, New York, 2023

It's almost trite to remark how cool Edward Ruscha is, but who's cooler?

And his work is equally cool. Words, cryptic phrases, photo series, paintings on drumheads, words in gunpowder, edible materials, blood: all of Ruscha's work expresses a level of confidence that looks like he doesn't care if you care (and is utterly OK with that).

Ruscha posed with his wife in 1971, fifty fucking years ago, shirtless and with a fully developed, but seemingly effortless, six-pack physique. He drives vintage cars (and a Tesla) and hails, along with his drawl, from Oklahoma. The whole thing would be terminally intimidating if he didn't seem like such a lovely guy. His longtime assistant has never heard him raise his voice in anger.

There's a bit of Dada in Ruscha. And more than a bit of pop. Plus Ferus Gallery. Plus post-pop. And maybe a bit of surrealism as well. It all adds up to virtually no one but Ed Ruscha.

Words as images. Words plus images. Images as words. Thoughts. Scraps of life. Documents of life. Continuous panoramas. It's all about re-seeing what you have already seen, but isn't that what every pop artist did? Turning the commonplace into the exalted?

Brillo boxes, comics, flags, scraps from the street all became art by virtue of someone noticing them.

Somehow Ruscha avoided the showiness of it all, quietly putting his work into the public consciousness. Books on gas stations, parking lots, buildings on the Sunset Strip. A type-face based on the Hollywood sign. But mostly just words. Wherever he trained his vision, we were enlightened.

Everyone knows what Andy Warhol looks like, and most know what David Hockney looks like (I saw him once at a garage on Twelfth Street waiting for his car, which turned out to be a vintage open Jaguar). But until recently I had no idea what Ruscha looked like, even though my wife, Carin Goldberg, has had a photo of him on our shelves for years. I thought it was Man Ray!

Ed Ruscha has managed to avoid the celebrity and tabloids and make, for his more than eighty years, prodigious amounts of art in a wide swath of media.

We know his art much better than we know him, as it should be.

17 December
Paul Cadmus

Broadway Barber Shop, New York, New York, opened 1904

When I first moved to New York City, I lived on Riverside Drive, just blocks from where Paul Cadmus was born and raised. I passed the Broadway Barber Shop at 2713 Broadway every day on the way to the subway. It was a perfect stage set for a Norman Rockwell (or Edward Hopper) painting: an exquisitely preserved relic of a lost world. It opened in 1904, and the last owner (who ran it for a mere forty years) died in 1999. It was deemed so important that it resides, in pieces, at the Museum of the City of New York.

That barbershop, where Paul Cadmus had his hair cut (I imagine, as he lived just a block away), spanned the twentieth century precisely as Paul Cadmus did. The barber's famous remark upon finishing a cut, "Now you look like a prince!" could be applied to Paul's canvases as well. He turned everything into a baroque painting, including, maybe especially, baroque eroticism (and homoeroticism).

Cadmus left school at fifteen (like every prodigy, it seems) to study at the National Academy of Design and later (like nearly every successful painter) at the Art Students League of New York. Thinking he could dodge the Great Depression, he and fellow painter and partner Jared French went to, of course,

France and other places. He returned to the States when money ran out, just in time to be hired by the Works Progress Administration (WPA) to paint murals in post offices.

He painted *The Fleet's In!* in 1934 for the PWPA (Public Works of Art Project). The work was so wild in content (carousing sailors and sex workers, both hetero and homo, in a riotous bulging-pants tableau) that it was removed from a show at the Corcoran it had been selected for. It hung in the assistant secretary of the Navy's house until it was moved to the super-elite Alibi Club. It should have been called "Hello, Sailor!" and, like virtually all of PC's work, it was anything but PG.

Cadmus turned the social realism of the 1930s into magic realism, while garnering the Artists Trade Union of Russia's designation as "one of the most important artists of the past four hundred years" (so maybe socialist realism?). But it is his thinly veiled homoerotic paintings and scenes of debauchery, all rendered exquisitely in egg tempera, that really defines his art.

Painted ten years before it inspired Jerome Robbins for his ballet *Fancy Free*, Paul Cadmus's *The Fleet's In!* seems like a model for all that followed.

Eastman Kodak, maroon/black No. 2 Beau Brownie, 1930

The worst film about a design giant has to be *Teague: Design & Beauty* on Walter Dorwin Teague. Here is a guy who started in art (at, of course, the Arts Student League of New York, like virtually everyone) and became an advertising star by making frames (also known as Teague borders), the drawn decorative embellishments that surrounded early print ads. He moved to product design by transforming Kodak cameras into gorgeous boxes with enameled art deco cases and colored gift packaging aimed to attract women and other users less enamored with the technical object and more interested in styled accessories. That alone is a fascinating transformation of a technology into an art and it, along with the subsequent design of new Kodak cameras, demonstrates an evolution from surface decor to whole-form remodeling.

In his graphic design days, Teague shared an office with Frederic W. Goudy, who is, in the film's telling, not even a factor in Teague's graphic development (though undoubtedly he was). Teague's designer son Dorwin was the impetus to streamlining and shape (not surface) as design, as in the Polaroid desk lamp (conceived by Edwin Land, who invented the

Polaroid Land camera that Teague designed) that was shaped to reduced glare.

Teague went on to design pavilions for Ford, General Electric, DuPont, and other giant US corporations for various US world's fairs, culminating in the 1939 New York World's Fair, where he pushed for its "World of Tomorrow" theme rather than a look backward at history. His pavilions are generally underappreciated, especially in light of Norman Bel Geddes's General Motors (GM) Pavilion, which completely changed the idea of an expo pavilion. Teague's Ford Pavilion exhibited the process of manufacturing autos and featured a half-mile/1.5-kilometer-long road with (very carefully chauffeured) new model Fords. His narrative extravaganza was dwarfed by the experiential invention at GM. And his National Cash Register Pavilion (with a giant cash register tallying the attendance) is pure kitsch.

This is pretty much where Walter Dorwin Teague was in the industrial design firmament: a successful design business just a few steps behind the real geniuses of industrial design in America.

19 December
Wally Olins

Personal logo

I have heard the name Wally Olins for years as yet another London-based, born-before-the-war icon of branding and identity and another clever wag about town. The difference between Wally and his erstwhile colleague Colin Forbes (besides the fact that Colin was still going strong at ninety-three) is Wally's apparently privileged upbringing. And, despite his protestations, his fully branded personality. And the Commander of the Most Excellent Order of the British Empire he got in 1999. So maybe they are nothing alike...

I've always thought (based on one early photograph I saw) that Colin would be played in the film version by Daniel Craig while Wally would probably be portrayed by (Sir) Ben Kingsley. Olins maintained his highly branded personality to the end, wearing "interesting" glasses and bow ties while saying, "I have not consciously branded myself at all. It is true that I wear a bow tie and funny spectacles, but it is not conscious branding."

I find that to be disingenuous in so many ways, but that kind of doublespeak is what I think separates more advertising-based design from more design-based identity. It is also a feint to distract from design made as a corporate-produced accessory, apart from design as made

by designers. The advertising model doesn't acknowledge that its version of design is produced by a relatively anonymous machine, rather than transparently promoting the people who actually designed it.

Forbes created an organization that stressed people, the personalities and the ideas they produced, rather than the structure in which they operated. Who knows (or cares) who created the designs that Olins's firm Wolff Olins or his later firm Saffron produced?

Olins and his former partner, Michael Wolff, while not indistinguishable, were both hairless men of a certain age, one with bow ties and one with scarves and T-shirts. More ironic is that occasionally in an article about Michael Wolff (the designer) you find a portrait of the other Michael Wolff, the exposé writer, who is also hairless with interesting glasses (and colorful socks, another trope of the design, or design-conscious, set).

Whoever they are, wherever they now are, they all sought to spin the world their way, with varying results.

20 December
Calvert Vaux

Bethesda Fountain terrace arcade, Central Park, New York, New York, 1864

Everyone knows (or should know) that Frederick Law Olmstead Sr. designed, as his very first landscape project, Central Park in New York City, winning the competition with his entry Greensward. It is now the most visited park (forty-two million visitors per year!) and most filmed location in the world (however they measure that). Everyone might not know that it is filled with Calvert Vaux's work, which has been thrilling us forever but usually without attribution.

The Bow Bridge, among the most graceful bridges ever devised, is a cast-iron beauty crossing the lake. So much of Central Park is based on an over-under arrangement that bridges and other devices are critically important; there are some thirty of them, not counting the wood ones.

More impressive is Vaux's Bethesda Terrace, a gorgeous termination to the Mall (the only geometric, tree-lined axis in the park) and a transition to the waterside plaza of the Bethesda Fountain. The "under" part is an arcade with a tiled ceiling, a bit of cool darkness linking the shade of the Mall and the blaze of the terrace.

The Belvedere Castle is a miniature (think Disneyland, all built at five-eighths

scale) folly marking a high point in the park. Its scale change makes it look even higher and farther away, and it is one of those buildings that we would have a hard time justifying today; "It's just there to look cool," is not necessarily what a client wants to hear. But happily, it was built and restored a hundred years later.

But Vaux did (much) more than Central Park: Hudson River mansions, Frederic Edwin Church's Olana, the Tombs prison, Jefferson Market Courthouse, the original Metropolitan Museum, the American Museum of Natural History, parks everywhere, and, somehow, lots of houses and buildings in Newburgh and Kingston (giving me renewed hope that Newburgh, once a hellhole of drugs and abandoned buildings, is on its way back to its former state of grace).

Calvert Vaux became partners with Andrew Jackson Downing (after Downing had tried to join Alexander Jackson Davis) following Downing's trip to London to find a simpatico architect. Vaux named his son Downing (think Donald Judd naming his son Flavin) after Downing died, and the rest is, for us, a very lucky set of collaborations.

21 December
Masaccio

Raising of the Son of Theophilus and St. Peter Enthroned, Florence, Italy, 1427

Imagine a time when the art and science of drawing in perspective was lost and then eventually found; things that seem self-evident to us now were once utterly mysterious. Perspective (and concrete) was known by the Romans and Greeks, but the process for creating a true perspective was lost until Filippo Brunelleschi reverse engineered it sometime after 1415. Masaccio, then a young prodigy in Florence, absorbed the system to achieve a new level of realism in art.

He had to hurry, as he lived only to twenty-six, poisoned by a rival artist. His early death only glorifies his few existing paintings and cements Masaccio as a young, dearly departed genius.

Is the century between Masaccio's relatively elementary use of perspective and somewhat primitive realism and, say, Michelangelo mastering it a case of purely technological advance (like the hundred years between the first telephone and the first cell phone)?

Masaccio's *Holy Trinity* in Santa Maria Novella verges on trompe l'oeil. Frescoes are very difficult, as they have to be painted on wet (fresh, or in Italian, *fresco*) plaster. Time is, of course, quite limited and corrections are nearly impossible, plus there is no underdrawing

as on canvas. For precision, Masaccio was said to have put a nail at the vanishing point and tied strings to it for all the linear perspective lines, then pressed those into the wet plaster. Upon that perspective grid, he proceeded to a composition that put people (patrons?) in front of the picture plane and the holy stuff in the illusory depth. This revolutionized image making, and you can still see the impression Masaccio's strings made in the plaster.

Giorgio Vasari, in reconstructing Santa Maria Novella 150 years later, built a wall in front of *Holy Trinity* for his own fresco, preserving Masaccio's until it was discovered in 1860. Vasari was said to have done the same with the lost Leonardo da Vinci mural a few minutes away at the Palazzo Vecchio.

As Mary McCarthy wrote of the *Holy Trinity*, "The fresco, with its terrible logic, is like a proof in philosophy or mathematics...being the axiom from which everything else irrevocably follows." The merger of technique and content. Cool shit for a twenty-five-year-old technocrat. Imagine if Masaccio had made it to thirty, or eighty.

22 December
Max Bill

Ulm stool, designed 1954

My favorite poster, hanging in a place of honor in our home, is Max Bill's 1960 announcement of Marcel Duchamp's exhibit at the Decorative Art Museum in Zurich. It is a perfect orange with a purple ink handprint of Duchamp in a white circle. For a while, my favorite watches (and I have about as many watches as I have posters: a lot) were Bill's series for Junghans. If I owned one of his clever little stool/bookshelf/tables, that might be my favorite too. He seemed to make things that were both perfectly Swiss and perfectly embraceable, not an easy task.

Oh, and books. The most precious and loved books I own are the *Le Corbusier: Complete Works*, which, of course, Bill designed. And when I just opened one volume, a small painting and note from my wife, Carin Goldberg, fell out; it was a gift before we were married. So, things I love inside things I love. Max Bill tends to do that to me. It hurt to learn that Sophie Taeuber-Arp died in Bill's cabin when a faulty stove filled it with carbon monoxide. Even that had personal repercussions.

And did I mention I have his light fixture with the amusing double-ended design? It never stops. What is so irritating about Max Bill is how easy he made it look. All the work, the variations, the sweating over details are concealed in the simple brilliance of the final form. When we do get that rare insight into his process (as in his logo and signage for the Corso movie theaters in Zurich that he did in 1934), it is overwhelming. He goes through all the variations, landing on such an unexpected, singular, and elegant solution, unhinted at in all the work leading up to it.

In the 1960s, he designed a bridge that is both an homage to and a comment upon (dare I say an improvement to?) those of Robert Maillart, the best bridge designer there ever was. On top of all that, much like finding a stunningly beautiful actress who is also brilliant as a writer, director, painter, singer, and scientist, Bill was super cool looking. He had, in his younger years, a zero-percent-fat David Mamet look.

And let's not forget his excellent entry into the both-names-as-first-names competition. Max Bill clearly wins that too.

23 December
Nancy Graves

Actual camels, unlike the artwork created by Nancy Graves in the 1960s and 1970s

Given who she hung out with, went to school with, and married, it's interesting to see how Nancy Graves chose her artistic directions, and we're lucky she did. Her range (moving past the minimalism of so many of her Yale colleagues, including, for a while, husband Richard Serra, and short of the realism of the others) puts her in a class of her own. Her work is occasionally weird, like her camels, but it's never doctrinaire or dull.

It's hard not to look at her work with context in mind. Graves created the lifelike taxidermy of camels and bones (entirely and obviously constructed of noncamel elements) while married to Richard Serra, creating a COR-TEN steel base in advance of Serra's use of the material that became his signature. Her father worked at a museum that was all about art and science, a mix not unlike Graves and Serra. While Serra was doing his "verb" sculptures ("to lift," etc.) and other explorations of pure material and physics with inorganic materials and forms, Graves was using almost entirely organic materials for her work (along with traditional casting, which Serra avoided). Seems like a Mary Matalin and James Carville relationship; opposites can attract (which would have been a good prompt for a Serra sculpture).

After their split, Graves became interested in (prophetically, as this is the 1970s) data, science, mapping, and archaeology and converted them to pointillist paintings. If her friends were converting art into data, she was converting data into art. And while some others were removing the hand from the work, using photographs or comics or geometry to define their art, Graves was doing the opposite.

In 1969, she was the youngest (and only the fifth) woman to have a solo show at the Whitney Museum, a distinction that says more about the Whitney than anything else. The show included the camels (probably all that was remembered from the show), and she later said, "The choice of the camel as form was a decision I didn't completely understand, but it makes sense with the work that came afterward."

It also made sense that Nancy Graves later married a veterinarian.

24 December
Joseph Cornell

"Why bother getting a passport, when I can do this anytime I feel like it?"

Joseph Cornell on how transporting his work was to him

Once you see a Joseph Cornell shadow box, the impulse to make one is almost unavoidable. But just try it and you'll see how magical the real ones are. That must have been how a friend, decades ago, found what she knew was a genuine Cornell at a garage sale. It was marked $5, and she spent some time bargaining the price down to $3.50; she immediately resold it for $15,000. My favorite part of the story is the price negotiation. This woman had either nerves of steel or a deeply ingrained sense of never paying retail. On the other hand, Cornell's *Medici Slot Machine* sold for $7.8 million (twice its pre-auction estimate), so maybe she didn't have a great sense of timing.

I tried making my own Cornell box with soda crates and type cases, but I think I was always more interested in the grid than the narrative. Plus, you know, my lack of talent.

Cornell led a very odd, quite interior life, moving into a house on Utopia Parkway, Queens, in 1929 with his overbearing mother and disabled brother. He never lived anywhere else and led an increasingly solitary life filled with regret. He made his work there, received visitors there, and cared for his family until their deaths in the 1960s.

On the other hand, he knew virtually every artist who swept through New York City and was even included in the landmark 1936 MoMA *Fantastic Art, Dada, Surrealism* show. He knew Marcel Duchamp, Salvador Dalí, Andy Warhol, Ad Reinhardt, Robert Motherwell, and many more; he was not so much a recluse, but certainly alone and lonely. That isolation, the sense of sadness, is clear in his work; everything is behind glass, untouchable, frozen, and unchanging.

His boxes made him famous, but he made films (by recutting and assembling existing movies), collages, Rorschach blot drawings, and more. His cataloging system for storing the results of his trips to Manhattan looking for "stuff" was staggering. It makes sense that he had masses of raw material waiting to become art; his work couldn't be conjured out of tubes of color.

He was the rare artist with no training, no expansive public persona, no posse of assistants and hangers-on, no SoHo studio. Today that would be a formula for failure, but Joseph Cornell succeeded despite, not due to, his personal quirks.

25 December
Paul Bacon

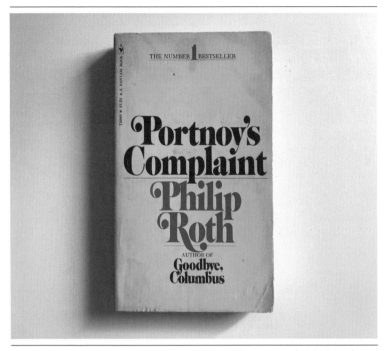

Cover of *Portnoy's Complaint* by Philip Roth, Bantam Books, 1978 (original 1969)

It may be obvious to some, but book and record covers matter. A lot. At a talk my wife, Carin Goldberg, was giving about the history of the book covers for *Ulysses*, a woman in the audience asked if Carin was the designer for Oliver Sacks's *The Man Who Mistook His Wife for a Hat* (she was). The woman told her that the cover was what launched Oliver's career as a writer. She should know; she was Sacks's editor and friend, and she runs the foundation in his name. Of course, it was his writing that made Sacks's career, but she credited the cover with a lot. (*The Man Who Mistook His Wife for a Hat* was originally titled *The Lost Mariner and Other Clinical Tales*, and the cover reflects that original title; when the title was changed the publisher kept the original type treatment, hence a very odd cover.)

Then there was the time Carin and I arrived at a book party just ahead of Kurt Vonnegut, who, when he learned that Carin had designed the complete reissue of his work, said, "Young lady, you have made me a *lot* of money!" They spent the rest of the evening in rapt conversation.

Paul Bacon designed the original cover for Vonnegut's *Slaughterhouse-Five*. The more than sixty-five hundred covers he designed started with record covers (just as Carin's did) for Blue Note and other jazz labels; eventually he designed a book cover for a friend.

Bacon is credited with the Big Book Look (BBL), which is either a huge deal or the worst thing to happen to books since *Reader's Digest*, depending on who you ask. BBL is a cover with the title and author's name really big and maybe a little conceptual image somewhere. It is the bête noire of current designers but did make the point that covers could sell books. This may have been a revelation in an industry that was famous for having no idea why certain books succeeded and other equally good books failed.

As is often the case, the first time you try to design something you haven't done before is often the best (my first restaurant design was Gotham, still open after thirty-eight years). This is true of Bacon's second book cover, for *Compulsion*. One-word titles are a thing (Carin collected them), and his cover is fantastic.

Paul Bacon had one great idea that kept him busy for fifty years and sixty-five hundred covers. Not bad for an idea.

26 December
Charles Babbage

Portion of the Analytical Engine built by Charles Babbage, 1837

While not a typical designer, Charles Babbage did design the first version of the most important device of this century (and maybe the last and next centuries): the computer.

His was analog (no electrical devices, no electronics, just steam) nearly a hundred years before Alan Turing, who in turn was about fifty years before the personal computer. So, Babbage had a jump on all that.

He did what any thinking designer would do: saw a problem and designed something to mitigate it. The problem: mistakes that "human computers" (that is, people doing math) made in tables for astronomy, tables that were used for navigating across oceans. Lives were at stake and accuracy was critical.

Babbage's solution was beyond imagination: a machine that calculated not only with perfect accuracy, but also to three to four times more decimal places. He thought up the idea, designed the machine, and built part of it, but he ran out of money when trying to erect a dust-free, fireproof factory for the twenty-five thousand parts required (comparable to the number of parts in a car). This was, in effect, chip manufacturing nearly two hundred years ago.

His next machine (Difference Engine #2) was *only* eight thousand pieces (maybe that's like an electric car), but that didn't get built either. Until, that is, 1991, when London's Science Museum made one out of four thousand pieces (somehow) that weighed three tons and, most importantly, *worked*! It was more than a steam-powered abacus; it could do complex calculations, even out of order, and store some results for later use. Its printed output was (and this is so great) on metal plates! Steampunk indeed.

Babbage's next leap was even more genius: a machine that could do what modern computers can do (much slower, with less memory, but *way* faster than human computers), solve complex formulations, not just precise calculations. The original machine had been called the Difference Engine with versions 1 and 2. The newest one was called the Analytical Engine and had a remarkable collaborator: Ada Lovelace, one of the few mathematicians at his level. Oh, and she was the daughter of Lord Byron.

Charles Babbage invented the future, and he knew it. That is Design.

"A technically perfect photograph can be the world's most boring picture."

Andreas Feininger, in *The Perfect Photograph*

Working for Le Corbusier for a year seems to have convinced Andreas Feininger that architecture was not for him, but photography was his natural métier. I went to school with some who made the same transition, feeling more like failures than (rightly) having dodged a bullet. Architecture can do that to you: imply that a choice to leave will always be a regret. Fucking bullshit.

Feininger saw architecture wherever he looked. It's interesting that his dichotomous focus was on the city and nature. He found structure in both, and there is an iconic quality to nearly every photograph he shot. It's partly the beautiful black-and-white images (and they are gorgeously printed) and partly the moment in which he worked. The city was almost always New York, where he moved, eventually, from Paris via Sweden, arriving as World War II began. It was an unequaled moment in New York City history, when smoke was abundant (great for photos, bad for lungs), ocean liners plied the Hudson River, and the city was chiaroscuro everywhere.

It was also a time before the streets were littered with news boxes, too many streetlights, and all the detritus of today. Feininger's images show a stark land of black and white, shadow and sun, filled with (or empty of) scores of people. It is such a nostalgic look, especially for those of us who never saw New York that way (which increasingly is everyone alive). For twenty years or so, from the start of World War II to the moment before the John F. Kennedy assassination, Feininger worked for *Life* magazine. His images memorialize America's finest moments (visually, that is, less so for anyone not white, Christian, and male).

Is there a more meta photograph than the one (it turns out to have been one of at least two) where the camera becomes the photographer's eyes? It's not Feininger's self-portrait, as I had always assumed, but of another photojournalist. That photo created the notion of human as camera, a perfect melding of the natural and manmade, of organic and mechanical.

Andreas Feininger created images that have defined not just an era, but a place and a world that has mostly vanished.

28 December
Vladimir Tatlin

Model of Tatlin's Tower (Monument to the Third International), 1920

In the one-hit-wonder column for postrevolutionary Russia is the Tatlin Tower (officially Monument to the Third International), designed just a couple of years into the Bolshevik era. It was to be a quarter mile/ four hundred meters high a decade before the Empire State Building approached that height, and it contained the Comintern (promoting world communism) within three enclosed buildings inside a spiraling steel structure.

But wait, there's more: four glass-enclosed stacked volumes, each a separate building that rotated at a different rate, were suspended within the double helix steel frame. At the bottom was a cube, containing an auditorium, one rotation per year; above that a small pyramid with administrative offices, one rotation per month; next a cylinder with information services, one rotation per day; and at the top a semisphere (dome) that could project messages onto the clouds as well as emit radio signals.

The tower was to be erected in Petrograd (before it was Leningrad, and now Saint Petersburg) but would have taken an insane amount of (unavailable) steel, not to mention it might not have stood. The jury is out on that.

It would have rivaled (and been 328 feet/100 meters taller than) the Eiffel Tower as a statement of national aspiration and pride (after Gustave Eiffel's work was mocked and despised before it was loved). That it didn't happen is almost as interesting as if it had. It might have been simply monstrous in scale, though the design (as sculpture) is fascinating as a smaller memorial rather than the world's largest vertical entry element (as it would be called at Disneyland).

Vladimir Tatlin did do other things: paintings (he visited Picasso's studio in 1913) located somewhere between futurism and constructivism, sculpture (including "corner counter reliefs" set into, you can guess, corners), fashion (and costumes for the theater), and set design. But he will always be known for his unconsummated tower, his submission to an imaginary competition for the Eighth Wonder of the World, for which I am pretty sure it would qualify.

29 December
James Gardner

Cover, *Britain Can Make It: The 1946 Exhibition of Modern Design*, Diane Bilbey, 2019

I never lie. (Except just then, perhaps.) But I love clever deceptions like magic tricks, camouflage, April Fools' jokes, materials disguised as other materials, and even the occasional perverse crossword. The early TV of my childhood, especially during off-hours (when the channels didn't just sign off) was rife with World War II documentaries. The war felt like a million years earlier, but it wasn't. The elaborate camouflage efforts that created Ghost Armies (and Navies and Air Forces) were a potent combo of both my fascinations. Created to fool the Axis powers into thinking the Allies had massive concentrations of troops and equipment in quantities and places where they weren't, they were the deep fakes of their day.

James Gardner was chief deception officer, Army camouflage, perhaps the coolest job in the British military short of breaking the Enigma codes (and I am utterly fascinated by them as well). I learned of this entire enterprise from my former Pentagram partner Kenneth Grange, who described James Gardner "as one of our stars" whose "modesty extended to not wasting time attending meetings." Vintage Grange.

Gardner designed inflatable rubber tanks, ships, and airplanes of phantom armies that so successfully deceived. He designed jewelry for Cartier (his first job) and drew amazing cutaway drawings of planes and ships (looking very much like the work of E. McKnight Kauffer because he studied under him). These drawings, Hugh Casson said, were how Gardner developed his X-ray ability of looking at virtually anything and understanding how it was made and how and why it worked. He also said G (as he was known) was "perhaps the most inventive, versatile, and prolific designer in the UK for more than half of the twentieth century."

James Gardner designed exhibitions for the Festival of Britain, an enthusiastic bit of deception to convince the British public that, indeed, it was worth celebrating. He may have started in jewelry, but after designing the public decorations for Queen Elizabeth's coronation was tasked to design the superstructure and interiors of the *QE2* ocean liner.

And all by not attending meetings.

30 December
W. Eugene Smith

Leica M3, similar to one of the cameras W. Eugene Smith used

Photographers are inherently collectors of images (of course), stories (usually), equipment (makes sense), and correspondences (perhaps). But W. Eugene Smith collected much, much more, like 2,500 LPs, 8,000 books, and 1,740 reels of audiotapes. His collected archive weighed twenty tons and filled a school gymnasium floor to ceiling.

Obsession may have been one of his problems. For his first assignment, Magnum asked him to take one hundred images in three weeks to document Pittsburgh's centenary; he spent three years and took more than twenty thousand photos. Descriptions of him invariably include hints at his obstreperousness: "compulsive," "obsessive," "alienating," "addicted," "huge ego," "self-sabotaging," "hard to work with," and "a nightmare to deal with."

When Smith was eighteen and about to graduate from high school, his father killed himself with a shotgun. This extraordinarily horrific public act just might have had an effect on young Gene. It doesn't seem that hard to connect this trauma to his lifelong obsession with pictures that have enormous emotional depth (it could have gone the other way; he might

have just shut down emotionally). Combine that with a domineering, stern mother (who lived with him for a while after he moved from Wichita to New York City) who gave him his first camera, acted as his darkroom assistant, and organized, for a while, his life, and it becomes easier to understand his quirks.

Credited with producing the first photo essays, Smith worked for *Newsweek* and *Life,* quitting or being fired from each until Magnum, the premier photo collective, found him. It's a sure thing that his antics didn't make anyone there very happy, but at least they understood his unique value. His addictions to alcohol and amphetamines (his cocktail of choice) might have destroyed his life except for the stream of people who genuinely loved him and undoubtedly loved his work. They tended to be those who didn't need, or expect, anything from him, dodging the pathological issues that made his work so difficult.

The title of the class he taught sums it up: "Photography Made Difficult." Not unlike his life.

31 December
Selma Burke

Selma Burke with bust of Booker T. Washington, 1935–1943

Born in North Carolina, one of ten children, Selma Hortense Burke attended a segregated one-room schoolhouse, studied to be, and moved to New York City as, a private nurse. She modeled for art classes to pay for her art school education at Sarah Lawrence College. She became part of the Harlem Renaissance, taught art, and worked under the Works Progress Administration Federal Art Project. She won two fellowships, traveled to and lived in Vienna and later Paris, where she met and studied under Henri Matisse (who praised her work) and with whom she shared a birthday (she was born thirty-one years after him!). She famously sculpted a bust of a German Jewish woman in response to the rising Nazi threat and left Europe shortly thereafter. When World War II started, she joined the US Navy and became a truck driver at the Brooklyn Navy Yard. As the war wound down, she found herself competing for and winning the commission to sculpt a bas-relief of President Franklin D. Roosevelt.

That commission became Burke's most famous. She couldn't find adequate photographic material for the piece and so requested a meeting with the president; she was granted a fifteen-minute appointment that stretched into four hours over two days of sketching FDR, two months before he died. Eleanor Roosevelt saw Burke's plaque and wasn't pleased (it depicted a young, vital FDR, not the aging and frail one Burke met). Selma convinced Eleanor that the artwork wasn't for her but for the nation and the future to remember him at his best, not as he died. By the end of 1945, when the plaque was unveiled, Burke had met two US presidents and its most famous first lady.

You can see her work by reaching in your pocket for a dime (a dime is a coin of US currency once used to pay for things); the portrait she sculpted was plagiarized by the mint for the ten-cent coin. FDR, who contracted polio in middle age, created a foundation dubbed the March of Dimes (a play on *The March of Time* radio program and newsreel) because lapel pins were sold for ten cents. His profile was added to the dime the year after Burke's portrait, now acknowledged to be the basis for the mint's design.

And that was just the first half of Selma Hortense Burke's remarkable life.

Acknowledgments

Michael Bierut: for suggesting, designing, pitching, designing again, securing permissions, and shepherding this book through the entire inscrutable process. Without Michael there would be no book.

Pentagram: Tamara, Camila, Melanie, Sachi, Paul, Claudia, Abby, Elyssa, and everyone else at Pentagram NY, without whom Michael Bierut might just be a guy with a huge pile of sketchbooks.

Jennifer Thompson: who edited this book and educated me about, among other things, *The Chicago Manual of Style* and (unsuccessfully) attempted to educate me as to why I shouldn't hate em dashes.

Princeton Architectural Press: for copy editor Clare Jacobson and managing editor Sara Stemen, and for publishing all the books I bought over the past four decades that helped me maintain my love of architectural history.

Lisa Naftolin and Jan Greben: for helping me get through the entire process, while a few other things were going on. Plus, providing valuable perspective about Eileen Gray and Jean Badovici.

Julian Biber: for choosing a design field that doesn't compete with everyone else we know.

Louie: for unquestioning companionship and for teaching us something new almost every day.

Carin Goldberg: for everything else.

My Instagram followers: whose encouragement kept me going for what seemed like an impossibly long time.

To all the creatives everywhere who were interesting enough to write about.

And for mothers everywhere, and anyone who has a birthday!

Notes

02 January
Rated the number one design: "100 Great Designs of Modern Times," Illinois Institute of Technology, March 16, 2020, https://id.iit.edu/wp-content/uploads/2020/03/100Great Designs.031620.pdf.

08 January
"Steel's constructive potential": Michael Sheridan, *The Furniture of Poul Kjaerholm: Catalogue Raisonné* (New York: Gregory R. Miller & Co., 2007), 16; "Profound essays": Sheridan, *Furniture of Poul Kjaerholm*, 9.

11 January
"I decided that if I was going": William L. Hamilton, "Mary Bright, 48, Curtain Maker Who Used Unorthodox Materials," *New York Times*, November 30, 2002, https://www.nytimes.com/2002/11/30/nyregion/mary-bright-48-curtain-maker-who-used-unorthodox-materials.html.

13 January
"Teaching is the only major occupation": Peter Drucker, *The Age of Discontinuity: Guidelines to Our Changing Society* (Abingdon, UK: Routledge, 2017), 310.

22 January
"Good taste": Francis Picabia, *Yes No: Poems and Sayings* (New York: Hanuman, 1990).

29 January
"My struggle against bourgeois society": John P. O'Neill, ed., *Barnett Newman: Selected Writings and Interviews* (Berkeley: University of California Press, 1992), 201; "Painting is over": Orianne Castel, "Barnett Newman's Painting without Compromise," Art Critique, April 19, 2019, https://www.art-critique.com/en/2019/04/barnett-newmans-painting-without-compromise/; "Signify the end": Castel, "Barnett Newman's Painting."

01 February
They recall her as a Mary Poppins figure: "About Vivian Maier," Vivian Maier, http://www.vivian-maier.com/about-vivian-maier/.

02 February
"It was purely intellectual": James F. O'Gorman, "Theodate Pope Riddle," Pioneering Women, accessed October 13, 2023, https://pioneeringwomen.bwaf.org/theodate-pope-riddle/.

05 February
"The best set that's ever been designed": Vincent Dowd, "Kubrick Recalled by Influential Set Designer Sir Ken Adam," BBC News, August 16, 2013, https://www.bbc.com/news/entertainment-arts-23698181.

12 February
"My concrete is more beautiful": "Revealing Details," Le Havre, World Heritage Site, accessed May 3, 2023, http://unesco.lehavre.fr/en/pass-on/revealing-details.

18 February
"I passed through successive": Paul R. Williams, "Blacks Who Overcame the Odds," *Ebony*, November 1986, abridgment from *American Magazine*, 1937, https://books.google.com/books?id=NdkDAAAAMBAJ&printsec=frontcover&dq=Ebony+Magazine++Nov+1986&hl=en&sa=X&ved=0ahUKEwjR2qvZqKvVAhXDxFQ KHSmoDBA4FBDoAQg7MAU#v=o nepage&q=Ebony%20Magazine%20%20Nov%201986&f=false.

04 March
"Gaudí: hit by streetcar": Edgar Tafel architectural records and papers, 1919–2005, Columbia University Libraries.

17 March
"I remember when I came to the States": Massimo Vignelli and Ed Benguiat, "Massimo Vignelli vs. Ed Benguiat (Sort Of)," interview by Philip B. Meggs, annotated by Julie Lasky, Design Observer, September 15, 2010, https://designobserver.com/feature/massimo-vignelli-vs-ed-benguiat-sort-of/15458.

19 March
"Realization of the complex structure": Charles Darwent, "Josef and Anni Albers: The Bauhaus Misfits Who Scaled Art's Peaks," *Guardian*, October 10, 2018, https://www.theguardian.com/artanddesign/2018/oct/10/bauhaus-josef-anni-albers-art.

29 March
"The secret of [his] success": Rem Koolhaas, *Delirious New York: A Retroactive Manifesto for Manhattan*, (Oxford, UK: Oxford University Press, 1978), 162.

31 March
"If he is honest enough": Cipe Pineles Golden, Kurt Weihs, and Robert Strunsky, eds., *The Visual Craft of William Golden* (New York: George Braziller, 1962), 79; "It is sometimes frustrating": Pineles Golden, Weihs, and Strunsky, *Visual Craft*, 13.

08 April
"On Quai Alexandre III": Letter from Le Corbusier, February 29, 1956, Jean Prouvé, https://www.jeanprouve.com/en/fiche/29-february-1956.

20 April
"Rachel Whiteread reveals": Sheila Wickouski, "A Puzzling and Playful Rachel Whiteread Retrospective at National Gallery of Art," Free Lance-Star (Fredericksburg, VA), December 26, 2018, https://fredericksburg.com/weekender/ a-puzzling-and-playful-rachel -whiteread-retrospective-at-national-gallery-of-art/article_041 dff5b-f319-5b de-b305-58ac6f8a1725.html.

25 April
"Herbert Matter is a magician": Paul Rand, "Introduction," in Herbert Matter, *Symbols Signs Logos: Trademarks by Herbert Matter* (n.p., ca. 1977).

29 April
"Constructing a fountain pen": Bruce Weber, "Jacob Jensen, Designer in Danish Modern Style, Dies at 89," *New York Times*, May 21, 2015, https://www.nytimes.com/2015/05/22/business/jacob-jensen-designer-in-danish-modern-style-dies-at-89.html?searchResultPosition=1.

31 May
"Architecture and war are not incompatible": Lebbeus Woods, "Manifesto," in Andreas Papadakis, ed., *Theory & Experimentation* (London: Academy Editions, 1993).

11 June
"To ennoble Photography": Julia Margaret Cameron, letter to Sir John Herschel, December 31, 1864, quoted in "Julia Margaret Cameron – An Introduction," V&A, accessed October 13, 2023, https://www.vam.ac.uk/articles/julia-margaret-camer-on-introduction#:~:text=My%20 aspirations%20are%20to%20 ennoble,devotion%20to%20 poetry%20and%20beauty.

14 June
"An object lesson": Ada Louise Huxtable, "Bold Plan for Building Unveiled; Edifice of 12 Stories for Ford Foundation Overlooks Garden," *New York Times*, September 29, 1964, https://www.nytimes.com/1964/09/29/archives/bold-plan-for-building-unveiled-edifice-of-12-stories-for-ford.html?searchResult Position=1; "All share a kind of ": Paul Goldberger, "Kevin Roche, Architect Who Melded Bold with Elegant, Dies at 96," *New York Times*, March 2, 2019.

Notes

02 July
"That encouraged the development": Charles W. Moore, introduction to Alexander Caragonne, *The Texas Rangers: Notes from the Architectural Underground* (Cambridge, MA: MIT Press, 1995); Examples of the art of building: José Parra-Martínez, María-Elia Gutiérrez-Mozo, and Ana-Covadonga Gilsanz-Díaz, 2020, "Queering California Modernism: Architectural Figurations and Media Exposure of Gay Domesticity in the Roosevelt Era," *Architectural Histories* 8, no. 1:14 (2020), http://doi.org/10.5334/ah.382.

08 July
But it wasn't until: Mark Lamster, *The Man in the Glass House: Philip Johnson, Architect of the Modern Century* (New York: Little, Brown, 2018).

11 July
"Extremely irritating conversationalist": Paul Ripley, "Death of Mr Whistler," *Times of London*, July 18, 1903, https://www.art renew al.org/Article/Title/obituary-of-james-mcneil-whistler.

23 July
"I had horrifying experiences": "Raimund Abraham, 76," *Baltimore Sun*, March 7, 2010.

01 August
"Julius wanted to invite different architects": Leslie J. Ergianian, "Modern Maverick: Raphael S. Soriano," 100 Years of Sephardic Los Angeles, accessed October 13, 2023, https://sephardi-closangeles.org/portfolios/modern-maverick/.

30 August
"The square": Lucy Davies and Cal Revely-Calder, "Bauhaus Design, an A to Z of the Movement," *Telegraph*, April 12, 2019, https://www.telegraph.co.uk/art/bauhaus-design-art-movement-centenary/.

01 September
"In an era": Rohan Varma, "Architecture as an Agent of Change: Remembering Charles Correa, 'India's Greatest Architect,'" ArchDaily, June 16, 2016, https://www.archdaily.com/789384/architecture-as-agent-of-change-remembering-charles-correa-india#:~:text=Charles%20Correa%20Associates-,In%20an%20era%20dominated%20by%20the%20"starchitects"%20and%20their%20iconic,organization%20and%20use%20of%20space.

03 September
"We should refrain": Louis Sullivan, "Ornament in Architecture," *Engineering Magazine*, August 1892.

08 September
"It is a sort of sculpture": Diana Rowntree, "Sir Denys Lasdun," *Guardian*, January 11, 2002, https://www.theguardian.com/news/2001/jan/12/guardianobituaries#:~:text=It%20is%20a%20sort%20of,was%20marked%20by%20a%20knighthood.

16 September
"Ever since my childhood": Jean Arp, *Jours effeuillés: Poèmes, essaies, souvenirs* (Paris: Gallimard, 1966); "I hereby declare": Jean Arp, "Declaration," 391 Issues, October 1921, https://391.org/manifestos/1921-declaration-jean-hans-arp/.

26 September
"It's never been": Fiona McCarthy, "Margaret Casson," *Guardian*, November 22, 1999, https://www.theguardian.com/news/1999/nov/23/guardianobituaries3.

03 October
"In mid-career": Denise Scott Brown, "Room at the Top? Sexism and the Star System in Architecture," in *Architecture: A Place for Women*, ed. Ellen Perry Berkeley and Matilda McQuaid (Washington, DC: Smithsonian Institution Press, 1989), 237–46.

07 October
"I never thought": Interview with Philippe Briet, catalog of the Jean Paul Riopelle exhibition *Peintures, estampes*, Musée des beaux-arts et Hôtel d'Escoville, Caen, May 2–July 15, 1984.

21 October
"I hope I haven't": Zorianna Kit, "Catherine Hardwicke Talks about Life after *Twilight*," Reuters, July 9, 2009, https://www.reuters.com/article/us-hardwicke-vref/catherine-hardwicke-talks-about-life-after-twilight-idUSTRE56869120090709.

28 October
"I find it difficult": Christine Mehring, "Public Options: The Art of Charlotte Posenenske," *Artforum*, September 2010, https://www.artforum.com/features/public-options-the-art-of-charlotte-posenenske-195269/.

14 November
"Color is the skin": Arthur Allen Cohen, *Sonia Delaunay: The Life of the Artist* (New York: Abrams, 1975), 84.

20 November
"Once you got Pop": Ananda Pellerin, "Andy Warhol's America," AnOther, March 2, 2011, https://www.anothermag.com/art-photography/912/andy-warhols-america.

21 November
"Akzidenz-Grotesk was not available": Wim Crouwel, Design-culture, posted February 8, 2016, http://www.designculture.it/interview/wim-crouwel.html.

25 November
"Johnson is the Lapidus of good taste": Gabrielle Esperdy, "'I Am a Modernist' Morris Lapidus and His Critics," *Miami Living*, July 19, 2020, https://www.miamilivingmagazine.com/post/morris-lapidus-moderist-architect-facts-history.

06 December
"I am troubled": Phyllis Birkby, "Designing for the Messiness of Life," *MS*, February 1981.

19 December
"I have not consciously branded myself": "Wally Olins," *Independent*, April 16, 2014, https://www.independent.co.uk/news/obituaries/wally-olins-authority-on-brandi ng-and-corporate-identity-who-changed-way-companies-and-even-countries-think-of-themselves-9265627.html.

21 December
"The fresco, with its terrible logic": Mary McCarthy, "A City of Stone – III," *New Yorker*, August 22, 1959, 48.

23 December
"The choice of the camel": Cathleen McGuigan, "Forms of Fantasy," *New York Times Magazine*, December 6, 1987, https://www.nytimes.com/1987/12/06/magazine/forms-of-fantasy.html.

24 December
"Why bother": Interview with Sarah Lea, "Joseph Cornell: Outside the Box," Christie's, October 25, 2018, https://www.christies.com/en/stories/joseph-cornell-outside-the-box-f623b0340703403ca762e7e74b9a7340.

27 December
"A technically perfect": Andreas Feininger, *The Perfect Photograph* (Amphoto: 1974).

Credits

Credits

02 March
Lowcarb23, https://commons
.wikimedia.org/wiki/File:Sudo
kunotready.jpg, https://creative
commons.org/licenses/by-sa/
4.0/legalcode

03 March
Paul Warchol/Pentagram

04 March
Courtesy of author

05 March
Louis I. Kahn standing against
north wall of Kimbell Art
Museum auditorium before
turning it over to its owner,
Kimbell Art Foundation,
August 3, 1972. Kimbell Art
Museum, Fort Worth, TX,
constructed 1969–72, Louis
I. Kahn (1901–1974), architect,
photograph by Robert Wharton
© 2022 Kimbell Art Museum,
Fort Worth

06 March
Pentagram

09 March
© Ezra Stoller/Esto

10 March
Paul VanDerWerf, https://flic.
kr/p/72RTrJ, https://creative
commons.org/licenses/by/2.0/

11 March
Library of Congress, Prints &
Photographs Division
[LOT 13411, no. 0338]

13 March
Library of Congress, Prints &
Photographs Division
[LC-DIG-ppmsca-00338]

14 March
Carl Emil Doepler, "Sectional
View of the Cliff Street Building"
(Harper & Brothers Building),
1855, from Jacob Abbott, *The
Harper Establishment; or, How
the Story Books Are Made* (New
York: Harper & Brothers, 1855).
The Metropolitan Museum of
Art, Gift of Joseph B. Davis,
1942 (42.105.22)

15 March
RIBA Collections

16 March
Aerial photograph by KLM
Aerocarto Schiphol-Oost,
24 February 1960

17 March
Courtesy of the Herb Lubalin
Study Center

18 March
LBJ Library photograph by
Robert Knudsen

19 March
Courtesy of the Western
Regional Archives, State
Archives of North Carolina

20 March
Courtesy of Mike Mills

22 March
Kamalpassi2102, https://
commons.wikimedia.org/wiki/
File:Pierre_Jeanneret_House_
in_Chandigarh.jpg, https://
creativecommons.org/licenses/
by-sa/4.0/legalcode

23 March
Courtesy of author

24 March
© The Regents of the University
of California, The Bancroft
Library, University of California,
Berkeley. This work is made
available under a Creative
Commons Attribution 4.0 license.
Courtesy of the Smithsonian
Libraries and Archives,
Washington, DC

25 March
Aline and Eero Saarinen
papers, 1906–1977, Archives
of American Art, Smithsonian
Institution

26 March
BrianPlrwin/Shutterstock.com

27 March
Courtesy of Mike Schwartz

28 March
Denis Esakov

29 March
Maciek Lulko (https://foto-ml.
pl/). "Rockefeller Center,"
(https://www.flickr.com/
photos/lulek/14192146714/in/
photolist-nC7pym-nC7sLJ-
nSeXUr-nS5Pxv), https://
creativecommons.org/licenses/
by-nc/2.0/

30 March
Werner Seligman

03 April
Pentagram

04 April
Library of Congress, Prints
& Photographs Division,
photograph by Carol M.
Highsmith [LC-USZ62-123456]

05 April
Fred the Oyster, https://
commons.wikimedia.org/
wiki/File:ABayer.png, https://
creativecommons.org/licenses/
by-sa/2.5/legalcode; typeface
digitized by The Foundry

07 April
Used by permission from the
Leon Krier Library and Archives,
held by the Architecture Library
of the Hesburgh Libraries,
University of Notre Dame,
Notre Dame, IN

08 April
Courtesy of author

10 April
Courtesy of Judith Turner.
Collection of SFMOMA
Accessions Committee Fund
purchase © Judith Turner

11 April
Photograph by Dody Weston
Thompson, used by permission
of Helen C. Harrison

12 April
Paul VanDerWerf,
https://flic.kr/ p/2o3gonF,
https://creativecommons.org/
licenses/by/2.0/

13 April
Robert Oo, https://flic.kr/
p/2hJbPA9, https://creative
commons.org/licenses/by/2.0/

14 April
Annik Wetter

15 April
Library of Congress, Prints
& Photographs Division
[LC-USZ62-110329 (b&w film
copy neg.)]

16 April
Huguette Roe/
Shutterstock.com

17 April
Courtesy of Princeton
Architectural Press

18 April
August Fischer, https://flic.
kr/p/HTkf8S, https://creative
commons.org/licenses/by-
nd/2.0/

19 April
Division of Rare and
Manuscript Collections,
Cornell University Library

20 April
Reading Tom, https://flic.
kr/p/LnhtqD, https://creative
commons.org/licenses/by/2.0/

21 April
© Eve Arnold/Magnum

22 April
Jonathan Simle (2004.26.180),
© ArtCenter College of Design,
Pasadena, CA

Credits

12 August
Lars Fasting, Per Kartvedt, Ron Herron, https://commons.wikimedia.org/wiki/File:Trøndelag_Teater_project_plate_14.jpg, https://creativecommons.org/licenses/by-sa/4.0/legalcode

13 August
Ville de Lyon, Archives municipales, Tony Garnier, cote 3SAT/2

14 August
Åke E:son Lindman, Lindman Photography

15 August
Courtesy of Dustin Kilgore/Yale University Press. © Yale University

16 August
THOR, https://commons.wikimedia.org/wiki/File:Alessandro_Mendini_Poltrona_di_Proust_Studio_Alchimia_1979_Musée_des_arts_décoratifs_Paris.jpg, https://creativecommons.org/licenses/by/2.0/legalcode

18 August
Courtesy of Seymour Chwast

20 August
Courtesy of author

21 August
Storyboard for animated bridge segment, Depatie-Freleng Studios

23 August
Courtesy of Eric Meola

24 August
The New York Public Library, https://digitalcollections.nypl.org/items/434b8be0-eb3c-013a-9d4c-0242ac110003

25 August
Courtesy of the Civita Institute

27 August
© The Regents of the University of California, The Bancroft Library, University of California, Berkeley. This work is made available under a Creative Commons Attribution 4.0 license. Courtesy of the Smithsonian Libraries and Archives, Washington, DC

28 August
Scott Meredith Literary Agency, Roger Tory Peterson Family

29 August
Courtesy of Michael Bierut

31 August
Landis Gores

01 September
© photograph by Meena Kadri, 2006

02 September
© photograph by Peter Vanderwarker

03 September
David Gleason (mindfrieze), https://commons.wikimedia.org/wiki/File:Getty_Tomb_Graceland_Sullivan_front.jpg, https://creativecommons.org/licenses/by-sa/3.0/legalcode

04 September
Library of Congress, Prints & Photographs Division [LC-D401-14278 (b&w film copy neg.)]

05 September
James Morris, © Claudio Silvestrin Architects

06 September
Humanscale 1/2/3, Humanscale 4/5/6, and Humanscale 7/8/9, by Niels Diffrient et al. © 2017 IA Collaborative Ventures, LLC - Series Humanscale. Reproduced with permission. For more information: www.humanscalemanual.com

07 September
Courtesy of Daniel Weil

08 September
Jim Osley, https://commons.wikimedia.org/wiki/File:32_Newton_Road,_Bayswater,_London_W2.jpg, https://creativecommons.org/licenses/by-sa/2.0/legalcode

09 September
Bengt Oberger, https://commons.wikimedia.org/wiki/File:Kotte_Poul_Henningsen.JPG, https://creativecommons.org/licenses/by-sa/3.0/legalcode

10 September
Library of Congress, Prints & Photographs Division, HABS CAL, 30-NEWBE, 1--1

11 September
heena_mistry, https://commons.wikimedia.org/wiki/File:Snowdon_Aviary_at_London_Zoo,_England-16Aug2009.jpg, https://creativecommons.org/licenses/by/2.0/legalcode

12 September
Hanne Therkildsen

13 September
Courtesy of Ralph Rapson & Associates

14 September
Tomislav Medak, https://flic.kr/p/8y9fd4, https://creativecommons.org/licenses/by/2.0/

15 September
John Owens, https://commons.wikimedia.org/wiki/File:McMath-Pierce_Solar_Telescope.jpg, https://creativecommons.org/licenses/by-sa/3.0/legalcode

17 September
Courtesy of David Shrigley

18 September
Darwin K. Davidson Photography

19 September
Aarne Pietinen Oy, courtesy of Helsinki City Museum

20 September
Fred Romero, https://flic.kr/p/Pv1MXg, https://creativecommons.org/licenses/by/2.0/

21 September
Courtesy of Sara Little Turnbull Center for Design Institute

22 September
Felix Odell

23 September
Paul Mehnert

24 September
Henry (Heintz) P. Glass (American, born Austria, 1911–2003). Folding Picnic Table Model, designed 1961. Painted wood, metal, textile, 6⅛ x 17¼ in. (15.6 x 43.8 cm). Brooklyn Museum, Modernism Benefit Fund, 2000.101.4. Creative Commons-BY (Photograph: Brooklyn Museum, 2000.101.4_bw.jpg)

25 September
Architas, https://commons.wikimedia.org/wiki/File:San_Carlo_alle_Quattro_Fontane_-_Dome.jpg, https://creativecommons.org/licenses/by-sa/4.0/legalcode

28 September
Billie Grace Ward from New York, USA, https://commons.wikimedia.org/wiki/File:Lincoln_Center_Operahouse_(25539636664).jpg, https://creativecommons.org/licenses/by/2.0/legalcode

Credits

29 September
Monica Pidgeon/RIBA
Collections

30 September
Steve Cadman, https://
flic.kr/p/5fjWRW, https://
creativecommons.org/licenses/
by-sa/2.0/

01 October
The Metropolitan Museum of
Art, New York, Harris Brisbane
Dick Fund, 1941

02 October
Courtesy of author

03 October
National Park Service

04 October
The Metropolitan Museum of
Art, New York, Gift of Edward
W. Root, Elihu Root Jr. and Mrs.
Ulysses S. Grant III, 1937

05 October
Balthazar Korab, courtesy
Maya Lin Studio

06 October
Courtesy of author

08 October
MikeJiroch, https://
commons.wikimedia.org/
wiki/File:Richard_and_Dion_
Neutra_VDL_Research_House_
II,_2300_Silver_Lake_Blvd._
Silver_Lake,_5093.jpg, https://
creativecommons.org/licenses/
by-sa/3.0/legalcode

09 October
André Cros, Archives
Municipales de Toulouse

10 October
Coweeczwech, https://
commons.wikimedia.org/wiki/
File:Kubistická_lampa_na_
Jugmanově_náměstí.jpg, https://
creativecommons.org/licenses/
by-sa/4.0/legalcode

12 October
© Ezra Stoller/Esto

13 October
Norbert Nagel, Mörfelden-
Walldorf, Germany, https://
commons.wikimedia.org/
wiki/File:Santa_Maria_del_
Rosario_Venice_2.jpg, https://
creativecommons.org/licenses/
by-sa/3.0/legalcode

15 October
Courtesy of author

16 October
Courtesy of Janet Odgis

17 October
Julius Shulman. © J. Paul Getty
Trust, Getty Research Institute,
Los Angeles (2004.R.10). Julius
Shulman Photography Archive

18 October
Courtesy of
House for an Art Lover

19 October
House and Garden magazine,
July 1935 and 2022. Beverly
Willis Architecture Foundation

20 October
The Metropolitan Museum
of Art, New York, The Elisha
Whittelsey Collection, The
Elisha Whittelsey Fund, 1960

22 October
Marion Schneider and
Christoph Aistleitner, https://
commons.wikimedia.org/wiki/
File:Graz_Kunsthaus_vom_
Schlossberg_20061126.jpg,
https://creativecommons.org/
licenses/by-sa/2.5/legalcode

23 October
© Ezra Stoller/Esto

24 October
Luca Ferri Fattoretto, https://
commons.wikimedia.org/
wiki/File:CASSINA_-_Nuage_
Charlotte_Perriand.jpg, https://
creativecommons.org/licenses/
by-sa/4.0/legalcode

25 October
Lundh/ArkDes

27 October
www.twin-loc.fr, https://
flic.kr/p/ctS67A, https://
creativecommons.org/licenses/
by-sa/2.0/

28 October
Courtesy of Estate of
Charlotte Posenenski and
Mehdi Chouakri, Berlin

29 October
Courtesy of author

31 October
Pivari.com, https://commons.
wikimedia.org/wiki/
File:Stazione_alta_velocita,_
Zaha_Hadid,_Napoli_Afragola.
jpg, https://creativecommons.
org/licenses/by-sa/4.0/
legalcode

01 November
Mike Peel (www.mikepeel.net),
https://commons.wikimedia.
org/wiki/File:At_New_York,_
USA_2017_119.jpg, https://
creativecommons.org/licenses/
by-sa/4.0/legalcode

02 November
Jason Leung (@ninjason)

04 November
National Numismatic
Collection, National Museum
of American History

06 November
Library of Congress, Prints
& Photographs Division
[C-USZ62-106358 (b&w film
copy neg.)]

09 November
Library of Congress, Prints
& Photographs Division
[LC-USZ61-1847 (b&w film
copy neg.)]

10 November
The Metropolitan Museum of
Art, New York, Harris Brisbane
Dick Fund, 1932

11 November
Carnegie Museum of Art,
Pittsburgh. Acquired through
the generosity of the Sarah
Mellon Scaife Family

12 November
Library of Congress, Prints &
Photographs Division,
HABS PA,51-PHILA,340--2

15 November
The Jon B. Lovelace Collection
of California Photographs in
Carol M. Highsmith's America
Project, Library of Congress,
Prints & Photographs Division

16 November
Courtesy of Alexander Isley

17 November
Used with permission from
the Eberly Family Special
Collections Library, Penn State
University Libraries

19 November
Macfadden Publications, Inc.,
photograph by Louise Dahl-Wolfe

20 November
Courtesy of Corita Art Center

21 November
Courtesy of Judith
Crouwel-Cahan

Credits

22 November
Library of Congress, Prints &
Photographs Division, NYWT&S
Collection [LC-USZ62-137159]

24 November
Library of Congress, Prints &
Photographs Division
[LC-DIG-ppmsca-41913 (digital
file from original item)]

25 November
Library of Congress, Prints &
Photographs Division, Gottscho-
Schleisner Collection [LC-
G613-T-66993 (interpositive)]

26 November
Library of Congress, Prints &
Photographs Division, NYWT&S
Collection [LC-USZC2-6148
(color film copy slide)]

28 November
Library of Congress, Prints
& Photographs Division,
photograph by Harris & Ewing
[LC-DIG-hec-07003 (digital file
from original negative)]

29 November
Charley/Shutterstock.com

30 November
marcobrivio.photography/
Shutterstock.com

01 December
Library of Congress, Prints
& Photographs Division,
Balthazar Korab Collection
[LC-DIG-ds-14573 (digital file
from original)]

02 December
© David Macaulay, courtesy
R. Michelson Galleries

04 December
Courtesy of author

05 December
Fagner Martins/
Shutterstock.com

06 December
Courtesy of Saskia Scheffer

07 December
MAVRITSINA IRINA/
Shutterstock.com

08 December
A Trip to the Moon (French:
Le voyage dans la lune) [Film],
G. Méliès [Director], Star Film
Company, 1902

09 December
Courtesy of Steven Holl
Architects

10 December
Library of Congress, Prints
& Photographs Division
[LC-USZ62-60375 (b&w film
copy neg.)]

11 December
Corporate Archives Porsche AG

12 December
Daniel Waters/
Shutterstock.com

13 December
Courtesy of MANITOGA/The
Russel Wright Design Center

14 December
Gillfoto from Juneau, Alaska,
United States, https://commons.
wikimedia.org/wiki/File:London_
Zoo_40393.jpg, https://creative
commons.org/licenses/by-sa/
4.0/legalcode

15 December
Courtesy of author

16 December
Pentagram

17 December
Matt Weber

18 December
Cquoi, https://commons.
wikimedia.org/wiki/
File:Kodak_2A_Beau_Brownie.
jpg, https://creativecommons.
org/licenses/by-sa/4.0/
legalcode

20 December
Vlad Hilitanu

22 December
Christos Vittoratos, https://
commons.wikimedia.org/wiki/
File:Ulmer-hocker.jpg, https://
creativecommons.org/licenses/
by-sa/3.0/legalcode

23 December
Vinnikava Viktoryia/
Shutterstock.com

25 December
Courtesy of Michael Bierut

26 December
© Science Museum Group

29 December
Courtesy of Paul Holberton
Publishing

31 December
Courtesy of the Smithsonian
Libraries and Archives,
Washington, DC

Index

Index

Index